NEW CULTURAL LANDSCAPES

While historical and protected landscapes have been well studied for years, the cultural significance of ordinary landscapes is now increasingly recognised. This groundbreaking book discusses how contemporary cultural landscapes can be, and are, created and recognised.

The book challenges common concepts of cultural landscapes as protected or 'special' landscapes that include significant buildings or features. Using case studies from around the world, it questions the usual measures of judgement related to cultural landscapes and instead focuses on landscapes that are created, planned or simply evolve as a result of changing human cultures, management policy and practice.

Each contribution analyses the geographical and human background of the landscape and the policies and management strategies that impact upon it, and defines the meanings of 'cultural landscape' in its particular context. Taken together they establish a new paradigm in the study of landscapes in all forms.

Maggie Roe is Senior Lecturer, Convenor of the Landscape Research Group, and Director of Programmes for MSc in Planning for Climate Change and for MA in Planning & Environmental Research at Newcastle University, UK. She is an editor of *Landscape Research*. Her research and publications focus on participatory and sustainable landscape planning, landscape policy analysis and landscape change. She has worked in Europe, North and South America, Bangladesh, China and India. Research and project funding bodies she has worked with include UNESCO, Council of Europe, British Council/DfID, AHRC, ESRC, NERC, DEFRA, SNH, Natural England, the Forestry Commission and the Environment Agency.

Ken Taylor AM is Adjunct Professor in the Research School of Humanities and the Arts and Program Advisor to the Institute for Professional Practice in Heritage and the Arts at the Australian National University; Emeritus Professor of Landscape Architecture and former Co-Director of the Cultural Heritage Research Centre, University of Canberra; and Visiting Professor, Silpakorn University, Bangkok.

NEW CULTURAL LANDSCAPES

*Edited by Maggie Roe
and Ken Taylor*

Routledge
Taylor & Francis Group

LONDON AND NEW YORK

First published 2014
by Routledge
2 Park Square, Milton Park, Abingdon, Oxon OX14 4RN

Simultaneously published in the USA and Canada
by Routledge
711 Third Avenue, New York, NY 10017

Routledge is an imprint of the Taylor & Francis Group, an informa business

British Library Cataloguing in Publication Data
A catalogue record for this book is available from the British Library

Library of Congress Cataloging in Publication Data
New cultural landscapes / [edited by] Maggie Roe, Ken Taylor.
   pages cm
Includes bibliographical references and index.
1. Cultural landscapes.   I. Roe, Maggie H.
GF50.N46 2014
363.6'9—dc23
                                            2013019978

ISBN: 978-0-415-59805-7 (hbk)
ISBN: 978-0-415-59806-4 (pbk)
ISBN: 978-1-315-86744-1 (ebk)

Typeset in Bembo
by Keystroke, Station Road, Codsall, Wolverhampton

MIX
Paper from
responsible sources
FSC   FSC® C013056
www.fsc.org

Printed and bound in Great Britain by
TJ International Ltd, Padstow, Cornwall

CONTENTS

CONTRIBUTORS

Tamer M. Abd El-Fattah Ahmed is a lecturer in the Department of Architecture, Alazhar University, Cairo, Egypt. He has worked in both academia and practice and obtained his PhD in Landscape and Urbanism from the School of Architecture Planning and Landscape, Newcastle University, in 2011. He lectures in urban planning, landscape and architectural design. His research focuses on liveable community issues and he is particularly interested in developing the links between urbanisation, liveability and landscape planning.

Brenda Barrett is the editor of the *Living Landscape Observer*, an online site that provides information and commentary on landscape scale conservation, historic preservation and sustainable communities. Former posts include Director of Recreation and Conservation at the Pennsylvania Department of Conservation and Natural Resources, the National Coordinator for Heritage Areas for the National Park Service, Washington, DC, and the Director of the Bureau for Historic Preservation at the Pennsylvania Historical and Museum Commission. She is an expert member of the ICOMOS International Scientific Committee on Cultural Landscapes.

Simon Bell is a forester and landscape architect. He is Professor and Head of the Department of Landscape Architecture in the Institute of Agricultural and Environmental Sciences at the Estonian University of Life Sciences in Tartu, Estonia and Associate Director of OPENspace, the Research Centre for Inclusive Access to Outdoor Environments based at Edinburgh College of Art, part of the University of Edinburgh.

Gerard Corsane is Dean for International Business Development and Student Recruitment in the Faculty of Humanities and Social Sciences and a Senior Lecturer in the International Centre for Cultural and Heritage Studies, Newcastle University, UK. Prior to 1999, he worked for ten years in South Africa with heritage organisations, museums and galleries participating in the exciting processes of transformation that occurred around the country's first democratic elections. His current research focuses on 'ecomuseums' and similar democratic projects located in various countries, particularly in South America, Southern Africa and the People's Republic of China.

Clive Davies is a visiting research fellow at Newcastle University and Director at MD² Consulting Ltd.; he works in the UK and internationally. Clive has over 30 years' experience working on environmental regeneration programmes encompassing management, strategy and practice. Professionally he acts as an advisor, mentor and project manager.

Peter Davis is Emeritus Professor of Museology in the International Centre for Cultural and Heritage Studies at Newcastle University, UK. His research interests include the history of museums, natural history and environmentalism; the interaction between heritage, landscape and concepts of place; and ecomuseums. He is the author of several books including *Ecomuseums: A Sense of Place* (2nd edition 2011).

Joe Duffy is Senior Lecturer in Filmmaking at Manchester School of Art and a practising artist working with film, photography and installation. His research interests are based around the locating of place within art practice, embodied landscapes, migration, mobility and narrativity. Current projects centre around the exploration of sublime landscapes and the apocalyptic imaginary.

Shelley Egoz is Professor in Place-Making, Department of Landscape Architecture and Spatial Planning, Norwegian University of Life Sciences. Her research interests focus on the symbolic and ideological power of landscape, in particular democracy, social justice and ethics associated with landscape, space and design. She is principal editor of *The Right to Landscape, Contesting Landscape and Human Right* (Ashgate, 2011).

Keven Francis is currently a PhD candidate at the Australian National University and a Management Consultant with K R Francis & Associates based in Gundaroo, NSW, Australia. His research investigates the shared management of cultural and natural landscapes, when considered as a single integrated environment.

Bronwyn Jewell is currently affiliated with the Queensland State Government, Australia. Much of this material was gathered while undertaking doctoral studies, at the School of Tourism, University of Queensland.

Susan McKinnon is currently lecturing with the University of Southern Queensland in Toowoomba, Australia, within the Marketing and Management Department. Her current teaching focus is Business Management Studies.

Robert Z. Melnick FASLA is former Dean and Professor of Landscape Architecture at University of Oregon, and senior cultural resource specialist with MIG, Inc, in Portland, Oregon. Co-editor of *Preserving Cultural Landscapes in America* (2000), he has published widely on cultural landscapes, receiving national awards for his writings and professional projects. In 1980 he was the first Historical Landscape Architect in the US National Park Service, subsequently co-authoring US National Register Bulletin 30 on rural cultural landscapes. His current research addresses the challenge of protecting cultural landscapes in the era of climate change.

Nora J. Mitchell holds masters degrees in Ecology and Environmental Planning and Policy. Her doctorate was in Landscape Studies from Tufts University. She is Adjunct Associate Professor in the Rubenstein School of Environment and Natural Resources at the University of Vermont. Previously, she was the founding director of both the National Park Service (NPS) Conservation Study Institute and the Olmsted Center for Landscape Preservation. She has worked nationally in the United States and internationally in cooperation with the UNESCO World Heritage Centre, IUCN and ICOMOS and has written extensively on cultural and protected landscape issues.

Mary G. Padua, ASLA, RLA is founding Chair and Professor at Clemson University's new Department of Landscape Architecture. She is an impassioned design educator and contemporary theorist on urbanism in modern China and the meaning of public space. She has taught on four continents and maintains MGP Studio, a critically minded design consultancy that interrogates international urban issues. She holds degrees from the Edinburgh College of Art, University of Edinburgh (PhD), UCLA (MA) and University of California, Berkeley (BA).

Maggie Roe is Senior Lecturer, convenor of the Landscape Research Group, and Director of the MSc in Planning for Sustainability and Climate Change and of the MA in Planning & Environmental Research at Newcastle University, UK. She is an editor of *Landscape Research*. Her research and publications focus on participatory and sustainable landscape planning, landscape policy analysis and landscape change. She has worked in Europe, North and South America, Bangladesh, China and India. Research and project funding bodies she has worked with include UNESCO, Council of Europe, British Council/DfID, AHRC, ESRC, NERC, DEFRA, SNH, Natural England, the Forestry Commission and the Environment Agency.

Suzanne Speak is Senior Lecturer in Planning and Director of the MSc in Planning for Developing Countries in the School of Architecture, Planning and Landscape at Newcastle University, UK. Her research focuses on issues of marginalisation and disadvantage, primarily in developing countries in a range of social and cultural contexts using innovative participatory methods. Work includes studies of sustainable development and the environmental implications of change. Recent research, on the nature, extent and experience of homelessness, was undertaken in nine countries. She has published extensively in international journals on housing and urban studies.

Ken Taylor AM is an Adjunct Professor in the Research School of Humanities and the Arts and Program Advisor to Institute for Professional Practice in Heritage and Arts, the Australian National University; Emeritus Professor of Landscape Architecture and former Co-Director, Cultural Heritage Research Centre, University of Canberra; and Visiting Professor Silpakorn University, Bangkok.

1

NEW CULTURAL LANDSCAPES

Emerging issues, context and themes

Maggie Roe and Ken Taylor

> It is the landscape as a whole – that largely manmade tapestry, in which all other artefacts are embedded ... which gives them their sense of place.
>
> *(Lowenthal 1975: 12)*

Introduction

Internationally there is a widening interest academically, professionally and in the community at large in the concept and meaning of landscape, rural and urban, as the setting for everything we do. Whilst there are many landscapes, we tend to refer to landscape in the singular, but that is expressive of a multitude of settings. Landscape is therefore a ubiquitous entity: we live in it, pass through it every day, and it thereby affects our lived experiences tangibly and intangibly. We shape it and it shapes us. It is a value-laden entity. We see landscape continuously; nevertheless landscape is not simply what we see, a kind of transient static scenery vacuously experienced with detached contemplation. Rather it is as Cosgrove suggests (1998 [1984]: 1):

> a way of seeing that has its own history, but a history that can be understood only as part of a wider history of economy and society; that has its own assumptions and consequences, but assumptions and consequences whose origins and implications extend well beyond the use and perception of land; that has its own techniques of expression, but techniques which it shares with other areas of cultural practice.

Variously described as an important but ambiguous term (Meinig 1979) and a slippery term (Stilgoe 1982), landscape, as Lowenthal (2007) declared, is everyone's heritage and an essential part of our patrimony. In this sense therefore and increasingly across the spectrum of interest in landscape the term 'cultural landscape' has firmly taken root. David Jacques' (1995) paper 'The Rise of Cultural Landscapes' tracked its emergence and significance to the international conservation community and criticised the shallow approach, evident until the early 1990s, to landscape evaluation based on visual or scenic aspects of landscape value. David Lowenthal (1978) had presaged this shift in his piece 'Finding Valued Landscapes'. The movement was coincidental with increasing appreciation of human values reflected in landscapes alongside the focus on landscape as process (Taylor 2012) and the inevitability of change over time.

Three forces may be seen to have helped drive the rise of the focus upon and interest in cultural landscapes. The first is the introduction twenty-one years ago in 1992 of three categories of cultural landscapes recognised by the World Heritage Convention process (Figure 1.1). The second is the European Landscape Convention which was adopted in 2000 and came into force in 2004 (Figure 1.2). The third is the alternative and changing views on the discourse into cultural landscapes as a bridge between culture and nature (Taylor 2012), seen not least in the IUCN Protected Areas Category V Landscapes with their biodiversity values (Dudley and Stolton 2012) and in community conserved areas (Brown and Kothari 2011) as discussed in Chapter 2 (Taylor and Francis).

Whilst this book is not about World Heritage cultural landscapes, consideration of these categories as a yardstick for identifying new cultural landscapes is helpful. By the term 'new cultural landscape' we do not solely mean new from scratch, although such landscapes exist and are created as for example in surface mining, in new urban areas, and by new landscape park designs. Our focus is also on how change creates new cultural landscapes incrementally where change adds new layers to an already layered composition, and may add new meanings to a materially changed or unchanged situation. We are also interested in how human values and ideologies affect the way people create changed landscapes.

Cultural landscapes fall into three main categories (UNESCO 2011) *Operational Guidelines for the Implementation of the World Heritage Convention* (Annex 3: p. 88)

1. The most easily identifiable is the clearly defined landscape designed and created intentionally by man. This embraces garden and parkland landscapes constructed for aesthetic reasons which are often (but not always) associated with religious or other monumental buildings and ensembles.
2. The second category is the organically evolved landscape. This results from an initial social, economic, administrative, and/or religious imperative and has developed its present form by association with and in response to its natural environment. Such landscapes reflect that process of evolution in their form and component features.
    They fall into two subcategories:

    i. A relict (or fossil) landscape is one in which an evolutionary process came to an end at some time in the past, either abruptly or over a period. Its significant distinguishing features are, however, still visible in material form.
    ii. Continuing landscape is one which retains an active social role in contemporary society closely associated with the traditional way of life, and in which the evolutionary process is still in progress. At the same time it exhibits significant material evidence of its evolution over time.

3. The final category is the associative cultural landscape. The inclusion of such landscapes on the World Heritage List is justifiable by virtue of the powerful religious, artistic or cultural associations of the natural element rather than material cultural evidence, which may be insignificant or even absent.

FIGURE 1.1   World Heritage cultural landscape categories

Source: UNESCO 2011; http://whc.unesco.org/archive/opguide11-en.pdf

Noting that the landscape has an important public interest role in the cultural, ecological, environmental and social fields, and constitutes a resource favourable to economic activity and whose protection, management and planning can contribute to job creation;

Aware that the landscape contributes to the formation of local cultures and that it is a basic component of the European natural and cultural heritage, contributing to human well-being and consolidation of the European identity;

Acknowledging that the landscape is an important part of the quality of life for people everywhere: in urban areas and in the countryside, in degraded areas as well as in areas of high quality, in areas recognised as being of outstanding beauty as well as everyday areas;

Noting that developments in agriculture, forestry, industrial and mineral production techniques and in regional planning, town planning, transport, infrastructure, tourism and recreation and, at a more general level, changes in the world economy are in many cases accelerating the transformation of landscapes;

Wishing to respond to the public's wish to enjoy high-quality landscapes and to play an active part in the development of landscapes;

Believing that the landscape is a key element of individual and social well-being and that its protection, management and planning entail rights and responsibilities for everyone.

FIGURE 1.2   Extract from the Preamble, European Landscape Convention

Source: CoE 2000a; http://conventions.coe.int/Treaty/en/Treaties/Html/176.htm.

Conceptions of cultural landscapes: cultural, culture and cultures, and landscape

Understanding the various ways cultural landscapes are conceived and experienced is of particular importance in considering what might constitute new cultural landscapes. In the academic world, there is a wide conception of cultural landscapes and, particularly once out of the area of heritage studies which focus primarily on layers of activity in the past that build up present-day landscapes, cultural landscapes are seen as living landscapes that reflect a range of relationships between humans and natural cycles. Although in the literature there is still an emphasis on cultural landscapes as 'a product of human management of one form or another' (Convery and Dutson 2008: 104), it is possible to identify other characteristics: an emphasis on thinking about a wider than site scale, about seeing the characteristics of landscape as being continually created by behavioural patterns (human and other species) and the way cultural landscapes portray an understanding of integrated, connected, complex relationships between species, places and the environmental conditions. Throughout such discussion the issue of language is important, particularly in relation to policy, because descriptions of cultural landscapes enshrine concepts and set out principles and approaches for landscape management.

Carl Sauer (1889–1975) is often attributed with coining the term 'cultural landscape'. However the term originates from the early twentieth century from the German geographer Otto Schlüter (1872–1959), Professor of Geography at the University of Halle. Sauer translated Schlüter's term *kulturlandschaft* into English and suggested that: 'the cultural landscape is fashioned from a natural landscape by a culture group. Culture is the agent, the natural area is the medium, the cultural landscape is the result' (Sauer 1925: 46). Raymond Williams (1921–88) in *Keywords* (1985 [1976]: 87–93) proposes three useful associations for the term 'culture': process of intellectual, spiritual and aesthetic development; a particular way of life relating to people, a period in history, or humanity in general in material and spiritual senses; and artistic activity. His view of culture is that it is a process which is traditional and creative; its nature is to have both the ordinary common meanings and the finest individual meanings.

There are a number of critics of the mechanistic view of landscape, notably Wylie (2007), and there has in recent years been a plethora of uses and combinations of the terms cultural and landscape. In the discipline of Geography 'cultures of landscape' and 'landscape cultures' are used to denote relationships between individual, community and national identities, and the design, representation and experience of landscape (see for example the work of Dennis Cosgrove, Stephen Daniels and David Matless). Based on these ideas it is possible to identify a number of helpful theoretical discussions that explore concepts of landscape that depart from linear thinking in time and space and pull together phenomenological, experiential and other ideas. Wylie (2007) provides an analysis of landscape as a 'series of tensions, between distance and proximity, observing and inhabiting, eye and land, culture and nature' that help to make the idea of landscape 'cogent and productive' (p. 216). Wylie (2007) reflects Cosgrove's thinking and, like cultural geographers such as Daniels, suggests a definition of landscape as a way of seeing or 'that *with which* we see' (p. 215) extended to an idea of landscape as a 'lifeworld' rather than a scene to view or a projection of cultural meaning.

Brown (2008) provides a review as to the useful meanings of the key terms 'culture' and 'landscape'. Definitions of the term culture have been highly contested in a similar way to those of 'landscape'. Culture is defined as both activity or meaning (as in allotment culture), outlook or tradition (as in Native American culture) and then there are 'cultures' which are used to suggest a separation or difference (as in Scottish versus English culture) which then leads to concepts of multiculturalism and cross-culturalism, suggesting states of human being that are changing. Such discussion is however not limited to humans, so animals have culture or cultures. Culture is also considered to be measurable and contain difference; arts are often referred to as 'high' culture while skills and crafts are 'low' culture. Designing landscapes is often described as an art, thus, does it follow that designed landscapes are considered as having higher cultural significance than those that have evolved through interaction with cultivators? Howard (2011) suggests that recent studies in landscape can be seen to be concentrating more on landscape as a reflection of the context of the time: 'a window onto the society and culture that produced it' (p. 22) and thus not neutral in that it also reflects a particular political and social agenda. Head (2012) indicates the importance of this, particularly in countries where people (particularly indigenous people) and cultures have been fenced into landscapes that are considered 'empty and natural' (p. 66), while in other examples people and cultures have been excluded from areas for precisely the same reasons in order to preserve what is seen as some kind of 'pristine' ecological condition. The way people describe or represent land-scapes tells us as much about the perceiver as the landscape itself, so studies on attitudes, preferences and behaviour are important in considering the values of cultural landscapes and these reveal considerable difficulties since there may not be a coherent cultural view of landscape that is not tempered by individual attitudes or beliefs. Two theories are much quoted in discussions about the meaning of culture as either something that is primarily acquired or something that is intrinsic to human life. Logan (2013) suggests that Matthew Arnold's (1822–88) *Culture and Anarchy* (1840) and Edward Tylor's (1832–1917) *Primitive Culture* (1871) provide different views on the same problem: 'Each redefines culture from a term limited to individuals to one that encompasses society as a whole. In doing so, each has difficulty actually defining culture' (p. 1). Logan also suggests that many interpretations of Arnold's work are in fact erroneous, and that Arnold's original thesis was 'that culture hinges on the willingness to question everything' (p. 5) and that culture is a process that is forever growing and changing. This is helpful in considering the composite term cultural landscape. Culture can be thought as having many characteristics now commonly attributed to landscapes, that is a 'dynamic, multiple contingent and contested process, worked out in everyday practice' (Head 2012: 67).

The emphasis on interaction rather than human impact in the creation of cultural landscapes has emerged as a result of the development of theories such as chaos, complexity and other ideas related to sustainability that have been applied to landscape issues. In the introduction to Salter's (1971) anthology of essays, the cultural landscape is defined as 'the artificial landscape man creates, remaking nature to better provide himself with his short-term needs of food, shelter, clothing, and entertainment' (unpag.). These essays emphasise the transformative processes by which humans, as agents of change, alter the land, primarily through actions related to mobility, husbandry (cultivation and management), and the organisation of space. In this description, the process is apparently one-way, with landscape as a product of human action. In many older writings, as exemplified in Salter's anthology, creating the cultural landscape is seen very much as a battle against nature; it is about taming, civilising and 'improving' the natural world. A renowned example of this is the way Capability Brown (1716–83) identified the 'capabilities' or potentials of the landscape for change according to the cultural taste and values of the time. There is an enduring view of nature as something to be tamed or colonised in a number of Western cultures, in particular in North America where there are common references to the 'Wild West' American frontier culture, and the early Puritan New World colonist culture of New England. As nature was 'tamed' by early colonists on the East Coast of the United States, a more benign view emerged as can be seen in the writings of Jonathan Edwards (1703–58), this mutated into an Edenic view of nature, such as those of Thoreau, Emerson and Muir, whose writings suggest that getting close to nature reveals transcendent truths that cannot be gained from 'civilisation'. Such work helped the development of wilderness versus civilisation thinking that promoted the National Park movement in the United States. Clarence Glacken's (1967) exploration of 'Nature and Culture in Western Thought from Ancient Times to the End of the Eighteenth Century' provides a narrative on these perceptions that have long been described as a nature/culture split.

The nature/culture debate does not seem to be in much danger of disappearing and there is still discussion founded on a separationalist concept of culture and nature, or humans versus nature. This is particularly reflected today in the language used in the restoration ecology and 'rewilding' debates in North America, that are now reaching into some, often academic, discussions in Europe focusing on environmental management and science (e.g. Bauer *et al.* 2009). As Convery and Dutson (2008) suggest, the rewilding idea has been put to good use for conservation management in landscapes in recent years, but this has often been at the expense of the understanding of the role of humans in the landscape, both over thousands of years as their case study of Ennerdale in the UK suggests, or in present and future sustainable planning. Such case studies suggest that a 'view from' human way of thinking in Western environmental planning perpetuates a separationalist attitude amongst scholars, policymakers and practitioners that may not actually be reflected in the reality of people's lives and is not revealed by the examination of many non-Western traditions (Taylor 2012; Silva and Chapagain 2013). The view of nature for human benefit can be seen entwined in the 'ecosystem services' concept which has gained considerable popularity in Europe and North America, particularly in policy circles.

It is suggested that the growth of interest in cultural landscapes in Europe resulted from a realisation of three key factors: first, new techniques that revealed historical information; second, the concern about loss of traditional agricultural landscapes; and, third, an understanding that simply ring-fencing landscapes did not ensure their sustainability (Head 2012; Birks *et al.* 1988). In New World contexts the cultural landscape label has been problematic in that many lands do not bear obvious (and to Westernised eyes) marks of either 'civilisation' or cultivation although such landscapes may have supported and had the presence of various cultures for many hundreds of years. In the case of Australia for example, Gammage (2011) demonstrates how Aborigines shaped the landscape on a continental scale over a period of forty millennia or more. Thus, although the term 'cultural' is still often used in opposition to 'natural', it is an unhelpful and erroneous continuation of an outdated idea that does not help when thinking about future cultural landscapes. Chapter 2 (Taylor and Francis) provides the context and further discussion on this important aspect of considering how the development of future cultural landscapes is affected by the continuation of the culture versus nature outlook. As is suggested in this chapter, many landscapes that are presently protected and managed under the 'cultural' label, such as National Parks, reflect predominantly western and colonial constructs of values that are in fact often alien to the indigenous populations, their culture and their landscape values. The idea of a 'pristine' ideal landscape is complex and still appears to be strong in some quarters and 'protection' of the landscape (primarily agricultural practice, material features and biodiversity) is often implemented as 'preservation' (not conservation). The implications of this for future cultural landscapes are important, particularly because change is inherent in landscape (as affirmed by the European Landscape Convention) (Figure 1.3) and thus management techniques need to respond to change in both environmental conditions and sociocultural conditions.

As John Wylie (2007) suggests, legions of geographers and others concerned with landscape continue to label landscape as natural and/or cultural and by doing so are still rephrasing 'the error of dividing landscapes up into two fields, into objective facts and layers of subjective meaning' (p. 10). He goes on to suggest that perhaps we 'should think about practices, habits, actions and events, ongoing processes of relating and un-relating that come before any separation of nature and culture'. Taylor (2012) and Selman (2012a) also emphasise the usefulness of considering landscape as process, integrating practices and relationships, to which could be added beliefs. Instead of landscape being the outcome of interactions of nature and culture, *practices* of landscaping – everyday things like walking, looking, gardening, driving,

> *In seeking the right balance between protection, management and planning of a landscape, it should be remembered that the aim is not the preservation or "freezing" of the landscape at a particular point in its lengthy evolution. Landscapes have always changed and will continue to change, both through natural processes and through human action. In fact, the aim should be to manage future changes in a way which recognises the great diversity and the quality of the landscapes that we inherit and which seeks to preserve, or even enhance, that diversity and quality instead of allowing them to decline.*

FIGURE 1.3 Extract from European Landscape Convention, Explanatory Report

Source: CoE 2000b; http://conventions.coe.int/Treaty/EN/Reports/Html/176.htm.

building – are in actuality the cause and origin of our ideas of what is 'nature' and what is 'culture' (Wylie 2007: 11). If we look at the processes and experiences of civilisation and cultivation in this way, it also provides a basis for considering how the term 'cultural' could help in identifying what matters to people about landscape. Wylie (2007) suggests that Ingold's concept of landscape as 'dwelling' is primarily seen in terms of practical activity 'by both humans and animals, that is rooted in an essential, ontological engagement with the material environment' (p. 158) and it is through interaction that the environment becomes meaningful, or becomes landscape. People are thus immersed within an active, practical and perceptual engagement, not a mind/body separation, but a series of relationships that are continually interacting and changing through activity (Ingold 2000).

Our interest in the following chapters of this book is to examine how such ideas and various landscape relationships and practices are relevant to future landscape planning, design and management. The idea of practice is particularly helpful in considering our own approach. Therefore, although there are often references in the literature to culture as something separate from nature, this debate is seen as somewhat old hat. There are however, interesting innovations within European research (e.g. Schneider *et al.* 2010) and the awareness from outside westernised cultures (e.g. Taylor 2009, 2013; Taylor and Lennon 2011) is providing scholars with new ways of understanding such relationships and alternatives to the Renaissance view that seems to have pervaded institutional thinking until very recently.

This book is therefore based on the premise that western (often colonial) influence upon (cultural) landscape protection and management has not been based on a holistic understanding of the culture–nature relationship and, in particular, has not fully understood the intangible values built up over generations within indigenous cultures in relation to landscapes. Chapter 2 (Taylor and Francis) suggests that the result of this is that there has been a degradation of past cultural landscapes as a result of the imposition of management regimes that do not fully understand the integrated nature of landscape. While this book does not aim to rewrite definitions of 'cultural landscape', it does take a holistic view of what cultural landscapes are and tries to understand what cultural landscapes of the future could be through this more integrated view and the contributions of various authors who interpret this idea using case studies from around the world. The development of the idea of future cultural landscapes triggers many questions; in particular how can we consider what future cultures and communities will value about landscapes? The following section provides a starting point for some of the key concepts from the literature as a preliminary to the arguments and case studies analysed within each chapter. The themes that emerge from the chapters are then picked up in Chapter 14.

New cultural landscapes: key concepts and themes

Landscape as process: quality and relationships

The European Landscape Convention (ELC) identifies that all landscapes are of potential value to communities; ordinary and degraded landscapes, water landscapes and seascapes, urban and rural areas are all recognised as 'landscape'. The idea of landscape can then be extended to include spatial concepts (urban areas, countryside, submerged), quality judgements (degraded, ordinary, outstanding beauty), uses (agriculture, transport, industrial), familiarity (everyday, foreign), perceptual (seascapes, skyscapes, waterscapes) and associative (wilderness, sacred).

In particular, the ordinary landscapes where most people live are seen as having potential value to someone, even though the quality may be low in terms of many of the commonly identified indicators, such as scenic beauty, biodiversity rating, range of use and accessibility. The emphasis here is very much on the value to 'someone' (communities, cultures and individuals). Landscape reflects interactions between and evolution of a society's internal and external social, economic and cultural characteristics, influenced by the natural environment's physical constraints and/or opportunities. This suggests that the adjective 'cultural' may be rendered as superfluous in reality as in the Chinese meaning of the word where all landscape is cultural (Han 2012). Is the term 'cultural landscape' therefore a tautology? It has been suggested that it is a metaphor that contains a dualistic construction of humans and the non-human world and that more relational perspectives are needed (Head 2012). This is not a simple issue but such arguments are in the end circular for an underlying aspect of some importance is how far does the concept of cultural landscape entail management and manipulation as opposed to simply experience?

In landscape management, quality has emerged as a key consideration. A number of agencies globally now suggest the need to understand and identify landscape quality and landscape quality objectives and such aims are enshrined within the European Landscape Convention. In spite of the emphasis on quality, there is little evidence to indicate that landscape quality is really what matters to people rather than, for example, familiarity. Thus there seems to be something missing in our present assessment of what actually matters to ordinary people about landscape. Are there commonalities around the world that can be identified and that help us understand what this missing understanding might be? This book uses the idea that all landscapes matter and thus recognises that *qualities* (rather than quality) of landscapes may be one useful starting point in considering what is important.

The American writer J.B. Jackson was one of the first to identify ordinary, everyday and not particularly special landscapes as cultural when thinking particularly of the highway/fast-food/traditionless areas that developed in the 1950s. Jackson (1984) suggests that much could be learned from 'the commonplace aspects of contemporary landscape' (p. ix) in relation to history, society and ourselves, intimating that the landscape is impacted upon by people thus changing those landscapes, and creating new landscapes, through often mundane and everyday actions. In this book authors have been set the task of thinking what constitutes a new cultural landscape and how a particular landscape develops or landscapes develop this characteristic of being new, or at least reshaped. We are interested in probing what possibilities there are for new types of cultural landscape and reshaped or developing new relationships with the landscape. In particular, the everyday and ordinary actions and building of meanings that may create what will be recognised as the cultural landscapes of tomorrow.

Critical to this discourse is the significance of the ordinary and everyday relationships that people have with landscape and landscape-making whereby landscape is viewed 'as a process by which identities are formed' (Mitchell 1994: 1). Ideas have also changed in relation to global definitions and categories of cultural landscapes. Everyday relationships are fundamentally important for the consideration of the designation of World Heritage cultural landscapes in the continuing and associative categories where the ordinary and the concept of Outstanding Universal Value (OUV)[1] are often coincidental. In this connection Francesco Bandarin reflected in relation to those cultural landscapes then inscribed on the World Heritage List 'most of them are living cultural landscapes' (Bandarin 2009: 3). He further drew attention to the fact that all three categories 'provide an opening of the

World Heritage Convention for cultures not or under-represented prior to 1992' (ibid.). Giving examples he speculates that none of these sites would have had a chance of being recognised prior to 1992.

Change

Certainly in the World Heritage categories, consideration of ongoing management is central to their inscription and maintenance of OUV and associated levels of acceptable change. Management in some form or other is also central to familiar everyday landscapes and does involve change over time as human values change. Landscape in real life is not like a picture, immutable. In turn this raises questions of: Does it matter if landscapes change? To whom does it matter? But change must be handled with consideration for those whose values are reflected in the landscape. Here J.B. Jackson's (1963) view that we should never tinker with the landscape without thinking of those who live in the midst of it, is an apt aphorism.

As the attention of policymakers has turned to this issue of landscape change and how it affects and is affected by communities who live within it, so there has been a growth in the development of tools to help measure and explain such change. The use of indicators and monitoring techniques show that change in the landscape is occurring at an increasing speed resulting in alteration to the quality, structure and character of many landscapes around the world with the effect of fragmentation, homogenisation, intensification, removal of diversity, alteration in habitats, species and genes, loss of traditional management cultures and uses and agricultural abandonment. At almost any stage during the known history of landscape, the impacts of such changes have been identified, discussed and the drivers attributed to a variety of, primarily human-induced, activities. But there has also been adaptation to change by communities (both human and other species), and the emergence of new landscapes and responses to change, or coping strategies (sometimes labelled *resilience*). Chapter 5 (Bell) provides a picture of Eastern European landscapes in flux and a population that is shifting to one that is much more urbanised and urban focused. The way people are living is changing rapidly and their reliance on the land and relationship with it is changing, thus the landscape is being abandoned in some areas and in others urbanised, or falling semiderelict, as the political landscape changes. Past writing sometimes describes indigenous communities in particular as having some kind of idealised relationship with the environment or land where equilibrium was reached, or some kind of ecologically constant harmony or 'balance'. Paradise myths support such portrayals, but these pictures have largely been shattered by new investigation and improved knowledge about natural cycles, so that although there is an understanding that long periods of ecological and cultural stability in landscapes can be observed, never-ending equilibrium is not a characteristic of natural or cultural systems (Diamond 2005). Resilience theory has provided us with the view that periods of extreme change are often followed by periods of adaptation, relative stability and less extreme change but that flux is normal and change is integral to natural systems including cultural landscapes. Reference to resilience in landscape literature generally refers to the way a system is able to cope with disturbance or change without the alteration of the 'essential characteristics' of the system (Plieninger and Bieling 2012). If a threshold is reached whereby change occurs, then the system may change character, new processes may be developed and a new 'basin of attraction' reached. Resilience theory provides the idea of the adaptive cycle and a basis for considering how landscape management can provide opportunities for greater sustainability within an understanding of perpetual change (slow and fast) and flux. The focus on resilience theory has encouraged the engagement of ecologists with the idea that consideration of human culture is important in the management approaches to conserve biodiversity in protected areas in particular. But Head (2012) suggests that what might appear as a more holistic approach actually provides an implicit rather than an explicit separation through the use of terms such as 'coupled systems' and 'integrative approach' that suggests two systems that need to be integrated.

In the literature there is a tension between the change that is integral to landscape that builds up layers of meaning for communities and provides the physical state that is perceived as valuable, and the notion that such identity may also be altered by undesirable change – such as globalisation and commodification of culture reflected in and reproduced by landscape planning, design and management. This is not a new discussion and has been highlighted by writers such as Matless and can be found in a number of critiques that compare writers such as Meinig (1979) and Hoskins (1985 [1954]) (see Wylie 2007; Matless 1993). There is a notion that there is 'good' change and 'bad' change in landscape that can be identified just as the extent of change can be measured against that which has occurred already. The concept of resilience is bringing in a slightly different view; that change is inevitable, but that it is the speed of change and the 'from what to what' that is important to consider. In relation to cultural landscapes the key question is, do existing management methods, local knowledge and ability of the landscape to support communities (as well as other species) change so quickly and to such an extent that knowledge and understanding, meanings, associations as well as physical features are lost? Is it possible to identify 'appropriate' change and thus is the idea of limits helpful in considering the acceptability of change to landscapes that alter perceptions of identity (Scazzosi 2011)? In particular, where future conditions become more uncertain, resilience theory may help in understanding how alternative states may be part of cultural landscape management planning (see Selman 2012b).

The idea of a transitional landscape, or one where identifiable periods of particular change can be identified between less unstable stages, is helpful in thinking about how culture(s) and landscapes evolve, and also in suggesting that there *are* periods where change may be minimal. Jackson (1980: 120) suggests that

> The notion of a kind of perpetual transition has the effect of making us appraise many things in terms of a familiar past instead of in terms of present-day realities. The widespread belief that ours is a transitional landscape is a case in point: we tend to see it not as it is, with its own unique character, but as a degenerate version of the traditional landscape, and to see its history as a long, drawn-out backsliding, the abandonment of old values, old techniques, old institutions, with nothing developing to take their place.

This suggests we should focus less on what we lose during periods of transition, but more on what we gain during periods of slow change. Various landscape character assessment and analysis methods are widely used around the world to provide a baseline against which desirable and undesirable change can be monitored (Figure 1.4). While such procedures are useful, the problem can be that they may emphasise the desirability of a static state of character rather than aid value judgements in relation to a natural process of change.

The idea of impact is also important in relation to interaction and change. Impact as a concept in landscape studies is generally represented as anthropocentric in origin or something

FIGURE 1.4 Contemporary cultural expression in Thessaloniki, Greece, reflects present values and sense of place in difficult economic times; it can be regarded as wall art or undesirable graffiti and will probably be a short-lived feature in the urban landscape (Maggie Roe).

that is 'done to' the landscape and negative in character and extent. A rather different take would be that humans interact with landscape in many ways and the impacts or effects of those interactions may be judged as large or small, positive or negative with regard to other species, to the practices, symbols, values, traditions, beliefs used in, on or about land depending on the values upon which such judgements are based. The identification of the traces of human impact, whether tangible or intangible, is the key to cultural landscape heritage designations. The problem here is to what extent such traces of individual or group ideas or actions need to be evident or remembered before a landscape is deemed valuable in cultural terms?

The way we view change in the landscape is particularly important in constructing a view of what a cultural landscape is and could be. For example, it is widely understood that the physical impact on landscape of tourism and the tourist industry can be significant, but the tourists' idea of particular landscapes is also important in changing their own and others' views. This in turn may have both material and perceptual implications for change in the landscape. Tourists can be considered as outsiders. As suggested in Chapter 6 (Jewell and McKinnon) a significant influence on the changing perception, association and the value of particular landscapes from the outside are representations of landscape in media such as films. Examining the imaginary landscapes portrayed in film, texts and other media can help in the understanding of how landscapes are often idealised, or become a part of cultural mythology. Such association or reinterpretation of landscape can be the catalyst for defining a new cultural landscapes on a global scale without individuals having any direct physical association with the material landscape. However such portrayals can also have considerable influence on material change in the landscape; for example a large tourism industry has built up around the location of the imaginary Hobbit landscapes for the *Lord of the Rings* films in New Zealand.

Past landscape imaginaries in media, such as books, often tell us more about the political or cultural desires of the imaginer, the social and economic uncertainties, or of a particular story rather than the material reality of landscape (e.g. Jefferies 2005 [1885]; Shelley 2004 [1826]). The power of mythology is often seen as a way to illuminate particular aspects of the human condition. Various forms of media have become useful not only in representing but exploring the relationship between individuals, communities and the landscape through use as new participatory and interactive tools for planning and design (Roe 2012a, 2012b). Can the scenarios and imaginaries now being produced be used to help us understand what is valued culturally and can they also be used to ascertain what people *might* value as new cultural landscapes?

The influence of imaginaries and media portrayals of landscape on the materiality of landscape suggests the importance of social and cultural systems on determining landscape change – even when there is great physical separation of interested communities. This suggests that new cultural landscapes could be seen primarily as the expression of social and cultural views and change, without necessarily a material interaction with real landscapes. If so, what implications does this have for the creation of new cultural landscapes? In Chapter 6, Jewell and McKinnon argue that a new heritage is created *by* and *for* tourists motivated by film portrayals of landscape, and interaction with film landscapes can help to redefine people's (or group) identities. In a world where we are increasingly reliant on and concerned with virtual representations of landscape, are there observations to be made particularly in relation to the relevance of particular material landscapes to present culture(s)?

As reflected in the principles of the European Landscape Convention, change is integral to landscape. In particular it emerges as a key issue within concepts of cultural landscapes; how landscapes and cultures or communities evolve over time, and how the actions of such communities, and interactions with the natural processes, create cultural landscapes. Thus within the idea of landscape as process, the creation of cultural landscapes can be regarded as an evolutionary condition that reaches from the past into the future. Although this book refers to the issues that arise from the designation and protection of existing cultural landscapes, the emphasis is not on the past, but on the future. Thus emerging ideas relating to present and future landscape change, culture(s), policymaking, planning, design and management are selected and discussed in the chapters. In particular the authors are asked to delve outside existing norms of thinking through their examination of how real landscapes are changing in material and other ways. There is a deliberate choice of both academic and practitioner contributors who, in a variety of ways, have and still do interact with past and present change in the landscapes, and are able to reflect upon the cultural landscape 'label', to contemplate what new cultural landscapes might be and how such landscapes might be emerging.

Interaction, consumption and practice

The vernacular history of the United States suggests that

> a landscape (whether urban or rural) gradually took form when people moved into a place, did what they could to survive and prosper with the resources at hand, and that

they soon organized themselves into a group for mutual help and protection and for celebration of one kind or another . . . landscapes grew and changed.

(Jackson 1980: 114)

While cultural landscapes can be seen to have originally evolved from such survival strategies which entailed intimate knowledge of the landscape, it seems that consumption rather than cultivation may be the driver of new cultural landscapes in a period that is often described as 'post-productive'. The literature is now providing increasing evidence of the importance of a holistic examination of the interactions people have with landscape. Schneider *et al.*'s (2010) study relating to farmers in Switzerland suggests that those working closely with natural cycles interpret natural events against the background of their 'entire life-world' (p. 337), thus the cultural, social and aesthetic considerations, so often ignored by the mass development of landscapes, are crucial in reflecting on management options for landscapes, not just financial, ecological and agronomic dimensions. The farmers made decisions that were not just about the materiality of the landscape, but were based on cultural and social values and norms, plus personal and professional ethics and identities which they regarded as integral to, not separate from, decisions about land management. Chapter 11 (Ahmed) describes how new cultural landscapes have been created out of the Egyptian desert around Cairo. The culture is about making the desert liveable. This is not necessarily a new or unusual objective for communities in arid lands, but these new landscapes around Cairo also represent a culture where landscape value is monetarised and where the product emphasises social exclusion. Perhaps the key change is that of landscape character and cultural meaning as developers expand into areas traditionally forbidden to the living.

The fundamental principles of sustainability reflect this idea that relationships between people and the environment matter; much of the concentration by policymakers on trying to increase environmental sustainability has been on how to create a greater awareness and closeness to natural cycles, functioning and attributes in order to increase our understanding of the significance of the present global environmental crisis. Chapter 9 (Duffy) focuses on another aspect of the post-productive potential for creating new cultural landscapes. Using examples from Indonesia, the chapter concentrates on two main areas of focus. The first is on *garbagescapes* landscape of consumption. In the UK we hide waste in big holes in the ground; in Indonesia the waste produced is seen as a resource. The people whose livelihoods depend on the waste build a new landscape, not of consumption but of recycling. These landscapes provide a living, have an identity, sounds, smells and a sense of place which can be revealed and is being revealed by artists. The new cultural landscapes that are thus exposed show that a new living is provided for communities from material rejected by others; the physical garbage provides a new landscape, with landform and features that act as a resource used in a similar way to those in other landscapes. It is argued that in both the *garbagescapes* and *disasterscapes* discussed in this chapter, there is beauty and meaning. But this is a very different meaning to that which the new landscape replaces.

Power and control: justice, politics, involvement and democracy

Ways of 'seeing' indicate much more than an ocular-centric idea (see Macpherson 2005) and the use of language is sometimes misunderstood. Olwig (1996) refutes much of the visual emphasis on landscape and explains it as something more material, embedded in considerations of law and justice. In the ordinary ways of using, experiencing and living in the landscape by people over long periods of time, or the customary use embedded within locality and culture (Wylie 2007; Olwig 2007), legal boundaries have made the 'social order visible in the landscape' (Jackson 1980: 115). Ownership and use of even small spaces help to define identity, status and 'most important of all, it establishes lasting relationships' (ibid.). The organisation of spaces signifies the values of a community, and as those values change so do the organisation of the spaces; clearly laws and customs affect the form of the landscape.

Eckersley (2006) describes an example of the appropriation of the material and visual landscape for political reasons by Hitler's administration in Germany in the late 1930s as a way of claiming ownership and control of German culture on behalf of the body politic. She goes on to describe how present-day German politicians understand the value of buildings in particular as a mirror of culture. Architectural development is not seen as passive in this relationship, but a moulder of culture (Brawne 2003). In the same way, the materiality of the cultural landscape provides spaces that reflect desires, emotions and identity and thus depict a culture's relationship with the material world as well as with others dwelling within that world. The experience and perception of such landscape portrays much about those dwelling in the landscape, and provides the pattern for passing on traditions, beliefs and customs.

In considering what new cultural landscapes might be, the principle of democracy as reflected in recent landscape policy and theory provides a useful and new basis for interpretation of the impact that changing cultural values might have on a future landscape. A more inclusive idea of landscape provides a more democratic concept for considering cultural landscapes. Politics cannot be separated from the consideration of cultural landscapes, although much is often left unsaid in cultural landscape studies on the subject. The broadening of the idea of value to include ordinary or everyday landscapes and not just those considered 'special', supports the idea that not only the landscape, but the culture(s) that conceive and create the landscape, matter. In the past, visual assessment and designed landscapes have had most attention in relation to the cultural landscape label, even though the origins of the term 'cultural' are much more mundane and can be traced back to ideas of cultivation, manipulation and management, rather than grand design.

Chapters 8 (Speak) and 10 (Egoz) suggest that revolution and migration may instigate the development of new cultural landscapes. In Chapter 8, Speak discusses how communities now living in squatter settlements and urban agricultural landscapes in India and other countries of the Global South have been forced to give up their rural homelands and in resettling create new landscapes. In so doing, landscape knowledge (agricultural production) is transported and reapplied, or reinterpreted in the creation of new cultural landscapes. In the story of Jewish settlers in Palestine, Egoz suggests that there was a return to ancient knowledge or myths linked to the landscape, because the location that they moved to afforded them the possibility of reconnecting with the biblical landscape. The new cultural landscape was based upon reviving cultural tradition, or perhaps reinvented cultural tradition, rather than reinterpreting knowledge to provide something novel in a new setting as in the cases that Speak discusses in relation to the Global South.

Egoz further suggests the ability of cultures to be selective (selective amnesia) in the use – and perhaps creation – of (landscape) myths upon which they create new landscapes. A number of chapters reflect the importance of how landscape stories are constructed by cultures and the way they are passed on. The exclusion and lack of justice in sociocultural systems is reflected in landscapes today as in the past. But these are often not fully recognised. Within these chapters there are difficult issues discussed of justice and democracy, and an indication of a growing awareness of individual and community rights and responsibilities in relation to landscape creation. Participatory working and involvement in landscape change has an increasing focus in both academic studies and landscape practice generally. Although much of this area of study is based on concepts of democracy and empowerment, it is also based on a realisation that healthy lifestyles, quality of life, individual and social well-being have a strong connection to the environmental conditions under which we live.

Linkage – past, present and future values

The interpretation of cultural landscapes as predominantly something that has been created through past actions and interactions between humans and the natural world owes much to the development of World Heritage Committee criteria on Outstanding Universal Value (Figure 1.5). All cultural landscapes that are considered for World Heritage designation have to meet criteria of authenticity and physical and/or contextual and/or environmental integrity (Fowler 2003). There are obvious difficulties with these judgements of landscape qualities and quality which are well rehearsed in the literature. In relation to the consideration of what future cultural landscapes might be, there are some particular issues to consider which are related to landscape change, as introduced above: do cultural landscapes reflect a certain snap-shot in time? Do cultural landscapes need to be 'working', as in physically productive and/or functioning in some way so as to retain 'authenticity', or can they just be 'valued', as in imaginary filmic landscapes? How can new cultural landscapes be created and continue to evolve while retaining their integrity and the identity of the culture(s) who dwell within them?

The discussion of heritage tends to assume that what is valued by present generations is often longevity in landscape management practices, evidence of settlement and character and function; that a sense of community identity can be linked to the character of the landscape and the landscape provides a basis for memories, associations, or as Jackson (1980) suggests, the provenance of roots. The idea that places need a working connection between past and present is embedded within much of this thinking about which landscapes are more significant than others. Although much discussion over the loss of what could be described as 'cultural capital' as reflected in landscape is about fear of the future, there is also an under-standing that past knowledge may be lost as we move away from a close relationship with the physical landscape that comes with direct contact with it through, for example, cultivation. A similar outlook can be found in relation to biodiversity conservation, where it is felt that loss of species – often as yet unrecognised – through environmental destruction could result in the loss of unidentified assets or environmental services.

Protection is often based on the idea that such landscapes are distinctive. But do cultural landscapes need distinctiveness to be significant, and does distinctiveness develop over time? The literature indicates that the various characteristics of perception of landscape commonly brought together under the concept of sense of place are important in the idea of what is valuable in cultural landscapes. This idea has its roots in the idea of *genius loci* and was much referenced in the eighteenth-century English Landscape School of design. Alexander Pope (1731) suggested that to design landscape well it is necessary to 'consult the genius of the place in all'. Originating from Roman thought, the *genius loci* is portrayed as a protective deity, something that exists without human presence in a place, and then variously defined and

Section 77: The Committee considers a property as having Outstanding Universal Value if the property meets one or more of the following criteria. Nominated properties shall therefore:

(i)   represent a masterpiece of human creative genius;

(ii)   exhibit an important interchange of human values, over a span of time or within a cultural area of the world, on developments in architecture or technology, monumental arts, town planning or landscape design;

(iii) bear a unique or at least exceptional testimony to a cultural tradition or to a civilization which is living or which has disappeared;

(iv)   be an outstanding example of a type of building, architectural or technological ensemble or landscape which illustrates (a) significant stage(s) in human history;

(v)   be an outstanding example of a traditional human settlement, land-use, or sea-use which is representative of a culture (or cultures), or human interaction with the environment especially when it has become vulnerable under the impact of irreversible change;

(vi)   be directly or tangibly associated with events or living traditions, with ideas, or with beliefs, with artistic and literary works of outstanding universal significance. (The Committee considers that this criterion should preferably be used in conjunction with other criteria);

(vii) contain superlative natural phenomena or areas of exceptional natural beauty and aesthetic importance;

(viii) be outstanding examples representing major stages of earth's history, including the record of life, significant on-going geological processes in the development of landforms, or significant geomorphic or physiographic features;

(ix)   be outstanding examples representing significant ongoing ecological and biological processes in the evolution and development of terrestrial, fresh water, coastal and marine ecosystems and communities of plants and animals;

(x)   contain the most important and significant natural habitats for in-situ conservation of biological diversity, including those containing threatened species of Outstanding Universal Value from the point of view of science or conservation.

Section 78: To be deemed of Outstanding Universal Value, a property must also meet the conditions of integrity and/or authenticity and must have an adequate protection and management system to ensure its safeguarding.

FIGURE 1.5   Criteria for the assessment of Outstanding Universal Value

Source: UNESCO 2011: Sections 77 and 78, pp. 20–21.

extended to an intangible and somewhat static quality of a material site that can be perceived intuitively by humans within a particular landscape. *Genius loci*, translated as the spirit of place, has been redefined as a dynamic relational concept where physical and spiritual elements give meaning, value, emotion and mystery to a place (UNESCO 2008). Rifaioglu and Neriman's (2008) review of these ideas suggests that humans give spirit to places through their actions and experiences within the places; that patterns of events in particular places add to the perception of sense of place. Sense of place indicates some kind of reaction and/or interaction with a particular place or landscape; this can be something quite benign that grows through a connection with a landscape over a long period, or it may be a sense that is gained over a very short exposure to landscape never previously visited or known. It can be applied to all kinds of landscapes – relating again to the ELC terminology – from the everyday to the extraordinary. Sense of place is seen as a key issue in landscape planning because the success of any planning action relies on how the communities value and thus manage the landscape. Participatory landscape practice and the growth of theoretical approaches and practical methods for carrying out such practice as well as the phenomenological 'turn' in landscape studies emphasising ideas of embodiment have led to a literature relating to experiential and interactive methods of revealing landscape relationships (see Wylie 2012; Thwaites and Simkins 2007). There is also discussion about whether the sensing body or the historical-cultural interpretations of landscape are generally predominant in the approaches that examine the relationship of humans and landscape (Wattchow 2012). Sense of place has become an important discussion in relation to the wider landscape (Roe 2012c) and there seems to be some relationship between participation in the landscape and the establishment of sense of place. There are also suggestions that only focusing on a local sense of place may result in the wider issues, such as those relating to sustainability in the landscape and cultural norms, being forgotten (Wattchow 2012). There is often a suggestion that reconnecting with the landscape and re-establishing perceptions of sense of place within communities is important, although the evidence base for this is still emerging and requires critical examination even though there are good examples of how this might occur (Selman 2012a). This relationship between sense of place and participation in the landscape is not yet clear, however interesting exploratory projects based on this notion, such as the PlaceBook Scotland website[2] where an eclectic collection of images, film, music and writing has been uploaded by the public to capture the sense of place of the Scottish landscape, suggest collective activities may be useful. Chapter 3 (Davies) and Chapter 4 (Mitchell and Barrett) provide insights as to how participatory processes and new partnership structures have been and continue to be significant in the production of new cultural landscapes in various contexts around the world including completely new landscapes established on former derelict areas and those with a long – but deteriorating – agricultural tradition.

It seems that the exhibition of linkages between past, present and future and the way change is revealed in the materiality of landscape features is often precisely what make cultural landscapes valued. This recognition of the importance of change or a continuum approach to cultural heritage and the idea that such heritage can contain ecological and cultural and historical information is revealed in studies of marine cultural sites (Mather and Jensen 2010) where wrecks have become integrated into marine ecosystems as habitat or as parts of the benthic environment. Studies suggest that an approach based on understandings of the dynamic nature of relationships that create what we see as cultural landscapes has helped in the recognition of the significance of ecological processes in the study and management of such marine landscapes. However, these landscapes are under severe threat of degradation and thus their potential for value may change (Figure 1.6). This theme is picked up by Melnick in Chapter 13 who critiques a head-in-the-sand approach to conserving the continuity of existing cultural landscapes where potential continuity is under threat.

While the sustainability agenda is influencing policy and practice as well as outlooks on consumption and landscape, the potential impact of climate change has re-emphasised the dynamic nature of landscape and the need for science-based understandings to open up to more social and cultural interpretation. Chapter 13 (Melnick) asks whether today's cultural landscapes will still be seen as cultural landscapes in the future under the impact of climate change and discusses how the response to climate change measures may result in the creation of new cultural landscapes. What makes existing cultural landscapes cultural/valued? Will changes in the material building blocks of such landscapes – species, soils, hydrology – result in the deterioration in people's perception of the value of cultural landscapes? Can

FIGURE 1.6 Underwater marine landscapes have long been valued by tourists for the cultural and ecological riches but integrated processes and values are only recently becoming clearer through research and the attention brought by changing marine conservation policies (Alistair Jenkins).

existing cultural landscape management encourage resilience and create new forms of sustainable cultural landscapes? The chapter discusses opinion, science and impact on our attitude to and practice of management and cultural landscapes as a continuum of the integration of past cultural practice and natural process; what happens when one of these is the driver of massive change?

Immense change is nowhere as apparent as in the new urban landscapes of China. Chapter 12 (Padua) considers what the new cultural landscapes might be in China. Given the central government's target to build 400 additional cities by 2020 (Liaw 2008) and a continuing mass migration of populations from rural areas to cities, how can designers create landscapes that will connect with and provide meaning to people? Should the cultural 'baggage' of migrating populations be reflected in new landscapes created for them, and if so how can this be done? How can designers provide meaning when the scale and rate of such change is so vast?

The importance of understanding changing relationships over time between humans and natural resources is revealed in the living landscape philosophy found in the ecomuseum approach discussed in Chapter 7 (Davis and Corsane). While the label 'museum' is still seen as indicating a somewhat static reference to the way heritage is presented, the ecomuseum movement is providing the possibility that new cultural landscapes may not necessarily be entirely new, but may be a new way of interpreting existing, often everyday, landscapes, or in considering a different scale of landscape significance since such approaches are often based on large areas. Ecomuseum approaches provide a more holistic way of understanding value and processes of landscapes. Can such approaches help protect valued landscapes as well as provide a viable future for them? The term 'cultural landscape' has become somewhat synonymous with the categorisation and protection of special landscapes and particularly protection and management of natural and cultural heritage as set out by the International Scientific Committee on Cultural Landscapes (ICOMOS) and the International Union for Conservation of Nature (IUCN). But these chapters provide some alternative ways of thinking about cultural landscapes.

Summary

This chapter reviews and establishes the key attributes that might lie behind the idea of new cultural landscapes. It provides some concepts for examining what new cultural landscapes might be. The objective of this book is to reflect on what people are passionate about in landscape and what provides the basis for that key connection with landscape that makes land something more than a useful resource. If we can get under the skin of what places mean to people then perhaps we can in future create and recreate landscapes that will be highly valued. The inspiration for the idea of new cultural landscapes is drawn from the heritage literature relating to the planning, design and management of existing and past cultural landscapes, particularly the way cultural landscapes are created by ideas, features, elements, processes, experiences and uses and how life is played out in cultural landscapes. But in the contributions to this book, inspiration is primarily gained through the experience of the authors who bring together their analysis from past and present to gaze into the future and consider new imaginaries, myths and conceptions of cultural landscape in both time and space. Imaginaries and envisioning are seen as important in this debate, in spite of suggestions that nostalgia from traditional and imagined landscapes can prevent the emergence of more sustainable landscapes (Selman 2012a). Greater sustainability cannot be achieved without landscapes being valued; desires and needs as expressed through imaginaries, and links to the traditions and practices of the past would seem to be important in this. The most relevant question is, perhaps, what will be valued in future? What will future landscapes reveal of our everyday relationships with each other and natural cycles? What culture(s) will be reflected, and how, in landscape? How can we manage existing and create new landscapes with material and symbolic elements of significance? (Figure 1.7) What will future populations understand from an analysis of the landscapes we are presently creating, how sustainable will they be and will these landscapes hold any meaning?

While identification, categorisation and protection of landscapes created by past cultures is important, this book is primarily interested in exploring conceptions of cultural landscape that might be useful in planning, managing and designing future landscapes. This book investigates the alternative view of cultural landscape; that is, not simply a 'cultural repository of evidence' (Howard 2011: 24), which seems to be a popular view of landscape, but something that is living, changing, reflective of contemporary concerns and lifestyles and where the direction of change can be determined through an interactive process between natural systems, including human interventions and actions. In particular, it aims to explore whether it is possible to identify some universalities in the complex relationships, values and qualities which constitute presently evolving landscapes that could lead to their recognition as 'cultural

FIGURE 1.7   The face of Northumberlandia: a massive earth sculpture created on derelict former coal extraction site. This new green space to the north of Newcastle upon Tyne aims to capture intangible and tangible values within a new public landscape (Maggie Roe).

landscapes'. If this recognition is possible, can we then propose how such understandings might be used to create future landscapes, through planning, design and management, that can be valued by communities, policymakers and practitioners in such a way as to justify the 'cultural landscape' label?

Notes

1   Outstanding Universal Value (OUV) means cultural and/or natural significance which is so exceptional as to transcend national boundaries and to be of common importance for present and future generations of all humanity. As such, the permanent protection of this heritage is of the highest importance to the international community as a whole. The Committee defines the criteria for the inscription of properties on the World Heritage List (UNESCO 2011: para 49, p. 16).
2   Placebook Scotland website: http://placebookscotland.co.uk/.

References

Bandarin, F. (2009) 'Preface', in *UNESCO World Heritage Papers 26*, Paris: UNESCO World Heritage Centre.
Bauer, N., Wallner, A. and Hunziker, M. (2009) 'The Change of European Landscapes: Human-Nature Relationships, Public Attitudes towards Rewilding, and the Implications for Landscape Management in Switzerland', *Journal of Environmental Management*, 90, 9: 2910–2920.

Birks, H.H., Birks, H.J.B., Kaland, P.E. and Moe, D. (eds) (1988) *The Cultural Landscape: Past Present and Future*, Cambridge: Cambridge University Press.

Brawne, M. (2003) *Architectural Thought and the Design Process: Continuity, Innovation, and the Expectant Eye*, Burlington: Elsevier.

Brown, S. (2008) *Cultural Landscapes and Park Management: A Literature Snapshot*, a report for the cultural landscapes: connecting history, heritage and reserve management research project, Sydney: Department of Environment and Climate Change, New South Wales, Australia.

Brown, J. and Kothari, A. (2011) 'Traditional Agricultural Landscapes and Community Conserved Areas: An Overview', *Management of Environmental Quality: An International Journal*, 22, 2: 139–153.

CoE (Council of Europe) (2000a) *The European Landscape Convention* text, online. Available at: http://conventions.coe.int/Treaty/en/Treaties/Html/176.htm.

CoE (Council of Europe) (2000b) *The European Landscape Convention: Explanatory Report*, online. Available at: http://conventions.coe.int/Treaty/EN/Reports/Html/176.htm.

Convery, I. and Dutson, T. (2008) 'Rural Communities and Landscape Change: A Case Study of Wild Ennerdale', *Journal of Rural and Community Development*, 3(1): 104–118.

Cosgrove, D.E. (1998 [1984]) *Social Formation and Symbolic Landscape*, London: Croom Helm.

Diamond, J. (2005) *Collapse, or How Societies Choose to Fail or Survive*, London: Penguin.

Dudley, N. and Stolton, S. (2012) *Protected Landscapes and Wildlife Biodiversity*, Gland, Switzerland: IUCN.

Eckersley, S.C. (2006) '(Re) Creating Positive Cultural Landscapes in Germany: The Role of Iconic Museum Buildings' paper presented at the Forum UNESCO University and Heritage 10th International Seminar *Cultural Landscapes in the 21st Century*, Newcastle upon Tyne, UK, April 2005. Available at: http://conferences.ncl.ac.uk/unescolandscapes/files/REIDsusannah%20Eckersley.pdf (accessed 17 April 2013).

Fowler, P.J. (2003) 'World Heritage Cultural Landscapes 1992–2002: A Review and Prospect', in *Cultural Landscapes: The Challenges of Conservation*, World Heritage Papers 7, Paris: UNESCO World Heritage Centre, pp 16–32.

Gammage, Bill (2011) *The Biggest Estate on Earth: How Aborigines Made Australia*, Sydney: Allen & Unwin.

Glacken, C. (1967) *Traces on the Rhodian Shore: Nature and Culture in Western Thought from Ancient Times to the End of the Eighteenth Century*, Berkeley: University of California Press.

Han, F. (2012) 'Cultural Landscape: A Chinese Way of Seeing Nature', in K. Taylor and J. Lennon (eds) *Managing Cultural Landscapes*, London: Routledge, pp. 90–108.

Head, L. (2012) 'Conceptualising the Human in Cultural Landscapes and Resilience Thinking', in T. Plieninger and C. Bieling (eds) *Resilience and the Cultural Landscape*, Cambridge: Cambridge University Press, pp. 65–79.

Hoskins, W.G. (1985 [1954]) *The Making of the English Landscape*, London: Penguin.

Howard, P. (2011) *An Introduction to Landscape*, Farnham: Ashgate.

Ingold, T. (2000) *The Perception of the Environment: Essays on Livelihood, Dwelling and Skill*, London: Routledge.

Jackson, J.B. (1963) 'Goodbye to Evolution', *Landscape*, 13, 2: 1–3.

Jackson, J.B. (1980) *The Necessity for Ruins and Other Topics*, Amherst: University of Massachusetts Press.

Jackson, J.B. (1984) *Discovering the Vernacular Landscape*, New Haven: Yale University Press.

Jacques, D. (1995) 'The Rise of Cultural Landscapes', *International Journal of Heritage Studies*, 1, 2: 91–101.

Jefferies, R. (2005 [1885]) *After London or Wild England*, Cirencester: Echo Library.

Liaw, L. (2008) 'Leaping Forward Getting Rich Gloriously, and Letting a Hundred Cities Bloom', *Architectural Design*, 78, 5: 6–15.

Logan, P.M. (2013) 'On Culture: Matthew Arnold's Culture and Anarchy, 1869', in D.F. Felluga (ed.) *BRANCH: Britain, Representation and Nineteenth-Century History* (Extension of Romanticism and Victorianism on the Net. Web). Available at: http://www.branchcollective.org/?ps_articles=peter-logan-on-culture-matthew-arnolds-culture-and-anarchy-1869 (accessed 7 February 2013).

Lowenthal, D. (1975) 'Introduction', in D. Lowenthal and M. Binney (eds) *Our Past Before Us: Why Do We Save It?*, London: Temple Smith, pp. 9–16.

Lowenthal, D. (1978) 'Finding Valued Landscapes', *Progress in Human Geography*, 21, 3: 373–418.

Lowenthal, D. (2007) 'Living with and Looking at Landscape', *Landscape Research*, 32, 5: 635–656.

Macpherson, H.M. (2005) 'Landscape's Ocular Centrism: And Beyond?', in G. Tress, G. Fry and P. Opdam (eds) *From Landscape Research to Landscape Planning: Aspects of Integration, Education and Application*, Heidelberg: Springer, pp. 95–104.

Mather, R. and Jensen, J. (2010) *Investigations into Block Island's Submerged Cultural Sites and Landscapes for the Rhode Island Ocean Special Area Management Plan 2010*, University of Rhode Island, 20 June 2010. Available at: http://seagrant.gso.uri.edu/oceansamp/pdf/appendix/05-Mather-Archeology Resources_reduced.pdf (accessed 19 November 2010).

Matless, D. (1993) 'One Man's England: W.G. Hoskins and the English Culture of Landscape', *Rural History*, 4, 2: 187–207.

Meinig, D.W. (1979) 'Introduction', in D.W. Meinig (ed.) *The Interpretation of Ordinary Landscapes*, Oxford and New York: Oxford University Press, pp. 1–7.

Mitchell, W.J.T. (1994) *Landscape and Power*, Chicago: University of Chicago Press.

Olwig, K. (1996) 'Recovering the Substantive Nature of Landscape', *Annals of the Association of American Geographers*, 86(4): 630–653.

Olwig, K. (2007) 'The Practice of Landscape "Conventions" and the Just Landscape: The Case of the European Landscape Convention', *Landscape Research*, 32, 5: 579–594.

Plieninger, T. and Bieling, C. (2012) 'Connecting Cultural Landscapes to Resilience', in T. Plieninger and C. Bieling (eds) *Resilience and the Cultural Landscape*, Cambridge: Cambridge University Press, pp. 3–26.

Pope, A. (1731) *An Epistle to the Right Honourable Richard Earl of Burlington, Occasion'd by his Publishing Palladio's Designs of the Baths, Arches, Theatres, &c. of Ancient Rome*. Available at: http://oll.libertyfund. org/?option=com_staticxt&staticfile=show.php%3Ftitle=2278&chapter=216011&layout=html& Itemid=27 (accessed 16 April 2013).

Rifaioglu, M.N. and Neriman, S.G. (2008) 'Understanding and Preserving Spirit of Place by an Integrated Methodology in Historical Urban Contexts', in *16th ICOMOS General Assembly and International Symposium: 'Finding the Spirit of Place – between the Tangible and Intangible'*, 29 September– 4 October 2008, Quebec, Canada. Available at: http://openarchive.icomos.org/64/ (accessed on 21 February 2013).

Roe, M.H. (2012a) 'Landscape and Participation', in P. Howard, I.H. Thompson and E. Waterton (eds) *The Routledge Companion to Landscape Studies*, Abingdon: Routledge, pp. 335–352.

Roe, M.H. (2012b) 'Participatory Landscape Practice', in T. Papayannis and P. Howard (eds) *Reclaiming the Greek Landscape*, Athens: MedINA, pp. 257–271.

Roe, M.H. (2012c) 'Making Sense of Place at the Landscape Scale', in I. Convery, G. Corsane and P. Davis (eds) *Making Sense of Place: Multidisciplinary Perspectives*, Woodbridge: Boydell, pp. 191–206.

Salter, C.L. (1971) *The Cultural Landscape*, Belmont: Duxbury.

Sauer, C. (1925) 'The Morphology of Landscape', *Geography*, 2, 2: 19–54.

Scazzosi, L. (2011) 'Limits to Transformation in Places' Identity: Theoretical and Methodological Questions', in Z. Roca, P. Claval and J. Agnew (eds) *Landscapes, Identities and Development*, Farnham: Ashgate, pp. 9–24.

Schneider, F., Ledermann, T., Fry, P. and Rist, S. (2010) 'Soil Conservation in Swiss Agriculture: Approaching Abstract and Symbolic Meaning in Farmers' Life-Worlds', *Land Use Policy*, 27, 1: 332–339.

Selman, P. (2012a) *Sustainable Landscape Planning: The Reconnection Agenda*, Abingdon: Earthscan/ Routledge.

Selman, P. (2012b) 'Landscapes as Integrating Frameworks for Human, Environmental and Policy Processes', in T. Plieninger and C. Bieling (eds) *Resilience and the Cultural Landscape*, Cambridge: Cambridge University Press, pp. 27–48.

Shelley, M. (2004 [1826]) *The Last Man*, London: Wordsworth Editions.

Silva, K.D. and Chapagain, N.K. (eds) (2013) *Asian Heritage Management: Contexts, Concerns and Prospects*, Abingdon: Routledge.

Stilgoe, J.R. (1982) *Common Landscapes of America 1580–1845*, New Haven: Yale University Press.

Taylor, K. (2009) 'Cultural Landscapes and Asia: Reconciling International and Southeast Asian Regional Values', *Landscape Research*, 34, 1: 7–32.

Taylor, K. (2012) 'Landscape and Meaning: Context for a Global Discourse on Cultural Landscape Values', in K. Taylor and J. Lennon (eds) *Managing Cultural Landscapes*, London and New York: Routledge, pp. 21–44.

Taylor, K. (2013) 'The Challenges of the Cultural Landscape Construct and Associated Intangible Values in an Asian Context', in K.D. Silva and N.K. Chapagain (eds) *Asian Heritage Management: Contexts, Concerns and Prospects*, London: Routledge, pp. 189–211.

Taylor, K. and Lennon, J. (2011) 'Cultural Landscapes: A Bridge between Culture and Nature', *International Journal of Heritage Studies*, 17, 6: 537–554.

Thwaites, K. and Simkins, I.M. (2007) *Experiential Landscape: An Approach to People, Place, and Space*, Abingdon: Routledge.

UNESCO (2008) *Quebec Declaration on the Preservation of the Spirit of Place, Adopted at Quebec, Canada, 4 October 2008*. Available at: http:whc.unesco.org/uploads/activities/documents/activity-646-2.pdf (accessed 21 February 2013).

UNESCO (2011) *Operational Guidelines for the Implementation of the World Heritage Convention*, Paris: UNESCO World Heritage Centre. Available at: http://whc.unesco.org/archive/opguide11-en.pdf (accessed 21 February 2013).

Wattchow, B. (2012) 'Landscape, Sense of Place: Creative Tension', in P. Howard, I. Thompson and E. Waterton (eds) *The Routledge Companion to Landscape Studies*, Abingdon: Routledge, pp. 87–96.

Williams, R. (1985 [1976]) *Keywords: A Vocabulary of Culture and Society*, revised edn, Oxford: Oxford University Press.

Wylie, J. (2007) *Landscape*, London: Routledge.

Wylie, J. (2012) 'Landscape and Phenomenology', in P. Howard, I. Thompson and E. Waterton (eds) *The Routledge Companion to Landscape Studies*, Abingdon: Routledge, pp. 43–65.

2

CULTURE–NATURE DILEMMAS

Confronting the challenge of the integration of culture and nature

Ken Taylor and Keven Francis

landscape 'is never simply a natural space, a feature of the natural environment . . . every landscape is the place where we establish our own human organization of space and time'.

(Jackson 1984: 156)

Introduction

With a focus on Australia and some reference to international practice this chapter examines culture–nature interplays and associated dilemmas. It addresses a number of points which are a crucial part of the critical culture–nature discourse. These include Indigenous Australian[1] values and spiritual integration with landscape within the spectrum of the deeply rich association between people and country;[2] alternative conceptions of cultural landscapes; and biodiversity as a driver of cultural landscape values in the culture–nature continuum. These are examined in the light of shifts over the past decade from what may be seen to be the myopically entrenched views of some conservationists for whom the idea that people shaping landscapes (country), as well as adding value such as biodiversity by their actions, is anathema.

Until the 1990s there was a clear, if to some of us, uneasy, division between cultural and natural heritage conservation. This was based on a hegemony of Western values where cultural heritage resided in monuments and sites and scientific ideas of nature and wilderness as something separate from people. Culture and nature were divided. Reflecting this, for example, cultural and natural World Heritage criteria were separate until 2005 when they were sensibly combined (UNESCO 2005).

Environmental ethics were central to the debate on natural values, in particular that of whether nature has instrumental value or intrinsic value. Instrumental value is assigned because of the usefulness of something; in contrast intrinsic value relates to values of things as ends in themselves (Feng Han 2006). To complicate matters further is the question of the origin of intrinsic value (ibid.). Is it subjective, created by human thought and value systems, or is it objective where value is endemic in its own right and simply waiting to be recognised objectively? Is nature valued as purely an object without any human interest or spiritual attachment? Entwined in our ideas of culture and nature is that of aesthetic appreciation. Here, few would argue that aesthetic value of nature and that of creations from the cultural domain which we can call works of art – and here we include human shaping of the landscape – both exist, but that the kind of value appreciation each encourages within a Western historical and philosophical perspective is often different (Berleant 1993). This schism has affected approaches to conservation where aesthetics of nature and culture are separated. But in the final analysis are not both cultural constructs and that to divide nature and culture is misleading?

Complicating matters even further was the emergence in the 1970s of deep ecology (Naess 2003) which inspired extension of the debate on nature preservation for its own intrinsic values. To preserve nature for its own sake was regarded as a mark of supreme respect, and amongst the avid wilderness lobby still is. Nature is concerned with the natural world; it is the phenomenon of the physical world – flora, fauna, natural environments and their physical components, and the processes that shape these – and excludes made objects and human interaction. In this concept even the word nature itself is a tool of separation and a means of valorising a Western perspective of framing nature as a fixed commodity, which is traded on the academic and commercial market.

The idea of wilderness: what do we mean by nature?

Central to the discourse on nature has been the concept of wilderness with its Western connotations of supreme value where people are visitors but not residents. Indeed as visitors they are often viewed by wilderness purists as a nuisance because they spoil the solitude experience. But the question here is, whose solitude and whose values?

Another question also is whether the very act of visiting and looking renders a place no longer wilderness as alluded to in Wallace Steven's poem, *Anecdote of the Jar*:

> I placed a jar in Tennessee,
> And round it was, upon a hill,
> It made the slovenly wilderness
> Surround that hill.
> The wilderness rose up to it,
> And sprawled, no longer wild.

Even more critical are the value systems that traditional communities worldwide associate deeply with so-called natural areas as part of their cultural beliefs, and the fact that many traditional communities live in or visit these so-called wilderness places as part of their life systems and may have done so for millennia. This prompts the question of what do we mean by nature? Is it the 1960s American model enshrined in the Wilderness Act with its connections to Protestant Christian, colonial, and postcolonial cultural associations from the English-speaking Western world? It is what Edward Said pithily refers to as the 'Puritan errand into the wilderness' (Said 1994: 63). Such concepts of nature have now assumed a global perspective where some so-called 'natural areas' are seen as conservation (preservation?) national park options with local inhabitants either evicted or marginalised to perform for tourists.

The role model for the national park approach rests in the United States' nineteenth national agenda of sublime, awe-inspiring natural wonders as a basis for national parks. They were regarded, as Nash (1973) critically explores, as symbolic of something special to the New World bequeathed by God to the civilising hand of white Christian immigrants who would look after them as God intended. That the first national park at Yellowstone had been the ancestral home of Native Americans was ignored in this heroic epic; their forced and brutal eviction swept under the carpet of civilising history. Tourism and cleansing contact with 'nature' for city dwellers overruled any rights and traditions of looking after the land of their ancestors that the original owners had. The continuing tragedy of this is that it is a pattern of land management that continues to the present day in the name of national parks.

Certainly criticisms of this model arose in the 1990s. Notably one criticism came from the Indian writer, Ramachandra Guha, in 1989 (in Feng Han 2006). He condemned wilderness as harmful to developing countries because its creation, which excludes people, ignores the needs of local communities. Twenty years ago he saw wilderness preservation areas as a new, American, imperialist project. As places for rich visitors they transfer resources from the poor to the rich. This is now having wider impacts as some places in Asia are declared the equivalent of Western-inspired national parks, opened for tourism that is either restricted or is mass tourism oriented but where local communities are evicted and sometimes man-made structures are demolished.

It is our view that we should recognise culture and nature as entwined components of landscape. The alternative of extracting humans is a distorted concept built on the Western paradigm of separating nature from human occupation and shaping of the landscape.

In the cultural landscape idea – landscape as a cultural construct (Taylor 2012) – culture and nature coexist within a humanistic philosophy of the world around us. It is an holistic approach to the human–nature relationship as opposed to the idea of human detachment from nature (Taylor and Lennon 2011). It is also a non-Western paradigm central to the Indigenous Australian concept of country and the bond between people, beliefs, ancestors and the total environment, beneath, on and above the land or water. In this paradigm there is no division between culture and nature as in the Western conceptual division, the activities of humans and nature are fundamentally bound for mutual survival. All country is part of a made world, a cultural landscape.

> Indigenous people have a holistic meaning for 'country', which encompasses land and landforms, water and marine resources, the plants, trees, animals, and other species which the land and sea support, and cultural heritage sites. The whole cultural landscape and the interrelationships within the ecosystem are encompassed in the term 'Country', and these relate to landowners under customary law in diverse ways, for example through links to totemic species.
>
> *(Hunt et al. 2009: 1)*

Who owns nature?

The forgoing discussion prompts the fundamental questions of who owns nature and for whom is it to be protected? Descola (2008) lucidly probes these questions in an essay that takes as its starting point how international policies for environmental protection are predicated on a very specific – narrow? – conception of nature from the European Enlightenment. He proposes that this conception is far from being shared by all peoples of the earth who value different cosmological principles. He calls for the preservation of biodiversity (which often drives the call for nature protection) within a paradigm of understanding plurality in the understanding of nature.

Underlying much of the debate on environmental conservation and the human–nature relationship is a focus on biodiversity protection, and to those concerned with human diversity, on cultural diversity. A notable UNESCO/IUCN international symposium in 2005 (UNESCO/IUCN 2006) served as a platform to address the developing interest in the link between environmental conservation, biodiversity and cultural diversity and for informed discussion on environmental conservation and sustainable development based on tradition belief systems. From a World Heritage perspective, for example, considerable attention over the last decade has swung towards an integrated concept of natural and cultural heritage (Rössler 2006). Reflective of this was the merging of cultural and natural criteria in the 2005 *Operational Guidelines* of the World Heritage Convention (UNESCO 2005), helping to 'provide a new vision [where] natural and cultural heritage are not separable' (Rössler 2006: 15).

Whose nature is it?

What we call wilderness is a civilization other than our own.

(Thoreau 1859, in Nash 1989: 37)

Emerging from the debate has been an increasing questioning in the literature and in professional practice of the idea that in the field of nature conservation people are considered to be 'disturbances of the natural ecosystem that result in some sort of loss of integrity' (Dove *et al.* 2005: 2). Traditional human activities are, *ipso facto*, seen as a negative, disturbing influence in this paradigm. Such a conservationist mantra remained unquestioned until recently, particularly in relation to the initiation and management of national parks. We are used to hearing the overused adjective 'pristine' in connection with a Western view of ecosystem preservation where there is a blinkered and historically insupportable assumption that anthropogenic disturbance has somehow negatively altered and debilitated what is supposed to be pristine. This is seen particularly in colonial settler societies, for example North America and Australia, but has spread to Asia where in some instances the instigation of national parks has been accompanied by removal or marginalisation of traditional communities and land-use management practices. 'Pristine' is associated with what some conservationists assume is a precolonial, untouched landscape as nature intended taking its cue from the assertion that 'Purely untutored humanity interferes comparatively little with the arrangements of nature' (Marsh 1864).

Two examples serve to illustrate our point. The first concerns Yosemite National Park where abandonment of fire as a traditional historic management tool as used by Native Americans resulted by the 1960s in a landscape that 'no longer resembled the "pristine" ecosystem that the park service set out to preserve' (Dove *et al. op cit*: 4). Solnit (1994, in Dove *et al. op cit*: 5), writing about the treatment of fire in the American landscape, quotes the following from a plaque in a restored valley meadow at Yosemite:

Two hundred years ago the Valley's meadows were much more extensive. Oak groves like the one across the way were larger and healthier. By setting fire to the meadows, and allowing natural fires to burn unchecked, the Valley's Native American inhabitants burned out the oak's competitors and kept down underbrush for clearer shots at deer. With leaf litter burned away, it was easier to gather acorns – the Indians' main food source. Without fires incense cedars are encroaching on the left side of the meadows and beginning to shade out the oaks, but now with controlled fires the NPS is reintroducing a natural process.

Even here the park service cannot accept that the process historically was never natural, that it was the fire management of the landscape by traditional owners that created the meadows and open woodland in the first place and contributed to the biodiversity of the area.

The second example comes from Australia. It is intimately associated as Gammage (2011) demonstrates with the traditional, carefully predetermined fire management by Aborigines. Over millennia Aboriginal management created a fecund and productive landscape scattered with trees, rich with an understorey of grass, interspersed with extensive grassy areas through which game and people could pass, treed areas where game could hide, and tracts of land farmed to raise crops such as yam vines. The result was a picturesque, park-like landscape that so delighted the early British explorers and settlers: for example Elizabeth McArthur summarised the landscape so created:

> The greater part of the country is like an English park, and the trees give it the appearance of a wilderness or shrubbery, commonly attached to the habitations of people of fortune, filled with a variety of native plants, placed in a wild irregular manner.
>
> *(Quoted in Taylor 2000a: 60)*

Notably the association between Aborigines and their country and the way it was managed did not escape some of the more astute early observers. In January 1847 the explorer Thomas Mitchell (1847, quoted in Gammage 2011: 186) observed:

> Fire, grass, kangaroos, and human inhabitants, seem all dependent on each other for existence in Australia; for any one of these being wanting, the others could no longer continue. Fire is necessary to burn the grass, and form these open forests ... But for this simple process, the Australian woods had probably continued as thick as those of New Zealand or America.

Of equal note is that a hardcore of Australian environmentalists and natural scientists today still, as Gammage (2011) reflects, deny the role of Aboriginal burning in spite of historical observational evidence from diaries and from images in colonial paintings. On 17 March 1841 Louisa Clifton (1993: 3 and 5) recorded in her diary as she arrived off the coast of Western Australia:

> We are laying within sight of the Australian shores ... A native fire has been distinguished on the shore ...
> I cannot easily cease to remember ... the native fires burning along the country, the smoke of which we only saw.

Australian colonial landscape paintings in the picturesque genre consistently show broad sweeps of open park-like landscapes that we now understand as a product of the process

FIGURE 2.1   Aborigines using fire to hunt kangaroos (Joseph Lycett ca.1817) (National Library of Australia PIC R5689).

of Aboriginal management dependent on predetermined sophisticated regimes of fires (Gammage 2011; Taylor 2000b). In some instances scenes of Aboriginal burning and hunting are depicted (Figure 2.1); in others we see smoke from fires dotted around the landscape. It was an Aboriginal cultural landscape that, soon after colonial occupation and cessation of carefully controlled regimes and mosaics of burning, degenerated into thick scrub and increasingly impenetrable woodland and forest prone to wildfires.

Culture–nature link

Sacred natural sites

The culture–nature discourse has been given a high profile in a recent theme issue of *Management of Environmental Quality: An International Journal* (Vol. 22, No. 2, 2011). In the opening overview paper on traditional landscapes and community conserved areas Brown and Kothari (2011) demonstrate the role of what they call 'living landscapes' in sustaining agro-diversity as well as inherent wild biodiversity values, ensuring ecosystems function, and supporting livelihoods and food security. Their findings are that:

> Across diverse settings, traditional agricultural landscapes, created by indigenous peoples and local communities, have been shaped by the dynamic interaction of people and nature over time. These landscapes, rich in agro-diversity as well as inherent wild biodiversity and cultural and spiritual values, embody human ingenuity and are continually evolving.
>
> *(Ibid.: 139)*

In addressing the challenge of conservation governance Brown and Kothari note the shift in conservation paradigms starting with the World Park Congress in Durban in 2003.[3] The latter produced the Durban Accord and Action Plan, the Message to the Convention on Biological Diversity, and over 30 specific recommendations. 'All these outputs strongly stressed the need to centrally involve indigenous peoples and local communities in conservation, including respecting their customary and territorial rights, and their right to a central role in decision-making' (Brown and Kothari 2011: 142).

The indivisibility of culture–nature is further explored by Verschuuren *et al.* (2010) in *Sacred Natural Sites: Conserving Nature and Culture.* The 27 essays in this excellent book are a welcome addition to the academic and professional literature on the relationship between people and nature. Its theme underscores the inextricable links between cultural diversity and biodiversity intimately existing between indigenous and traditional communities and their landscapes. The concern for the links relates closely to the work of IUCN where sacred natural sites play a particularly important role, demonstrating the special relationship between nature and people.

One aspect highlighted in *Sacred Natural Sites* is the increasing challenge in conservation management of the rights of traditional owners. It is articulated clearly by Studley (2010: 117):

> The sacred dimension can and does play an important role in landscape care and nature conservation but eco-spiritual values continue to be ignored as a result of the mono-cultural myopia of dominant western research epistemologies. Intangible values only make sense when research epistemologies are predicated on pluralism, holism, multi-culturalism and post-modern logic and science.

In some countries in the developing world mimicking the Western wilderness ethic, the incidence of traditional people and local communities being removed or marginalised in some national parks and World Heritage areas has regrettably occurred. Instances are recorded in various chapters in *Sacred Natural Sites.* Following this line of thought, it is notable that a submission under the title *Joint Statement of Indigenous Organizations on Continuous Violations of the Principle of Free, Prior and Informed Consent in the Context of the World Heritage Convention* was made to the 2011 World Heritage Committee meeting.[4] In this connection it is instructive to consider the indigenous people/landscape relationship through the IUCN concept of protected landscapes. IUCN recognises six such categories (I–VI) for which its Commission on National Parks and Protected Areas takes responsibility. A protected area is defined as 'an area of land and/or sea especially dedicated to the protection and maintenance of biological diversity, and of natural and associated cultural resources, and managed through legal or other effective means' (IUCN 1994). The six categories and management focus are:

  I   Strict protection: Ia) Strict nature reserve and Ib) Wilderness area.
 II   Ecosystem conservation and protection (i.e. national park).
III   Conservation of natural features (i.e. natural monument).
IV   Conservation through active management (i.e. habitat/species management area).
  V   Landscape/seascape conservation and recreation (i.e. protected landscape/seascape).
VI   Sustainable use of natural resources (i.e. managed resource protected area).

It is noted that the National Park Category II is intended to focus primarily on ecosystem protection and visitor opportunities (Dudley 2008). Nevertheless it is also noted (ibid.: 16, note 3):

> that the name 'national park' is not exclusively linked to Category II. Places called national parks exist in all the categories (and there are even some national parks that are not protected areas at all). The name is used here because it is descriptive of Category II protected areas in many countries. The fact that an area is called a national park is independent of its management approach. In particular, *the term 'national park' should never be used as a way of dispossessing people of their land.*
>
> *(Our emphasis)*

Not dispossessing a local ethnic community in a national park is exemplified in Doi Inthanon national park near Chiang Mai, Thailand, where Hmong hill-tribe people are allowed to live in their traditional villages continuing traditional lifestyle and crafts. Further they are allowed to undertake intensive market gardening raising produce for urban markets (Figure 2.2).

It is the practice whereby traditional owners who have managed the landscape often for hundreds, even thousands, of years, are dispossessed in the name of national parks that is, in our view, insupportable. It involves, all too often, extinguishing human rights and spiritual attachment to landscape. Accompanying this is the ignoring of the fact that rich biodiversity

FIGURE 2.2 Doi Inthanon national park, Chiang Mai, Thailand, showing intensive market garden activity within the wider landscape (Ken Taylor 2010).

is often linked to traditional cultural practices and what in effect is conservation management based on local knowledge systems and deep attachment to the land.

In 1992, with key support from ICOMOS and deepening international interest in the cultural landscape construct, UNESCO introduced three categories of cultural landscapes of Outstanding Universal Value for World Heritage recognition and inscription.[5] Their purpose is to link culture and nature, tangible and intangible heritage, and cultural diversity and biodiversity (Figure 2.3). Enlarging on this the current *Operational Guidelines* for the World Heritage Convention propose that:

> Cultural landscapes often reflect specific techniques of *sustainable land-use*, considering the characteristics and limits of the natural environment they are established in, and a specific spiritual relation to nature. Protection of cultural landscapes can contribute to modern techniques of sustainable land-use and can maintain or enhance natural values in the landscape. The continued existence of traditional forms of land-use supports biological diversity in many regions of the world. The protection of traditional cultural landscapes is therefore helpful in maintaining biological diversity.
>
> *(UNESCO 2008: Annex 3, para. 9)*

By mid-2012 eighty cultural landscapes had been inscribed on the World Heritage List. As Bandarin (in UNESCO 2009) reflects most of these are living cultural landscapes and

FIGURE 2.3 World Heritage listed (1994) Cordilleran Rice Terraces, Batad, Philippines (Ken Taylor 2012).[6]

over time cultural landscape categories (including relict and associative) provide an opening of the World Heritage Convention for cultures not or under-represented prior to 1992. Bandarin (in UNESCO 2009) quotes as examples the inscription of the Kaya Forest Systems in Kenya, or Chief Roi Mata's Domain in Vanuatu, the Kuk Early Agricultural site in Papua New Guinea or the tobacco production of Vinales Valley in Cuba, reflecting that none of these sites would have had a chance prior to 1992 of being recognised as cultural heritage on a global scale. Herein lies the major importance of the inclusion of the cultural landscape category in the operations of the Convention. Of the 80 inscriptions only 17 are located in the Asia-Pacific region. In contrast many inscribed properties in the region listed as natural sites are in fact cultural landscapes and offer considerable scope for renomination and re-inscription as happened in 1992 with Tongariro (New Zealand) and 1994 with Uluṟa-Kata Tjuṯa National Park (Australia) (Taylor 2012).

An Australian perspective

In the Australian context, the division between culture and nature continued along the North American convention of managing natural landscapes under the philosophy of separation of people from their land. In part this can be considered a continuance of the British colonisation of Australia in 1788 and the forced or coercive removal of Indigenous Australians from their traditional lands by successive governments. In contemporary Australian landscape management, there is a move to recognise the necessity to manage both the natural and cultural aspect of landscape as one integrated environment. This is being led by the engagement with Indigenous Australians. 'Indigenous people do not generally separate natural resources from cultural heritage, but refer to both in a holistic way when talking about "looking after country"' (Hunt *et al.* 2009: ix).

The revision of landscape management terminology such as Natural Resource Management (NRM), when dealing with cultural and natural landscapes, has been progressive but slow in the Australian context. The term Cultural and Natural Resource Management (CNRM) is starting to be used to replace NRM, as utilised in 2011 Indigenous Cultural and Natural Resource Management Futures (Altman *et al.* 2011). Contributing to this shift in terminology is the policy development of the Australian government in seeking to improve the well-being of Indigenous Australians. Associated research, supported by the Australian government, such as the Healthy Country, Healthy People project (Garnett and Sithole 2007), considers an integrated approach to deliver both environmental and cultural outcomes through Indigenous CNRM.

The potential of the leadership in Indigenous landscape management is that it may translate into general landscape management models and provide meaningful cultural and natural sustainability. With regard to cultural sustainability the reference is related to sustaining the integrity of Indigenous authority, maintenance and evolution of their own intangible and tangible cultural heritage. In considering cultural and natural landscape management several Australian national models seek to link culture and nature more closely in properties that involve shared management with Indigenous Australians. These include, but are not limited to, National Parks and Indigenous Protected Areas, which both can be considered as shared management models linking culturally divergent stakeholders into a partnership for mutual benefit.

The term shared management, in the context of this discussion, is considered a philosophical and dynamic practical process. It incorporates interactions between groups, and individuals who have a common interest in a landscape, but a different understanding of its significance through their own cultural paradigm. It can also be expressed as joint or collaborative management where different parties manage a cultural and natural landscape together, with separate degrees of authority over the landscape management dependent on circumstances. In considering shared management the space of interaction is the common ground where each party is engaged with the other in dialogue. This meeting place is where participants can work cooperatively together, whilst still recognising the hidden conflicts of interest generated through secret sacred cultural practice, commercial in-confidence, government confidentiality, cabinet in-confidence and other interests held by the parties.

National parks

Uluṟu-Kata Tjuṯa National Park, previously known as Uluṟu (Ayers Rock-Mt Olga) National Park is a demonstration of a significant Australian national park model. The park is managed under a joint management arrangement with the Aṉangu[7] who were granted freehold title to the park on 26 October 1985, through their organisation Uluṟu-Kata Tjuṯa Aboriginal Land Trust. Subsequent to the granting of title, and on the same day, the park was leased to the Australian government for a period of 99 years. The current 2010–2020 Plan of Management (Director of National Parks 2010) states on its cover *Tjukurpa katutja Ngaṟantja,* which translates into *Tjukurpa*[8] *above all else* or *Tjukurpa our primary responsibility*. Here the management of nature and culture blur into one holistic concept of interdependence of people and the environment.

Whether the policies and programmes implemented at this location have been successful or not is not necessarily the primary issue, as this can be considered simply a reflection of a historically unaware government policy response to shared landscape management with Indigenous Australians. This is particularly so when informed by colonialist and wilderness perspectives. The most opportune issue is the continuing development of the underpinning philosophy of integration, which has become established within a Western management model supported by local Indigenous knowledge. The integration of cultural and natural landscape management at Uluṟu-Kata Tjuṯa National Park further pushes Western landscape management in that it also demonstrates a contemporary approach that recognises the integration of the intangible heritage of Tjukurpa and the tangible physicality of its entwined geological, biodiversity and human interaction.

An extension to this approach of landscape management modelling, where culture and nature are fundamentally intertwined, is the consideration that intangible and tangible heritage portray a symbiotic relationship, holding the physicality of landscape and its cultural interpretation. Detaching the intangible from the tangible causes a shift in understanding of place and is demonstrated when the same tangible heritage, such as the geological mount Uluṟu (Ayers Rock), is shared by different cultures with different intangible heritage understandings, interpretations and value within each party's particular cultural paradigm. The Aṉangu relate to Uluṟu experientially through Tjukurpa, whilst others including settlers and Indigenous Australians not traditionally linked culturally to the site, attach an intangible value to the mount through their own history and interpretation. The Aṉangu and non-Aṉangu understandings of place attachment, aesthetics and phenomena, linked to Uluṟu-Kata

Tjuta National Park's landscape, are often separated by cultural divisions. They identify different intangible heritage values and a different understanding of what natural conservation is appropriate and what processes are needed to maintain site-specific cultural landscape integrity.

Cultural values in opposition

Such potentially disparate cross-cultural interpretations of a landscape's heritage values can paint a dark picture for sustainable joint management. They also reflect the potential crippling consequences of a lack of common valorisation of the intangible and tangible heritage of place held by the partners. In regard to Uluru-Kata Tjuta National Park, this outlook needs to be questioned as a general position, when there exists such a vast array of entwined shared history and a stated partnership intent that 'Anangu and Piranpa[9] will work together as equals, exchanging knowledge about our different cultural values and processes and their application' (Director of National Parks 2010: i).

A demonstration of the complexity, collaboration and conflict emerging within the realm of intangible heritage interpretation of the tangible is the issue of tourists climbing Uluru. The Anangu, with assistance from park officials (both Anangu and Piranpa), some tourist operators and many supporters, have been attempting to close the Uluru climb for decades. Many people have been injured and more than 30 people have died attempting to climb the very steep Uluru path (Director of National Parks 2010: 90). Senior Anangu have continued to make statements about the Uluru climb, including Kunmanara[10] Nguraritja (ibid.: 90):

> That's a really important sacred thing that you are climbing . . . You shouldn't climb. It's not the real thing about this place. The real thing is listening to everything. And maybe that makes you a bit sad. But anyway that's what we have to say. We are obliged by Tjukurpa to say. And all the tourists will brighten up and say, 'Oh I see. This is the right way. This is the thing that's right. This is the proper way: no climbing'.

In the face of these deaths, injuries and cultural petitions 'Many people feel that Uluru is a national icon and that all Australians have a "right" to climb it' (Reconciliation Australia 2010). The 2010–2020 Plan of Management (Director of National Parks 2010: 92) attempts to address the issues and commits to permanently closing the Uluru climb under specific conditions.[11] Whether these conditions will ever be met and the commitment fulfilled will largely rely on the will of politicians in the face of intense commercial and nationalist lobbying.

A tangible consequence of the continuation of the climb at Uluru is the physical degradation of the rock surface being continually etched by the feet of thousands of tourists. The climbing track is now a scar visible for several kilometres and the etching continues. The landscape in this example is managed within a joint management framework under cultural and natural World Heritage criteria. The result is that the intangible heritage of the Anangu has been detached from the tangible and replaced by the intangible heritage perceptions of another culture. Under this alternative regime the management of the mount's physical degradation is seen as acceptable when linked to the new intangible nationalistic or colonial heritage that proclaims the right to climb Uluru and view the landscape from above.

Thus the intangible heritage of the Anangu has been subverted by the intangible heritage of the settler within a domain of joint or shared management. Whilst the management of Uluru and the actions of the dedicated park officials recognised the integration of culture and nature plus the relationship between intangible and tangible heritage, still the contradiction of the climb exists. Here another important aspect to cultural and natural landscape management arises: the disparity that can exist between heritage policy intent, its interpretation and implementation.

In the face of such contradictions, and in the light of a landscape management model that has received international acclaim through being awarded the UNESCO Picasso Gold Medal (1995) for World Heritage management, more innovative management solutions are needed. These must provide governance, policy and process models that deliver sustainable and meaningful outcomes for all parties, whilst supporting biodiversity and cultural integrity.

Indigenous Protected Areas

An alternative cultural and natural landscape management model is the Indigenous Protected Area (IPA) concept, which is part of the Australian government's Indigenous Australians Caring for Country programme (Figure 2.4) (Department of Sustainability, Environment, Water, Population and Communities 2011). The first declared IPA was in 1998 at Nantawarrina in central South Australia. It covers an area of approximately 23 million hectares. The declaration of the Nantawarrina IPA marked 'the first time that a formal Protected Area has been set up voluntarily in Australia by an Indigenous community rather than through government legislation' (Muller 2003: 30). Today there are over 50 declared IPAs across Australia. A recently declared location is the Mandingalbay Yidinji Indigenous Protected Area, which includes the environments of mangroves, wetlands, rainforest, beaches, reef and islands. It was declared in November 2011 and was the first IPA to be established over existing government protected areas.

The shared management aspect within this model is built into the relationship of the government providing funding based on an understanding of negotiated outcomes. The Indigenous partners and government often have divergent views on the priority of such outcomes, which include: Indigenous health, education, economic and social benefits; biodiversity; cultural resource conservation; cultural maintenance. The partners' different priorities are illustrated in the comparison of the two statements below, which are published on the same departmental web page (ibid.).

FIGURE 2.4 Yolngu at Garanhan (Macassan Beach), Laynhapuy Indigenous Protected Area, located in north-east Arnhem Land in northern Australia (Nicholas Hall, 2006).

The government states:

> An Indigenous Protected Area is an area of Indigenous owned land or sea where traditional owners have entered into an agreement with the Australian Government to promote biodiversity and cultural resource conservation. Indigenous Protected Areas make a significant contribution to Australian biodiversity conservation.

The Nari Nari Tribal Council from the Toogimbie IPA in New South Wales states:

> Our vision is to protect and enhance our culture and history, while encouraging and protecting the natural environment and conserving biodiversity.

The Indigenous priority is clearly towards Indigenous culture and history, which in Indigenous understanding is integrated with nature. The government's statement however emphasises biodiversity and references culture as a resource in relation to the broader Australian estate.

The dissimilarity in emphasis and referencing articulated by the two parties reflects an underlying difference in management priority. This has the potential, even with the current goodwill and respect, to produce conflict and misunderstanding within the IPA model, particularly when the financial viability of the IPA projects relies on Indigenous compliance with government funding conditions.

In considering the Australian government national parks and Indigenous Protected Area models for cultural and natural landscape management, it appears evident that significant progress has been made to address the contradictory Western wilderness construct of separation of natural heritage management from cultural heritage management. In addition the importance of the interdependence, rather than separation, of the intangible understandings of tangible heritage is gaining recognition. This bodes well for the creation of understandings and intellectual foundations on which new cultural landscapes can be created, managed and protected.

Conclusion

The international discourse plus the actions of UNESCO and IUCN illustrate a philosophy leading towards more holistic practices in the management of cultural and natural landscape, particularly when encompassing shared management with traditional cultures. A more informed understanding is emerging that recognises the need to address the artificial separation of culture from nature and intangible from tangible heritage. As yet, the reduction of these separations is more akin to straddling the problem rather than reducing the chasm of division.

To implement this philosophical change there needs to be a movement beyond the debate of whether there is validity in the integration of culture/nature and intangible/tangible within landscape management. There needs to be an investigation into the governance and management of landscapes where they are treated as integrated environments.

Two questions, among many, arise from the struggle facing Indigenous people and governments working in the arena of shared management of cultural and natural landscape management. What are the governance structures and processes that can lead professional practice in the management of cultural and natural landscapes, when such landscapes are perceived and managed as a single integrated environment? How can the recognition of the symbiotic relationship of intangible and tangible heritage, within management policy and process, contribute to continued cultural maintenance, sustainable development, conservation and biodiversity?

Notes

1 Indigenous Australians include the diverse range of Australian Aboriginal and Torres Strait Islander cultures.
2 The term 'country' encapsulates the fertile human meaning of interrelationships between people and places, as in Indigenous Australian culture and in the European notion of 'landscape' and its human associations.
3 Organised by IUCN's World Commission on Protected Areas.
4 See UNESCO WHC Decision 35 COM 12E.
5 See (UNESCO) World Heritage Centre – Cultural Landscapes: http://whc.unesco.org/en/culturallandscape/.
6 Note: the Rice Terraces were placed on the World Heritage in Danger List in 2001as a result of changes taking place that were seen to affect adversely the Outstanding Universal Value of the Terraces. The *Report on the Joint World Heritage Centre/ICOMOS Reactive Monitoring Mission to the Rice Terraces of the Philippine Cordilleras 13/24 March 2011* recommended to the 2011 meeting of the World Heritage Committee that they remain on the list pending recommended management actions: Decision 34 COM 7A.26, WHC-11/35.COM/7A.Add. See http://whc.unesco.org/en/decisions/4102 (accessed 18 March 2012)
7 'Anangu is the term that Yankunytjatjara and Pitjantjatjara Aboriginal people from the Western Desert region of Australia use to refer to themselves . . . it has come into common use in the region as a term referring to Aboriginal people, as opposed to non-Aboriginal people, as well as Aboriginal people who come from other parts of Australia' (Anangu Tours 2011).
8 'Tjukurpa or Wapar is our law, culture, history, and our world view all bundled into one. Our ancestors have lived around Uluru (Ayers Rock) for many thousands of years, maintaining Tjukurpa, the law of the ancestors. Our grandparents taught us our Tjukurpa, just as their grandparents taught them. The term, Tjukurpa/Wapar, includes many complex but complementary concepts.
Tjukurpa/Wapar encompasses:

- Anangu religion, law and moral systems;
- the past, the present and the future;
- the creation period when ancestral beings, Tjukaritja/Waparitja, created the world as it is now;
- the relationship between people, plants, animals and the physical features of the land; and
- the knowledge of how these relationships came to be, what they mean and how they must be maintained in daily life and in ceremony.

. . . Tjukurpa is the foundation of Anangu life.
(There is not a single word in English that conveys the complex meaning of Tjukurpa. This is why at Uluru-Kata Tjuta National Park we use the Pitjantjatjara word. The Traditional Owners who speak Yankunytjatjara use the word Wapar to mean the same complex body of Law and beliefs)' (Anangu Tours 2011).
9 Piranpa is a Pitjantjatjara/Yankunytjatjara term meaning, literally, 'white', but now used to mean non-Aboriginal people (Director of National Parks 2010: 175).
10 Kunmanara is a Pitjantjatjara/Yankunytjatjara 'substitute used name when the name of a living person is the same as, or sounds like, the name of someone recently deceased' (Director of National Parks 2010: 175).
11 The conditions for the closure of the tourist climb at Uluru are stated in Section 6.3.3 (c) of the Uluru-Kata Tjuta National Parks Management Plan 2010–2020 (Director of National Parks 2010: 92). Section 6.3.3 (c) states:
'The climb will be permanently closed when:

- the Board, in consultation with the tourism industry, is satisfied that adequate new visitor experiences have been successfully established, or
- the proportion of visitors climbing falls below 20 per cent, or

- the cultural and natural experiences on offer are the critical factors when visitors make their decision to visit the park.'

References

Altman, J., Kerins, S., Hunt, J., Ens, E., May, K., Russell, S. and Fogarty, B. (2011) 'Indigenous Cultural Resource Management Futures', *CAEPR Topical Issue No. 9/2011*, Canberra: Centre for Economic Policy Research, ANU.

Anangu Tours (2011) 'Anangu Culture – Tjukurpa', online. Available at: http://www.Ananguwaai. com.au/Anangu_tours/law.html (accessed 29 November 2011).

Berleant, A. (1993) 'The Aesthetic of Art and Nature', in S. Kemal and I. Gaskell (eds) *Landscape, Natural Beauty and the Arts*, Cambridge: Cambridge University Press, pp. 228–243.

Brown, J. and Kothari, A. (2011) 'Traditional Agricultural Landscapes and Community Conserved Areas: An Overview', *Management of Environmental Quality: An International Journal*, 22, 2: 139–153.

Clifton, L. (1993) *Journal*, typescript copy (MS 2801, National Library of Australia), in M. Ackland (ed.) *The Penguin Book of 19th Century Australian Literature*, Ringwood: Penguin Books.

Department of Sustainability, Environment, Water, Population and Communities (2011) *Indigenous Protected Areas*, online. Available at: http://www.environment.gov.au/indigenous/ipa/index.html (accessed 4 December 2011).

Descola, P. (2008) *Who Owns Nature? Books & Ideas*, 21 January 2008. Available at: http://www. booksandideas.net/Who-owns-nature.html (accessed 15 September 2010).

Director of National Parks (2010) *Uluru-Kata Tjuta National Park Management Plan 2010–2020*, Department of Sustainability, Environment, Water, Population and Communities, Australian Government.

Dove, M.R., Sajise, P.E. and Doolittle, A. (eds) (2005) *Conserving Nature in Culture: Case Studies from Southeast Asia*, New Haven: Yale University Southeast Asia Studies.

Dudley, E. (ed.) (2008) *Guidelines for Applying Protected Area Management Categories*, Gland, Switzerland: IUCN.

Feng Han (2006) *The Chinese View of Nature: Tourism in China's Scenic and Historic Interest Areas*, PhD submitted in part-fulfilment of the requirements for the Degree of Doctor of Philosophy, School of Design, Queensland University of Technology, Brisbane.

Gammage, B. (2011) *The Biggest Estate on Earth: How Aborigines Made Australia*, Sydney: Allen & Unwin.

Garnett, S. and Sithole, B. (2007) *Sustainable Northern Landscapes and the Nexus with Indigenous Health: Healthy Country Healthy People*, Canberra: Land and Water Australia.

Hunt, J., Altman, J.C. and May, K. (2009) 'Social Benefits of Aboriginal Engagement in Natural Resource Management', *CAEPR Working Paper No 60/2009*, Canberra: The Centre for Aboriginal Economic Policy Research (CAEPR), The Australian National University, Canberra.

IUCN (1994) *Guidelines for Protected Area Management Categories*, Gland, Switzerland, and Cambridge, UK: IUCN.

Jackson, J.B. (1984) *Discovering the Vernacular Landscape*, New Haven: Yale University Press.

Marsh, G.P. (1864) *Man and Nature*, New York: Charles Scribner.

Marsh, G.P. (1864) 'Introduction', in Fairbrother, N. 1970, *New Lives New Landscapes*, Harmondsworth: Penguin Books, p. 11.

Muller, S. (2003) 'Towards Decolonisation of Australia's Protected Area Management: The Nantawarrina Indigenous Protected Area Experience', *Australian Geographical Studies*, 41, 1: 29–43.

Naess, A. (2003) 'The Deep Ecology Movement: Some Philosophical Aspects', in A. Light and H. Rolston (eds) *Environmental Ethics: An Anthology*, Oxford: Blackwell Publishing, pp. 262–274.

Nash, R. (1973) *Wilderness and the American Mind*, New Haven: Yale University Press.

Nash, R. (1989) *The Rights of Nature: A History of Environmental Ethics*, Madison: University of Wisconsin Press.

Reconciliation Australia (2010) 'Climbing Uluru'. Available at: http://www.reconciliation.org.au/ home/resources/factsheets/q-a-factsheets/climbing-Uluru (accessed 24 September 2011).

Rössler, M. (2006) 'World Heritage: Linking Culture and Nature', in UNESCO/IUCN, *Conserving Cultural and Biological Diversity: The Role of Sacred Natural Sites and Cultural Landscapes*, Proceedings UNESCO/IUCN International Symposium, United Nations University, Tokyo 30 May–2 June 2005, Paris: UNESCO, pp. 15–16.

Said, E. (1994) *Culture and Imperialism*, London and New York: Vintage Books.

Studley, J. (2010) 'Uncovering the Intangible Values of Earth Care: Using Cognition to Reveal the Eco-spiritual Domains and Sacred Values of the Peoples of Eastern Kham', in B. Verschuuren, R. Wild, J. McNeely and G. Oviedo (eds) *Sacred Natural Sites*, London and Washington, DC: Earthscan, pp. 107–118.

Taylor, K. (2000a) 'Colonial Picturesque: An Antipodean Claude Glass', in A. Hamblin (ed.) *Visions of Future Landscapes: Proceedings of Australian Academy of Science 1999, Fenner Conference on the Environment*, 2–5 May 1999, Canberra, 2000, pp. 58–66.

Taylor, K. (2000b) 'Culture or Nature: Dilemmas of Interpretation', *Tourism Culture & Communication*, 2, 2: 69–84.

Taylor, K. (2012) 'Landscape and Meaning: Context for a Global Discourse on Cultural Landscapes Values', in K. Taylor and J. Lennon, *Managing Cultural Landscapes*, London and New York: Routledge, pp. 22–44.

Taylor, K. and Lennon, J. (2011) 'Cultural Landscapes: A Bridge Between Culture and Nature?', *International Journal of Heritage Studies*, 17, 6: 537–554.

UNESCO (2005) *Operational Guidelines for the Implementation of the World Heritage Convention*, Paris: UNESCO World Heritage Centre.

UNESCO (2008) *Operational Guidelines for the Implementation of the World Heritage Convention*, Paris: UNESCO World Heritage Centre.

UNESCO (2009) *World Heritage Cultural Landscapes A Handbook for Conservation and Management. World Heritage Papers 26*, Paris: UNESCO World Heritage Centre.

UNESCO/IUCN (2006) *Conserving Cultural and Biological Diversity: The Role of Sacred Natural Sites and Cultural Landscapes*, Proceedings UNESCO/IUCN International Symposium, United Nations University, Tokyo, 30 May–2 June 2005, Paris: UNESCO.

Verschuuren, B.W., Wild, R., McNeely, J. and Oviedo, G. (2010) *Sacred Natural Sites: Conserving Nature and Culture*, London and Washington, DC: Earthscan in association with IUCN.

3

OLD CULTURE AND DAMAGED LANDSCAPES

The new cultural landscapes of post-industrial sites in Britain

Clive Davies

Introduction

A visitor to Ironbridge Gorge in the English West Midlands chancing upon its mature broadleaved woodlands and meandering river can be forgiven for mistaking this as an ancient landscape befitting the Ironbridge World Heritage Site. Two centuries ago this area was the crucible for the industrial era and the landscape was far from pristine as shown in Philip James de Loutherbourg's 1801 painting *Coalbrookdale by Night*.[1] This firey scene, reminiscent of Dante's *Inferno*, depicts the Madeley Wood Furnaces which were used in the manufacture of the components of the famous Iron Bridge. Opened in 1781, this was the first bridge of its kind in the world. The iron manufacturing furnaces located around the Ironbridge Gorge and a scattering of other sites in England can claim to be close to the 'big bang' of the Industrial Revolution. The bridge is now seen as a symbol of the revolution and the area regarded as the birthplace of industry.[2]

This revolution instigated fundamental economic and social changes, impacts of which transformed the landscape of Britain and gradually the rest of the world (Ashton 1964). New cities emerged and extractive industries expanded of which, in Britain, coal mining was the most notable. Two centuries after this revolution began, the threat of the exhaustion of natural resources, growing expectations of less arduous labour, the coming of new technologies and neo-liberal economic policies combined to alter the way industry functions and the character of the impacts upon the landscape. Communities familiar with the Dickensian world of industrialised landscapes with their smoke stacks and back-to-back housing began to encounter a new physical and cultural post-industrial landscape which featured large areas of damaged land. The traditional certainties linked to the way of life, the former landscape and the working-man's culture felt out of place in the modern world and these were seen primarily as social and political problems that could be solved by modernisation of communities and removal of the vestiges of this culture from the landscape.

Viewing damaged landscapes requires perspective; from a young age we are taught that humans have been shaping and exploiting landscapes since the pre-Neolithic period with the Mesolithic and Neolithic settlers of approximately 7,000 years ago identified as particular agents of large-scale change (Goudie 1990). Thus the various types and the extent of human impact on the development of the landscape has long been recognised and debated and a fair proportion of so-called damaged landscapes are now listed as world heritage sites by UNESCO. Given this long historical landscape perspective it is necessary for our story to have a focus. In this chapter the focus is on post-industrial damaged landscapes close to cities and the landscape-led regeneration that has occurred in damaged areas as a result of former industrial activities which generated urbanisation and population growth. It draws heavily on the British and wider European experience and on my personal 33 years' experience as a practitioner of environmental and landscape planning primarily focused on such issues.

Post-industrial landscape regeneration

The European continent's experience of landscape change provides lessons relevant to global landscapes, primarily because it was the first continent to industrialise but also the first, along with the United States, to have entered a post-industrial era (Hancock 1971). It may be contrary to this analysis but still necessary to report that Europe is still industrialised. However the nature of this industry is radically different to that of 40 years ago; the new focus is on clean technologies, high-end engineering and the service sector. As the European landscape was the first to suffer radical transformation by the industrial era, it is this continent that has been one of the first to face up to the need to restore and give new purposes to damaged industrial landscapes. These post-industrial landscapes range from pocket-sized compartments vacated by factory units to entire landscape systems and the physical damage reflects the dislocation and damage existing in their communities (Roe 2007).

Mining has been a noteworthy producer of damaged land throughout the world. For example the proportion of landscape now suffering from polluted land and water in Europe has a close association with the impact of present and historic mining (Jordan and Szucs 2011). In particular, the decline of the coal-mining industry has had an important impact on the rise in damaged land (Figure 3.1). The relationship between the state of such 'pollution' landscapes and societies has been shown to be complex with communities developing risk management strategies to cope with dwelling in such places (Castán Broto *et al.* 2007). Mining is also regarded as a highly political activity associated with social inequalities that are often expressed in the way landscape is managed and changed (Roe 2011).

In Britain during the pinnacle of the industrial era coal mining, along with steel making, canals, railways, cotton and shipbuilding were the key industries. Coal had been mined in Britain since before the Roman invasion. Flint axes have been found embedded in coal and there is also evidence of Roman coal stores on Hadrian's Wall in Northumberland in northern England (UK Coal 2012). The gradual development of the steam engine by Thomas Savery, Thomas Newcomen and James Watt led to a huge demand for coal. In Britain coal mining reached its zenith in 1913 and production fluctuated through most of the twentieth century, but by the mid 1970s the industry was in a sharp decline.

In many cases the legacy of coal mining presented new opportunities for landscape change. The closure of the Nottinghamshire coalfield in the English East Midlands during the early 1990s left derelict coal-mine sites across the county. An agreement signed between UK Coal and Nottinghamshire County Council involved turning the former pit sites into country parks by planting millions of trees, landscaping and providing new cycle tracks and footpaths. Over the last 30 years Nottinghamshire has gained 14 new country parks on the site of former coal mines which provide opportunities for biodiversity through the creation and management of low-intensity landscapes such as new broadleaved woodland, wetlands and species-rich

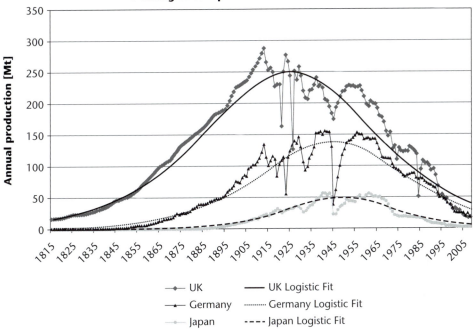

Peaking of coal production in selected countries

FIGURE 3.1   The peaking of coal consumption in selected countries (Hook et al. 2010) (note should be made of the rapid decline from 1980 mirrored both in Britain and Germany. This coincides with the rise in damaged landscapes in both countries. Key: diamond line: UK; circle line: Japan; triangle line: German Hard Coal; smooth (upper) line: UK logistic fit; dashed (lower line): Japan logistic fit; dotted (middle line): Germany logistic fit).

grassland as well as recreation opportunities (Nottinghamshire County Council n.d.). The experience in Nottinghamshire demonstrates the regenerative potential of landscape and is proof that landscapes that once reflected a coal-mining culture can be transformed into new cultural landscapes which reflect a desire for regeneration and a new beginning.

Five key drivers for contemporary landscape-led regeneration can be identified:

- market failure;
- ameliorating the longer-term impacts on communities that find themselves in the wrong place;
- opportunities presented for urban planning and policymaking;
- sustainable development, Local Agenda 21[3] and the Green Infrastructure approach;
- availability of resources.

The loss of an extractive industry such as coal mining means that large sites on which the industry was based, including coke and steelworks, and coal villages which developed to service the industry, are often now not in a good location to attract new investment from possible alternative industry or businesses. In the UK this has been a particular problem in relation to the demise of the coal industry in the North of England, the Midlands and South Wales. The costs of land reclamation, the retraining of the workforce and new markets far away have led to short- and long-term market failure. No one wants to redevelop these sites or harness the energies of such communities because initiatives are not regarded as economically viable. However in this kind of situation and often for political reasons which generate a desire to improve the image of such areas, landscape regeneration that provides new public parks and green spaces can be seen as an attractive solution. Such solutions are not necessarily permanent. Greening a landscape as preparation for future economic development when the macroeconomic cycle is right is a practical response to real world economics and this intention can be embedded in urban green space strategies (Greenkeys 2008).

Regenerating community landscapes

A landscape that is improved in terms of its accessibility and functions can ameliorate the longer-term impacts on communities that find themselves in the wrong place after the main means of their economic support has collapsed. In England, the Index of Multiple Deprivation (IMD) is maintained by the Department of Communities and Local Government (DCLG) and is used by policymakers and planners as the principle measure of poverty in a community. The overall index is constructed from a set of domain indicators which are weighted and combined together. These include income deprivation, employment deprivation, health deprivation and disability, education, skills and training, barriers to housing and services, crime and the living environment including an outdoors living sub-domain (DCLG 2011). The spatial relationship between damaged landscapes and the IMD is close; of the 20 most deprived communities in England in 2010 all but one has experienced significant landscape damage through deindustrialisation (DCLG 2011). Using landscape as a way to tackle deprivation is challenging as the expectations of local communities can be very high and such expectations may not be linked to the potential impact that an improved landscape can provide. However landscape expectations, identified through consultation processes, can reveal demands for playing fields, allotment gardens, nature reserves, public parks and community woodlands. Communities often look to local authorities and other public agencies to act as leaders on such initiatives.

Capital funds for the regeneration and creation of new landscapes during the period between 1980 and 2010 were relatively easy to source, normally by utilising public regeneration monies. In contrast, resources for long-term management, or finances for running costs, were scarce and this has led the new landscapes that were created on regeneration sites to deteriorate and lose their intended functionality and community appeal. In England recreation provision is a non-statutory service and therefore frequently takes a disproportionately large funding cut when budgets are tightened. This trend has exacerbated the landscape management problem. The way out of this problem has been to design-in low-cost and nature-based sustainable management at the expense of creative high-cost landscape design; a solution that has long since proven its worth.

Creating a landscape infrastructure approach to regeneration sites

In Britain, an extensive network of damaged sites has provided urban planning and policy-makers with the opportunity to make large-scale structural and modal changes to the urban infrastructure. Exemplified by former mineral railway lines which have been used to create new cycleways, tramways or road corridors, post-industrial damaged sites have also been developed into housing regeneration sites and new retail parks accompanied by new structural landscaping. In Britain the programme of Garden Festivals starting in Liverpool in 1984 and finishing in Ebbw Vale in 1992 was used to regenerate large areas to offer a public spectacle followed by redevelopment to other economic end uses. An example of this regenerative potential is the site of the Stoke Garden Festival (1986) which became a major retail and entertainment facility fortuitously timed at the start of a major growth phase in consumerism.

In Britain the commitment at the Rio Earth Summit in 1992 effectively placed sustainable development at the centre of the country's economic policy agenda. In recent years, Green Infrastructure planning has been seen in the UK as a useful tool to deliver more sustainable landscape planning and achieve a number of the aims of sustainable development including, most recently, the need to respond to climate change mitigation and adaptation (Benedict and McMahon 2002, 2006; Handley *et al.* 2007; Kambites and Owen 2006; Llausàs and Roe 2012). Damaged landscapes have been recognised as a significant opportunity for implementing a Green Infrastructure approach which is conceived as 'an interconnected network of protected land and water that supports native species, maintains natural ecological processes, sustains air and water resources and contributes to the health and quality of life for … communities and people' (Williamson 2003: 4), most notably by providing the nodal points where ecological corridors converge. Planning for Green Infrastructure has now been adopted as an important way of enabling societies to sustain the ecosystem services essential for sustainable urban living and to fulfil multiple functions including economic benefits (Ahern 2007; AMION 2008). The Landscape Institute (2009) believes that the Green Infrastructure approach has a critical role in meeting many landscape challenges and that this is achieved through multifunctional landscapes that provide opportunities for more connected natural areas.

Community involvement in the creation of new landscapes

British governments and the European Union (EU) have made resources available for the reinstatement of damaged landscapes. The restoration of damaged landscapes normally takes place within the context of physical regeneration (PNE Consulting 2008). This refers to all activities classified as capital expenditure and which are mainly focused upon land, buildings and environmental improvements. In England the National Audit Office reports that the English Regional Development Agencies' (RDAs') physical regeneration programmes have helped to generate additional regional wealth and that between 1999 and 2010 the eight RDAs outside of London spent £5 billion on physical regeneration programmes. For every pound of RDA spend on physical regeneration, an estimated £2.80 was secured from elsewhere, including £1.51 from the private sector (National Audit Office 2010). More broadly, regeneration is understood as the holistic process of reversing the economic, physical and social decline of places where market forces alone will not suffice (Scottish Government 2011). In response to such understandings, the regeneration of damaged landscape is also now linked to social and community participation programmes. In Britain such programmes involve a mass movement of conservation volunteers, trainees, the intermediate labour market (ILM) and restorative justice teams. This has provided low-cost labour for local landscaping initiatives often in partnership with local community groups.

In Europe regeneration of damaged landscapes is closely associated with the practice of urban fringe land management since many of the most derelict and damaged landscapes are found in these areas. These areas have attracted much attention from geographers and sociologists as well as landscape planners. There have been many attempts to define both urban and rural in both policy and the academic literature. The late Ray Pahl proposed the concept of a rural–urban continuum to articulate the differences between the way people view urban and rural areas (Pahl 1966). The concept of a rural–urban continuum is useful in landscape management in order to understand the kinds of opportunities and functions that damaged landscapes might be restored for; examples of land-use types are shown in Figure 3.2.

By the late 1980s in England, the urban fringe had become recognised as a discrete area which was neither entirely urban nor rural but exhibited characteristics of both (County Planning Officers' Society 1992). Half a century after Pahl's work the discussion received new traction in the Countryside In and Around Towns initiative (Countryside Agency and Groundwork UK 2005) which focused on the role of the urban fringe and identified a number of spatial characteristics and key functions (Table 3.1) the combination of which, it was argued, provided the potential for regarding such areas as having particular qualities and benefits that could not be described as entirely rural or solely urban.

In Europe, although much of the literature concerns multifunctionality in rural areas; urban fringe landscapes have also provided a useful testing ground for multifunctionality in relation to landscape management in practice. There is a continuing discussion concerning the particular qualities of such landscapes and the relevant policies that encourage or restrict the development of multifunctionality. When a landscape performs a wide range of social, economic and environmental functions, that landscape can be considered as offering multifunctional benefits. In reality most landscapes are multifunctional even if land management practice is focused on a single major purpose such as farming and food production since clearly farming supports many other benefits including visual amenity and biodiversity. However landscape can be positively managed to increase multifunctionality and

Built urban	Countryside in town	Urban fringe	Rural fringe	Rural	Remote rural
High-rise buildings Bridges Central Business District Shopping centre Factories Houses Roads Rail	Urban parks Green spaces Green corridors (e.g. ex-railway lines) Street trees Private gardens Allotment gardens Urban woodland	Ring roads Arable farming Livery and equestrian Country parks Community forests Landfill sites Out-of-town retail parks Airports	Horticulture Arable and pastoral farming Farm shops Garden centres Woodlands Approach roads Commuter villages	Arable and pastoral farming Villages Forests and woodlands Visitor economy, e.g. B&B, restaurants, cafes	Hill farming Hamlets and scattered farmhouses Watersheds Forests Reservoirs Bogs and mires Moorland

Urban rural ecotone based on UK experience [C. Davies 2012]

FIGURE 3.2 An urban rural ecotone drawing together the urban–rural continuum and contemporary terminology (after Pahl 1966).

TABLE 3.1 The ten key functions for the countryside in and around town, Countryside Agency and Groundwork UK (2005).

A bridge to the country	Networks of footpaths, bridleways and cycle ways form continuous green corridors between town and country.
A gateway to the town	The countryside in and around towns creates a powerful first impression and needs to be managed and maintained to be attractive and welcoming.
A health centre	Green space close to where people live and work provides an invaluable respite from the stresses of urban living.
A classroom	Hands-on learning in a variety of 'outdoor classrooms', supporting all parts of the national curriculum with a particular relevance to environmental education and rural studies.
A recycling and renewable energy centre	Woodlands absorb large quantities of atmospheric pollution, especially 'particulates'. Flood plains and water meadows protect urban residents from flooding.
A productive landscape	Farmers close to urban areas are close to their markets. Towns and cities benefit from farmers' markets – cutting down 'food miles' and promoting healthy eating.
A cultural legacy	The countryside in and around towns can be rich in history; buildings and structures, archaeology and landscapes, can all tell a story of the area.
A place for sustainable living	The need for new development, especially for affordable homes, means the area around towns can be a prime location for the selective expansion of urban areas.
An engine for regeneration	Residents in the urban edge can be involved in creating and managing environmental improvements to make their neighbourhoods more 'liveable'.
A nature reserve	Woodlands, wetlands, meadows and a broad array of other natural habitats can produce a marked increase in biodiversity both around and within urban areas. People would be better able to appreciate nature, encountering more wildlife, more often.

this approach offers added benefits resulting in a diverse, dynamic and versatile environment (Countryside Agency and Groundwork UK 2005).

It is however the case that not all landscape functions are complementary and that conflict of functions arise. An example of this is in the recreation facilities offered by landscapes. Individual landscape consumers often seek different experiences from a given landscape; some consumers are looking for peace and tranquillity whilst others wish to use the same space for active sport. Managing conflict is an inevitable consequence of multifunctional landscape management and community participation has emerged as the most important tool in managing conflict with solutions including temporal or spatial zoning (Sheppard and Meitner 2005).

Leadership in landscape-led regeneration is normally found in local-authority-led countryside management partnerships. In the UK the major vehicle for funding such initiatives is the Heritage Lottery Fund (HLF) which reports that more than 70,500 hectares of land of importance for wildlife has been acquired and restored and over £70m has been awarded to 55 Landscape Partnerships across the UK (Heritage Lottery Fund n.d.). The development of landscape-led regeneration partnerships is of significant historical interest as there has been a discernable move towards ever-stronger partnering arrangements over the last 30 years.

A pathfinder for this approach was Operation Groundwork launched in 1984 in St Helens, North West England (Groundwork Federation n.d.(a)). It was described by the then UK Environment Secretary Michael Heseltine as 'an entrepreneurial team, which could act independently as an enabler to mobilise all the resources in the community – public, private and voluntary'[4]. A key focus was community-led regeneration with an emphasis on environmental and landscape improvements. The approach was soon adopted elsewhere leading to an England-wide network of locally managed Groundwork Trusts. The initial focus was on small-scale damaged landscape units initially referred to as *bomb sites* due to their resemblance to the bombed sites of Second World War Britain. One of the most significant early developments of Groundwork was NUVIL (new uses for vacant industrial land). The aim was to bring damaged land back into productive use through good landscape design.

Based on the experience of Groundwork Trusts, the Countryside Commission and Forestry Commission sought to emulate the approach at the landscape scale with the added challenges of working across municipal boundaries, entire landscape systems and tackling the high level of dereliction in the urban fringe. The result, launched in 1989, was an ambitious programme to create Community Forests around major urban settlements in England. The concept was described in their joint publication *Forests for the Community* (Countryside Commission and Forestry Commission 1989). By 1994 12 Community Forest partnerships were working in the countryside around some of England's largest settlements. The working method used by the new Community Forests was based on a landscape-scale approach with zoning used to differentiate landscape prescriptions; these were described as Local Management Zones (LMZ). Guidance in advice papers issued by the Countryside Commission set out a framework for landscape-scale decision making though a partnership approach. Community Forests were described as ahead of their time and their approach to land planning influenced later approaches. Central to the Community Forest concept was that of a planned approach with a Community Forest plan required to turn ideas into reality. Advice papers were issued by the Countryside Commission which set out, for newly appointed project teams and local partners, the main strategic features of Community Forests (Table 3.2).

Landscape design in Community Forests was intended to create new woodlands and other natural landscapes for multiple uses. However by the mid 1990s this terminology was to become more generally referred to as multipurpose forestry. The landscape design advice for the preparation of Community Forest plans (Countryside Commission 1990) was not included in the original guidelines and was added in 1992. It gave passing consideration to cultural landscapes but it was not, at the time the advice manual was in active use, considered to be a central issue (Table 3.3). The key issue was to provide opportunities for often deprived, local communities in terms of spaces for recreation, learning and training. There was a considerable emphasis on encouraging communities to get close to nature, to become involved in creating these new landscapes as well as regenerating the derelict and damaged areas. In cultural terms, the emphasis was therefore primarily on provision of the physical opportunities and support for the growth of a new culture of landscape participation and landscape creation in such areas.

Over their first decade (1989–1999) Community Forest practice in England evolved to become closely associated with a contemporary re-presentation of heritage frequently borrowing from local recollections of industrial heritage. Many of the features such as the mining equipment relating to past activities in the landscape had been removed as the economic situation relating to these activities deteriorated. The landscape was in effect sanitised.

TABLE 3.2 Strategic characteristics of Community Forests in England adapted from the advice manual for the preparation of Community Forest plans (Countryside Commission 1990)

Advice Paper	Topic	Notes
1	Philosophy of zoning	Underlying principles for identifying zones within a community forest according to land use characteristics.
2	Process of plan preparation	To ensure the Community Forest Plan is the basis for land use planning and analysis.
3	Economic factors affecting implementation	Land valuation and net annual incomes especially linked to landowning sector.
4	Planning issues	Land cost and availability and project management. Reference made to biological resources and capital. This is an early reference to what would later develop into the Green Infrastructure approach and Ecosystem Services.
5	Nature conservation and habitat creation	Changes in land management.
6	Involving local communities	Focuses on the theme of resolving different perspectives and the rights of local people to participate in the planning process.
7	Designing community forests for the less able	Design principles.
8	Design issues relating to safety and fear in parks and woodlands	Design principles.
9	Community Forests and archaeology	Respecting heritage and creatively using land management changes to secure greater public access to heritage features.
10	Monitoring and evaluation	How the performance of community forests would be measured. Focused on woodland planting and management, recreation and leisure, landscape, nature conservation, education, regional economic development, farm diversification, statutory planning and other strategic plans (embedding of Community Forest policies within).
11	Management plans: source of published information (added 1992)	Based on Management Plans, Countryside Commission, England, CCP206 (1986).
12	Landscape Design in Community Forests (added 1992)	Distillation of Forestry Commission Community Woodland design guidelines (Forestry Commission 1991).

In the development of projects Community Forest teams became active in trying to retain some of these features and the Community Forest projects tried to encourage reflection on the cultural memories and meanings that were associated with the former landscapes in the new landscapes that were being created. Throughout this period an ongoing discourse between key actors on project teams and national sponsors raged over the extent of landscape restoration to be pursued (Figure 3.3).

TABLE 3.3 Cultural landscapes are not referred to directly in landscape design in Community Forests (added to later editions of CCP 271 Countryside Commission (1990) in 1992).

Forest Design process	Reference made to (i) landscape context, (ii) existing land use, (iii) existing areas of archaeological or historic importance
Involving people	Respecting local wishes and identifying preferred landscapes
Visual design principles	The 'spirit of the place' – to be identified, strengthened and not destroyed

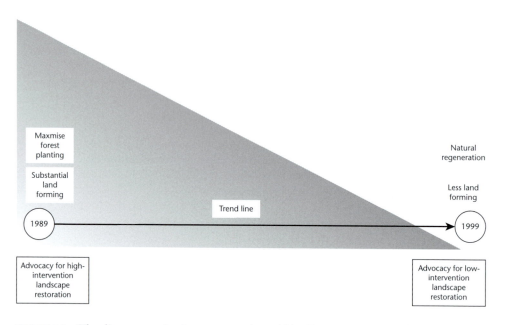

FIGURE 3.3   The discourse on landscape restoration within Community Forests between 1989 and 1999.

Land supply was the greatest challenge faced by Community Forests hence the opportunity to create new cultural landscapes was driven principally by land opportunity. Where opportunities and local community wishes coincided, projects emerged with the intention that they would, as far as possible, be sustainable. A key aspect of sustainable land management was considered to be the involvement of local people in long-term management. This commitment would be essential once project teams had withdrawn to develop other projects elsewhere. A variety of tools and features was used to engage the public and create a new sense of place. Sculptural artwork was a popular tool and was described as 'an advance coloniser for landscape change to come' (Pollard n.d.).

By 2000 the majority of damaged land available for restoration by Community Forests had significantly diminished in extent. Some had been restored by Community Forest partners while other land had been reclaimed for the booming housing market or for new industrial estates to meet the needs of the service sector. Dwindling interest from national partners, the rise of regional structures following the arrival of the 1997 Labour government and a policy shift from conservation towards a wider focus on sustainable development led to a substantial refocusing of Community Forest projects. Most notable was the role of Community Forest teams in introducing the green infrastructure approach and then applying it to regional regeneration. Across the country the results were variable but it led to new opportunities in some areas, notably in North West England, where the Regional Development Agency embraced the concept. Despite local successes the sense was that the role of the Community Forests in creating new cultural landscapes, in terms of participatory opportunities for local communities and reflection of the cultural aspects of landscape, had passed its zenith and the future lay in addressing hard-edge environmental problems such as climate change adaptation and making the planning system more responsive to environmental concerns. At the same time interest was growing in landscape partnerships.

New mechanisms for reclaiming damaged landscapes

In Britain examples can be found of a number of formal and informal landscape partnerships which have been formed over the last 30 years to address reclamation and restoration issues in landscapes. The landscape partnership approach has been shown to be very successful in motivating communities around a heritage theme with tangible outcomes. In 1997 14 organisations in North East England came together to launch a £10m 'Turning the Tide' project funded by the Millennium Commission. This sought to restore a coal-damaged coastline through a series of projects focused on former colliery sites and involving local communities (Durham County Council 2002). The coastline has been transformed, through 100 separate projects over 13 years, to a valued cultural and natural area from a colliery waste dumping ground. Formerly, communities had little or no access to the coast and it reflected a wider malaise in the social and economic conditions of the area. This coastline is now well used for recreation and contains important, nationally significant grassland habitats. It is also a designated Heritage Coast[5] and in 2011 it received special mention in the Council of Europe Landscape Awards for its 'excellent model for the regeneration of degraded coastal areas' (Durham Heritage Coast Partnership 2012). The award particularly noted the way local communities had been mobilised to create a new landscape and a new identity.

Following recognition of the success of such schemes, the Heritage Lottery Fund in the UK has established a Landscape Partnerships (LP) grant programme which is normally delivered by a partnership made up of regional, national and local organisations with an interest in an area, community groups and members of the community. The programme is based around a portfolio of smaller projects, which together provide long-term social, economic and environmental benefits for both rural and urban areas. The area of countryside has to have a distinctive landscape character and is recognised and valued by local people. The area of countryside should be no smaller than 20 km² and no larger than 200 km². The emphasis is primarily for public benefit, not private gain, and landscape partnerships must deliver evenly across four programme outcomes: (1) conserving or restoring the built and natural features that create the historic landscape character; (2) increasing community participation in local heritage; (3) increasing access to and learning about the landscape area and its heritage; and (4) increasing training opportunities in local heritage skills.

In these partnership schemes community consultations have shown that local people are eager to celebrate the former industries that were the reason for the establishment of their settlements. In response, landscape managers have looked to artists to provide the community with links to the past and at the same time a view of the future. Art has the ability to act as a focal point for landscape regeneration but the early involvement of communities appears essential in winning acceptance for artwork in localities. This does not always sit agreeably with artists who, with some justification, feel that artwork is a personal statement rather than a corporate expression of a community creative process. Furthermore artists can point to successful landscape icons such as Anthony Gormley's *Angel of the North* (1998) in Gateshead as a demonstration of bold statements and artist leadership (Gateshead Council 2012). However in the same region an entirely different approach was developed by the Great North Forest partnership (Roe 2005). From the outset the Great North Forest project team wished to use artwork as an advance coloniser to develop artistic and cultural links between local people and their environment, creating new features within the countryside, marking special places and celebrating the rich local landscape. The Marking the Ways initiative in the Great North Forest was launched in 1992 when a series of artworks and sculpture trails were commissioned. The sculpture initiatives included outreach programmes working with local communities to connect them with their environment and walks, festivals, and working with poets and film-makers to explore their relationship with the surrounding landscape. The project worked well at the community level and attracted the attention of the academic community and local politicians, but the media and regional impact was much less.

Based on this analysis it appears that a mixture of community-based and iconic artwork projects grouped together into a project-wide landscape art programme is required for artwork to make an impact on landscape-led regeneration at different levels. Community-based art projects are a vehicle for general community involvement especially in the early stages of a new landscape regeneration initiative when there may be few results to show in terms of physical landscape change. It also demonstrates intent to involve the community in all aspects of landscape regeneration and provides the opportunity for the community to identify the heritage drivers that matter to local people. It is also a learning framework to develop the governance rules which will be used by a project throughout its life. Iconic projects are needed for opposite reasons, notably to attract the attention of the media and through them the wider community including business and local opinion formers. They also inspire regional and national actors that something notable is happening in a given neighbourhood. This can bring long-term revenue funding benefits and assist future fundraising.

Landscape artwork can provide a motivation for the public to visit landscapes, even on otherwise immature sites. This includes day tourism as well as recreational activities linked to health improvement. Exercise facilities can be achieved by linking artworks together to create a long-distance trail. Consequently landscape artwork has the potential to generate income by providing services to visitors such as hospitality and car parking. In the context of cultural landscapes, artwork can borrow physically and inspirationally from former land uses and cultural activities (Konijnendijk 2008). Materials such as brick, stone and metal can be salvaged and incorporated into new sculpture. Some of the most outstanding examples are found in the Emscher Landscape Park in the Ruhrgebeit Germany (Ruhr.2010 GmbH 2010). The *sky staircase* by Hermann Prigan at the Halde Rheinelbe tip has become justly famous for the reuse of materials and land-forming. The *Tetrahedron* is an example of an iconic landscape artwork at the Emscherblick tip. In Germany urban natural regeneration or rewilding of damaged landscapes (Kowarik and Körner 2005) has been used as a successful landscape planning tool. This is the predominant land management approach at Hansa Coking Plant in Dortmund (Figure 3.4), a site where nature is returning to industry demonstrated by rail sidings now recolonised with birch woodland and exotic species flourishing between large industrial structures.

FIGURE 3.4   Hansa Coking Plant in Dortmund has become internationally renowned for the natural recolonisation of industrial structures (Clive Davies).

Community benefits and involvement in reclamation of damaged landscapes

At the UNESCO meeting on the Convention concerning the protection of the world cultural and natural heritage held in Christchurch, New Zealand in 2007 (UNESCO 2007), the word community was added to the strategic objectives identified by the World Heritage Committee for promoting the implementation of the World Heritage Convention. Among the justifications for this was that heritage protection without community involvement and commitment is an invitation to failure. The first step in the process of community involvement is to define the relevant communities. There are two principal types of community; communities of neighbourhood (or place) and communities of interest (Agyeman 1996) and often these groups can overlap (Roe 2012). Where the focus of landscape regeneration is based around a site then the community of neighbourhood will usually predominate. For landscape-scale regeneration projects community involvement is generally developed through communities of interest, such as schools, local history groups, voluntary organisations and umbrella groups. The purpose of community involvement is twofold; first to get the physical landscape improvements agreed and implemented and second to develop capacity in the community which in turn can assist in long-term landscape management.

Practice has shown that damaged landscapes present a real opportunity for community involvement. In the case of communities of neighbourhood, residents may have seen their landscape turn from an industrial past, through a period of decline then headlong into dereliction. To these communities the opportunity to shape their locality after facing many hardships (such as the loss of jobs, decline of money in the community, eyesores and other environmental problems such as pollution) can be a transformative experience. It can also help militate against antisocial behaviour which frequently accompanies dereliction. Having a theme for community involvement, determined within the community through a *Planning for Real* exercise (Neighbourhood Resource Centre for Central England n.d.), can provide a focus for landscape-led solutions.

One such focus is the need for better local facilities for recreation. There is now a general understanding of the wide range of cultural services and benefits that ecosystems can provide[6] and that the built environment can facilitate or constrain physical activity. Green space within the built environment offers many opportunities for beneficial 'green exercise' such as walking, running and cycling (University of Essex iCES 2012). Use of planning agreements between local authorities and developers has been used to create such facilities and a revenue stream for ongoing maintenance; West Park, Darlington, UK, is such an example (Figure 3.5).

Physical and social features of the environment also affect behaviour and there are clear documented associations between people's interaction with green space and a variety of psychological, emotional and mental health benefits including a positive effect on stress and general quality of life (Natural England 2009). However short distance and good and easy access to green spaces are crucial parameters in the use of green spaces (Harrison *et al.* 1995).

FIGURE 3.5   Extreme cycling at West Park, Darlington, UK, is an example of a green exercise facility created with a planning agreement and involving the local authority, housing developer, voluntary groups and local stakeholders (Clive Davies).

Local communities may wish to develop new green spaces to influence the neighbourhood's social capital through these kinds of health benefits, but also through the provision of facilities such as providing a meeting place for users to develop and maintain neighbourhood social ties. The formation of such ties and the presence of green vegetation in urban areas also significantly contribute to residents' sense of safety and belonging. The local landscape has also been found to perform an important role in children's development; attention span and cognitive skills in children are facilitated by exploratory and imaginative play. Wild urban nature spaces with opportunities for den making and the collection and use of natural materials are ideal environments for this purpose and create inspiring, even mythical, landscapes for all ages. Sheffield General Cemetery, UK, is an outstanding example of wild urban nature and an active volunteer group supporting it (Figure 3.6). Interaction with the landscape at an early age can provide the potential for important learning experiences and a relationship with local landscape that forms the basis for lifelong attitudes towards the environment (UKNEA 2011).

Communities without a strong local presence of skilled professionals whose knowledge they can call on often need support from community development workers and landscape designers/architects to bring about the improvements needed. In England, organisations such as the Conservation Volunteers (TCV 2013) have become specialists in involving local people in the environment whilst Groundwork Trusts (Groundwork Federation n.d.(b)) specialise in creating local partnerships to provide a whole-project service involving local participation, design, securing funding and implementation.

FIGURE 3.6   Wild urban nature at Sheffield General Cemetery is an example of a setting where the juxtaposing of urban nature and monumental stonemasonry creates an almost mythical landscape which is ideal for children's exploration and encouraging imaginative skills (Clive Davies).

Conclusions

Damaged landscapes have become and are becoming new cultural landscapes in a number of ways. Perhaps a key issue is the opportunity that these landscapes provide for communities which have lost opportunities for interacting with, or which have turned their back on, the landscape. At first viewing, damaged landscapes may appear as incongruous intrusions into a wider setting, yet there is another story to tell. If left undisturbed, these areas can regenerate into celebrated heritage landscapes; they are also the settings for creative regeneration projects and using artwork and other tools they can be the canvass on which cultural links can be painted between a bygone era and the future. The narrative on landscape-led regeneration processes in Britain, as elsewhere, tells its own story of partnering and community participation and mirrors the development of governance and political ideas. The opportunities provided by damaged landscapes have, in Europe at least, been instrumental in making cities better places to live and work and have encouraged nature to recolonise urban areas. The latter has been especially important during 30 years when the land use of truly rural countryside has become progressively more intensive. In large-scale damaged landscapes, large-scale benefits can be seen, not only from the physical change, but also in the building of community-based partnerships where a mosaic of projects add up to new governance mechanisms for decisions on landscape change over large areas. Damaged landscapes have also provided a livelihood for many professionals, including artists, ecologists, project managers and landscape architects. Indeed those, like the author, who have been part of the story have been privileged to share in the reshaping of their communities.

Notes

1   P.J. de Loutherbourg, *Coalbrookdale by Night* (1801) Oil on canvas, 68 × 106.5 cm. Science Museum, London.
2   See Ironbridge Gorge World Heritage Site information at: http://www.ironbridgegorgewhs.co.uk/welcome.html.
3   Local Agenda 21 (LA21) in the UK describes the strategy and action programme by which local authorities implemented the Agenda 21 action plan agreed at the so-called Earth Summit, the United Nations Conference on Environment and Development (UNCED), held in Rio de Janeiro, Brazil, in 1992. This aimed to implement sustainable development at a local level in partnership with local communities. Sustainable development is based on the idea that the quality of people's lives, and the state of communities, is affected by a combination of economic, social and environmental factors. A key concept of this was for community involvement in environmental decision making as a necessary prerequisite for sustainability (Agyeman and Evans 1997).
4   http://www.groundwork.org.uk/who-we-are/history.aspx (accessed 23 August 2013).
5   Heritage Coast is an English landscape designation which represents stretches of the most beautiful, undeveloped coastline, which are managed to conserve their natural beauty and, where appropriate, to improve accessibility for visitors (Natural England 2012).
6   The UK National Ecosystem Assessment (particularly Chapter 16) identified the importance of the cultural services and goods that ecosystems and environmental setting can provide and reviewed the key research evidence for the many claims concerning such services (UKNEA 2011).

References

Agyeman, J.A. (ed.) (1996) *Involving Communities in Forestry*, Edinburgh: Forestry Commission.
Agyeman, J. and Evans, R. (1997) 'Government, sustainability and community', *Local Environment*, 2, 2: 117–118.
Ahern, J. (2007) 'Green infrastructure for cities: the spatial dimension', in V. Novotny and P. Brown (eds) *Cities of the Future*, London: IWA Publishing, pp. 267–283.

AMION (2008) *The Economic Benefits of Green Infrastructure – an Assessment Framework for the NWDA*, online. Available at: http://www.naturaleconomynorthwest.org.uk/download.php?The%20Economic%20Benefits%20of%20Green%20Infrastructure%20-%20An%20Assessment%20Framework%20for%20the%20NWDA.pdf (accessed 06 November 2013).

Ashton, T.S. (1964) *The Industrial Revolution, 1760–1830*, Oxford: Oxford University Press.

Benedict, M.A. and McMahon, E.T. (2002) 'Green infrastructure: smart conservation for the 21st century', *Renewable Resources Journal*, 20(3): 12–17.

Benedict, M.A. and McMahon, E.T. (2006) *Green Infrastructure: Linking Landscapes and Communities*, Washington, DC: Island Press.

Castán Broto, V., Tabbush, P., Burningham, K., Elghali, L. and Edwards, D. (2007) 'Coal ash and risk: four social interpretations of a pollution landcape', *Landscape Research*, 32, 4: 481–497.

Countryside Agency and Groundwork UK (2005) *The Countryside in and Around Towns*, CA207, Wetherby: Countryside Agency Publications.

Countryside Commission (1986) *Management Plans – A Guide to their Preparation and Use*, Cheltenham, Countryside Commission.

Countryside Commission (1990) *Advice Manual for the Preparation of a Community Forest Plan*, CCP 271, Cheltenham: Countryside Commission.

Countryside Commission and Forestry Commission (1989) *Forests for the Community*, CCP 270, Cheltenham: Countryside Commission.

County Planning Officers' Society (1992) *Planning in the Urban Fringe*, Middlesbrough: Cleveland County Council.

DCLG (Department of Communities and Local Government) (2011) *The English Indices of Deprivation 2010*, London: DCLG, online. Available at: http://data.gov.uk/dataset/index-of-multiple-deprivation (accessed 20 April 2012).

Durham County Council (2002) *The Durham Coastal Footpath*, Durham: Durham County Council.

Durham Heritage Coast Partership (2012) Durham Heritage Coast Website, online. Available at: www.durhamheritagecoast.org/DHC/usp.nsf/pws/Durham+Herigate+Coast+-+Durham+Heritage+Coast+-+Welcome (accessed 27 June 2012).

Forestry Commission (1991) *Community Woodland Design Guidelines*, Edinburgh, Forestry Commission.

Gateshead Council (2012) *Angel of the North*, online. Available at: http://www.gateshead.gov.uk/Leisure%20and%20Culture/attractions/Angel/Home.aspx (accessed 26 February 2012).

Goudie, A. (1990) *The Human Impact on the Natural Environment*, Oxford: Blackwell.

Greenkeys (2008) *Greenkeys @ Your City – A Guide for Urban Green Quality*, online. Available at: http://www.greenkeys-project.net/media/files/flyer_greenkeys_manual_11042008.pdf?PHPSESSID=163162364c1e48 (accessed 14 March 2013).

Groundwork Federation (n.d.(a)) *History*, online. Available at: http://www.groundwork.org.uk/who-we-are/history.aspx (accessed 26 February 2012).

Groundwork Federation (n.d.(b)) *Communities*, online. Available at: http://www.groundwork.org.uk/ (accessed 26 February 2012).

Hancock, M.D. (1971) 'The United States, Europe, and post-industrial society', *Comparative Politics*, 4, 1: 133–146.

Handley, J., Pauleit, S. and Gill, S. (2007) 'Landscape, sustainability and the city', in J.F. Benson and M.H. Roe (eds) *Landscape and Sustainability*, London: Routledge, pp. 167–195.

Harrison, C.J.B., Burgess, J., Millward, A. and Dawe, G. (1995) *Accessible Natural Greenspace in Towns and Cities*, English Nature Research Report 153, Peterborough: English Nature.

Heritage Lottery Fund (n.d.) *Land & Biodiversity*, online. Available at: http://www.hlf.org.uk/ourproject/projectsbysector/landandbiodiversity/Pages/index.aspx (accessed 25 February 2012).

Hook, M.W.Z., Werner, Z., Schindler, J., Aleklett, K. (2010) 'Global coal production outputs based on a logistics model', *Fuel*, 89, 11: 3546–3558.

Jordan, G. and Szucs, A. (2011) 'Geochemical landscape analysis: development and application to the risk assessment of acid mine drainage. A case study in central Sweden', *Landscape Research*, 36, 2: 231–262.

Kambites, C. and Owen, S. (2006) 'Renewed prospects for green infrastructure planning in the UK', *Planning Practice and Research*, 21(4): 483–496.

Konijnendijk, C.C. (2008) *The Forest and the City: The Cultural Landscape of Urban Woodland*, Springer, Netherlands.

Kowarik, I. and Körner, S. (2005) *Wild Urban Woodlands: New Perspectives for Urban Forestry*, Berlin and Heidelberg: Springer.

Landscape Institute (2009) *Green Infrastructure: Connected and Multifunctional Landscapes*, London: Landscape Institute.

Llausàs, A. and Roe, M.H. (2012) 'Green infrastructure planning: cross-national analysis between the north east of England (UK) and Catalonia (Spain)', *European Planning Studies*, 20, 4: 641–663.

National Audit Office (2010) *Regenerating the English Regions: Regional Development Agencies' Support to Physical Regeneration Projects*, London: National Audit Office.

Natural England (2009) *Health and Natural Environments: An Evidence Based Information Pack*, online. Available at: http://www.naturalengland.org.uk/Images/health-information-pack_tcm6-31487.pdf (accessed 20 June 2013).

Natural England (2012) *Heritage Coasts*, online. Available at: http://www.naturalengland.org.uk/ourwork/conservation/designatedareas/heritagecoasts/default.aspx (accessed 12 July 2012).

Neighbourhood Resource Centre for Central England (n.d.) *Planning for Real*, online. Available at: http://www.planningforreal.org.uk/ (accessed 26 February 2012).

Nottinghamshire County Council (n.d.) *Coal Tips*, online. Available at: http://www3.nottinghamshire.gov.uk/atoz/c/coal-tips/ (accessed 25 February 2012).

Pahl, R.E. (1966) 'The rural-urban continuum', *Sociologia Ruralis*, 6(3): 299–327.

PNE Consulting (2008) *The Third Sector and Physical Regeneration*, Newcastle upon Tyne: PNE.

Pollard, D. (n.d.) *Advice to Great North Forest Partnership on Artwork in the Great North Community Forest*, unpublished.

Roe, M.H. (2005) *Community Forestry and Landscape Identity: Planning New Forest Landscapes*, UNESCO Landscapes Conference, Newcastle University, online. Available at: http://conferences.ncl.ac.uk/unescolandscapes/files/ROEMaggie.pdf (accessed 26 February 2012).

Roe, M.H. (2007) 'The social dimensions of landscape sustainability', in J.F. Benson and M.H. Roe (eds) *Landscape and Sustainability*, 2nd edition, Oxford: Routledge, pp. 58–83.

Roe, M.H. (2011) 'Editorial: landscape and mining', *Landscape Research*, 36, 2: 189–190.

Roe, M.H. (2012) 'Making sense of place and landscape planning at the landscape scale', in I. Convery, G. Corsane and P. Davis (eds) *Making Sense of Place Multidisciplinary Perspectives*, Woodbridge: Boydell & Brewer, pp. 191–206.

Ruhr.2010 GmbH (2010) *New in Europe – The Ruhr Metropolis*, from European Capital of Culture 2010, online. Available at: http://www.essen-fuer-das-ruhrgebiet.ruhr2010.de/en/home.html (accessed 26 February 2012).

Scottish Government (2011) *Achieving a Sustainable Future: Regeneration Strategy*, Edinburgh: Scottish Government.

Sheppard, S.R.J. and Meitner, M. (2005) 'Using multi-criteria analysis and visualisation for sustainable forest management planning with stakeholder groups', *Forest Ecology and Management*, 207, 1–2: 171–187.

TCV (2013). TCV Community Network, online. Available at: http://www.tcv.org.uk/community (accessed 23 August 2013).

UK Coal (2012) *Community and Environment*, UK Coal, online. Available at: http://www.ukcoal.com/how-mining-began (accessed 27 February 2012).

UKNEA (United Kingdom National Ecosystem Assessment) (2011) Technical Report, online. Available at: http://uknea.unep-wcmc.org/Resources/tabid/82/Default.aspx (accessed 06 November 2013).

UNESCO (2007) *Convention Concerning the Protection of the World Cutlural and Natural Heritage*, World Heritage Committee, 31st Meeting (pp. WHC-07/31.COM/13B), Paris: UNESCO.

University of Essex iCES (2012) *Green Exercise*, online. Available at: http://www.greenexercise.org/ (accessed 26 February 2012).

Williamson, K.S. (2003) *Growing with Green Infrastructure*, Doylestown: Heritage Conservancy.

4

ENVISIONING NEW CULTURAL LANDSCAPES

Agricultural traditions and adaptation

Nora J. Mitchell and Brenda Barrett

Introduction

In the last three decades, the concept of cultural landscapes has been applied to an increasingly diverse array and larger scale of places, including working agricultural landscapes.[1] Conservation of lived-in vernacular cultural landscapes has ushered in a number of important debates. Tensions around the nature and pace of landscape change, the role of governmental designation and management, and the need for more integrative strategies and new types of governance for conservation efforts are issues that have fuelled debate and critical discussion. The shifting social, economic and ecological context for working cultural landscapes has also seen other issues emerge such as climate change and globalization, dramatically influencing the viability of land uses. Over the last ten years, new initiatives for agricultural landscapes in the United States have evolved to meet these challenges.

This chapter argues that these initiatives, generated by adaptation of a cultural landscape concept to working agricultural lands, now offer insights and guidance for new cultural landscapes of the future. Analysis of several of these emerging efforts demonstrates a variety of promising approaches that create locally based economic initiatives for food systems and heritage-based tourism, reuse and reinvestment of heritage infrastructure, more integrated strategies across public and private sectors and between conservation and other community goals, and stronger partnership networks for governance for larger landscape scales. Amidst an increasingly rapid pace of change, landscape has been used as an integrating concept for an adaptive management approach advancing community development often at a regional scale. These efforts, and others, collectively begin to envision an approach and characteristics for new cultural landscapes.

Evolution of a cultural landscape concept: the promise and challenge of agricultural landscapes

Over the last 30 years there has been increasingly wide recognition of landscapes as cultural heritage in the United States and in many other countries (Taylor and Lennon 2012; Rössler 2003, 2006). During this evolution, the concept has expanded to include lived-in vernacular, cultural landscapes including but not limited to agricultural landscapes. Many designations around the world have recognized the heritage value of lived-in cultural landscapes represented by the distinctive character created by local time-honoured traditions that shape the landscape and sustain the culture and way of life. The tangible heritage and associated intangible values are understood to result from the presence of people in these landscapes over time, and are often linked to traditional ownership and management systems. Long-term land management and the sustained interaction of people and their environment have been recognized for supporting both cultural and biological diversity (Amend *et al.* 2008; Brown *et al.* 2005). These landscapes represent continuity with the past and are characterized by a layering of material evidence from previous generations and ongoing cultural activity. For example, traces of earlier field patterns may exist within contemporary landscapes along with adaptive reuse of agricultural buildings. Consequently, agricultural landscapes, like other types of vernacular cultural landscapes, are 'essentially a palimpsest portraying traces of successive periods of occupation and transformation' (Selman 2010: 161). Attention to such working landscapes is also timely and urgent, since the loss of agricultural land is a growing concern both in the United States and also in Europe (Dramstad and Fjellstand 2011).

In 1992, the UNESCO World Heritage Committee recognized three categories of cultural landscapes as a type of heritage that represents interaction of humans and their environment. Organically evolved landscapes (Category Two) were identified as one of three types of cultural landscapes (UNESCO 2011). Some of these evolved cultural landscapes continue to 'retain an active social role in contemporary society closely associated with the traditional way of life, and in which an evolutionary process is still in progress' and exhibit 'significant material evidence of its evolution over time' (UNESCO 2011: 88). Many of the cultural landscapes on the World Heritage List belong to this second category of landscapes and include a variety of rural, agricultural landscapes (UNESCO World Heritage Centre n.d.; Taylor and Lennon 2012; Fowler 2003).

The International Union for the Conservation of Nature (IUCN) has, for many years, recognized Protected Landscapes and Seascapes as one management category (Dudley 2008; Phillips 2002). Designation of protected landscapes, known as Category V, recognizes the importance of people interacting with their environment to sustain places that have biodiversity values and often cultural values as well (Amend *et al.* 2008; Brown *et al.* 2005).

In the United States, the National Park Service (NPS) has developed guidance for listing cultural landscapes in the National Register of Historic Places, a list of the nation's properties worthy of preservation. In the 1990s, the National Register recognized historic vernacular landscapes (sometimes termed rural historic landscapes) that provided guidance on evaluating significance and management of agricultural landscapes (McClelland *et al.* 1999; US Department of the Interior, NPS 1996; Birnbaum 1994). In addition, the agency has adopted policy on management of cultural landscapes, including agricultural areas, within Congressionally designated areas within the National Park System (US Department of the Interior, NPS 1998, 2006).

All of these designation strategies recognize the significance of agricultural landscapes and set documentation standards to assess their importance and serve as a foundation for management. With recognition of landscapes as heritage, an historic preservation framework began to be used to guide management of agricultural landscapes; this has created some challenges (Buggey and Mitchell 2003, 2008; McEnaney 2001). Generally, historic preservation tenets seek to minimize resource change in order to retain the property's important characteristics. In contrast, there is a continuing need to adapt and evolve agriculture in response to changing markets, the available labour force and variations in climate. Agricultural ways of life and landscapes change in order to survive. Traditional field patterns and farm buildings, for example, may change in response to changing agricultural uses. Certain changes in agrarian practices on the ground can also place natural resource protection and agricultural interests at odds with each other. Dynamism of agricultural landscapes also stimulates the need to ask the fundamental question about the point at which heritage values of a changing landscape have been lost.

As agricultural landscapes are shaped by cultural, socio-economic and ecological systems, a variety of drivers influence the viability of types of farming and generates land use change and adaptation over time. Today, many of these drivers are national and international and the resulting landscape transformations become increasingly dominated by and, in many cases, increasingly vulnerable to exogenous market forces (Arler 2011; Selman 2010). Another 'widespread problem is that the drivers which produced our distinctive heritage are increasingly obsolete, yet contemporary drivers do not seem to be creating landscapes which are intuitively pleasing or characteristically place-sensitive' (Selman 2010: 162). For example, current economic systems based on the commodity market can result in farm consolidation, creating a change in scale of agriculture and the loss of individual farmsteads.

Agricultural landscapes are often much larger than areas traditionally designated in the United States for conservation. To work effectively at this larger scale, the goals for conservation are often integrated with those for community development such as quality of life, nature conservation and economic vitality. This broadened agenda involves many more landowners, organizations and levels of government and requires coordination, partnerships and new forms of governance at the appropriate scale.

Given these challenges, it is important to develop a management strategy that will recognize landscape character and values and the need for working landscape change, as well as consider the relationships with the geographic, social and economic context that are needed to sustain existing cultural landscapes into the future. The World Heritage Committee, for example, requires a management plan or documentation for a management system as part of any proposed site to the World Heritage List (UNESCO 2011; Mitchell *et al.* 2009).

Several European countries have programmes with a long track record for conserving lived-in regional landscapes. Areas of Outstanding Natural Beauty (AONB) in the United Kingdom (specifically England, Wales and Northern Ireland) and Parcs Naturels Régionaux (Regional Natural Parks, or PNR) in France have pioneered the process of landscape-scale planning and management. In the United Kingdom, AONB designations include agricultural values and they also take recreational opportunities and development into account (English Heritage 2009) to encourage the realization of multifunctional landscapes. In France, the focus is increasingly on the conservation of traditional agricultural products and practices. The AONB and PNR programmes recognize rural landscapes for the high quality of their agricultural and natural values, and they focus on the long-term conservation of landscape character. Both programmes also incorporate the social and economic interests of local communities, having learned over time that landscape conservation cannot succeed without benefiting and having the support of the people who live in the region (Barrett and Taylor 2007).

Agricultural landscape conservation case studies: innovations in practice

In North America, agriculture has a deep past stretching back to native peoples and subsequently was the foundational activity of European settlement (Conzen 1990). In the United States, 50 per cent of the land cover of the contiguous 48 states is dedicated to agrarian purposes such as cropland or grazing land. Consequently, many of the nation's landscapes are agricultural in nature (Lubowski *et al.* 2006). These places include the iconic landscapes of farms and forests of New England to the wide expanses of the Midwestern prairies and the extensive ranches in the west. Even so, this type of cultural landscape is under-represented in the national historic designation schemes due, in part, to the management challenges associated with working cultural landscapes (as discussed in the previous section). Some of the most difficult conservation challenges stem from landscape dynamism and the resulting change over time in response to social, ecological and economic forces, and the large scale of many vernacular landscapes with many owners, crossing many jurisdictions.

The following three case studies offer some new strategies that address these challenges in innovative ways. The new models consider designated landscapes as well as recognition of the value of the everyday working landscape. These examples offer promise for conservation of large-scale vernacular landscapes as an important component of regional community-based strategies and suggest ways to consider future new agricultural landscapes as dynamic and valuable places.

Case study 1: working landscape initiatives at Cuyahoga Valley National Park: from park system to food system

Cuyahoga Valley National Park preserves the rural landscape along 20 miles of the meandering, northward flowing Cuyahoga River and the Ohio & Erie Canal between the large urban populations of Cleveland and Akron in Northeast Ohio (Cuyahoga Valley National Park n.d.). The historic canal brought commerce in the early 1830s, and shaped the character of the region as canal-related industries and agriculture became the dominant occupations. Many of the small towns, villages and farms that made up this nineteenth-century landscape still exist today.

Historically, between 60 and 90 per cent of the area now within the national park boundaries was used for farming. By the late 1990s less than 4 per cent of the land within park boundaries was still farmed (around 1,180 of the park's nearly 33,000 acres) (Kelsey 2002). At the time the park was created in 1974, small working farms still existed in the valley, but many were in declining condition. As a result, farmsteads were being converted to other purposes and the agricultural character of the valley was being lost. In response, the US National Park Service acquired some properties to protect them from future development. However, acquisition, without the means to continue agricultural land use, did not arrest the deterioration of farm fields or associated buildings. The park and the local communities became concerned about the growing loss of this agricultural heritage and decided to work together to revitalize some of the remaining farms that had operated in the valley from the mid-nineteenth to the mid-twentieth century.

Inspired by the European approach to maintaining working agricultural cultural landscapes in national parks, the partners advanced an initiative to encourage privately supported, economically viable, and environmentally friendly approaches to agricultural practices within the national park setting. In 1999, a new non-profit organization, the Countryside Conservancy, was created to coordinate this initiative and bring necessary technical expertise on sustainable agriculture as well as support the reuse and adaptation of farm properties (Countryside Conservancy n.d.). Importantly, its mission (see below) also encompasses ongoing collaboration with farmers and engaging the community through a variety of pro- grammes and activities. The goal is to revitalize 15 farms averaging 100 acres or less, and as of 2011, 12 farms have been leased (Cuyahoga Valley National Park n.d.).

> Countryside Conservancy mission statement:
>
> We envision Northeast Ohio filled with thriving farming and food entrepreneurs: where farms are viable businesses, farmland is a treasured resource, and local food is commonplace.
>
> We support up-and-coming farmers, share innovative land-use and business models, facilitate networking opportunities and advocate community-based agriculture.
>
> We connect communities and farmers, provide alternate market choices, and create venues that foster civic engagement through fun and informal education. This program promotes living, working farms in a national park that represent the rural heritage of the Cuyahoga Valley, while also protecting the park's resources.
>
> *(Countryside Conservancy n.d.)*

The Countryside Conservancy, in partnership with the national park and other partners, has developed a network of sustainable farms, value-added strategies, and new markets for their products. The Conservancy was able to work with the farmers on sustainable agriculture, defined as agriculture that is economically profitable, socially responsible and ecologically healthy (Kelsey 2002). This approach is suited to farms that are small in scale and intensively managed such as those in the national park. Sustainable agriculture produces high-quality, high-value, specialty products for direct, local, retail sale. Consequently, a key step forward was opening seasonal farmers' markets to serve as an outlet for food and crafts produced by farms in the region (Figure 4.1). The farmers' markets support the economic vitality of farms, make quality food available to local residents, and also provide an opportunity for visitors to the park to learn first-hand about rural heritage and contemporary stewardship.

In addition to revitalizing farms during its first decade, the Countryside Conservancy also developed a series of educational programmes to support new farmers, as well as to engage and educate the general public. Through diverse activities, the Conservancy has built social capital by strengthening relationships within the region and developing a sense of community among the farmers who cooperate with each other (NPS Conservation Study Institute n.d.).

More recently, the Conservancy has begun to connect their work to community-based food systems in Northeast Ohio that address growing concerns around food security. Food security is a term for making healthy food accessible to all, including low-income people, through building local food systems (Community Food Security Coalition n.d.). Food systems revitalize local economies by supporting local, regional, sustainable farmers and other businesses to work more effectively together as an economic system (Local Food System n.d.). The Conservancy's programmes contribute to local food systems in many ways, by helping farmers find land, connecting local growers to chefs and consumers, providing access to food for low-income community members, and sharing the importance of local food systems with the public (Countryside Conservancy n.d.). In addition, the Conservancy is actively engaged in

FIGURE 4.1   Cuyahoga Valley farmers' market supports the farming economy and builds community (courtesy of and used with the permission of the US National Park Service).

regional and statewide efforts, such as the Ohio Food Policy Advisory Council, to support local farm economy and access to healthy local food (Countryside Conservancy, Ohio Food Policy Advisory Council n.d.).

In summary, this initiative, to conserve the agricultural heritage in a national park and the surrounding valley, has transformed the landscape into a contributor to the economic vitality and well-being of the region. The resulting new and revitalized cultural landscape reflects the agricultural legacy and, through adaptations that address critical current social concerns, is building community strength and resilience.

Case study 2: Iowa's landscape of silos and smokestacks: an agricultural heritage partnership

Located in the heart of America's tall grass prairie, northeastern Iowa includes some of the world's most fertile soil. Across a gently undulating terrain, the landscape breaks into hills,

FIGURE 4.2 Silos and Smokestacks National Heritage Area: a northeastern Iowa agricultural landscape (courtesy of and used with the permission of Silos and Smokestacks National Heritage Area).

valleys and bluffs as it approaches the Mississippi River at its eastern border (Figure 4.2). Native Americans farmed the valleys and managed the upland prairie with fire to improve habitat for game. Europeans arriving in the 1850s divided up the lands into individual farms. Many of these new settlers were immigrants from all corners of Europe. In the twentieth century technological changes such as seed hybridization, food processing and preservation, and widespread mechanization expanded agricultural production. The region's increased productivity helped supply world markets with food and grain. Local universities further developed the area as a centre of agribusiness innovation. Located in urban areas were packing houses, farm equipment factories, and transportation links to the growing areas which helped to support an agricultural economy (NPS 1995).

As in all agriculturally based economies, the region was buffeted by fluctuations in climate, the national economy and world markets. By the end of the twentieth century it also faced other difficulties. This part of Iowa struggled with the loss of established food processing facilities, which had adverse impact upon the vitality of the urban centres. The farming population was aging, some prime agricultural land was falling out of production, and there was farm consolidation that changed both the appearance of the landscape and affected community vitality. More positively, the region still had a strong tradition of family farming and farmers were well-known for their work ethic and traditional values.

In 1991, community leaders in one of the depressed urban centres surveyed the region's assets as part of an economic revitalization scheme. The survey found that the city's heritage and economic well-being was inextricably linked to the larger rural landscape. The effort called itself 'Silos and Smokestacks' to reflect the geographic connection between agriculture (silos) and industry that constituted the agribusiness that helped feed the world (smokestacks). Following on from this work, the NPS was asked to study the potential national signi-ficance of the region. The resulting NPS Special Resource Study determined that northeast Iowa had made significant contributions to the story of national and international agriculture and proposed designation of a 17-county area as a new entity to be called a heritage partnership to tell this story (NPS 1995).

One year later Congress designated a substantially larger region, 37 counties in all, as an agricultural heritage partnership that became known as Silos and Smokestacks. This legislation also authorized a new local management entity made up of representatives from volunteer associations, private businesses and state and local political subdivisions to interpret and promote the natural and cultural resources that contributed to the region's significance. Similar to a National Heritage Area, the partnership was a large lived-in landscape, which was to be managed locally with the federal government's role limited to financial and technical assistance (NPS 2004).

In the beginning, the Silos and Smokestacks partnership faced many challenges. These included the scale of the initiative, which was over 20,000 square miles. Another was the rural agrarian culture, which places a high premium on individual action and on self-reliance. To overcome community concerns about the role of the national government in this new heritage designation, the original legislation authorized the Department of Agriculture to serve as the lead federal agency, given that this department was the traditional federal agency liaison to the farm community (NPS 2004). However, the project stalled when the department could not envision itself in this new and unfamiliar role as a provider of heritage assistance.

Despite these setbacks, the Silos and Smokestacks partnership persevered and built a strong partnership network. In 2000, the NPS was designated as the lead federal partner and the region became part of the agency's National Heritage Area programme. This programme now has 49 Congressionally designated areas that receive assistance from the NPS (NPS National Heritage Areas, n.d.; National Park System Advisory Board 2006; Barrett and Mitchell 2003; Barrett and Wood 2003). The heritage area focused on interpretation of the agricultural story in order to implement the partnership network in a way that respected the area's traditional values of independence and voluntarism. The primary goals were to add economic value through increased heritage tourism and to share the story with residents and visitors (Silos and Smokestacks National Heritage Area 2003).

> Vision
> The partnership preserves and promotes the story and makes a positive economic impact by encouraging tourism and heritage based development. Through an integrated story tied to every site, visitors leave with an understanding of the value and importance of American agriculture through authentic experiences. Ownership of the Heritage Area rests in the communities, residents and stakeholders of the region. Together they achieve the Heritage Area's mission.
>
> *(NPS 2004: 3)*

Over the last ten years, this focus on telling the story and adding economic value has been well received within the 37 counties. The area has 108 formal partnerships built on existing and valued community assets that strengthen the sense of regional identity. It has connected these partner sites around a series of broader interpretive themes and built the capacity of the organizations with targeted grants, workshops and technical assistance. Linking the areas' identity to the NPS brand, regional signage programmes and multiple social media campaigns have helped promote the heritage value of this very large landscape. A recent evaluation documented that over three million people visit heritage sites a year. It also found that the heritage area responded to demand for youth programming by adding a substantial educational component with a focus on history of farming, reading the landscape, and the impact of agricultural programmes and policies. There have been 1,000 participants in training programmes and 500,000 visits to the award-winning web-based 'Camp Silos' (Raymond 2012).

In conclusion, the Silos and Smokestacks National Heritage Area has developed a collaborative approach where partners work together towards common goals. It is also able to tackle emerging issues through new partnerships, for example, flood assessment studies with Leopold Center for Sustainable Agriculture, tours to introduce winemaking in the region, and supporting food security through heritage plants and breeds exchanges (Silos and Smokestacks National Heritage Area n.d.). This strategy has overcome the initial concerns of residents about governmental designation and outside control of agricultural resources. For National Heritage Areas, the NPS's role is to be one of the partners offering guidance, limited funding and strong brand recognition (NPS National Heritage Areas n.d.). The nationally significant cultural landscape is still managed by the people that live in it, but with a much greater appreciation of the place they call home.

Case study 3: shaping the future of Vermont's working landscape: a marriage of tradition and innovation

Communities in Vermont have a strong place-based identity linked to the traditional livelihoods of farming and forestry. The roots of this identity can be traced back to the late eighteenth- and early nineteenth-century settlement pattern of dispersed small villages with a white church spire nestled in mountain valleys, surrounded by fields and forests managed for self-sufficiency (Klyza and Trombulak 1999). This created a 'classic agrarian landscape' remarked upon as early as 1803, by the Reverend Timothy Dwight, president of Yale College, evoking a bucolic ideal landscape scene for his readers (Albers 2000). The landscape character of Vermont today remains from the first half of the nineteenth century, shaped by the transition to a commercial farm-based economy that has been primarily dominated by dairying (Albers 2000) (Figure 4.3).

Tourism started early in the nineteenth century and was driven, in part, by a romantic view of nature and an idyllic image of Vermont which was cultivated through paintings that reinforced the central role of the landscape in the state's culture and identity (Albers 2000). Beginning in 1946, *Vermont Life* magazine reinforced the image of rural life. Since the 1950s, Vermont's pastoral landscape (second only to the ski industry) has been important to its economy. In 1997, tourism was the number two industry in Vermont (behind manufacturing) (Klyza and Trombulak 1999).

> By the end of World War II, the majority of Vermonters had never plowed a field or run their hands down the smooth, glossy flanks of their own cows. Yet Vermont's sense of itself remained tied to the hard-won nature of its farming.
>
> *(Albers 2000: 274)*

FIGURE 4.3 Third-generation dairy farm in a central Vermont valley (courtesy of and used with the permission of US National Park Service).

The vernacular landscape is also important symbolically, as part of the state's heritage and identity and is embedded in its culture.

Over the decades since the 1870s, Vermont agriculture has been integrated into regional, national and international markets. Farmers responded by shifting from Merino sheep in the 1830s, successfully, to butter and cheese production in the late nineteenth and early twentieth centuries, and to fluid milk in the commodity market in the mid-twentieth century (Klyza and Trombulak 1999). In spite of these changes which were in response to competition from the west and to market opportunities, there has been a general decline in the agricultural sector in Vermont's economy and also in acres farmed and the number of farms.

Public concern over this decline in agriculture that accelerated in the 1970s and 1980s prompted a number of responses over the ensuing years to retain farmland for its contributions to the state's economy, the sense of place and recognition that the working landscapes also support a growing tourism industry. Discussions on the future of the Vermont landscape have a long history, beginning with the Commission on Country Life in 1929 (Vermont Council on Rural Development 2009). In 2007, the Vermont Council on Rural Development (VCRD) created the Council on the Future of Vermont as a two-year initiative to envision the future of Vermont, based on public opinion and research. Over 3,900 Vermonters participated through an extensive array of engagement opportunities including a series of public forums, focus group meetings, online contributions to the website, and statewide polling efforts as well as meetings with over 300 statewide organizations (VCRD 2009).

This effort produced many insights, however, the primary finding was that overwhelmingly Vermonters are united in their support of the working landscape that is central to their personal identification and love of Vermont (VCRD 2009). Attachment to the working landscape is integral to a broader set of values including community, environment, hard work, independence, and Vermont's identity defined by centuries of traditions. Vermonters also expressed their concerns for the future of agriculture and some of the other cultural values they cherish. Based on these responses and other information from research, VCRD crafted a broad vision for the future (VCRD 2011; see also concurrent effort, Vermont Sustainable Jobs Fund 2011).

This vision became the foundation for VCRD's Vermont Working Landscape Partnership and an Action Plan (VCRD 2010). The focus of the Partnership is on

> the rural land-based economy centering on agriculture and forestry to conserve and enhance the Vermont brand, support the prosperity of rural communities, maintain Vermont as a pre-eminent tourism destination, and steward the state's character for the next generation of Vermonters.
>
> *(VCRD 2010: 1)*

The Action Plan takes a more integrated approach to the landscape than previous efforts and acknowledges that this can only be accomplished through broad-based partnerships between many individuals, organizations and businesses. One element of this ambitious programme and policy development, a Working Lands Enterprise Investment Bill was just signed into law by the Vermont legislature to support and stimulate innovations for economic development in agricultural and forest products businesses (VCRD 2012). According to VCRD executive director Paul Costello, 'This bill ... lets the nation know that agricultural and forest products entrepreneurs are welcome here. Vermont will be known as the "value-added" state. This initiative is an economic development strategy that supports rural prosperity' (Costello 2012, pers.comm.).

This work by VCRD and a concurrent effort by Vermont Sustainable Jobs Fund (2011) has created an environment for a renewed investment in sustaining the working landscape of Vermont, incorporating ongoing successful programmes and also launching new initiatives. Since 1977, for example, the Vermont Land Trust (VLT) has conserved over 250,000 acres, including more than 700 working farms (VLT n.d.). Since 1995, the Vermont Fresh Network has been advancing partnerships between farmers, chefs and consumers to grow markets for local food (Vermont Fresh Network 2013).

These ongoing efforts, combined with a growing partnership with a vision and plan for the future of Vermont's working landscape, began to illuminate opportunities for diversifying agriculture and growing the market for local products. A number of entrepreneurial businesses began making award-winning farmstead cheeses and using place-based labels that capitalized on Vermont's image as a healthy, wholesome source of food. Some young business school graduates began creating new regional agricultural infrastructure such as a cave for aging cheese. Leaders in Hardwick, Vermont, began intentionally building their local food systems to connect individual entrepreneurs and retain more money locally (Hewitt 2009). All of this is creating a momentum and additional opportunities for a growing value-added local market and advancing the ability to expand the percentage of locally grown food while reducing the dependence on imports.

Given the growth in farmers' markets, farm stands, and community-supported agriculture within the state, the growing artisan cheese industry, vineyards, and other specialty agricultural operations, former Secretary of the Vermont Agency of Agriculture, Food and

Markets, Roger Allbee, has called this a 'Renaissance of Vermont Agriculture' (Vermont Sustainable Jobs Fund 2011: 3). The growing network of agricultural producers and other business as a food system combined with the statewide effort to develop a supportive framework of policies and programmes holds great promise for the future of Vermont's working landscape.

Reflections on recent initiatives: insights for envisioning new cultural landscapes

These case studies and other recent experience with conservation of working agricultural landscapes illustrate some new directions and many of these initiatives are being led by local people and communities in order to intentionally shape the future of these places. These rural places may be designated as national parks, national heritage areas, World Heritage Sites, protected landscapes or simply recognized as everyday landscapes that are of value to people and part of their communities and their region. While there is no one solution to meeting the serious social and economic challenges facing rural agricultural regions, these case studies suggest some key interrelated components integral to a strategy for guiding change. These components – articulating a shared sense of place, building a common vision, harnessing the drivers, and designing new collaborative forms of governance – are dimensions of social capacity for adaptation in a rapidly changing world.

Articulating a shared and evolving sense of place

Attachment to traditional working landscapes by people within a region is not simply nostalgia, but rather about landscape identity, memory and sense of place (Taylor and Lennon 2012; Le Du-Blayo 2011). These case studies demonstrate the importance of articulating a shared understanding of sense of place by people that live in these agricultural regions. In Cuyahoga Valley National Park, the values of the farm properties within the national park became a subject of discussion when the decline of agriculture resulted in abandonment. The local communities used this shared sense of loss of this rural community as motivation for seeking an alternative path and in partnership with the NPS brought many farms back to life using environmentally sustainable agricultural practices. In the examples from Silos and Smokestacks National Heritage Area and Vermont, the people of these regions articulated their rural identity and used recognition by the state or national governments as part of their strategy for sustaining the character and intangible community values of these traditional agricultural places.

Many different methods were used in these and other examples to identify and describe landscape character and the complexity of values from the communities' point of view. Even so, certain historic documentation approaches, such as the National Register for Historic Places, may overlook certain landscape 'markers with special meanings for residents' (Morgan et al. 2006). Therefore it is critical to strive to represent the range and types of values communities hold for their landscapes. The participatory, dialogue-based approach used in the Vermont case study also illustrates how this sense of place serves as a foundation for creating strategies for the future of the rural landscape. As a sense of place evolves over time as landscapes and communities change, it is important to periodically renew a shared perspective articulated through an organizational and management framework tailored to the situation (Antrop 2006).

Building a shared vision as a foundation for coordinated action

Implicit in many of the lived-in landscapes that convey a special sense of place is a sense of shared purpose that is often based on generations of people working the land. Making this shared vision explicit emerged in these case studies as an important element of a strategy at the landscape scale. In the Silos and Smokestacks example, the interpretive plan, prepared with a high level of public engagement, was completed prior to adopting the final management plan for the region. As each partner organization helped to shape the interpretive plan, they better understood their contribution to the story of the region. In the Vermont example, the community engagement process, led by the Council on the Future of Vermont, elicited articulation of not only a shared sense of place, but also the shared hopes for the future of the working landscape, the associated cultural traditions, and civil society. In the Cuyahoga Valley, the initial vision for reclaiming the declining farmsteads gained momentum with each farm revitalization, and their vision expanded to engaging youth, creating a stronger sense of community, and building a better food system for northeastern Ohio.

In each of the case studies, a vision or mission statement served as a touchstone for defining success, looking forward to the next generation. The Silos and Smokestacks Management Plan, for example, stated the desired outcome of implementing the mission and vision for the region as: 'Preserving the integrity of the cultural landscape and local stories means that future generations will be able to understand and define who they are, where they come from and what ties them to their home' (NPS 2004: 3).

Evaluations of three of the US National Heritage Areas has shown the importance of creating a statement on the broad range of values of a place through some type of collaborative process as one of the first steps in taking action to conserve large landscapes (Barrett 2008; Copping *et al.* 2006; Tuxill *et al.* 2005, 2008). Development of an expansive definition of values that encompasses natural and cultural heritage as well as regional character and vitality, broadens the goals for the future that is more centred around preserving a sense of place than on preserving specific features of the cultural landscape.

Harnessing economic drivers to help manage change

Each case study acknowledged the significant and fundamental challenge of maintaining the economic vitality of these agricultural communities, given the strong influences from a variety of economic drivers originating beyond the region, many at the national and international level. Vernacular working landscapes in many countries face a similar issue from exogenous drivers (Arler 2011; Le Du-Blayo 2011; Selman 2010). The case study communities demonstrate several approaches that assert local adaptation of these drivers or capitalize on opportunities presented by current economic and social trends.

Heritage tourism, for example, can, if strategically managed, bring visitor dollars into the local economy without major disruption of the farming system. Vermont has a very long history of heritage tourism as an economic driver and has recognized that the state's working landscape is a critical asset for this important part of their economy. Silos and Smokestacks identified tourism as a new opportunity and focused on building tourism infrastructure as a priority. Branding the region and its partnership with the NPS was an important aspect as well as developing new programmes to expand the capacity of both local heritage sites and new heritage entrepreneurs.

The current interest in local foods and concerns with food security create opportunities for agricultural regions to market local, high-quality food as a way to add value to their products and to promote the place where food is grown (Slow Food n.d.; Krupp 2010; Diamant *et al.* 2007a, 2007b). As illustrated in examples from Cuyahoga Valley and Vermont, initiatives are building a growing regional economy based on fresh produce and farmstead products such as cheese and meats, emphasizing buy-local strategies. Marketing campaigns that connect agricultural landscape heritage with artisanal cheeses and other products at the state and regional level appeal to locals and visitors. In Vermont, young business entrepreneurs are reusing existing infrastructure such as farm buildings and also adding new regional infrastructure such as caves for aging cheese and facilities for meat processing (Vermont Sustainable Jobs Fund 2011). Importantly, traditionally managed working landscapes can also help with global climate change, as many of the traditional forms of agriculture and forestry are more climate friendly and potentially more resilient than many of the modern large-scale industrialized systems (Worldwatch Institute 2009). Agriculture and land use can 'simultaneously provide food and fiber, meet the needs of nature and biodiversity, and support viable livelihoods for people who live there' (Scherr and Sthapit 2009: 33). While farmers in the United States are an aging population, fortunately, there is a resurgence of interest by young people and, as illustrated in all three case studies, there are now many programmes that connect a new generation of farmers with agricultural land.

Designing models for collaborative governance at the landscape scale

Cooperation in a community context is an important tradition in many agricultural communities. As all of these case studies illustrate, this tradition is foundational to deliberately build partnership systems over larger landscape scales for the purpose of creating shared identity and a vision for the future, and for sustaining the efforts to reach those goals over time.

As each case demonstrated, working at a larger scale can enhance effectiveness in adapting economic drivers and can be beneficial to regional initiatives such as heritage tourism or marketing agricultural products. Existing governmental structures, based on political jurisdictions, often do not coincide with the business and social networks on the landscape and often do not match the scale of threats or opportunities. Participatory processes and democratic models of governance can complement these and other existing structures.

In the Cuyahoga Valley, a partnership between a private non-profit organization, the Countryside Conservancy, and the NPS grew to engage many other partners in the surrounding communities and with the state, as their goals became more comprehensive. In Vermont, a statewide organization created an environment for communities across the state to envision a shared future and importantly to use state government to support agreed-upon goals and to encourage regional strategies for markets and agricultural infrastructure development. In Iowa's Silos and Smokestacks, national legislation authorized a partnership management model to lead the regional effort for the conservation of place using economic and interpretive strategies that rely on heritage assets.

This type of regional collaborative governance has been documented in other National Heritage Areas across the country, demonstrating that community-based efforts can support people working together to retain their shared values and essential character of places by planning for the future and managing change (Laven *et al.* 2013; Copping *et al.* 2006;

Tuxill *et al.* 2005, 2008). The European Landscape Convention also addresses landscape quality and democracy, according to a variety of models in different countries (Arler 2011). Using an inclusive, community-based conservation approach builds social capital and the capacity at the regional level to imagine and enact new directions for sustainability of communities, including strengthening their ability to cooperate, as well as continually adapt and be resilient to change (Laven *et al.* 2013; Barrett and Taylor 2007; Borrini-Feyerabend *et al.* 2007; Goldsmith and Eggers 2004).

Conclusions

These case studies and other similar experiences illustrate that conservation of vernacular landscapes can incorporate the changing nature of agricultural places while retaining heritage character and the cultural traditions which are important aspects of sense of place. The continuing leadership and ongoing adaptation by communities, whose culture created their agricultural landscapes, remain vitally important to sustaining and intentionally shaping these landscapes into the future. Collaborative efforts at a regional landscape scale can be strategic investments for successfully harnessing economic drivers and capitalizing on partnership networks for joint economic and social initiatives. Regional collaboration is particularly important as a response to national and international market drivers. These locally based collaborative strategies respect cultural traditions and ecological systems while continually adapting to rapidly changing socio-economic environments. New models of governance at a regional scale can create environments for an enhanced level of sustained collaboration, integration of conservation with multiple community goals, and innovation. Governance that draws on cultural identity and generates a shared vision for the future can strengthen community capacity for managing change. Policies and landscape designations can provide critical context and incentives for advancing this approach. The case studies demonstrate the supportive role of government and international efforts, for example, at the state level through agricultural initiatives in Vermont, at the national level through US National Heritage Areas or recognition of regional landscapes in the UK and France, or international frameworks such as the European Landscape Convention.

These examples illuminate several of the key characteristics for envisioning new cultural landscapes and offer lessons for putting participatory and locally led governance into action in designated landscapes as well as everyday landscapes. This approach holds promise for other large-scale landscapes such as river basins, forested ecosystems and other types of protected areas. Creating new cultural landscapes through collaborative models of adaptation at the landscape scale can address many of the most challenging issues faced by communities today, revitalizing them and contributing knowledge for a more sustainable society.

Note

1   The focus of this chapter is on agricultural landscapes with heritage value that continue to be lived-in and remain in operation often incorporating physical change over time in response to their social, environmental and economic context. In the US National Park Service (US Department of the Interior, NPS 1998) and in the *Operational Guidelines for the Implementation of the World Heritage Convention* (UNESCO 2011: 88), the terms 'vernacular' and 'organically evolved' are used respectively for this category of cultural landscapes that includes agricultural and other types of working landscapes. Each of these typologies also makes a distinction between those where the 'evolutionary process is still in progress' or, in other words, where the traditional landscape work is ongoing,

described in the *Operational Guidelines* as 'continuing evolved' and those where the process is no longer ongoing, as 'relict' (UNESCO 2011: 88). In this chapter, we interchangeably use the terms vernacular, lived-in, working and agricultural to describe the type of new cultural landscape that is the subject of this chapter.

References

Albers, J. (2000) *Hands on the Land: A History of the Vermont Landscape*, Cambridge, MA and London: The MIT Press.

Amend, T., Brown, J., Kothari, A., Phillips, A. and Stolton, S. (eds) (2008) *Values of Protected Landscapes and Seascapes Series Volume 1: Protected Landscapes and Agrobiodiversity Values*, Gland, Switzerland: IUCN Protected Landscapes Task Force and GTZ, online. Available at: http://data.iucn.org/dbtw-wpd/edocs/2008-001.pdf (accessed 15 May 2012).

Antrop, M. (2006) 'Sustainable Landscapes: Contradiction, Fiction or Utopia?', *Landscape and Urban Planning*, 75: 187–197.

Arler, F. (2011) 'Landscape Democracy in a Globalizing World: The Case of Tange Lake', *Landscape Research*, 36, 4: 487–507.

Barrett, B. (2008) 'Valuing Heritage: Re-examining Our Foundations', *Forum Journal*, 22, 2: 30–34.

Barrett, B. and Mitchell, N. (eds) (2003) 'Stewardship of National Heritage Area', *George Wright Forum* 20, no. 2, online. Available at: http://www.georgewright.org/node/381 (accessed 15 May 2012).

Barrett, B. and Taylor, M. (summer 2007) 'Three Models for Managing Living Landscapes', *CRM: The Journal of Heritage Stewardship*, 4, 2: 50–65, online. Available at: http://crmjournal.cr.nps.gov/Journal_index.cfm?CFID=5380437&CFTOKEN=43847865 (accessed 7 May 2012).

Barrett, B. and Wood, E.B. (eds) (2003) 'Regional Heritage Areas: Connecting People to Places and History', *Forum Journal*, 17, 4: 4–51.

Birnbaum, C.A. (1994) *Protecting Cultural Landscapes: Planning, Treatment and Management of Historic Landscapes, Preservation Briefs No. 36*. Washington, DC: National Park Service, online. Available at: http://www.nps.gov/history/hps/tps/briefs/brief36.htm (accessed 8 May 2012).

Borrini-Feyerabend, G., Johnstone, J. and Pansky, D. (2007) 'Governance of Protected Areas', in M. Lockwood, G.L. Worboys and A. Kothari (eds) *Managing Protected Areas: A Global Guide*, London: Earthscan.

Brown, J., Mitchell, N. and Beresford, M. (eds) (2005) *The Protected Landscape Approach: Linking Nature, Culture and Community*, Gland, Switzerland and Cambridge: IUCN, International Union for the Conservation of Nature.

Buggey, S. and Mitchell, N.J. (2003) 'Cultural Landscape Management Challenges and Promising New Directions in the United States and Canada', in *Cultural Landscapes: The Challenges of Conservation, World Heritage Papers 7*, Paris: UNESCO World Heritage Centre, pp. 92–100, online. Available at: http://whc.unesco.org/documents/publi_wh_papers_07_en.pdf (accessed 29 April 2012).

Buggey, S. and Mitchell, N. (2008) 'Cultural Landscapes: Venues for Community-based Conservation', in R. Longstreth (ed.) *Cultural Landscapes, Balancing Nature and Heritage in Preservation Practice*, Minneapolis and London: University of Minnesota Press, pp. 150–179.

Community Food Security Coalition (n.d.) Online. Available at: http://www.foodsecurity.org/views_cfs_faq.html (accessed 26 April 2012).

Conzen, M.P. (ed.) (1990) *The Making of an American Landscape*, Boston: Unwin Hyman.

Copping, S.E., Huffman, P.B., Laven, D.N., Mitchell, N.J. and Tuxill, J.L. (eds) (2006) *Connecting Stories, Landscapes, and People: Exploring the Delaware & Lehigh National Heritage Corridor Partnership*, Conservation Study Institute Publication #9. Woodstock: Conservation Study Institute, online. Available at: http://www.nps.gov/csi/pdf/D&L%20Report.pdf (accessed 28 April 2012).

Costello, P. (2012) 'Working Lands Investment Bill Signing Today!' E-mail (15 May 2012).

Countryside Conservancy (n.d.) Online. Available at: http://www.cvcountryside.org/ (accessed 26 April 2012).

Countryside Conservancy, Ohio Food Policy Advisory Council (n.d.) Online. Available at: http://www.cvcountryside.org/food/food-policy-council.php (accessed 26 April 2012).

Cuyahoga Valley National Park (n.d.) Online. Available at: http://www.nps.gov/cuva.

Diamant, R., Mitchell, N.J. and Roberts, J. (2007a) 'Place-based and Traditional Products and the Preservation of Working Cultural Landscapes', *CRM: The Journal of Heritage Stewardship*, 4, 1: 6–18.

Diamant, R., Roberts, J., Tuxill, J., Mitchell, N. and Laven, D. (2007b) *Stewardship Begins with People: An Atlas of Places, People, and Handmade Product*, Conservation Study Institute Publication #14, Woodstock: Conservation Study Institute in cooperation with Eastern National.

Dramstad, W.E. and Fjellstand, W.J. (2011) 'Landscapes: Bridging the Gaps between Science, Policy and People', *Landscape and Urban Planning*, 100: 330–332.

Dudley, N. (ed.) (2008) *Guidelines for Applying Protected Area Management Categories*, Gland, Switzerland: IUCN, online. Available at: http://data.iucn.org/dbtw-wpd/edocs/PAPS-016.pdf (accessed 29 April 2012).

English Heritage (2009) *A Strategy for English Heritage's Historic Environment Research in Protected Landscapes (Areas of Outstanding Natural Beauty and National Parks)*, online. Available at: http://www.english-heritage.org.uk/publications/historic-environment-research-in-protected-landscapes/ (accessed 29 April 2012).

Fowler, P.J. (2003) *World Heritage Cultural Landscapes 1992–2002, World Heritage Papers 6*, Paris: UNESCO World Heritage Centre, online. Available at: http://whc.unesco.org/documents/publi_wh_papers_06_en.pdf (accessed 28 April 2012).

Goldsmith, S. and Eggers, W.D. (2004) *Governing by Network – The New Shape of the Public Sector*, Washington, DC: Brookings Institute.

Hewitt, B. (2009) *The Town that Food Saved: How One Community Found Vitality in Local Food*, New York: Rodale.

Kelsey, D. (2002) 'The Countryside Initiative at Cuyahoga Valley National Park', *Forum Journal*, summer 2002: 35–43.

Klyza, C.M. and Trombulak, S.C. (1999) *The Story of Vermont: A Natural and Cultural History*, Hanover and London: University Press of New England.

Krupp, R. (2010) *Lifting the Yoke: Local Solutions to America's Farm and Food Crisis*, Milton: Whetstone Books.

Laven, D.N., Jewiss, J.L. and Mitchell, N.J. (2013) 'Towards Landscape-scale Stewardship and Development: A Theoretical Framework of U.S. National Heritage Areas', *Society and Natural Resources*, 26, 7: 762–777.

Le Du-Blayo, L. (2011) 'How Do We Accommodate New Land Uses in Traditional Landscapes? Remanence of Landscapes, Resilience of Areas, Resistance of People', *Landscape Research*, 36, 4: 417–434.

Local Food System (n.d.) Online. Available at: http://localfoodsystems.org (accessed 26 April 2012).

Lubowski, R.N., Vesterby, M., Bucholtz, S., Baez, A. and Roberts, M.J. (2006) *Major Uses of Land in the United States, 2002/EIB-14* Economic Research Service, Washington, DC: United States Department of Agriculture, online. Available at: http://www.ers.usda.gov/publications/eib14/ (accessed 7 May 2012).

McClelland, L.F., Keller, J.T., Keller, G.P. and Melnick, R.Z. (rev) (1999) *National Register Bulletin 30: Guidelines for Evaluating and Documenting Rural Historic Landscapes*, Washington, DC: US National Park Service, online. Available at: http://www.nps.gov/nr/publications/bulletins/nrb30/ (accessed 8 May 2012).

McEnaney, M. (2001) 'Working the Land: Understanding and Managing Our Nation's Agricultural Legacy', *Cultural Resource Management*, 24, 7: 41–43, online. Available at: http://crm.cr.nps.gov/archive/24-07/24-07-12.pdf (accessed 8 May 2012).

Mitchell, N., Rössler, M., and Tricaud, P. (2009) *World Heritage Cultural Landscapes: A Handbook for Conservation and Management, World Heritage Papers 26*, Paris: UNESCO World Heritage Centre; online. Available at: http://whc.unesco.org/en/series/26/ (accessed 28 April 2012).

Morgan, D.W., Morgan, N.I.M. and Barrett, B. (2006) 'Finding a Place for the Commonplace: Hurricane Katrina, Communities and Preservation Law', *American Anthropologist*, 108, 4: 706–718.

National Park Service (1995) *Cedar Valley: A Special Resource Study*, Washington, DC: National Park Service, online. Available at: http://www.nps.gov/history/history/online_books/mwro/special_resource_study.pdf (accessed 26 April 2012).

National Park Service (2004) *America's Heritage Partnership Management Plan*, Washington, DC: National Park Service, online. Available at: http://www.nps.gov/heritageareas/FAQ/Partnershipplan.pdf (accessed 26 April 2012).

National Park Service Conservation Study Institute (n.d.) 'The Future of Working Cultural Landscapes: Parks, Partners and Local Products, 21–22 October 2008', full report, online. Available at: http://www.nps.gov/csi/pdf/Working%20Cultural%20Landscapes%20Report%20Full.pdf (accessed 29 April 2012).

National Park Service National Heritage Areas (n.d.) Online. Available at: http://www.cr.nps.gov/heritageareas/htm (accessed 29 April 2012).

National Park System Advisory Board (2006) *Charting a Future for National Heritage Areas*, Washington, DC: National Geographic Society, online. Available at: http://www.nps.gov/civic/resources/Commission_Report.pdf (accessed 15 May 2012).

Phillips, A. (2002) (ed.) *Management Guidelines for IUCN Category V Protected Areas Protected Landscapes and Seascapes*, Gland, Switzerland: IUCN, online. Available at: http://data.iucn.org/dbtw-wpd/edocs/PAG-009.pdf (accessed 15 May 2012).

Raymond, M. (2012) NPS National Coordinator for National Heritage Areas, personal communication (30 April 2012).

Rössler, M. (2003) 'Linking Nature and Culture: World Heritage Cultural Landscapes', in M. Rössler (ed.) *Cultural Landscapes: The Challenges of Conservation, World Heritage Papers* 7, Paris: UNESCO World Heritage Centre, pp. 10–15, online. Available at: http://whc.unesco.org/documents/publi_wh_papers_07_en.pdf (accessed 29 April 2012).

Rössler, M. (2006) 'World Heritage Cultural Landscapes', *Landscape Research*, 31, 4: 333–353.

Scherr, S. and Sthapit, S. (2009) 'Farming and Land Use to Cool the Planet', in Worldwatch Institute, *2009 State of the World, Into a Warming World*, New York and London: W.W. Norton & Company, pp. 30–49.

Selman, P. (2010) 'Learning to Love the Landscapes of Carbon-Neutrality', *Landscape Research*, 35, 2: 157–171.

Silos and Smokestacks National Heritage Area (n.d.) Online. Available at: http://www.silosandsmokestacks.org (accessed 25 April 2012).

Silos and Smokestacks National Heritage Area (2003) *Interpretive Plan*, online. Available at: http://www.silosandsmokestacks.org/home/uploads/documents/SSNHAInterpretivePlan.pdf (accessed 25 April 2012).

Slow Food (n.d.) Online. Available at: http://www.slowfood.com/ (accessed 26 April 2012).

Taylor, K. and Lennon, J. (eds) (2012) *Managing Cultural Landscapes*, London: Routledge.

Tuxill, J.L., Mitchell, N.J. and Huffman, P. (eds) (2005) *Reflecting on the Past, Looking to the Future, Sustainability Study Report for the John H. Chafee Blackstone National Heritage Corridor*, Conservation Study Institute Publication #7, Woodstock: Conservation Study Institute, online. Available at: http://www.nps.gov/csi/pdf/Blackstone%20Final%20Report.pdf (accessed 26 April 2012).

Tuxill, J.L., Huffman, P.B., Laven, D.N. and Mitchell, N.J. (eds) (2008) *Shared Legacies in Cane River National Heritage Area: Linking People, Traditions, and Landscapes, A Technical Assistance Report for Cane River National Heritage Corridor Commission, Report Summary*, Conservation Study Institute Publication #15, Woodstock: Conservation Study Institute, online. Available at: http://www.nps.gov/csi/pdf/Cane%20River.pdf (accessed 26 April 2012).

UNESCO (2011) *Operational Guidelines for the Implementation of the World Heritage Convention*, Paris: UNESCO, World Heritage Centre, online. Available at: http://whc.unesco.org/en/guidelines (accessed 26 April 2012).

UNESCO World Heritage Centre (WHC) (n.d.) World Heritage List, online. Available at: http://whc.unesco.org/en/list (accessed 29 April 2012).

US Department of the Interior, National Park Service (1996) *The Secretary of the Interior's Standards for the Treatment of Historic Properties and Guidelines for the Treatment of Cultural Landscapes*, Washington, DC: National Park Service, online. Available at: http://www.nps.gov/tps/standards/four-treatments/landscape-guidelines/index.htm (accessed 8 May 2012).

US Department of the Interior, National Park Service (1998) *Director's Order #28: Cultural Resource Management*, Washington, DC: National Park Service, online. Available at: http://www.nps.gov/policy/DOrders/DOrder28.html (accessed 8 May 2012).

US Department of the Interior, National Park Service (2006) *Management Policies*, Washington, DC: National Park Service, online. Available at: http://www.nps.gov/policy/mp2006.pdf (accessed 8 May 2012).

Vermont Council on Rural Development (VCRD) (2009) *Imagining Vermont: Values and Vision for the Future, A report of the Council on the Future of Vermont*, Montpelier: Vermont Council on Rural Development, online. Available at: http://vtrural.org/programs/policy-councils/future-of-vermont/final-findings-council-future-vermont-imagining-vermont (accessed 26 April 2012).

Vermont Council on Rural Development (VCRD) (2010) *Vermont Working Landscape Partnership Action Plan*, Montpelier: Vermont Council on Rural Development, online. Available at: http://vtworkinglands.org/programs/policy-councils/working-landscape/working-landscape-platform-and-action-plan (accessed 26 April 2012).

Vermont Council on Rural Development (VCRD) (2011) *Vermont's Working Landscape, Investing in Our Farm and Forest Future: The Action Plan of the Vermont Working Landscape Partnership*, Montpelier: Vermont Council on Rural Development, online. Available at: http://vtworkinglands.org/sites/default/files/library/files/working%20landscape/WLActionPlan-final-sm.pdf (accessed 26 April 2012).

Vermont Council on Rural Development (VCRD) (2012) http://vtworkinglands.org/programs/policy-councils/working-landscapes/bill (accessed 15 May 2012).

Vermont Fresh Network (2013), online. Available at: http://www.vermontfresh.net/ (accessed 27 November 2013).

Vermont Land Trust (VLT) (n.d.) Online. Available at: http://www.vlt.org/land-weve-conserved (accessed 28 April 2012).

Vermont Sustainable Jobs Fund (July 2011) *Farm to Plate Strategic Plan: A 10-Year Strategic Plan for Vermont's Food System, Executive Summary*, revised edition, Montpelier: Vermont Sustainable Jobs Fund, online. Available at: http://www.vsjf.org/projects/2/sustainable-agriculture (accessed 26 April 2012).

Worldwatch Institute (2009) *2009 State of the World, Into a Warming World*, New York and London: W.W. Norton & Company.

5

CULTURES IN FLUX

Simon Bell

Introduction: the irony of fate

There is a film made in the 1970s and shown every New Year's Eve on television in the former Soviet Union in which a young doctor gets drunk at a party and ends up on a flight home – he is heading to Moscow. When he lands and leaves the airport, still drunk, he gets into a taxi, gives the driver his home address and when he arrives at a block of flats he takes the lift up and uses his key to enter a flat, whereupon he falls asleep in the bed. A short time later a young woman enters the flat and screams in fright. The doctor wakes up and demands to know who she is and what she is doing in his flat. She tells him that no, this is her flat. After some incoherent argument it transpires that it is indeed her flat – in Leningrad, not Moscow. The doctor's own girlfriend is waiting for him in Moscow ready to celebrate the new year while the boyfriend of the girl in Leningrad arrives home for their own party, only to find another man there. What has happened is that in both Moscow and in Leningrad – and indeed in many other cities across the then Soviet Union – residential landscapes had become practically interchangeable and someone could find themselves in an almost identical place, where even their front door key would fit. Such was the standardisation of blocks of flats organised into massive housing areas, divided hierarchically into *Mikrorayon, Dom, Korpus* and *Kvartirye*, that there was no sense of local identity. The doctor had got on the wrong flight and just went to what seemed like the area where he lived, but was actually the sector of a different city. The irony of fate of the title (*Ironya Sudby*) is that the doctor and the young woman meet in these circumstances and fall for each other.

The story is fictional but it could have happened and it has been introduced here to set the scene for this chapter which examines the landscapes of Eastern Europe and the dramatic changes which continue to have an impact on the cultural landscape of urban and rural areas alike. To understand these landscapes in flux it is necessary to understand the massive social, political and economic changes that have occurred in the area – the former Eastern Bloc and parts of the former Soviet Union – over the last century because it is the legacies of these changes that continue to be felt today. It is also worth raising the question of what a cultural landscape means in these areas, taking into account the legacy of the Communist era and the changes it wrought on the landscape. In particular there is the question as to whether there is a traditional cultural landscape left in Eastern Europe and what values the new post-Communist landscape represents and for whom.

Everywhere in the post-Communist world people's relationship with the landscape and living environment has been changing along with the landscape itself – the two factors go hand in hand. In common with other countries or regions undergoing rapid changes, one of the most significant is a move away from rural areas to cities and the embrace of the urban lifestyle.

This chapter explores the dynamics of these landscapes in flux, based on the recent work[1] of the author and other colleagues working on aspects of landscape change, land use change, urban development and landscape perception. Owing to the importance of the Communist legacy the chapter will start with a brief overview of the main features of the dynamics which have affected the landscapes of the region from pre-Communist to post-Communist times so as to set the context. Then the main contemporary influences will be presented, illustrated by some case studies derived from recent research in rural and urban landscapes and people's changing relationship with the land. Finally a reflection on the source of identity with the emerging cultural landscape will be offered.

A landscape of empires

A hundred years ago, back in 1912, the landscape – political as well as economic – of Eastern Europe was very different from today. It largely belonged to the territory of three empires: Austria-Hungary, Germany and Russia. Poland as a country did not exist as it had long been partitioned between all three empires, and many countries existing today were merely nations or ethnic territories within them. The countryside landscape of these areas was almost entirely divided up into estates owned by gentry, aristocracy or nobility and farmed by tenants living in small clustered villages or scattered farmsteads. In many cases these were the first generation of free peasants after the abolition of serfdom. In Livonia – what was to become Latvia and Estonia – the Imperial government was Russian, the landowners Baltic German and the peasantry Latvian or Estonian (Boruks 2003). These Livonian landscapes comprised manor houses, often in a kind of Gothic architecture, and estate complexes, with a landscape park, a set of estate buildings made of stone or timber and a (usually) Lutheran church (Figure 5.1). The estate was set in a scene of scattered wooden farmsteads with roofs of wooden shingles or thatch located in clearings among extensive forest. Gravel roads wound their way amongst the fields and lines of oak trees, orchards and ponds added variety.

The Polish lands had developed a pattern of narrow strip fields constantly subdivided between sons and with linear villages along the country roads. Churches and other religious features were common; a similar situation was found in Lithuania. In the German parts, the roads and houses were much more substantial and the peasants better off than in Russian territory. Russia proper also had estates (*usadby*) and villages (*posyelkii* or *derevyanii*) of former serfs living in small log houses with ornate window frame decoration straggling along a dirt road with gardens behind and a small church with onion domes providing a focal point. Forest was omnipresent but in many areas had been cleared so that there was a very low proportion of forest cover.

FIGURE 5.1 A twentieth-century manor house at Vecauce in Latvia, designed in a kind of 'Hanseatic Gothic' style and now part of the Latvian Agricultural University (Simon Bell).

The landscape of independence

The outbreak of the First World War in 1914 heralded enormous upheavals. First, compared to the Western Front, the Eastern Front was a much more mobile sector with huge Russian, Austrian and German armies devastating massive areas. Wooden houses burned easily and large areas were destroyed by fighting. However, the main result was the complete collapse of all three empires and their replacement with a patchwork of nation states. Poland was resurrected, the three Baltic states gained independence (Lithuania, Latvia and Estonia) and Czechoslovakia, Hungary and Austria emerged from the ashes of the Austro-Hungarian Empire. Prussia was still part of Germany but the eastern part was separated from the rest by the Danzig corridor.

On achieving independence land reform was carried out in the three Baltic states. The German-owned estates were broken up and the land given to the farmers who became freeholders. This led to an agricultural revolution and high levels of production, especially of dairy products. During the mid-1930s the proportion of agricultural land in Latvia, for example, was 57.3 per cent and forest 26.6 per cent. The population of the country was 1.9 million of whom 62.8 per cent lived in the countryside (a density of 18.5 persons per square kilometre). It was a similar story in Estonia and Lithuania.

The arrival of Communism and the establishment of the ideological landscape

The countryside of the kolkhoz

The period of the Second World War was also disruptive for Eastern Europe. For the Baltic states, forcible incorporation into the Soviet Union as a result of the Molotov-Ribbentrop Pact in 1940, occupation by Germany following the invasion of the Soviet Union by Nazi Germany in 1941 and finally reconquest and occupation once more by the Soviet Union were catastrophic. The result of the fierce fighting was damage to large parts of the territory, destruction of houses and estate buildings, abandonment of land in some districts, and a large-scale loss of population through deportations (to Siberia) in 1940–41, war casualties and exile (possibly amounting in total to one-third of the pre-war population in all countries).

Further deportations of so-called *kulaks* (the name for rich peasants which means 'closed fist' in Russian) took place in 1949 under Operation *Priboi* (Operation Surf – the code name in Latvia) which removed many of the original farmers from the land and sent them to Siberia. The exiled people, or rather the survivors, came back to their countries in 1953, following the death of Stalin, but they were not allowed to return to their land or houses, as they were still branded as enemies of the people. In order to replace the lost populations and to provide labour for factories, large numbers of ethnic Russians, Ukrainians, Belorussians and other Soviet people were brought in, changing the ethnic make-up and balance, a situation which is still present today. Around half of the Latvian population are not ethnically Latvian, for example, and speak Russian as their first language. The Russian speakers are mainly found in urban areas of which some, such as the city of Daugavpils in Latvia or the industrialised north-eastern part of Estonia, are almost wholly Russian speaking.

The other countries of what became known as the Eastern Bloc fell under the indirect rule of the Soviet Union but were to follow a similar ideology and trajectory, especially collectivisation of agriculture, except in the case of Poland. Here collectivisation was a failure due to fierce resistance by farmers, except in the Recovered Territories of western Poland which had been part of Germany (Upper Silesia for example). Here the changes wrought by collectivisation as described below did not take place.

The largest physical, social and economic change to the rural landscape occurred during the collectivisation phase when farms were nationalised and amalgamated into the industrial agricultural unit known as the collective farm, the *kolkhoz* (short for *kollektivnoe khoziaistvo*) or *sovkhoz* (*sovietskoe khoziaistvo*) (Serova 1991). These had been forced on the peasantry in the Soviet Union in the 1930s at great human cost, especially in the Ukraine where widespread starvation had occurred. They were run as a business and all the former landowners (who were not deported to Siberia as *kulaks*) became members. In a way it reintroduced a kind of serfdom because collective farmers – *kolkhozniki* – could not obtain permits to travel without good reason or to obtain train tickets, so they were unable to move away very easily.

In Russia villages were generally nucleated and it was easy for the collective farm authorities to exert social control over the *kolkhozniki*. In the Baltic states farms were traditionally scattered across the landscape, so in order to make the villagers conform to the ideology of collectivisation the previous dispersed settlement pattern was changed as people were moved into blocks of flats constructed in the new village centres (Grave and Lūse 1990).

FIGURE 5.2   Silos placed on the top of a hill to emphasise the Socialist progress of the *kolkhoz* at Vecpiebalga, Latvia (Simon Bell).

Each *kolkhoz* tended to specialise in one type of production. For this, large facilities were constructed in the *kolkhoz* centres, such as barns, heating plants for the houses and flats, grain silos, intensive pig sheds, dairy facilities, machine tractor stations and storage units (Melluma 1994). These structures, like many others we shall see later in the chapter, were built of industrial materials to standard designs. This saw large constructions of steel, white brick and asbestos cement roofs appear in the landscape; structures such as tower silos were often located on high points in the landscape so as to make an impression and to advertise progress (Figure 5.2).

Owing to the introduction of machinery such as tractors large-scale modification of the farm layout was also undertaken, facilitated by the removal of ownership boundaries following nationalisation of land (Melluma 1994). Areas capable of being improved ('meliorated') by drainage or levelling to allow large machines to operate were brought into production in large contiguous fields that ignored the original field patterns or former ownership boundaries. Huge wetland or swamp areas were also drained and if houses were in the way they were demolished. Land deemed marginal and inefficient for mechanised agriculture was left uncultivated and allowed to become colonised with forest. This led, as we shall see, to major increases in forest cover in some areas. The old houses of former landowners were in many cases left empty, some were demolished to make way for large fields while others remained in use, perhaps as storage or where some people (not the original owners) continued to live. Some forest areas were also drained and improved in terms of productivity.

In Eastern Germany – the so-called German Democratic Republic or DDR – the Communist system mimicked the Soviet system with collectivisation forced on the farmers between 1958 and 1960 under the Second Five-Year Plan. The large open plains of the country lent themselves to this type of agriculture.

The city of the krushchevka

Urban areas were also heavily damaged in the war and afterwards there was a massive need for housing which only really got underway in the Soviet Union in the 1960s under Nikita Krushchev (hence the nickname *krushchevka* for a particular type of building). A limited number of standardised designs of blocks of flats were built in huge numbers to rebuild damaged towns and cities but also to extend them, leading to vast areas of such developments and their successor designs from the Brezhnev and Gorbachev eras. The original designs were built in the same white brick used on collective farms, factories and other buildings although later on concrete panel construction was also used.

These urban landscapes (Figure 5.3) were laid out in the *mikrorayon* (micro-region), *korpus* (building), *dom* (section or staircase) and *kvartirye* (apartment or flat) system as noted in the introduction and, in each *mikrorayon* there were also schools, nurseries, sports facilities and green areas – at least in theory – making a self-contained residential area. The urban expansion areas can be enormous and dwarf the scale of the original towns to which they were attached (Anon. 1989).

The landscape of polluting industry

Another legacy of Soviet times and the Eastern Bloc is the landscape of industry. Massive steelworks were developed in Poland at Nova Huta, oil shale was extracted in Ida-Virumaa in Estonia and huge brown coal (lignite) mines were excavated in Saxony in the DDR, for example. These were in most cases much more polluting than in Western Europe and also resulted in complex and messy industrial landscapes of housing, factories, railways and power

FIGURE 5.3   An area of Soviet-era housing in Lasnamae, Tallinn (Simon Bell).

stations. Brown coal, when used in power stations, caused acid rain which led to forest death or *waldsterben* in West Germany. There were also many military bases and installations littering the landscape.

The ideological landscape

Eastern Europe, as it underwent these transitions and changes, ceased to follow the kind of trajectory found in Western Europe as described by Antrop (2005), such as *traditional landscapes* or *landscapes of the revolutionary era*. The impact of central planning to a standardised model, the setting of norms for all aspects of life (floor space per person, green areas per person, etc.) and the pre-eminence of the state over the individual led to the development of rural, urban and industrial landscapes which expressed the Communist ideology. This, in European terms, is a different type of landscape both in scale and in intensity of change as well as in its social and visual manifestation. Differences existed, the biggest being the case of Poland, and there was some reflection of national characteristics in Eastern Bloc countries, but as the national Communist parties took their lead in political and economic spheres from the Soviet Union so too did they follow in planning and architecture, agriculture and industry.

The ideological landscape might have persisted had the whole system not come crashing down following the events in Berlin of November 1989. This shook the foundations of the political and economic systems to their core and led to the first series of post-Communist transformations which, although centred on political, social and economic aspects, soon had widespread effects on the landscape and set in train a dynamic process which can still be felt. Truly, these areas have become landscapes in flux.

Landscapes in the post-Communist era

The landscape of systemic collapse

In the former Eastern Bloc from 1989 onwards and in the former Soviet Union (FSR) – here focusing on the Baltic states as the only parts of the FSR to join the European Union (EU) – political collapse also meant economic and, to a large extent, social collapse. Markets for poor-quality products ceased to exist and state-owned factories went bankrupt or were privatised, often being sold to foreign companies if they were deemed economically viable. This meant that large areas of industry soon lay derelict but with factories still standing since there was no money to demolish them.

In the former DDR, reunification meant that large amounts of capital were pumped into the economy of the region so as to reincorporate it into the newly enlarged Germany. Because it became one big country people were free to move from the east of Germany, where the labour market collapsed, to the west and they did this in droves, especially younger women, leaving the men behind in many places. The phenomenon of the shrinking city started about this time, leading to major urban problems (see the discussion on Leipzig-Halle on p. 94).

The *kolkhoz* system, too, was an early casualty and with the restoration of the Baltic states people soon wanted to get their family land back, hence a process of land restitution started soon after the new countries established themselves. As the difficulties of moving away from the *kolkhoz* ceased, people also started to leave the countryside for the cities, especially if they wanted an education or to take up whatever jobs were available for educated people.

This movement of people has since become one of the major drivers of landscape change in both rural and urban areas, with land abandonment taking place in the former and shrinkage in some of the latter.

Rural landscapes

The emptying countryside

Entry into the EU by most of the Eastern European countries in 2004 opened the floodgates to mass migration from East to West. Internal migration from countryside to city had, as noted above, been underway from the start of the post-Communist period, but international labour migration became the most common type. Migration for whatever reason is generally understood to occur due to the combined effect of push and pull factors. Push factors are those which originate in the home country such as unemployment or low wages; pull factors are those of the destination country such as job prospects, higher wages and the presence of established immigrants from the home countries providing social support systems. Labour migration tends to be undertaken by younger and educated or skilled people who find that there are not many prospects at home. Rural young people who went to the cities for education found insufficient employment possibilities back home in the rural areas or in the cities of their home country where, although the economies started to boom in the mid-2000s, there were too few jobs, so they left to work in Western Europe. The booming building trade and the leisure and hospitality sector were prime targets for migrant workers and the 'Polish plumber' became a well-known figure in the media. Other people, slightly older and less skilled but willing to work in industries such as agriculture, horticulture, forestry and food processing where seasonal labour shortages were a problem, also migrated, sometimes seasonally but also permanently. These groups all originated in the countryside so that at times the rural population consisted mainly of old people and school-age children or farms which were managed by wives while husbands worked abroad.

A study of the effects of migration on the landscape categorised rural and urban areas into different types depending on their likely future viability (Bell *et al.* 2010). Table 5.1 presents the types from this categorisation which are relevant to the discussion here: note the other countries where these types also occur or are predicted to occur.

The emptying landscape of countries like Latvia has also been affected by the repercussions of land restitution. The people who lost their land when they were deported to Siberia, or their descendants, as well as those who went into exile, were able to get their land back if they could prove it has been in their family. Most of the farmland in the Baltic states was restored to the owners or family members. This meant that the large-scale collective farms became subdivided into the original ownerships. The farmhouses may or may not have survived or may have been derelict and some land had become forest during *kolkhoz* times. Older people who lived once more in their original homes, from which they had been evicted in 1949, often became small-scale subsistence farmers. Many others, often the descendants of the original owners, who got back the land, already lived in cities or even abroad, being exiles and living in the United States, Canada, the UK or Australia. Many of them were not interested or capable of farming the land which started to become abandoned. Abandonment had already started in the hiatus between the closing of the *kolkhozes* and the restitution process. In countries as forested as Latvia or Estonia vacant land left uncultivated, meadows left uncut or pasture left ungrazed soon becomes colonised by tree seedlings and quickly turns to scrub

TABLE 5.1 Landscape types resulting from migration pressures (Bell *et al.* 2010).

Type	Migration character	Land use change character	Locations where this change takes place
Abandoned rural	Flow of young people to cities, flow of working age people to cities or abroad, older residents left behind.	Land abandonment: fields lie uncultivated, empty farms, forest colonising abandoned land, landscape becoming progressively wilder.	Eastern Europe (Baltics to main cities), parts of Poland, Bulgaria and Romania, Portugal and Spain, parts of Swiss, Austrian, Italian and Greek mountains.
Extensified rural	Flow of young people to cities, general depopulation out of the region.	Extensification of agriculture and forestry: more land farmed by fewer people, extensive modes of farming and industrial forestry. May be some tourism development in places.	Eastern Finland, Eastern Germany, parts of Romania, Italy, central Sweden, Hungary, eastern France, Iceland.
Stagnant urban	Moderate population change from inward and outward migration, net effect being slight reduction in population. Some non-EU immigration substitutes for the loss of national population.	Some decay of urban infrastructure, reduction in development pressures, increase in brownfield land.	Central Germany, parts of Eastern Europe, ex-industrial cities across Europe.
Shrinking urban	Net out-migration from failing cities to other more economically active regions or countries. May be in-migration at a rate that does not balance out-migration.	Reduction in development pressure, vacant housing in less desirable areas, increase in brownfield sites.	Eastern Germany, Baltics, regional cities in Eastern Europe.

and eventually to forest (Busmanis *et al.* 2001) (Figure 5.4). This was especially the case in the less fertile areas where the farms had originally been small, whereas in the flatter open arable plains most land remained in cultivation.

A study of the changing landscape in a selection of rural municipalities in Latvia was undertaken in the year immediately preceding the country's membership of the EU (Bell *et al.* 2009b). Comparing maps from 1900 and 2000 showing forest, farmland and settlements together with an assessment of the character of the landscapes of these areas demonstrated just how much they had changed, the main driver of which could be traced to the effects of Soviet central planning. The maps were updated to 2007 to show the then extent of abandonment which gave an idea of the rate of change the sample areas were then undergoing (Figures 5.5a and 5.5b). Table 5.2 shows two contrasting examples of these changes and Table 5.3 shows the resulting landscapes with an evaluation of the changes in progress.

FIGURE 5.4   An area in Latvia where forest is starting to colonise fields no longer used for agriculture (Simon Bell).

TABLE 5.2 Summary of land use change factors for two sample areas

Location	Topography	Soil type and quality	Percentage of farmland in the 1900s	Proportion of land suitable for amelioration	Resulting land use change	Percentage of farmland in 2000
Dzerbene	Hilly, with cooler climate and more snow in winter	Luvisols or Cambisols, loamy sand or sandy loam	53.6	Very little	Reduction in amount of farmland and increase in area of forest. Scale of forest increased	30.0
Vecsaule	Flat plains, lowland	Luvisols and Stagnosols on loamy soils except in the north-eastern part with Arenosols and Cambisols on sandy soils	73.8	Large areas of fens suitable for drainage	Overall area of farmland reduced but substitution of poor land by drained fens	63.1

Source: Bell *et al.* 2009b.

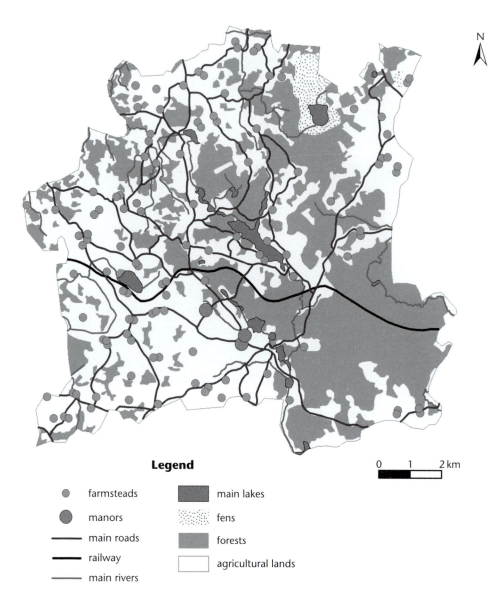

Legend

- ● farmsteads
- ● manors
- —— main roads
- ▬▬ railway
- —— main rivers
- ▨ main lakes
- ▦ fens
- ▨ forests
- ☐ agricultural lands

0   1   2 km

FIGURE 5.5a   Main land use classes in the rural municipality of Dzerbene in Latvia in 1900.

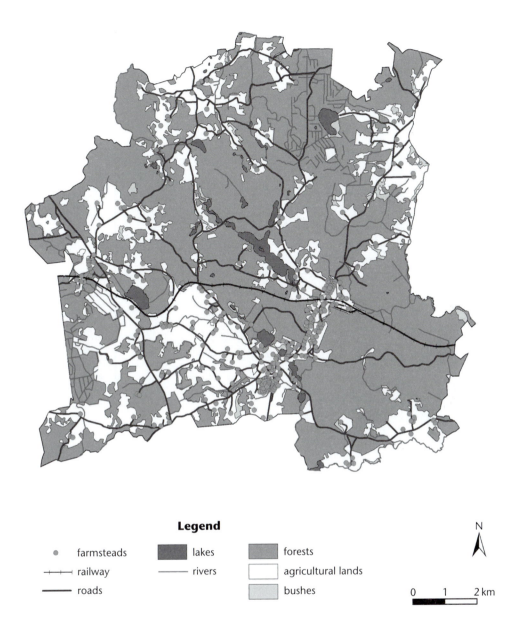

Legend

● farmsteads	▮ lakes	▮ forests
┼┼┼ railway	── rivers	☐ agricultural lands
── roads		▮ bushes

N

0   1   2 km

FIGURE 5.5b   The same area in 2000. Note the significant increase in forest and the development of a concentrated nucleated settlement pattern.

TABLE 5.3 Summary of the landscape character aspects assessed for two sample areas

Pagast	Landform	Land use pattern	Landscape scale	Settlement pattern	Landscape condition	Key features
Dzerbene	Hilly landform with lakes in hollows. Rolling, rounded landforms of moraine origin.	Farmland tends to be on the ridges. Heavily forested elsewhere, with a lot of forest cutting taking place. Strong mosaic pattern in the main farming areas.	The small areas of farmland give a small-scale feel contrasted with wide views from the open ridges.	Much settlement concentrated in the centre and along the main roads. Away from the centre there remain numbers of old farmsteads set back from the roads.	The old collective farm infrastructure is derelict. The older wooden houses which still dominate often have asbestos roofs and are in need of repair. Much land is abandoned and covered with bushes.	Several interesting lakes, an important manor house and church and the river Gauja give a sense of identity to the pagast.
Vecsaule	Flat with some low undulations in places.	Farmland is the dominating element with forest in isolated patches. Some wetlands still remain.	The open character and smaller isolated quality of the forest patches produces a large-scale landscape.	Settlement is in part distributed across the landscape, though tending to be aligned along roads.	Collective farm elements are derelict. Some land is abandoned and covered in bushes. Houses are in a mixed condition. Lines of bushes are starting to appear along the lines of the drainage ditches.	The landscape is not notable for special features. Some wetlands and a small lake give some character.

Source: Bell *et al.* 2009b.

FIGURE 5.6   A ruined *kolkhoz* centre, where the buildings are abandoned and useful materials have been stripped from them (Simon Bell).

Another factor which results in a generally deteriorated landscape character is the large number of ruins, especially in the village centres. These are mainly of buildings which became redundant after the collapse of the *kolkhoz* system and which were often stripped of usable or salvageable materials (Figure 5.6). In one of the study areas summarised above in the tables, Dzerbene, a single 3 km stretch of public road revealed the existence of many ruins of different varieties: a white-brick pig house with a collapsed roof of asbestos; an old estate building from the pre-war period; an old wooden farmhouse collapsed and rotten; a white-brick pig house with the roof removed; an unfinished block of flats from the late 1980s and other similar examples. If this is what can be found on a single stretch or road in one village it suggests that there are huge numbers of these ruins all over the countryside (Bell 2009).

The changing forest landscape

Once people got the land back again one of the major assets on it was often the timber. Many of the areas which turned into forest in the 1940s or 1950s were approaching an age where they could be harvested and since many people in the countryside were short of cash they liquidated their timber assets. This has led to widespread changes to the forest landscape all over Latvia and Estonia. Because of the fragmented ownership pattern and the small size of harvest units the effect has been to fragment the forest quite significantly. Often the harvest units are quite geometric in shape but are usually seen at close quarters from roads passing through them (Figure 5.7). In the late 1990s the issue of forest expansion onto abandoned land and the effect of harvesting on the landscape of Latvia was the focus of a project and guidance was produced but owing to the small size of ownership units it has proved difficult to effect any kind of landscape-scale planning (Bell and Nikodemus 2000). Some abandoned land has

FIGURE 5.7 Forest felling to produce timber is another driver of landscape change (Simon Bell).

been purposely planted but most just reverts to forest in an unplanned way increasing the enclosure of the landscape and taking over valuable meadows which are not only part of the cultural landscape but also important habitats.

Managing landscape change

Once the Eastern European countries joined the EU they gained access to agri-environment funding under the EU Common Agricultural Policy. It then became possible for farmers to obtain payments to cut meadows, even if there was no production from them, in order to maintain them and prevent scrub taking over as the first step along the successional path towards forest. After some years a study was undertaken to review the effectiveness of the policy of Single Farm Payments and Less Favoured Area Payments (Nikodemus *et al.* 2010). This showed that larger farmers were more active in taking up the payments but that these were not usually in locations where the worst problems of land abandonment were occurring, which was the smaller, older farmers whose land was most at risk of abandonment. These farmers were much less likely to apply for the payments, possibly because the paperwork was onerous and because they would need help to do it properly. The study concluded that if the system could be refined and made more effective then land at risk of abandonment and reverting to forest could be brought back into management (ibid.). However, land already covered in scrub does not qualify for payment unless the scrub is removed and this costs money that many people do not have. Thus the payment system only allows existing fields to be maintained, not the restoration of meadowlands.

The most economically viable agricultural landscapes are still effectively managed and the farms are often large and sometimes let to foreign farmers. Investments tend to be in machinery, and new farm buildings are not a common sight anywhere in the Baltics. Most buildings are still either the older ones from pre-Soviet times or reused *kolkhoz* structures with some updating.

Perceptions of the countryside landscape

As part of the research into landscape change urban and rural residents of Latvia were asked about their perceptions of the landscape (Bell 2009). It turned out that, for many, the traditional countryside landscape is strongly connected with being Latvian. People were able to name or describe a kind of archetypal Latvian landscape which can be found in limited places and in the smaller-scale surroundings of the older farmsteads (Figure 5.8), but it is also the case that the landscape is presently largely a relic of Soviet times with recent changes overlaid on it and there is no real larger-scale traditional landscape left. This raises questions in the context of the European Landscape Convention[2] as to what landscape should be managed or conserved in the Baltic states. The current younger generation which has reached adulthood has no direct memory of Soviet times and the landscape they know is

FIGURE 5.8   An archetypal timber country farmhouse in Latvia, the kind of scene which has a strong place attachment for people, with oak trees, orchard, haycocks and storks (Simon Bell).

the post-Soviet one. If they have strong place attachment it might be to the family farmstead which might be associated with summer vacations and weekends. If this is quite traditional then it may also represent the quintessential Latvian cultural landscape to the younger generation also, while the general scene of fields and forests acts as a sort of background to the farmstead.

Urban landscapes

Shrinking cities

The emptying rural landscape has, in many areas, been accompanied by the emptying of cities. In Eastern Germany this has been an especially significant phenomenon. What has happened can be illustrated by the city region of Leipzig-Halle, recently studied by Bauer *et al.* (2013).

The severe disruptions of the two world wars were followed by the foundation of the Communist German Democratic Republic (DDR) in Eastern Germany. During DDR times, following the central planning processes, the Leipzig-Halle region was developed as a centre for the chemical industry. Major urban reconstruction after the extensive war damage was followed by urban expansion as new housing areas were created. These consisted of large blocks of flats constructed to standardised designs, much as elsewhere in other Communist countries as noted earlier. From having been part of the relatively closed economic system of the DDR and its uneconomic and inefficient state-owned industries, soon after the German reunification of 1989 a major deindustrialisation process occurred, when the region's economy suddenly faced national and international competition. This led to massive unemployment and a flight of people to Western Germany in search of work and a better life, leading to a shrinking population. In economic terms, the region shows a decline in investment rates and public finances with high unemployment rates. In Leipzig, for example, 90,000 of the 100,000 industry jobs in 1990 disappeared shortly afterwards; in and around Halle the large Leuna and Buna petrochemical plants almost completely shut down. The unemployment rate in the entire area remains at about 20 per cent, despite all the out-migration.

The Leipzig-Halle region as a whole experienced population loss since the 1970s, which is still continuing so in that respect shrinkage is nothing new. Since 1990 Leipzig and Halle developed differently. Through suburbanisation and out-migration Halle lost 20 per cent of its population between 1990 and 2000 and has a continuing declining tendency. Leipzig's population decline of 12 per cent between 1990 and 2000 changed into a gentle population increase rate of 2.7 per cent. Today, with the exception of Leipzig city centre, which has been rejuvenated to some extent, a general shrinking tendency can be seen in the Leipzig-Halle region. Thus, growth and shrinkage occur next to each other, conveying the impression overall of a stagnating region.

The demographic growth-shrinkage patterns described above have been accompanied by changes in residential, commercial and infrastructure patterns. While the immediate post-Communist transformation period with the sudden explosion of urban sprawl has passed, moderate development in the peri-urban zone still continues. At the same time, considerable parts of the inner city have faced a population outflow leading to residential vacancy (Figure 5.9); large urban brownfields following demolition of vacant and redundant buildings (including some derelict apartment blocks in city centre locations); and massive underutilisation of urban infrastructure such as the water supply system which still distributes

FIGURE 5.9   Socialist-era apartment blocks which were renovated in the 1990s following German reunification but which are largely empty following the movement of people either to West Germany or to the suburbs (Simon Bell).

water to areas no longer occupied by buildings. In urban cores, land use changes in the period from the early 1990s until now mainly consist of infill development – mostly residential – next to vacant sites and urban brownfields. In the inner peri-urban and outer peri-urban zones, different forms of residential and commercial sprawl can be found. Conflicts have arisen between the inner peri-urban areas which belong to the city and the outer ones belonging to the municipalities surrounding the core of each city in terms of land preparation for development and attracting people to live there in order to counteract population shrinkage. This kind of tension between municipalities came about with reorganisation of local government and is a major feature of other city regions in Eastern Europe, such as Warsaw, Riga and Tallinn.

What this means of course is that many people wish to live in leafier suburbs and to get away from the monotonous flats and this reflects patterns found elsewhere in Europe where a more individualistic and less communitarian approach to lifestyle is emerging, in part as a backlash to the enforced communal conditions of Communism. Residential choice is a clear indicator of people's desires as the next section also shows in a contrasting context.

Urban sprawl and suburbanisation

It is not always the case that cities are shrinking in Eastern Europe: Warsaw, the capital of Poland, is the country's economic powerhouse. In a recent study by Grochowski *et al.* (2013) it can be seen that the city and, more particularly, its surrounding municipalities are expanding. This is largely due to migrants from other areas in Poland attracted to Warsaw for employment, as the city made a successful transformation from an industry-dominated to a

FIGURE 5.10 New apartments built out in the countryside around Warsaw but with no associated infrastructure such as roads, schools or shops (courtesy Mirosław Grochowski).

service-sector-dominated economy back in the 1990s. However, they do not move to the Warsaw Metropolitan Area but to the surrounding municipalities. These municipalities have allowed virtually uncontrolled development in order to raise income from increased taxation. Furthermore, they have little power to prevent development as spatial planning is underdeveloped in Poland. However, while it is easy to build a house, no infrastructure has been provided. This means that many people commute along roads choked with traffic and there are inadequate schools and shopping facilities in many of these areas. Farmland is gradually becoming covered with low-density scattered housing and habitats are fragmented (Figure 5.10). This is exacerbated because of the land use and land ownership patterns typical of Poland – the long narrow strips which are owned by an individual farmer and which are unsuitable for any land use other than agriculture, but are sold by farmers for piecemeal development.

The reason for the lack of strong control is an understandable backlash against the centralised planning of Communist times. Thus there was an overcorrection in the system exacerbated by the development of a three-tier local government system: regions (*wojewodztwo* – *voivodship*), counties (subregional unit – *powiat*) and municipalities (local unit – *gmina*). Thus there has been an explosion in local democracy but inadequate tools to coordinate development and to prevent sprawl over the city region scale. This has led to a chaotic landscape where it is difficult to determine whether one is in a city or a form of countryside.

The problem of sprawl and ex-urban development can also be found in Riga (capital of Latvia) and Tallinn (capital of Estonia). In Riga most people live in flats dating to the Soviet era. When the economy started to boom, in the mid-2000s until the crash of 2008, many better off people wanted to move to a more suburban type of area. Developers bought land in the municipalities surrounding Riga and built housing estates or subdivided land and set up the infrastructure to allow people to buy a plot and build their own house. There are now a number of these 'ex-urbs' which have been studied by Zigmunde (2010) and shown to have very little connection to the surrounding cultural landscape or to offer any significant ecological benefits. It is a kind of gentrification of the countryside. A similar issue affected

Tallinn, although here it was also business and commercial premises that started to spread out along the main roads, permitted by the municipalities surrounding Tallinn city.

The future landscape of flux

This chapter demonstrates that the massive upheavals that followed the collapse of Communism were largely the result of the release of artificial constraints on the economy and society imposed by the state and its central planning and closed economy. The landscape of the Communist era changed as a result of all these different forces being unleashed, often in a rather chaotic and uncoordinated way, as each newly independent country experimented with democracy and capitalism for the first time since the 1930s. The massive movements of people, land abandonment, the collapse of industry, the desire to move to greener living areas and the low level of spatial planning controls have led to a cultural landscape in which pre-Communist, Communist and post-Communist elements haphazardly coexist. The current generations, who do not remember Communist times and who are very mobile and versatile, risk losing a sense of identity in this landscape of flux.

A landscape made up of several distinct zones or major types can be postulated for much of the Eastern European space, although to different degrees in different places (especially relevant to the Baltic states):

- Historical urban cores developed to provide tourism services (much like Tallinn is today).
- A ring of Soviet/Communist-era flats which may gradually become vacant and be redeveloped but not for quite a time except in places like Leipzig where there are many vacant areas at present.
- Modern suburbs of a rather chaotic nature which may continue to develop once the credit crisis subsides and which may not benefit from improved planning for quite a time to come since there are no moves to reform the local government or planning systems.
- Countryside within commuting distances which may remain agricultural but with increasing numbers of hobby farmers.
- The best land remaining in agriculture and increasingly resembling the mechanised and intensive farmland of Central Europe but with ruins of Communist times still present unless a programme of demolition and removal is undertaken.
- Marginal rural areas in the most attractive places becoming more and more managed through subsidies to be diversified into some organic production, tourism and nature protection.
- Abandoned land turning into large areas of forest and managed for timber, this being a valuable product of the Eastern European countries such as the Baltic states.

What seems certain is that these areas will remain in flux for the foreseeable future and they may never settle into the kind of relatively stable cultural landscape found in many other areas. Populations are still in decline, people are still migrating, so the drivers remain in place. How people will identify with the landscape of flux is also an open question. The countryside seems to be important in many countries as a source of identity but it seems as if the image of the countryside and its reality are moving further and further apart. Returning immigrants may see places changing significantly between their departure and return and this may cause some kind of dislocation, a loss of place attachment.

Notes

1 The research included the author's doctoral work on landscape change in Latvia, together with the EU-funded Sixth Framework project PLUREL (peri-urban land use relationships), as well as various smaller research projects.
2 European Landscape Convention: http://www.coe.int/t/dg4/cultureheritage/heritage/landscape/default_en.asp.

References

Anon. (1989) 'Строительные нормы и правила. Градостроительство. Планировка и застройка городских и сельских поселений', СНиП 2.07.01—89, *Construction Rules and Regulations. City-Planning, Planning and Development of Urban and Rural Settlements*, SNiP 2.07.01—89.

Antrop, M. (2005) 'Why landscapes of the past are important for the future', *Landscape and Urban Planning*, 70(1–2): 21–34.

Bauer, A., Röhl, D., Haase, D. and Schwarz, N. (2013) 'Leipzig-Halle – Ecosystem services in a stagnating urban region in Eastern Germany', in S. Pauleit, S. Bell, K. Nilsson and C. Aalbers (eds) *Peri-urban Futures*, Berlin: Springer Science, pp. 209–239.

Bell, S. (2009) *Landscape Change, Landscape Perception and the Latvian Countryside*, PhD thesis, Estonian University of Life Sciences, Tartu.

Bell, S. and Nikodemus, O. (2000) *Handbook of Forest Landscape Planning and Design*, Riga: State Forest Service.

Bell, S., Nikodemus, O., Peneze, Z. and Kruze, I. (2009b) 'Management of cultural landscapes: what does this mean in the Former Soviet Union: a case study from Latvia', *Landscape Research*, 34, 4: 425–455.

Bell, S., Peneze, Z., Montarzino, A., Aspinall, P. and Nikodemus, O. (2009a) 'Rural society, social inclusion and landscape change in central and eastern Europe: a case study of Latvia', *Sociologia Ruralis*, 49, 3: 295–326.

Bell, S., Alves, S., Silveirinha de Oliveira, E. and Zuin, A. (2010) 'Migration and land use change in Europe: a review', *Living Reviews of Landscape Research*, 4, 2. Available at: http://www.livingreviews.org/lrlr-2010-2.

Boruks, A. (2003) *Land, Agriculture and Peasantry in Latvia*, Jelgava: University of Agriculture of Latvia.

Busmanis, P., Zobena, A., Grinfelde, I. and Dzalbe, I. (2001) *Privatisation and Soil in Latvia*, land abandonment paper presented at seminar on Sustainable Agriculture in Central and Eastern European Countries: The Environmental Effects of Transition and Needs for Change, Slovakia: Nitra.

Grave, Z.L. and Lūse, M. (1990) 'Designing and practice of rural settlement in Latvia', *Proceedings of the Latvian Academy of Sciences*, 7: 76–85 (in Russian).

Grochowski, M., Korcelli, P., Kozubek, E., Sławiński, T. and Werner, P. (2013) 'Warsaw – spatial growth with limited control', in S. Pauleit, S. Bell, K. Nilsson and C. Aalbers (eds) *Peri-urban Futures*, Berlin: Springer Science, pp. 131–167.

Melluma, A. (1994) 'Metamorphoses of Latvian landscapes during fifty years of Soviet rule', *Geojournal*, 33, 1: 55–62.

Nikodemus, O., Bell, S., Peneze, Z. and Rasa, I. (2010) 'The influence of European Union single area payments and less favoured area payments on the Latvian landscape', *European Countryside*, 2:1.

Serova, E.V. (1991) *Agricultural Cooperation in the USSR*, Moscow: Agropromizdat.

Zigmunde, D. (2010) *The Aesthetic and Ecological Interaction of the Urban and Rural Landscape*, PhD Thesis, Latvia University of Agriculture, Jelgava.

6

THE COMMERCIAL AND DREAM LANDSCAPE CULTURES OF FILMS

Bronwyn Jewell and Susan McKinnon

Introduction

This chapter explores concepts of identity within the commercial and dream landscapes created by films and film tourism and the cultures that such landscapes help to establish. Film tourism is created by the people who connect to a film and its ideology. Therefore the 'heritage' of the story, place, time and characters can be seen as constructing a particular identity and culture via a feeling of belonging. This has implications for both the physical landscape and the creation of commercial or dream landscape cultures. The chapter establishes the metaphorical new cultural landscape of filmgoers as an important influence on the creation of new associations and change in the structure of the physical landscape upon which these filmgoers depend.

Films, identity and the creation of cultural landscapes

It is important to understand what makes people passionate about connecting to a film, the heritage the storyline creates for the individual and for the physical landscape, and in turn the creation of an identity that helps build links between like-minded individuals, forming a new cultural community. Understanding these new identities and communities and the role films play in this, has practical implications for the tourism industry. The psychological mechanisms by which global and personal connections are created need to be understood by countries in order to provide an appropriate design of effective and strategic communications (Clayton and Opotow 2003) wishing to attract film tourists. Identity is a discourse about the individual and community (Billig 1995). The individual and thus the greater cultural identity and dream landscape created by films can be compared to a nation's myths. Myths are a part of culture in establishing the foundations of a collective's beliefs and views of itself (Schöpflin 2000). Billig (1995) posited that beliefs about and the feeling of naturalness regarding belonging to a nation are the results of specific moments in history. Films can also be seen as a specific moment in time and the 'history' of the storyline helps create for the individual a sense of community, a 'nation' and a cultural identity.

According to Bloch (2001), one of the fundamental drives of the human race is to belong (to family, a community or a nation) and it is this concept of belonging that underpins our understanding of culture. Thus, as humans, we often define ourselves according to how different 'we' are from 'them' and 'our' culture is from 'theirs'. Culture is important in the creation of identity, and the basis of identity is related to a range of identifiers which include feelings, thoughts and actions within an immediate social/cultural context. According to Rocker (1998), the German philosopher Immanuel Kant (1724–1804) believed that culture was the final purpose of nature, where humans transcended their natural crudity and ascended into a consciousness of self and social worth. Culture is an important element of national identity that defines and reinforces feelings of belonging and community amongst groups and individuals (Henderson 2002), providing an awareness of shared culture and the differences between and from other groups (Eisenstadt 1998; Gilbert 1988).

The idea of heritage is strongly associated with identity and thus culture, since the inheritance of actions and practices within a particular context forms the basis of our understanding of heritage. Identity can be defined in terms of both the individual and the cultural group. Self-identity is related to cultural heritage, both through personal and societal histories (Schöpflin 2000; Lowenthal 1996; Lerner 1985). Heritage commonly speaks of 'our' people; it binds the individual to the group through common ways of life and culture and can be seen as an almost genetic inheritance that is transmitted free from outside influence (Billig 1995). The physical components of heritage or, in the case of films, the physical landscape, help to validate the very existence of a culture and its community, often providing the materiality for understanding timelines, supporting feelings of ownership and providing credence to culture (Henderson 2002; Smith and van der Meer 2001; Renfrew and Bahn 1996; Boniface and Fowler 1993).

Lowenthal (1993) posited that these feelings are provided by physical talismans. Mountains, rivers and woodlands become more than familiar elements in a landscape; they can become a part of an ideology or heritage through association with birthplaces, battle sites and national shrines. Victorious invading forces would destroy the character and features of the defeated locale in order to quash the losers' spirit. This connection can be seen in films such as the *Lord of the Rings* trilogy where the filmgoer can become emotionally involved in the battles and in the invading forces trying to defeat and destroy the landscape, as well as identify with the spirit of the defenders. Some film enthusiasts go even further and visit New Zealand and the locales where the trilogy was filmed to re-enact the battle scenes (Herbert 2001).

National and community identities are generally seen as complex social constructs, created from sharing material and spiritual interests, information, knowledge, beliefs, values, ideas, customs and practices between individuals and their perception of their surrounding natural environment over time and space (Hopkins 2001; Chanock 1998; Billig 1995; Jones 1993). The links between national identity and landscape are highly contested, particularly in relation to how elements in the landscape help construct community identities (Agnew 2011). Billig (1995) and Hopkins (2001) suggest that national identity is embodied within the fabric of social life, an ideological creation rather than a psychological state; and Poole (1999) described national identity as an 'imagined political community'. However, whether constructed or inherent, or perhaps both, the important point for the argument in this chapter is that an individual's and a community's sense of identity is frequently found to be connected to land and this is reflected in the way films use landscapes and in the associations that film tourists have between certain films and particular landscapes.

Particular events in a nation's history help to provide the basis for national identity. An example of this is Anzac Day, which helps to define the Australian identity through collective remembrance of those fallen during war. Anzac stands for 'Australian and New Zealand Army Corps'. Anzac Day does not glorify war but respects those who gave their lives. The battle of Gallipoli in Turkey (April 1915–January 1916), fought during the First World War, is seen as a battle where the Turkish victors sowed the seeds for the creation of the Turkish Republic and where Australia became a nation through defeat (Kapferer 1988). A defeat which, according to records and now an extensive folklore for Australians, came about due to external circumstances beyond the Australian soldiers' control. It was also the landscape where Australia's first sniper was 'born' (Hamilton 2008). According to Kapferer (1988: 155), Anzac Day represents male 'mateship', which 'is an egalitarian principle of national sociality and reciprocity between equals'. Although the acronym of Anzac stands for a body, or corps, of soldiers, the Anzac tradition stresses the Australian soldier's individuality. The importance given by Australians to Anzac Day suggests the credence given by the nation is one made up of a collection of individuals and by the idealistic characteristics of these individuals.

The 1981 film *Gallipoli*, which starred Mel Gibson and Mark Lee, showed the lives of Australian young men who signed up for the First World War and their part in the Gallipoli campaign, their personal and collective characteristics; larrikinism, lack of subordination, free spirit and the loss of innocence from war. The final part of the film occurs at the Battle of the Nek on 7 August 1915 and shows the futility of war. The film's final scenes are extremely powerful. Although many other powerfully emotional films regarding Australian soldiers in the world wars and other conflicts have been made over the years, the emotions that the film *Gallipoli* stirred has seen the place in Turkey where the Anzacs fought and died for seven months become a consecrated place of memorial. The film has been seen to re-emphasise the Anzac myth and contribute to the growing culture of remembrance in Australia and generally around the world. Originally the Turkish people could not understand why young Australians would come to a place where their Australian forbears were defeated. However, the film has helped to create a sense of 'knowing' about what has occurred and has created a connection to a landscape across time, place and space, stimulating imagination, self-knowledge and identity for many Australians (Jewell and Crotts 2001; Lerner 1985; Vaughn 1985). Over time, the number of Australians travelling to this site has grown to such a size that the landscape has become both cultural and highly commercial with visitors admitting to being attracted by both commemorative and leisure pursuits (Scates 2006).

On the 25 of April each year, Anzac Day is commemorated within Australia and at Gallipoli in Turkey. Both nations have now become involved in the building of this cultural and commercial landscape. Turkish and Australian government officials and military attend the Dawn Service laying wreaths and giving speeches with emotional songs or poems to stir national pride and further enhance Australian national identity. Australian War Memorial staff and an Australian event company work in collaboration with the Turkish government and local villages. The Turkish government has also built a road to the site for easier access, graves with headstones are now visible, and local villages were commissioned by the event company to construct demountable stands for the Dawn Service. The villages hire the demountable stands during the rest of the year to individuals and companies holding events within Turkey. This landscape has become both a commemorative and a commercial landscape fuelled by the tourists encouraged to visit by the various media representations of events at this place.

Films and the creation of communities and places

In terms of films, the stories of both imaginative and real places can create a heritage, a timeline and cultural landscape for the individual. As Jewell and McKinnon (2008) proposed, this may explain the activities of the fans of films such as *Star Trek*, *Star Wars*, *Harry Potter* and more recently the *Twilight* film series. Enthusiasts not only dress as their favourite characters but also attend meetings, exhibitions, conventions and film screenings to create new, or strengthen existing, friendships, and exchange memorabilia and information regarding their heritage, culture and community. These like-minded individuals who identify and belong to a cultural group have even aided in the development of film-inspired new languages such as Klingon. There are many events held each year with the intent of providing an outlet for film fans to become their ideal film creation. However, the ultimate event held since the early 1970s is the annual three-day Comic-Con International in San Diego, and Wonder-Con in San Francisco. Here fans can become involved in panel discussions, seminars and workshops; an outlet for fans of a variety of entertainment forms, including films and fantasy worlds (Figure 6.1).

While there is a certain level of pleasure that can be derived from differing forms of entertainment (Brown 1997: 13), this can sometimes 'sweep us into what appears [to be] consuming and fanatical behavior'. Such activities can also provide means of recreational relief. They are seen to provide the opportunity to express one's self and one's relation with others within a constantly evolving and complex everyday society (Brown 1997). These

FIGURE 6.1   Convention gathering of enthusiasts, Anime Expo LA 2011 (courtesy Sandra Westerbladh)

FIGURE 6.2   Hobbit landscape near Mata Mata, New Zealand: the use of the New Zealand landscape as the film set of the *Lord of the Rings* and *Hobbit* has been a significant pull for tourists. Not only has it raised the profile of the New Zealand landscape for tourists wanting an 'authentic' experience, but it has brought the character of the landscape, and its identity to prominence on a global scale (Susan McKinnon).

conventions and meetings can provide a form of community and self-expression for the fan who can relate to like-minded individuals, by dressing as their favourite film character. In engaging with these activities they become part of a particular and alternative cultural group. The activities by fans can create changes in the physical location of where a film was made, turning a dream landscape into reality (Figure 6.2). Although based on an imaginary Middle Earth and not a real place, the film versions of the *Lord of the Rings* trilogy have created a specific film-induced tourism industry for New Zealand (Heath 2005). Owing to the large number of tourists visiting New Zealand to view the scenery as portrayed in the trilogy, tours have now been created specifically to cater for the 150+ locations utilised. Fans can visit Hobbiton and see the houses where Bilbo, Frodo and the other hobbits live and re-enact their favourite scenes from the films in the actual locations.

Cultural groups seek to maintain, sustain and nurture their culture from which the community can organise and draw meanings regarding their existence (Schöpflin 2000).

Films allow the creation of identities to emerge within groups of individuals globally. A cultural heritage is thus created through the sharing of beliefs, ideas, values and experiences. Heritage and history created from films provide personal and collective memories, expanding knowledge and inspiring imagination and creativity (Lerner 1985; Vaughn 1985). The interaction between individuals at meetings, exhibitions, conventions and film screenings strengthens socially constructed boundaries in a similar way to that found in other cultural groupings.

Social Identity Theory (SIT) is a useful way of examining the new cultures, heritage and identities created by films. At the most basic level, SIT is one of categorisation. That is, it is a general theory that assumes that psychological elements are a key aspect in group behaviour and therefore group identity (Billig 1995). In order for a group to exist, individuals need to identify with the group, making categorical distinctions between 'us' and 'them'. In other words, individuals become members of an 'ingroup' as opposed to an 'outgroup'. According to Billig (1995) SIT presumes that psychological features are universal and not linked to socio-historic contexts. Identifying oneself as a Jedi knight, Hobbit, or wizard, attending conventions, wearing the appropriate clothes and enacting scenes with other like-minded individuals in your 'cultural' group, normalises behaviour which in everyday life might be seen as unusual.

The environmental psychological concept of place-identity appears to be compatible with the broader models of SIT's collective identity. Place-identity is seen as a construct of feelings, memories, conceptions, interpretations and ideas about a particular physical setting that is created by communication between people and provides connectivity to a place, guiding actions and meanings (Holmes 2003; Dixon and Durrheim 2000). Place-identity has also been defined in terms of the way that humans attempt to control their environment which creates and sustains a coherent sense of self and a sense of belonging. It is the human interaction with and usage of the natural and built environment that creates place-identity suggesting that the environment is not simply a setting but rather it is actively incorporated into a sense of self and identity (Holmes 2003; Dixon and Durrheim 2000, 2004). This interaction, usage, construct and creation of the physical environment into a cultural landscape helps reinforce the psychological elements and the collective identity as noted in SIT – the distinction between and of the 'ingroup' and the 'outgroup'.

This concept of place-identity appears to be in some agreement with Rocker's (1998) perception of culture being a conscious resistance by humans against nature and the attempts to control nature through the creation of fire, weapons, tools and clothes. This attempt to control could be said of the film tourist who is creating a new cultural landscape by imposing and constructing new realities – the heritage created by the film – upon the physical landscape. The suggestion is therefore that humans may promote this through the way that they mould and interact with their environments, primarily through the use of creating cultural landscapes. Middle Earth is an imaginary world, yet it has created meaning and emotions that are real to audiences globally. In turn, this cultural dream landscape has become a reality for the film tourist due to the reconstruction by the New Zealand tourism authorities of the Hobbiton houses.

There is some disagreement regarding the conceptualisation of place-identity in the literature, however there appears to be four components of which place-identity is comprised. First, place-identity occurs from a deep-seated familiarity which has arisen from humans' habituation of the surrounding physical environment (Dixon and Durrheim 2004; Manzo 2003). Second, 'affective-evaluation': over time the individual expresses preferences for and attachment to a particular environment and a sense of belonging. A third component is how the self is expressed or symbolised in the material environment and can operate at a collective level (Dixon and Durrheim 2004; Manzo 2003). Finally, the physical environment plays a role in which humans can find self-expression, self-worth and self-coherence. The environment allows individuals to de-stress, restore a sense of self, provide emotional, spiritual, aesthetic and intellectual fulfilment, and self-expression in the forms of achieving goals, desires and aspirations (Dixon and Durrheim 2004; Clayton 2003; Manzo 2003).

Jewell and McKinnon (2008) suggested that travelling specifically to a film's location setting as a result of fascination with a film could be seen as a psychological need to connect with or belong to a film's plot line, whether it is one of fantasy, conspiracy theory or romance. By doing so, film fans seem to be employing at least two of the components identified above and are thus invoking a strong sense of place and identity through their connection with the particular landscape. Interestingly, according to Manzo (2003), the literature has tended to explore and focus on positive aspects of place-identity and not negative or ambivalent feelings and experiences towards the environment. Horror films, such as the 2005 Australian film *Wolf Creek*, can have the potential of creating a negative experience and perception of a film's physical location. Backpacking in outback Australia to see, explore and experience a different culture may be influenced by the storyline of three young backpackers held captive, tortured and murdered by a serial killer. The marketing of the film, 'based on a true story', can further heighten for the film-going public a sense of dislocation to the film's landscape. The film has created a cultural landscape and an identity that the film tourist does not want to connect or belong to.

It would therefore appear that culture and identity are intertwined with the natural and built environment rather than being separate from it and this provides a strong source of connection and sense of belonging over time. Kim and Richardson (2003: 233) believed that 'popular motion pictures may be particularly critical elements of popular culture in creating place image since they often serve to mystify places by imbuing them with myth and meaning through drama'. It is to this end that film tourism could be seen as helping to create new cultural groups and, in turn, new forms of cultural landscape and place identities. The construction of new groups and new landscapes influences individuals and communities within societies to visit destinations as is seen, for example, by young Australians to Gallipoli and by *Harry Potter* fans to Alnwick Castle in the UK (Figure 6.3) which is the setting for much of the filming of Hogwarts School. From this, the new cultural landscapes become highly commercial at the place where the film was set, although not necessarily filmed (as in the case of Gallipoli), and vice versa; sometimes the commercialism results in visits to places where the film was filmed, rather than the fictional landscapes of the film, which cannot be physically visited (as in the case of *Harry Potter*). While Comic-Con and Wonder-Con are destinations where the physical landscape is simply a conference-type setting that provides various meeting opportunities for fans, others, such as Disneyland in France, have become popular school visit destinations for children. A re-creation of the fictional landscape of the films in a highly commercial setting and a landscape which reflects values predominantly based on recreation.

FIGURE 6.3   Alnwick Castle, Northumberland: the first two Harry Potter films (2001 and 2002) used the castle as Hogwarts School. This led to an increase in public interest and visitor numbers to Alnwick. 'Harry Potter Days', including events such as 'broomstick training', ensure that over 800,000 visitors a year help to support this major visitor attraction and retain the iconic status of this landscape. The castle has also been used as a location for other films including *Elizabeth* (1998) and *Robin Hood, Prince of Thieves* (1991).

Authenticity in film tourism destinations

Film tourism can be defined as a 'tourist visit to a destination or attraction as a result of the destination's being featured on television, video, or the cinema screen' (Hudson and Ritchie 2006a: 387) or 'a specific pattern of tourism that drives visitors to see screened places during or after the production of a feature film or a television production' (Roesch 2009: 6). There have been many attempts to categorise film tourism by researchers in leisure and tourism studies which has led to the development of phrases including: film tourism, film-induced tourism, teletourism, symbolic pilgrimage, media tourism, cinematic tourism, cultural tourism, popular media-induced tourism and cult geography (Iwashita 2007; Law *et al.* 2007; Hudson and Ritchie 2006a, 2006b; Beeton 2004, 2005; Macionis 2004; Singh and Best 2004; Tzanelli 2004; Hills 2002).

As well as attempting to categorise film tourism, many authors have discussed the influence of films, the ways viewers gain images, information and consciousness of destinations, which, in turn, affect their decision-making process, and the behaviour of the film-induced tourist.[1] The development of these new terminologies has moved film tourism from its niche tourism market into a more mainstream tourism research outlet. Beeton (2005: 53) emphatically states this via underlining the concept of film-motivated tourism as a direct successor to literary tourism by drawing a parallel with 'mainstream' tourism: 'Film is to literary tourism what the Boeing 747 was to mainstream tourism—a major booster for mass tourism. We have moved from small, niche-based personal pilgrimage literary tours to the mass (and at times over-full) visitation of film sites'. Film, in this conception, is a new technology, which may increase the convenience and popularity of tourism, but does not reshape the fundamentals of the tourist experience. Regardless of the undeniable power of visual tourism images via film and television (Morgan and Pritchard 1998), symbols also play a role in endorsing a destination's image, for instance, Big Ben (United Kingdom), the Eiffel Tower (France), Red Square (Russia), the Statue of Liberty (United States) and the Opera House (Australia) (Kotler and Gertner 2004).

The concept of the 'tourist gaze' as identified by Urry (2002) can be used in relation to film tourists. This concept can be employed not only to understand physical tourism experiences with a film-based background but also in understanding how such a view can act as the catalyst of 'viewing representations of other lands or even periods', so that 'the traditional room with a view becomes a seat with a view' (Gibson 2006: 158). Image is seen to play an important part in how tourist destinations are viewed, in how decisions are made concerning holidays and in the development of motives for holiday travel (Bolan *et al.* 2007). Urry (1990: 3) suggested that tourist 'places are chosen to be gazed upon because there is anticipation' created by the potential tourist whilst a decision is being made. This anticipation is constructed and sustained by a variety of activities linked to film, television, literature, magazines, records and videos. These 'non-tourist' practices construct and reinforce the tourist gaze. The viewing by a potential tourist seems to show a greater sensitivity to the visual elements of a landscape or townscape than is normally found in everyday life (Urry 2002). In particular, films and television play a key role in influencing people's images and perceptions of a destination prior to their arrival at the destination. Butler (1990) argued that films used as visual media are more important to tourists than printed sources of information as they tend to be more reliable. This is supported by Schofield (1996) who maintained that media images are not perceived to have the bias that is found in printed marketing material. Thus films can positively enhance the awareness of destinations and affects the tourist decision-making process (Macionis 2004).

Tourists are increasingly visiting destinations and attractions resulting from those places being depicted or featured in film or television (Hyunjung and Chon 2008; Iwashita 2007; Connell 2005) as suggested in relation to the impact of the film *Gallipoli*. Kim and Richardson's (2003) study evaluated the effects a film can have on a destination's image and suggested that although films tend to have a significant impact on people, it is only for a short while. This suggests that longer-term impact must rely on drivers other than the film. Furthermore, it was found that it was the moving image that was important as destinations shown in films are deemed to be more important than printed images from the films. Films can be seen as an effective tool to change the image of places that people hold and thereby affect people's interest in visiting a particular destination. This effect can be either positive or negative, depending largely on the tourist's personal cognitive and affective images.

For instance, it has been indicated that one in five tourists visit the United Kingdom as a result of the country being portrayed in a film (O'Connor *et al.* 2006) such as the *Harry Potter* film series. Interest is also still strong for the *Lord of the Rings* film locations in New Zealand, with approximately a dozen tourist operators offering location tours, ranging from half a day to a ten-day intensive location tour (Roesch 2009). This is not a new phenomenon; the roots of film tourism can be seen as far back as 1949 with the release of films such as

The Third Man (1949), *Niagara* (1953), *To Catch a Thief* (1955), *Bridge on the River Kwai* (1958), *Lawrence of Arabia* (1962) and *The Sound of Music* (1965). All of these films inspired the earliest film tourists to seek their own adventures related to the locations shown (Roesch 2009). Although the primary purpose of a film production is not to induce viewers to visit locations, effective motion pictures enhance the charm of these locations and have been identified by a number of researchers as having a particularly effective impact on audiences when the storyline and the site are intimately interrelated[2] as can be observed at the site of the *Sound of Music* which is still achieving over 300,000 film tourists per year (Roesch 2009).

Films, locations and the search for authenticity

Authenticity is a complex concept in the context of mediated representations and externally managed tourist experiences. Taylor (2001: 8) pointed out that 'there are at least as many definitions of authenticity as there are those who write about it'. However there are two main themes that can be identified when considering the concept of authenticity in relation to film tourism. When something is seen to be authentic, it is *known* to be real, but there is also *staged authenticity*, when something is portrayed as real, even though it is not. Cohen (2004) listed both of these as reasons for travelling with the reaction to the type of authenticity they experience that is important. The search for authenticity can encourage people to look back in time in order to try and gain the feeling of experiencing an event or an ideal as it once was. It can also encourage a visit to what is regarded as a natural place where everything has remained relatively untouched by human impact. However, another major pull in the search for authenticity is travelling to see something that appears to be real that would not be experienced in daily life. When experiencing staged authenticity, tourists are often aware that they are experiencing something that is not genuine and that the show or scenery has been put together in order to entertain tourists. However, this is not always the case and several types of staged authenticity can be identified.

Tourists are generally seen as people travelling for pleasure and demanding authenticity. Today's modern tourists tend to 'seek authenticity in various degrees' (Cohen 2004: 106) with motives being novelty, prestige and fantasy (Macionis and Sparks 2006) and the choice of travel destination may have been arrived at by a combination of information gathered prior to the visit about sites and people, cultures and habits. An audience's attitudes are influenced through the consumption of films, particularly when they are repeatedly exposed to films (Soliman 2011) but sources of information such as family or friends, guidebooks as well as something seen in a film or on television are all potential motivations for film destination travel. The choice of destination is often related to imaginary places; ideas and expectations are related to the imagery of authenticity expected by the potential tourist. Further, Macionis (2004) believed that while some individuals seek out specific film locations depicted in a film, others will be motivated by a more general desire relating to films, or the novelty of visiting a film location, or being provided with the opportunity to participate in a group film tourism activity. Thus film-induced tourists are often persuaded by the particular images they have seen in a film whilst some want to visit the destination to find the authentic images and experiences they have seen in the film (Roesch 2009).

Films have been shown to increase the awareness of the places they depict (Kim and Richardson 2003), increasing the number of tourists to destinations portrayed in a film. The release of the film *Crocodile Dundee* was connected to increases in tourism figures to

Australia (Gartner 1996). Interest in the film influenced the use of Paul Hogan, the lead character of the film, as the spokesperson for Tourism Australia's most famous tourism campaign. Television documentaries can have the same effect on a destination's image (Gartner 1996). Popular film locations include New Zealand (*Lord of the Rings* trilogy), Forks in Washington State (*Twilight*), the Greek Island of Cephalonia (*Mamma Mia* and *Captain Corelli's Mandolin*), Thailand (*The Beach*), Malta (*Troy* and *Gladiator*), Kenya (*Out of Africa*), Newfoundland (*The Shipping News*), England (*Harry Potter* series) and walking tours of Montmarte in Paris (*Amelie* and *Moulin Rogue*). Within the realm of television, the now discontinued *The X-Files* television series still draws a high number of tourists to the Vancouver region. Reijnders (2011: 5) questioned whether tourists to the region are 'ascribing meaning to the represented landscape … or should the answer be sought in the landscape itself'. With the continuing number of visitors to Vancouver seeking *X-File* shooting locations, this would tend to lead to the conclusion that the stories presented in the television show are anchored to the landscape. The storylines have created a sense of connection to and identification with the characters by way of creating a cultural landscape filled with aliens and conspiracy. Perhaps the individual is seeking their own adventure and encounter with an alien.

Morgan and Pritchard (1998) believed that creating a tourism destination in a film can be construed as the ultimate in tourism product placement. The film tourism market seems to provide a broad appeal with a diverse range of goods for consumption. It offers the chance to walk the *Bridges of Madison County* in the United States of America, visit the birthplace in Tunisia of Luke Skywalker, from the *Star Wars* films, follow the Hobbits' journey to Middle Earth in *Lord of the Rings* and be swept up in the intrigue of the *Da Vinci Code* conspiracy from Italy to Paris to England. One of the positive benefits that has arisen from a tourist marketing point of view is the creation of new destinations for the worldwide film-going public. This makes these film locations an extraordinary force in destination marketing and a 'really successful film can boost tourism by 50% over a four to five year period' (International Tourism Trade Fairs Association 2011: 6).

However, when looking for an authentic film experience, the film tourist may be disappointed to discover that their imagined or cinematic-inspired tourist adventure is not in the country they understood to be the setting of the film. Films are often made in cheaper or more accessible film location alternatives that look like, but may be far away from, the original landscape. So the question remains as to whether the historical accuracy of certain film locations is a necessary element for providing authenticity in films? Examples of film locations that are used in this way are Moscow, Russia, used as Berlin, Germany, and Paris, France, for *The Bourne Ultimatum* (2007), New Zealand and Australia portrayed as the American countryside for *Wolverine* (2009) and New Zealand portrayed as Japan in the film *The Last Samurai* (2003).

Reijnders (2011: 14) believed that film locations can 'serve equally well as the setting for memorialising and reliving a fictional event'. Thereby the allocation of a believably authentic location becomes more relevant to the memorialisation of the film rather than the use of specific historical locations that may be depicted in the story (Reijnders 2011). The 2006 film *Kokoda* is based upon the story of conscripts in the Second World War sent to Papua New Guinea to fight against the Japanese in the 1942 Kokoda Track Campaign, considered to be Australia's most significant campaign of the Second World War. The film's opening scene shows the men trudging along a muddy track in the jungle. Australians who have fought, lived and worked in Papua New Guinea were surprised to find that the film was not filmed in the actual location but instead was filmed in Australia's Gold Coast Hinterlands. Each year, Australians walk the track in the footsteps of the Australians who fought and died. Rather than detract from the fact it was filmed in Australia, the authentic portrayal of the landscape, the mud, the rain, the conditions and the fighting, help create an emotional connection to the soldiers portrayed and their lives. In comparison, although the cultural landscape of Gallipoli is authentic, it has become commercialised and reshaped from what it originally looked like and portrayed by the film. However, the visitor sees past the commercialisation and, during Anzac Day Dawn Service, feels the connection to those who fought and died there.

The construction of film and dream landscapes

The film franchises of *Harry Potter*, *Star Wars*, *Twilight* and *Lord of the Rings* reinforce the notion of a new, emerging culture and cultural landscape for the locations they were filmed in. As noted, the desire to visit locations of these films influence individuals to travel. These kinds of films are about the construction of alternative worlds and realities. Herbert's (2001) assessment is that visitors are not concerned with the distinction between reality and fiction but rather the features that involve imagination and awareness.

When tourists visit their chosen destination, their image of the destination will usually change as they tend to learn something new that they have not read about or seen before they arrived. Kim and Richardson (2003) found that tourists identifying with a film want the same experience of the destination as that shown by the characters in the film. According to Beeton (2001), there is ample anecdotal evidence that tourists re-enact fantasies portrayed in films and television programmes at those film locations. Films can thereby create the viewpoint by which the viewer experiences the destination. However visitors are also likely to connect to the destination in ways separate from the film's influence while looking for signs to remind them of the film. Kim and Richardson (2003) suggested that because television and film viewing now seems to be a normal and expanding experience, the influence the media has on a destination's image is likely to increase and some destinations will even alter reality to fit the image that is seen on the screen.

Television programmes or motion pictures in a prime destination not only bring in money to the location during the actual filming, but can also inspire people to visit the location for years afterwards. One of the most recent destinations that has benefited from film-induced tourism is New Zealand, which has capitalised on being the backdrop to the *Lord of the Rings* (2001–2003) trilogy. Malta is another destination that added a new dimension to their tourism marketing product by advertising the filming of such epic films as *Troy* and *Gladiator*. Using its landscape and historical buildings as a backdrop, the Malta Tourism Authority also recently created a new online Malta Movie Map (Naudi 2005). Kim and Richardson (2003) found that those who are exposed to a destination's image in a film responded more favourably to the destination's image of the featured location than those who were not exposed. O'Connor and Bolan (2008) explored the integration of film-induced tourism and destination branding upon locations in Northern Ireland featured in the film *The Chronicles of Narnia: The Lion, the Witch, and the Wardrobe* (2005). Their findings highlighted that destinations can brand themselves more effectively when there is a definitive association with the film, as has been previously witnessed in New Zealand and the *Lord of the Rings* films.

Finally, it is expected that media-induced tourism will grow rapidly to become in fashion as viewing numbers grow. As more viewers become interested in cinematographic history, the demand for film tour experiences will rise. Defining a film icon as a film's symbolic meaning or theme, Riley *et al.* (1998) indicated that film scenes expressing intimate and humane storylines, dramatic conversation and attractive characters all encourage travel to sites seen on the film screen. Macionis (2004) proposed that a difference between the three concepts of place (location attributes, landscapes, scenery), personality (cast, characters, celebrity) and performance (plot, theme, genre) be made in order to identify whether different or distinct motivations drive or induce film travel behaviour. Interestingly, it would appear the films involving fantasy, action, adventure, alternate worlds, good fighting evil, and magic have the greatest emotional connection to people. Perhaps these new cultural landscapes being created from the film industry with a flow-on effect on the tourism industry are the desire to escape everyday life and reality, constructing for the individual new identities and realities and, thus, a connection to a greater community and cultural group.

Conclusion

The traditional meaning of heritage is related to an individual's inheritance of goods and values from the past involving traditions, ideas and values (Yale 1997; Watts 1995), but now involves both tangible and intangible aspects (Smith and van der Meer 2001; Lowenthal 1996; Pearson and Sullivan 1995). In terms of film tourism, the storyline and film's landscape provides a heritage and connection for like-minded individuals and therefore a sense of place in the scheme of life. It is clear that tourists are now visiting landscapes as a result of their being featured in films. Films can engage the audience, constructing alternative worlds, new realities and perceived truths based on stories, interpretations of historical experiences and/or tangible remains of past events.

As noted, one of the deepest drives of the human race is to belong, whether to family, community or a nation and part of this is to gain identity. Identity is a social construct, an ideology of what it means to be part of a group. The concepts of both belonging and identity are seen as important in the consideration of the actions of film fans. Film franchises such as *Star Wars*, *Harry Potter* and *Lord of the Rings* can create for a person an imagined 'heritage' and a yearning for the 'romance' that a storyline can create. These films create commercial and dream landscape cultures for the destinations where they were filmed, influencing individuals to travel, creating place-identities, social identities and providing the opportunities for like-minded individuals to build connections (Jones 2002; Riley *et al.* 1998; Lerner 1985).

Visitors are often not concerned with the reality of the destination but rather the features as seen in the film which allows them to connect to the film, its storyline and characters. This construction of a place-identity from the physical location portrayed in a film can create a sense of belonging for the filmgoer (Holmes 2003; Dixon and Durrheim 2000). This kind of place-identity and the development of commercial and dream landscapes occurred even before the advent of globally successful films (Figure 6.4). Places described in novels connected people emotionally to a destination, compelling them to visit and become part of the story via their imagination (Herbert 2001; Squire 1996). However films have created a greater awareness of many more destinations and have enhanced this desire to connect with such places to a wider global audience. This desire provides opportunities to share activities, experiences and meanings with others and belong to a new community of interest which may also be linked by concern for particular places.

FIGURE 6.4 The house used as the location for the film of the novel *Anne of Green Gables* on Prince Edward Island, Canada. The novel was written in 1908 by L.M. Montgomery and relates the adventures of the orphan Anne Shirley. Based on the locale and surrounds of Cavendish, Prince Edward Island, the story is set in the fictional town of Avonlea. This children's novel which has been translated into over 20 languages, inspired a literacy-related tourism industry well before the novel and sequels were adapted into numerous films and television series. The power of the novel's landscape and subsequent celluloid imagery, has led to development of specific tourist attractions where visitors can eat and drink foods as described in the novels, pose for photos dressed as their favourite character, and be married in the grounds of Green Gables farm.

A successful film can generate and increase tourism visitation. Destinations such as the United Kingdom and New Zealand have seen visitor numbers increase after each release of a *Harry Potter* or *Lord of the Rings* film. In remote locations where scenes were filmed for the *Lord of the Rings* trilogy, visitor numbers have increased as they seek to re-enact scenes (Voight 2005). Visitors who have connected to this new cultural identity and landscape have been shown to make repeat visits, with each visit making Middle Earth seem more real as they are able to experience the same sounds and sights as seen in the film (Buchmann 2004).

Places have been given new value as information about them is delivered to people via films and television. The subsequent relationship that is built is often about bringing to life history or, for some, creating a new heritage and identity to connect to. The values that are created help maintain and reproduce social relationships within and between participants who may be from both local and global communities (Carroll 1999). The effects of film tourism can also affect the very landscape visitors have come to see. Landscapes such as Gallipoli which once were inaccessible and protected by their remoteness are now being made accessible by improved infrastructure such as roads. Although mitigation plans may be in place to lessen the impact of large visitor numbers, allowing visitors easy access to an area causes degradation due to the simple allowance of visitation and its flow-on effects such as rubbish and noise. The visitors thereby have impact on the very landscape that they have come to see (Sorupia 2005).

Film tourism has become a considerable driver of development for the creation of commercial and dream landscapes creating an interaction between the feelings, ideas and interpretations of an individual, and the economy of a destination. The images formed by watching a film and the pull that films have on us, often creates the landscape of the film as a 'must see'. Perhaps, as noted, the main function of these landscapes created and used by the film industry – both real and imagined – is that they respond to the desire to escape everyday life and reality, constructing for the individual new identities and new realities.

Notes

1   See 'further reading' section for useful references here.
2   See 'further reading' section.

References

Agnew, J. (2011) 'Landscape and National Identity in Europe: England versus Italy in the Role of Landscape Identity Formation', in Z. Roca, P. Claval and J. Agnew (eds) *Landscapes, Identities and Development*, Farnham: Ashgate, pp. 37–50.

Beeton, S. (2001) 'Horseback Tourism in Victoria, Australia: Cooperative, Proactive Crisis Management', *Current Issues in Tourism* 4, 5: 422–439.

Beeton, S. (2004) 'Rural Tourism in Australia—Has the Gaze Altered? Tracking Rural Images through Film and Tourism Promotion', *International Journal of Tourism Research* 6, 3: 125–135.

Beeton, S. (2005) *Film-induced Tourism*, Clevedon: Channel View.

Billig, M. (1995) *Banal Nationalism*, London: Sage Publications.

Bloch, N. (2001) 'The Accidental Empire', *Earthwatch Institute Journal* 20, 2: 11–15.

Bolan, P., Crossan M. and O'Connor, N. (2007) 'Film and Television Induced Tourism in Ireland: A Comparative Impact Study of Ryan's Daughter and Ballykissangel', in 'The Media and the Tourist Imagination', *Proceedings of the 5th DeHaan Tourism Management University Conference*, Nottingham Business School, 12 December 2006, pp. 226–252.

Boniface, P. and Fowler, P. J. (1993) *Heritage and Tourism: In the 'Global Village'*, London: Routledge.

Brown, J.A. (1997) 'Comic Book Fandom and Cultural Capital', *The Journal of Popular Culture* 30, 4: 13–31.

Buchmann, A.S. (2004) 'From Erewhon to Edoras – Tourism and Myths in New Zealand', *International Tourism and Media Conference Proceedings*, Melbourne: Tourism Research Unit, Monash University, pp. 114–121.

Butler, R.W. (1990) 'The Influence of the Media in Shaping International Tourist Patterns', *Tourism Recreation Research* 15, 2: 46–53.

Carroll, L. (1999) 'Communities and Other Social Actors: Rethinking Commodities and Consumption in Global Historical Archaeology', *International Journal of Historical Archaeology* 3, 3: 131–136.

Chanock, M. (1998) 'Globalisation: Culture: Property', in G. Couvalis, H. Macdonald and C. Simpson (eds) *Cultural Heritage: Values and Rights*, Bedford Park, South Australia: Flinders University Press, pp. 47–60.

Clayton, S. (2003) 'Environmental Identity', in S. Clayton and S. Opotow (eds) *Identity and the Natural Environment: The Psychological Significance of Nature*, Cambridge, MA: The MIT Press, pp. 45–65.

Clayton, S. and Opotow, S. (2003) 'Introduction: Identity and the Natural Environment', in S. Clayton and S. Opotow (eds) *Identity and the Natural Environment: The Psychological Significance of Nature*, Cambridge, MA: The MIT Press, pp. 1–24.

Cohen, E. (2004) *Contemporary Tourism Diversity and Change: Tourism Social Science Series*, Boston: Elsevier.

Connell, J. (2005) '"What's the Story in Balamory?": The Impacts of a Children's TV Programme on Small Tourism Enterprises on the Isle of Mull, Scotland', *Journal of Sustainable Tourism* 13, 2: 228–255.

Croy, W.G. (2010) 'Planning for Film Tourism: Active Destination Image Management', *Tourism and Hospitality Planning and Development* 7, 1: 21–30.

Dixon, J. and Durrheim, K. (2000) 'Displacing Place-identity: A Discursive Approach to Locating Self and Other', *The British Journal of Social Psychology* 39, Part 1: 27–44.

Dixon, J. and Durrheim, K. (2004) 'Dislocating Identity: Desegregation and the Transformation of Place', *Journal of Environmental Psychology* 24, 4: 455–473.

Eisenstadt, S.N. (1998) 'World Histories and the Construction of Collective Identities', in P. Pomper, R.H. Elphick and R.T. Vann (eds) *World History: Ideologies, Structures, and Identities*, Oxford: Blackwell Publishers Ltd., pp. 105–125.

Gartner, W. (1996) *Tourism Development: Principles, Processes and Policies*, New York: Van Nostrand Reinhold.

Gibson, S. (2006) 'A Seat with a View: Tourism, (Im)Mobility and the Cinematic-travel Glance', *Tourist Studies* 6, 2: 157–178.

Gilbert, A. (1988) 'The New Regional Geography in English and French-speaking Countries', *Progress in Human Geography: An International Review of Geographic Work in the Social Sciences and Humanities* 12, 2: 208–228.

Hamilton, J. (2008) *Gallopoli Sniper: The Life of Billy Sing*, Sydney, Australia: Pan MacMillan.

Heath, M. (2005) 'Movie Tourism in New Zealand', The Cultured Traveler. Available at: www.theculture dtraveler.com/Archives/AUG2005/Movies_New_Zealand.htm (accessed 16 June 2006).

Henderson, J.C. (2002) 'Heritage Attractions and Tourism Development in Asia: A Comparative Study of Hong Kong and Singapore', *International Journal of Tourism Research* 4, 5: 337–344.

Herbert, D. (2001) 'Literary Places, Tourism and the Heritage Experience', *Annals of Tourism Research* 28, 2: 312–333.

Hills, M. (2002) *Fan Cultures*, London: Routledge.

Holmes, S.J. (2003) 'Some Lives and Some Theories', in S. Clayton and S. Opotow (eds) *Identity and the Natural Environment: The Psychological Significance of Nature*, Cambridge, MA: The MIT Press, pp. 25–41.

Hopkins, N. (2001) 'Commentary – National Identity: Pride and Prejudice?', *The British Journal of Psychology* 40, 2: 183–186.

Hudson, S. and Ritchie, B. (2006a) 'Promoting Destinations via Film Tourism: An Empirical Identification of Supporting Marketing Initiatives', *Journal of Travel Research* 44, 2: 387–396.

Hudson, S. and Ritchie, B. (2006b) 'Film Tourism and Destination Marketing: The Case of Captain Corelli's Mandolin', *Journal of Vacation Marketing* 12, 3: 256–268.

Hyunjung, H. and Chon, K. (2008) 'An Exploratory Study of Movie-induced Tourism: A Case of the Movie The Sound of Music and its locations in Salzburg, Austria', *Journal of Travel and Tourism Marketing* 24, 2–3: 229–238.

International Tourism Trade Fairs Association (2011) *Travel Daily News International*. Available at: http://www.traveldailynews.com/ (accessed 1 December 2011).

Iwashita, C. (2007) 'The Influence of Films and Television on the Destination Image of Japanese Tourists to the UK: Truth or Consequences', in *The Media and the Tourist Imagination*, Proceedings of the 5th DeHaan Tourism Management Conference on Culture, Tourism, and the Media, Nottingham Business School, 12 December 2006, pp. 205–225.

Jewell, B. and Crotts, J.C. (2001) 'Adding Psychological Value to Heritage Tourism Experiences', *Journal of Travel and Tourism Marketing* 11, 4: 13–28.

Jewell, B. and McKinnon, S. (2008) 'Movie Tourism – A New Form of Cultural Landscape?', *Journal of Travel and Tourism Marketing* 24, 2–3: 153–162.

Jones, M. (1993) 'The Elusive Reality of Landscape: Concepts and Approaches in Research', in J.M. Fladmark (ed.) *Heritage: Conservation, Interpretation and Enterprise*, papers presented at The Robert Gordon University Heritage Convention. Wimbledon: Donhead Publishing Ltd, pp. 17–41.

Jones, M. (2002) 'Tourism: Keeping Up With the Indiana Joneses', TRI Hospitality Consulting, online. Available at: http://www.trimideast.com (accessed 28 June 2006).

Kapferer, B. (1988) *Legends of People – Myths of State: Violence, Intolerance and Political Culture in Sri Lanka and Australia*, Washington and London: Smithsonian Institute Press.

Kim, H. and Richardson, S. (2003) 'Motion Picture Impacts on Destination Images', *Annals of Tourism Research* 30, 1: 216–237.

Kotler, P. and Gertner, D. (2004) 'Country as Brand, Product, and Beyond: A Place Marketing and Brand Management Perspective', in N. Morgan, A. Pritchard and R. Pride (eds) *Destination Branding: Creating the Unique Destination Proposition* (2nd edn), Oxford: Elsevier Butterworth-Heinemann, pp. 40–56.

Law, L., Bunnell, T. and Ee Ong, C. (2007) 'The Beach, the Gaze and Film Tourism', *Tourist Studies* 7, 2: 141–164.

Lerner, G. (1985) 'The Necessity of History and the Professional Historian', in S. Vaughn (ed.) *The Vital Past: Writings on the Uses of History*, Athens, GA: University of Georgia Press, pp. 104–115.

Lowenthal, D. (1993) 'Landscape as Heritage: National Scenes and Global Changes', in J.M. Fladmark (ed.) *Heritage: Conservation, Interpretation and Enterprise*, papers presented at The Robert Gordon University Heritage Convention, Wimbledon: Donhead Publishing Ltd, pp. 3–15.

Lowenthal, D. (1996) *The Heritage Crusade and the Spoils of History*, London: Penguin Group.

Macionis, N. (2004) 'Understanding the Film-induced Tourist', in W. Frost, G. Croy and S. Beeton (eds) *International Tourism and Media Conference Proceedings*, Melbourne: Tourism Research Unit, Monash University, 11–13 July, pp. 86–97.

Macionis, N. and Sparks, B. (2006) 'Film-induced Tourism: An Incidental Experience', in S. Beeton, G. Croy and W. Frost (eds) *International Tourism and Media Conference Proceedings*, Melbourne: Monash University, 11–13 July, pp. 120–128.

Manzo, L.C. (2003) 'Beyond House and Haven: Toward a Revisioning of Emotional Relationships with Places', *Journal of Environmental Psychology* 23, 1: 47–61.

Morgan, N. and Pritchard, A. (1998) *Tourism Promotion and Power: Creating Images, Creating Identities*, Chichester: John Wiley and Sons.

Naudi, C. (2005) *Promoting Malta as a 'Hollywood in the Mediterranean'*. Available at: http://www.mta.com.mt/index.pl/industry_local_articles (accessed 17 November 2011).

O'Connor, N. and Bolan, P. (2008) 'Creating a Sustainable Brand for Northern Ireland through Film-induced Tourism', *Tourism Culture and Communication* 8, 3: 147–158.

O'Connor, N., Flanagan, S. and Gilbert, D. (2006) 'A Stakeholders Perspective: The Impact of Television Induced Tourism in Yorkshire, UK', in S. Beeton, G. Croy and W. Frost (eds) *International Tourism and Media Conference Proceedings*, Melbourne: Monash University, 11–13 July, pp. 153–166.

Pearson, M. and Sullivan, S. (1995) *Looking After Heritage Places: The Basics of Heritage Planning for Managers, Landowners and Administrators*, Melbourne: Melbourne University Press.

Poole, R. (1999) *Nation and Identity*, London: Routledge.

Reijnders, S. (2011) *Places of Imagination: Media, Tourism, Culture*, Burlington: Ashgate.

Renfrew, C. and Bahn, P. (1996) *Archaeology – Theories Methods and Practice* (2nd edn), London: Thames and Hudson Ltd.

Riley, R., Baker, D. and Van Doren, C.S. (1998) 'Movie Induced Tourism', *Annals of Tourism Research* 25, 4: 919–935.

Rocker, R. (1998) *Nationalism and Culture* (English Translation), Canada: Black Rose Books.

Roesch, S. (2009) *The Experiences of Film Location Tourists*, Bristol: Channel View Publications.

Scates, B. (2006) *Return to Gallipoli: Walking the Battlefields of the Great War*, Melbourne: Cambridge University Press.

Schofield, P. (1996) 'Cinematographic Images of a City: Alternative Heritage Tourism in Manchester', *Tourism Management* 17, 5: 333–340.

Schöpflin, G. (2000) *Nations, Identity, Power*, New York: New York University Press.

Singh, K. and Best, G. (2004) 'Film-induced Tourism: Motivations of Visitors to the Hobbiton Movie Set as Featured in the Lord of the Rings', in S. Beeton, G. Croy and W. Frost (eds) *International Tourism and Media Conference Proceedings*, Melbourne: Monash University, 11–13 July, pp. 98–111.

Smith L. and van der Meer, A. (2001) 'Landscape and the Negotiation of Identity: A Case Study from Riversleigh, Northwest Queensland', in M. Cotter, B. Boyd and J. Gardiner (eds) *Heritage Landscapes: Understanding Place and Communities*, Lismore: Southern Cross University Press, pp. 51–63.

Soliman, D.M. (2011) 'Exploring the Role of Film in Promoting Domestic Tourism: A Case Study of Al Fayoum, Egypt', *Journal of Vacation Marketing* 17, 3: 225–235.

Sorupia, E. (2005) 'Rethinking the Role of Transportation in Tourism' *Proceedings of the Eastern Asia Society for Transportation Studies* 5: 1767–1777.

Squire, S.J. (1996) 'Literary Tourism and Sustainable Tourism: Promoting "Anne of Green Gables" in Prince Edward Island', *Journal of Sustainable Tourism* 4, 3: 119–134.

Taylor, J.P. (2001) 'Authenticity and Sincerity in Tourism', *Annals of Tourism Research* 28, 1: 7–26.

Tzanelli, R. (2004) 'Constructing the "Cinematic Tourist": The "Sign Industry" of The Lord of the Rings', *Tourism Studies* 4, 1: 21–42.

Urry, J. (1990) *The Tourist Gaze*, London: Sage Publications.

Urry, J. (2002) *The Tourist Gaze* (2nd edn), London: Sage Publications.

Vaughn, S. (1985) 'History: Is it Relevant?', in S. Vaughn (ed.) *The Vital Past: Writings on the Uses of History*, Athens, GA: University of Georgia Press, pp. 1–14.

Voight, P. (2005) *The Lord of the Rings: A Case Study*, New Zealand: Investment New Zealand.

Watts, P. (1995) 'Maintaining Our History and Our Heritage: Working Together', *Historic Environment* 11, 4: 9–11.

Yale, P. (1997) *From Tourist Attractions to Heritage Tourism* (2nd edn), Huntingdon: Elm Publications.

Recommended further reading

On the categorisation of film tourism

Beeton, S. (2001) 'Smiling for the Camera: The Influence of Film Audiences on a Budget Tourism Destination', *Tourism, Culture and Communication* 3, 1: 15–25.

Beeton, S. (2002) 'A (de-)marketing Approach to Enhancing Capabilities for Film Induced Tourism', in L. Bennington (ed.) *Enhancing Business and Government Capability, 16th Australian and New Zealand Academy of Management Conference*, Victoria, 4–6 December 2002, pp. 1–8.

Connell, J. and Meyer, D. (2009) 'Balamory Revisited: An Evaluation of the Screen Tourism Destination-Tourist Nexus', *Tourism Management* 30, 2: 194–207.

Crouch, D. (2007) 'The Media and the Tourist Imagination', in The Media and the Tourist Imagination, Proceedings of the 5th DeHaan Tourism Management Conference on Culture, Tourism and the Media, Nottingham Business School, 12 December 2006, pp.67–79.

Croy, W.G. and Buchmann, A. (2009) 'Film-induced Tourism in the High Country: Recreation and Tourism Contest', *Tourism Review International* 13, 2: 147–155.

Daye, M. (2007) 'Developing a Framework for the Study of Tourism and the Media', in *The Media and the Tourist Imagination*, Proceedings of the 5th DeHaan Tourism Management Conference on Culture, Tourism, and the Media, Nottingham Business School, 12 December 2006, pp. 80–96.

Kim, S. and Richardson, S. (2001) 'Impacts of Popular Motion Picture on Destination Perceptions', in N. Moisey, N. Nikerson and K. Andreck (eds) *Proceedings from the 32nd Annual Conference of The Travel and Tourism Research Association*, Fort Myers, FL, 10–13 June, pp. 9–12.

Liou, D. (2010) 'Beyond Tokyo Rainbow Bridge: Destination Images Portrayed in Japanese Drama Affect Taiwanese Tourists' Perception', *Journal of Vacation Marketing* 16, 1: 5–15.

Image, tourism and the effectiveness of films

Crompton, J.L. (1979) 'Motivations for Pleasure Travel', *Annals of Tourism Research* 6, 4: 408–423.

Croy, W.G. (2004) 'Teaching Tourism, Image, and Media Relationships', in W. Frost, G. Croy and S. Beeton (eds) *International Tourism and Media Conference Proceedings*, Melbourne: Monash University, 11–13 July, pp. 24–38.

Echtner, C.M. and Ritchie, B. (1993) 'The Measurement of Destination Image: An Empirical Assessment', *Journal of Travel Research* 31, 3: 3–13.

Paul, W. (2007) 'Pottery, Pride or Parochial Prejudice? The Impact of Media Indifference on Tourism Development in Stoke-on-Trent', in *The Media and the Tourist Imagination. Proceedings of the 5th DeHaan Tourism Management Conference on Culture, Tourism, and the Media*, Nottingham Business School, 12 December 2006, pp. 163–204.

Warnick, R., Bojanic, D. and Siriangkul, A. (2005) 'Movie Effects on the Image of Thailand among College Student Travelers', in *Proceedings of the Northeastern Recreation Research Symposium*, Bolton Landing, New York, 10–12 April, pp. 355–364.

7

COMMUNITIES, HERITAGE AND NEW CULTURAL LANDSCAPES

Ecomuseological approaches

Peter Davis and Gerard Corsane

Introduction

This chapter describes the main features of ecomuseological approaches as a prelude to analysing their actual and potential impacts on the perception of cultural landscapes and how these spaces and places are sometimes rebranded into 'new' landscapes by local communities. Ecomuseological approaches recognise the interplay between nature and culture as a dynamic process, welcoming change while also conserving aspects of natural and cultural heritage seen to be important to local communities. They provide a system that helps to shape sense of place; they inform and change attitudes and perceptions of the cultural landscape. Individuals, communities and democratic processes lie at the heart of the eco-museum philosophy; by encouraging interest groups and individuals to work together to contribute to understanding, celebrating and even improving the environment, new images of places are created. Sometimes these images are formed by using marketing tools, 're-branding' for economic purposes to encourage tourism for example, but usually (and more importantly) these actions, through inclusive processes and gains in cultural capital, engender a local sense of pride and belonging. These ideas are explored here using four case studies of initiatives that have the word 'ecomuseum' in their titles and two examples of projects that do not include the term ecomuseum in their name, but which have instinctively followed integrated approaches, principles and practices that are very similar to those of the ecomuseum. All these examples indicate the 'added value' that ecomuseological-like approaches give to the perception and (re-)development of cultural landscapes. Many of the landscapes described are already regarded as significant, beautiful, spectacular and/or fascinating by local people and outsiders, but it is argued that by adopting ecomuseological-like approaches and principles new layers of experience can be created, changing the ways in which places are perceived and promoted.

Ecomuseums: a brief introduction

The word 'ecomusée' (ecomuseum) was devised in September 1971 by the French museologist Hugues de Varine to express new museological approaches to community–heritage–place interactions. Early definitions included many of the key concepts – local identity, territory, landscape, a sense of history and continuity – that appear to be important in creating a sense of belonging. Georges Henri Rivière's (1985) definition emphasised the importance of communities in their creation and the idea of the ecomuseum having 'limitless diversity', that it is a malleable concept where no two ecomuseums are necessarily the same as each is the specific result of a very individualistic response to a unique set of contexts and local needs and drivers. An imaginative definition came from the Canadian museologist René Rivard (1985) who compared the traditional museum (= building + collections + experts + public) to the ecomuseum (= territory + heritage + memory + population). This definition encapsulates a key feature of the ecomuseum, that of a territory (a cultural landscape) within which material heritage features are conserved and interpreted *in situ*, and where intangible cultural heritage is highly valued. Here the idea of the museum as building is discarded in favour of 'museum as place'. In addition to considering the history of the ecomuseum movement and attempts to define ecomuseology, the authors of this chapter, along with other colleagues, have reflected on various examples from around the world and have identified 21 possible characteristics or indicators of ecomuseums, which can be viewed as key ecomuseological principles (Corsane *et al.* 2007; Corsane 2006). However, not all ecomuseums display the full set of possible characteristics and those that are displayed by individual ecomuseums will be found in different proportions and ratios. More recently Davis (2007: 199) reflected on the importance of sustaining landscapes and their communities in particular, defining the ecomuseum as 'a community-driven museum or heritage project that aids sustainable development'.

Although the ecomuseum appears to defy an accepted definition, the flexibility of ecomuseological approaches has led to its widespread adoption. More than 400 are currently found worldwide, on every continent (Borrelli and Davis 2012). Now fully established in Europe, and especially in France, Spain, Portugal, Italy and Sweden, the concept is presently emerging strongly in Eastern Europe. In South and Central America new ecomuseological approaches and practices are very strong, while in Canada (notably Quebec) there is significant interest. In Asia the recent growth is especially marked; there, the processes of creating ecomuseums have been frequently linked to meeting demands for sustainable tourism and representing indigenous and ethnic minority nationality cultures, while encouraging heritage conservation and interpretive practices that will ultimately benefit local people.

Put simply, ideally the ecomuseum is a cultural landscape, a territory with shared characteristics that are valued and cared for by local people – even when input, facilitation and direction in varying degrees also comes from other stakeholder groups including government bodies, professional heritage management groups and business organisations. The heritage within these territories is not solely that designated by official conservation agencies, but that which is recognised and given significance by local people and authorities with heritage conservation interests. As such they sometimes fall outside the 'Authorised Heritage Discourse' (Smith 2006) and provide an alternative view of what 'place', 'cultural landscape' and 'heritage' are. Each ecomuseum celebrates what Common Ground (Clifford and King 2006: ix) refer to as 'local distinctiveness' – 'Everywhere is somewhere. What makes each place unique is the conspiracy of nature and culture; the accumulation of story upon history upon natural history' (ibid.: ix). Hence every ecomuseum seeks to inform visitors that they are in a distinct cultural landscape, encouraging exploration and discovery.

Case studies of ecomuseums and ecomuseum-like initiatives

The following first four subsections describe different examples of ecomuseums from around the world. In addition, there are two further subsections that introduce initiatives, which although they do not refer to themselves as being ecomuseums, have followed similar processes to those where ecomuseological approaches and principles have overtly been used. These six case studies provide interesting examples that demonstrate how the use of ecomuseological-like approaches and principles can influence perceptions of places, creating new cultural landscapes in the minds of local communities and tourists. They have been chosen to demonstrate the diversity of environments (urban and rural), scale (regional landscapes, local scale) and heritage focus (nature, culture, intangible, political conflict). They have all been subject to investigation by the authors, working with local communities and the other key stakeholders and shareholders.

Kalyna Country Ecomuseum, Alberta, Canada: the rebranding of a cultural landscape

Kalyna Country, an area of some 15,000 square kilometres east of the provincial capital of Edmonton, markets itself as 'the world's largest ecomuseum'. The region was one of the first parts of Canada's Far Western Plains visited by Europeans who opened up the territory to the fur trade. Major pioneer settlement took place from 1880 to 1920, primarily by immigrants from Eastern European countries, and especially Ukraine; these people shaped the contemporary landscape, which is dominated by agriculture, with some mining and forestry. Balan (1994: 11) noted that 'although assimilation, depopulation, urbanisation and technological change have substantially transformed the complexion and the demographic profile of the region, its fundamental make-up and distinctive features remain largely intact'. A strong sense of identity is created by markers that 'claim' the landscape as Ukrainian, specifically the onion domes of Eastern Rite churches (Figure 7.1). The idea for the ecomuseum emerged when plans were being made in Edmonton to mark the one-hundredth anniversary of Ukrainian settlement in Canada in 1992. The ecomuseum was seen as a process that could link heritage sites in the area, promoting its Ukrainian heritage; consequently initial projects included self-guided car tour brochures, a telephone hotline advertising public events, the introduction of a community events calendar and providing moral and practical support for local heritage initiatives. Local activist Jars Balan suggested the title 'Kalyna Country' be adopted; the Kalyna Country Ecomuseum Trust Society was formed in June 1992, with an executive board that included members from the Ukrainian, Romanian, English and Cree communities.

The ecomuseum is named after the Ukrainian word for a native cranberry, *Viburnum opulus*; the kalyna berry was recognised by early Ukrainian settlers in the late nineteenth century as a food source found in their former homeland. It has particular resonance as the plant has been used as a symbol of Ukrainian independence since the tenth century, and features strongly in the country's literary, musical, artistic and folk traditions. Chosen as the name and logo for the ecomuseum (Figure 7.2), the kalyna has taken on new meaning, and has become a potent symbol for the region.

The ecomuseum, although a means of introducing visitors to the many existing heritage sites in the region, is not directly responsible for their management. The Trust acts as a catalyst, encouraging joint working and promotion between the varied heritage sites, which include

FIGURE 7.1   The Orthodox Ukrainian church at Lamont, Alberta, Canada. Such 'onion-dome'
churches are a significant feature of the plains landscape of Kalyna Country
(Jars Balan).

historic properties, a Ukrainian Cultural Heritage Village, some 23 local museums and
40 designated wildlife sites (including Elk Island National Park). Emphasis is placed on
encouraging individuals and organisations to work together towards shared goals; the
ecomuseum is identified as a means of uniting diverse communities and interest groups
under the umbrella of the Kalyna Country theme and concept. Balan (1994) stressed that
a key goal was to forge a sense of identity among residents of the region and as a result
involvement of the local community has been an essential factor in the success of the project.

From small beginnings the Kalyna Country Ecomuseum sought to promote cultural
tourism and ecotourism. In a region facing population decline with limited economic
prospects the ecomuseum combines a conservation strategy with an economic tourism and
community development strategy. Using the 'Kalyna' label – creating a new cultural landscape
in the eyes of tourists and local people alike – has been remarkably successful in terms
of increasing tourist numbers and economic well-being. The formation of an independent
body in response to legislation regarding tourism marketing, the Kalyna Country Destination
Marketing Organisation, was, for a time, an element that supported and promoted an integrated network of heritage sites under the 'Kalyna' banner. This marketing role has now been
reclaimed by the Ecomuseum Trust following reorganisation of tourism strategies in Alberta.
However, their joint efforts in producing the Kalyna guide, and ensuring its profile through

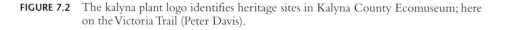

Welcome to the Victoria Trail

From this point, signposts mark a 58km drive which
follows sections of the original Victoria Trail, part of a
heavily travelled overland route from Fort Garry
(Winnipeg) to Edmonton dating from the 1820s.
Remnants of the 1862 Methodist Mission to the Cree,
the 1864 Hudson's Bay Company fur trade post, the
predominantly Métis riverlot Settlements, and
subsequent homesteads of East Europeans and British
are still visible along the Trail. Watch for churches,
cemeteries, houses, barns, fencelines, and changes in
the route of the road itself. All these provide clues to the
rich history of the Victoria Trail.

*Much of this route is not paved, and is subject to
varying weather conditions. Please exercise
appropriate caution, and respect private property.*

FIGURE 7.2   The kalyna plant logo identifies heritage sites in Kalyna County Ecomuseum; here
on the Victoria Trail (Peter Davis).

tradeshow displays, the website and other marketing endeavours has evidently created a new vision for this area of Alberta. Balan (pers. comm. 1/2012) states:

> For many locals, the name Kalyna Country has been adopted as a regional identity, meaning people now refer to living in Kalyna Country. A recent example was that a newly formed regional health unit took the name 'Kalyna Country' as part of their title ... because it best captured the region that the unit was serving. We also have a performing arts festival run by a separation association that uses the name Kalyna Country Performing Arts Festival, and the there have been a number of businesses and groups that have similarly incorporated Kalyna Country in their names. It is no longer necessary to always explain to residents and visitors that they are in Kalyna Country, as many of them are now fully aware of it.

The success in promoting 'Kalyna' has meant some job creation, both in marketing and administration for the Trust, in addition to obtaining grants for projects that have enabled contract work to be commissioned. Perhaps less measurable are the economic benefits that have accrued to businesses and communities in the area thanks to Kalyna Country's promotional endeavours. However, Balan (pers. comm. 1/2012) states that 'We know from feedback that some operators of tourism businesses (like a riverboat guiding company and some bed and breakfasts) have attracted customers by advertising with us and associating themselves with the Kalyna Country project'.

The one concern here is that some of the other major ecomuseum goals, including initiating and sponsoring research, education, conservation and cultural projects, have been less successful because of the emphasis on tourism promotion. There have been some recent cultural achievements, however, including providing funds to the Beaverhill Museum to plant kalyna bushes and other native plants in a garden attached to their building, restoring an historic French Canadian home and assisting a museum to digitise its photographic collection.

In this ecomuseum, a fascinating territory, rich in biodiversity, museums, objects, heritage sites, traditions, festivals, craft skills and local memories, has been subsumed into a fabricated 'identity', a new cultural landscape. Although 'Kalyna Country' is now widely accepted as a term that identifies this region, it is difficult to know whether these changes in status will have lasting and important benefits for heritage conservation and interpretation, tourists and local people.

Ceumannan Ecomuseum, Staffin, Isle of Skye, Scotland: new approaches to natural heritage

Trotternish is the most northerly of Skye's peninsulas and is arguably one of the most spectacular landscapes in Britain (Figure 7.3). The Staffin area is one of rugged mountain scenery hiding secluded grassy plateaus and small freshwater lakes, and has a dramatic coastline with stacks, pinnacles and hidden coves. The coastal rocks are predominantly Jurassic age with Tertiary exposures, rich in fossils and supporting colonies of breeding seabirds and populations of rare plants.

In 2004 the Staffin Community Trust was awarded almost £200,000 to develop an ecomuseum in north-east Skye. It became the first ecomuseum in Scotland (and indeed the

FIGURE 7.3   'The Table' is a remarkable landscape feature in the Ceumannan Ecomuseum, Staffin, Isle of Skye, Scotland (Caileen MacLean).

first in the UK at that time), assisted by funding from a variety of European, national and European sources, and the Heritage Lottery Fund. The Trust, which includes representatives from local voluntary groups and organisations, took responsibility for development, with aims to stimulate economic growth, encourage social activities in the community, improve local services and strengthen sense of place. Inaugurated in 2008, ecomuseum supporters have undertaken a range of ambitious projects. Aware of the wide range of natural and cultural assets that attract geologists, naturalists and walkers, projects have been largely devoted to historical and environmental themes.

The Staffin Ecomuseum promotes some 13 sites of interest to visitors and local people by encouraging them to discover the area on waymarked trails. These include Flodigarry with its Viking connections, scattered crofts at Brodaig, Quiraing, the massive rock face that towers above Staffin, dinosaur footprints on the shore at An Corran, and the Staffin Museum at Ellishadder which houses excellent collections of local geological specimens. This low-key ecomuseum could be a model for many others in the UK to follow. It is closely linked to community identity, local history, memory, sense of place and economic development. As the Trust's chairman, Donald MacDonald, noted:

> We are extremely positive about the outcomes of the *Ceumannan* [ecomuseum] project and feel that the paths which have been created are beneficial to both locals and visitors. We believe the interpretation will open up the landscape for us all and will allow the community to focus on its key strengths, which are scenery, history and culture.

Our discussions have focussed in many ways on how to expand this project and how we can further enhance our community infrastructure.

(Schmidt pers. comm. 3/2010)

Although the goals of this ecomuseum echo those of Kalyna, the fact that it is on a much smaller scale appear to have contributed to its success. The natural landscape has been 'rebranded', it has been given the 'ecomuseum' label as a means of drawing attention to its distinctive character, yet this image has been delivered in a sensitive and inclusive manner.

Cortemilia Ecomuseum, Piedmont, Italy: rebuilding a community through appreciation of the cultural landscape

Murtas and Davis (2009) have described in detail this Italian ecomuseum, but because of its significance a brief précis is included here to demonstrate how inclusive ecomuseological approaches can revitalise small communities and lead to a new appreciation of local landscapes.

Cortemilia was renowned for its high-quality agricultural produce, but had suffered from economic decline, emigration and the abandonment of farmland. The valley had also suffered severe chemical pollution from a local factory and in 1994 a terrible flood emphasised the fragility of a landscape that had seemingly lost its purpose. The terraced hillsides, formerly sites of vines and orchards, lay ruined, a visual metaphor for environmental and societal erosion. In 1996, following the closure of the chemical factory, an opportunity arose to assess the future of the community. It was then that an ecomuseum approach was proposed as a way forward, using the town's cultural assets, but focusing on the locally distinctive terraced landscape, with its links to land use, history and local memories.

From the beginning it was evident that conservation, maintenance and rebuilding of the terraced landscape would be impossible without a revolution in local perception about their environment. For that reason the project had at its core the *contemporary* interpretation of the values linked to the terraced landscape, with the revitalisation of the local community being the most important goal. As a consequence the ecomuseum project sought to involve as many people as possible in the local community, people of different ages, those with varied interests and specialists with local knowledge, including associations. This intensive and demanding process required many hours of meetings, discussions and persuasion, engendering belief in the project and deciding upon activities that could be successfully achieved. Much of this initial work focused on working with local people to help them discover that there were valuable local heritage resources in their everyday lives that belonged to everyone. Initially most of the inhabitants were very vague about what heritage assets they had, often citing the main church and the town's medieval tower, or unable to give any meaningful response. Little evidence was provided of the thousands of tangible and intangible elements that made, and make, the Cortemilia area distinctive. Hardship, depression and lack of trust in authority had meant that even the predominant feature in the local cultural landscape, the terraced hillsides, seemed to have been erased from memory.

Initial projects in the ecomuseum focused on local material culture and memories, approaching local inhabitants willing to contribute their objects, reminiscences and ideas to contribute to small exhibitions held in the town. These were shown in a marquee in the main village square during the summer months and focused on the distinctive features of the area, including vernacular architecture, local vegetable crops, local recipes and individual personal stories linked to everyday objects. These exhibitions enabled the ecomuseum team to gain a better understanding of local beliefs and knowledge, breaking stereotypical perceptions of history and that of the town itself and contributing to the shaping of a common cultural heritage and a recognition of its importance. Luigi Porro, an 88-year-old farmer and the main 'character' in an exhibition about chestnuts said:

> It was the first time I was asked to relate my experience, the experience of a life spent working in agriculture. I felt important and I believe that it is very important to collect this not written knowledge. If the old people die nobody will know about this area and its traditional uses.
>
> *(Cited in Murtas and Davis 2009: 156)*

Having made good connections in the town and a broad acceptance of their mission the ecomuseum staff moved on to restoration projects linked directly to the terraced landscape. An historical building in the old town centre was restored and reused as an interpretation centre, library, a venue for temporary exhibitions, video projection and meetings, putting the heart back into the town's historic centre. The restoration of this traditional stone building, which now also acts as the headquarters for the ecomuseum, led to other vernacular buildings located in the same square being renovated. What was once a dismal tarmac car park is now a charming pedestrian square, paved with stone and used for exhibits, theatre and film projection. Giuseppe Canobbio, owner of a pastry shop on the square, recalled his feelings:

> My first shop and laboratory was on a corner of the square. It was a very modest and small place, but my hazelnut cakes are and were so appreciated that a lot of clients coming from a lot of places came there. They all complain about the square and the feeling of abandonment that they had. Now the building with the ecomuseum offices offers a good restoration example and the square has become pedestrianised, everybody is really happy. Now that the square is so beautiful my family and I have decided to leave the old shop and to buy a bigger building on the square. We decide that it is worth investing in the old village.
>
> *(Quoted in Murtas and Davis 2009: 156)*

The ecomuseum went on to restore a farmhouse, its adjacent vineyards and orchard. Sitting atop a superb terrace it is now used by the local community, hosts school visits, specialist groups and general training courses. The vineyard has its own niche production of quality wine and the restored terraces are farmed for local varieties of vegetables and fruits, conserving rare varieties.

These projects, and many others, have led to the creation of new social networks and a growing sense of community; local people appear to better understand their heritage and recognise that their cultural landscape has contemporary cultural and economic value. Symptomatic of this is the rebranding of Cortemilia based upon the now restored and actively used terraced landscapes; it appears local people have re-created the town and its environs not simply through delivering successful heritage projects, but by capitalising on a renewed sense of purpose and a revitalised sense of place.

Hüsamettindere Ecomuseum, Turkey: incomers and vernacular architecture

The idea of creating an ecomuseum in this small village in Anatolia was proposed by a group of people who had bought vernacular buildings there as holiday homes; most of them live and work in Istanbul, some 200 km distant. Initially led by Tunca Bokesoy, the Hüsamettindere Ecomuseum Association for the Preservation of Cultural and Natural Heritage was formed in 2005 with the principal aims of restoring the architecture of this old village (Figure 7.4) and documenting disappearing local culture, including its craft skills, folklore and traditions. The ultimate goal is to keep the village 'alive' by encouraging low-level tourism to a very special environment and to set an example that might encourage similar action in the many hundreds of semi-abandoned villages in rural Turkey.

It might be imagined that imposing such ideas onto a rural community by 'outsiders' is fraught with problems, notably significant potential for feelings of resentment and interference. However, a recent (November 2011) visit by one of the authors (PD) allayed any such fears,[1] indeed it was clear that a remarkably close link had been formed between the local farmers, their families and the Association members. Much of the success of the project lies with the inclusive and personal approach adopted by the Association's current leader, Funda Inanduğçar, who has encouraged connections based on friendship, recognising the need to ensure joint responsibility and ownership of ecomuseum goals. In conversations with her and her team

FIGURE 7.4 Conserved traditional houses in the Hüsamettendere Ecomuseum, Turkey (Hüsamettindere Ecomuseum Association).

it was clear much had already been achieved, including the restoration of some 20 wooden houses, the renovation of village wells, carrying out oral recordings with local residents about their traditional ways of life, making general environmental improvements, producing a 'landscape map' and creating a website (www.ekomuze.org).

The ecomuseum is ambitious in its goals. In the near future the 'landscape map' will be reworked to create a Parish Map, working with local people to identify heritage sites and places of interest. Restoration projects will include turning the abandoned village school into a library and cultural centre. The team have excellent connections with the local administration and the support of the Mayor of Mudurnu, the nearest large town, and recognise the importance of working alongside the authorities, especially with regard to developing signage for the ecomuseum and new visitor facilities such as car parking. A major future plan is to promote local organic crop production, including honey, and to 'eco-label' local foods, working with a local university to develop these ideas. A longer-term goal is to fully document local biodiversity, recognising that the mountain landscapes, a rich flora and interesting wildlife will attract ecotourists; the Association is aware that to develop sustainable tourism it has to develop a niche market.

The main reason for the decline in the village was due to emigration, largely young people moving to urban centres to find work. In addition, many local residents have been rehoused in new homes nearby which do not require dedicated conservation and regular maintenance. The cultural landscape was changing rapidly as the old houses, fields and village infrastructure went into decline. It might be argued that the Ecomuseum Association are simply maintaining an old cultural landscape through their actions, but our conclusions are that a new community – based on a combination of traditional knowledge of residents and new ideas brought by homeowners – is creating a new tapestry of cultural connections and an entirely different landscape.

Iwokrama protected rainforest area and the North Rupununi, Guyana: following principles similar to those in ecomuseology to promote natural and indigenous cultural landscapes

The Iwokrama protected rainforest area (Figure 7.5) and the North Rupununi in Guyana, South America, are an interesting example of a territory where a multilayered sense of place has developed over time (Corsane and Bowers 2012: 249) and where there have been shifts towards the representation of new cultural landscapes as areas for sustainable conservation and responsible eco- and heritage tourism that benefit all of the stakeholders and shareholders. It is also a territory where the artificial division between nature and culture is being blurred, and where work has been started to promote the value of Amerindian intangible cultural heritage alongside the tangible heritage resources (Bowers and Corsane 2012).

> While the cultural landscapes are shifting from one of traditional land use by the local indigenous communities to an area of modern development centred on tourism, Iwokrama and the NRDDB continue to work to promote the responsible use and safeguarding of the local natural heritage. However, as development moves forward and the cultural landscapes continue to change, equal attention will also need, and is currently starting, to be focussed on safeguarding cultural heritage as well.
>
> *(Bowers pers. comm. 3/2012)*

FIGURE 7.5 View of rainforest from Turtle Mountain in the Iwokrama protected area, with the Essequibo River in the background (Gerard Corsane).

The Iwokrama protected area, or reserve, in Region 8 of Guyana takes its name from the sacred mountains of the Amerindian Makushi people, who make up the majority of the inhabitants in the one village within it and those villages in the North Rupununi wetlands and savannahs in Region 9 to the south of the protected area. This area, which was 'gifted' to the international community in 1989, is in the centre of the country. It is made up of nearly one million acres of rainforest and has the Iwokrama River Lodge and Research Centre at the reserve's north-eastern border on the Essequibo River. This facility is close to the Kurupukari ferry crossing of the river and is just off the main road running from Guyana's capital city Georgetown, on the northern coast, via Linden, to Lethem on the western border that Guyana has with Brazil. In 1996, the *Iwokrama International Centre for Rain Forest Conservation and Development Act* was passed by the National Assembly of Guyana, establishing the Iwokrama International Centre for Rainforest Conservation and Development (IIC), with its administrative headquarters in Georgetown, which oversees the management of the protected area.

In undertaking its activities, the IIC has intuitively followed ecomuseological approaches and its work shares many of the principles of the ecomuseum ideal, without overtly being aware of them. It has worked closely with key stakeholders and shareholders internationally, nationally and locally. At the local level, it has engaged with the North Rupununi District Development Board (NRDDB) established in 1996, with some support from the IIC, as a democratic body that has representation from the local Amerindian villager communities.

Together, the IIC and the NRDDB have fostered the development of more inclusive, participatory and empowering processes to safeguarding, managing and interpreting the natural and cultural heritage resources *in situ* in the overall geographical territory. In these processes, there is an acknowledgement of the need for joint ownership and collaboration and a number of the local people put in a substantial amount of voluntary time and work in order to progress the shared aims of the stakeholders and shareholders. With this participation and engagement at the local level, there is an important focus on promoting local identities and sense of place, which is a key for promoting the territory as a destination for tourism. In addition, the worth of intangible cultural heritage resources are recognised – including the particular knowledge systems, cultural expressions and traditional practices passed down through the generations in the Amerindian communities. Along with this, work has been undertaken, and is continuing to be done, to research people's interactions with the natural, economic, social and cultural environments and landscapes, both in historical and current contexts. Here, the research needs to be multidisciplinary and even interdisciplinary and it is being conducted by academics as well as by local 'specialists', who should be seen as having equal status for their invaluable indigenous knowledge.

In their collaborative work the IIC and NRDDB, together with the other partner stakeholders and shareholders, have unconsciously followed many of the principles and practices of the ecomuseum ideal, as noted above. In this work there has been a certain amount of 'mutual moulding' where all the partners have had positive influences on the part played by each in creating new cultural landscapes. Although the work of the IIC has principally concentrated on sustainable rainforest management and scientific research in the protected area in Region 8, the NRDDB has focused more on helping to develop sustainable alternative livelihoods for the local Amerindian communities, both in the protected reserve and in the North Rupununi wetlands and savannahs of Region 9. Combined, they and the other stakeholders and shareholders have created new cultural landscapes: where natural and cultural heritage elements are starting to be reintegrated to promote a unique sense and spirit of place; where there is a certain amount of balance in the recognition of the values of intangible and tangible cultural heritage resources, especially in relation to indigenous knowledge systems and how they have informed culturally based uses of the natural resources; where an understanding of indigenous cultural heritage is used to affirm local identities; where scientific research has been enhanced with indigenous knowledge systems in the study of the earth sciences, biodiversity and climate change; and, where there is an ideal of bringing together conservation and responsible tourism to promote sustainability.

However, with an assumption held among some people in the local communities that tourism could be used to bring economic benefit and modernisation as a 'quick fix' to help in poverty reduction and alleviation, there may have been an emphasis in the first mid-1990s tourism ventures on developing the product. However, thinking is becoming more informed and there has been an increasing interest placed on process over product, in order to bring benefits to all involved and to the world at large.

The new cultural landscapes that have been emerging in this territory within Guyana are ones that do have value and meaning for locals, tourists, researchers and those involved in conservation at all levels. However, along the way the processes have not always been straightforward or easy, and, at times, there have been contestation and imbalances in the power dynamics between the various stakeholders and shareholders. Nevertheless, the partners do appear to be committed to negotiation and their work can be seen as a model for developing more integrated landscape policy and planning procedures to ensure future natural and cultural landscape quality.

Robben Island Museum, South Africa: using ecomuseological-type approaches at a National Monument, National Museum and World Heritage Site

Robben Island in South Africa has had a place within human history that goes back a long way. As an example of a cultural landscape that has been undergoing recent (re-)development and shifts, it can be noted that 'Robben Island is a complex place with a multiple layering of significant physical, social, cultural and political landscapes' (Corsane 2006: 399). Although it has a long history, including other periods when it was used as a place of banishment, the island is probably most known to people today as being the political prison for black male activists incarcerated in the three decades from 1960 for their involvement in the struggle against Apartheid in South Africa (Figure 7.6). It lies in Table Bay, north-west of Cape Town and is just under 7 km to the west of Bloubergstrand on the Atlantic coast of the Western Cape province. The departure point for a trip out to Robben Island is now the Nelson Mandela

FIGURE 7.6   Part of the display in the Nelson Mandela Gateway to Robben Island. The display area with the photograph of the island on the back wall is the size of an individual cell in the old maximum security prison. Note also in the jar to the left, the limestone cuttings taken from the infamous quarry where the political prisoners worked in hard labour (Gerard Corsane).

Gateway to Robben Island at the Victoria and Alfred Waterfront harbour of Cape Town, which has been developed as a key tourist destination. The boat trip from this departure point to Murray's Bay at the island is over 11 km and the island itself is about 5.4 km long and 2.5 km wide. As an island, the place appears to have a naturally constituted territory where the over-layered natural, cultural and political history landscapes can be managed as a contained protected area.

After the first South African democratic elections in 1994, the new government started a process of consultation about the future of Robben Island and in 1996 it was declared as a National Monument. In the following year, on Heritage Day, 24 September 1997, it was officially opened by the then president, Nelson Mandela, as the Robben Island Museum – giving the island the added standing of being a National Museum and a Declared Cultural Institution in South Africa. Further, in December 1999, it obtained World Heritage status and was added to the UNESCO list of World Heritage Sites. With all of this, the perceptions of the overlaid landscapes of Robben Island have been changing. From a place of banishment that many South Africans may have tried to 'blank out' of their consciousness during the Apartheid years with selected social amnesia, the island has from 1996 become a place of 'special' and protected landscapes that has been projected centre stage into the public psyche of the new 'rainbow nation'. With the key driver of 'transformation' of South African society, the new government supported Robben Island as a beacon for this. It soon became a national symbol and international icon for freedom and the triumph of the human spirit.

These changes in perceptions and the new meanings and values invested into the Robben Island landscapes were particularly evidenced at the official opening of the Robben Island Museum in 1997. During his address on this occasion, Nelson Mandela, an ex-political prisoner of the island himself, posed an important question about the changing perceptions and new meanings of Robben Island and then provided a reply. He said:

> How do we reflect the fact that the people of South Africa as a whole, together with the international community, turned one of the world's most notorious symbols of racist oppression into a world-wide icon of the universality of human rights; of hope, peace and reconciliation? . . . I am confident that we will together find a way to combine the many dimensions of the Island, and that we will do so in a manner that recognises above all its pre-eminent character as a symbol of the victory of the human spirit over political oppression; and for reconciliation over enforced division.
>
> *(Mandela 1997: 3)*

It was through following ecomuseological-like principles during its initial period of re-development as a museum and World Heritage Site, that Robben Island Museum became the first 'cultural and conservation showcase for the new South African democracy' (Corsane 2006: 416; Robben Island Museum 2001: 2; Mandela 1997: 3). The 21 characteristics or indicators of ecomuseology have been mapped on to the processes and practices used (Corsane 2006) in the first five years, when Robben Island's landscapes were being re-conceptualised and when public perceptions were being reshaped, as the island shifted from being a place of banishment to a destination for tourism. During this time, the management processes encouraged the local communities of ex-political prisoners and ex-warders to be involved in decision-making around the redevelopment activities. Public participation that was appropriate and sympathetic to the symbolic nature of the landscapes was facilitated and encouraged and there was a sense of joint ownership, with the various stakeholders being considered and brought into discussions about developments. Although work was undertaken to develop tourism products, an emphasis was placed on the importance of allowing for responsible and sensitive processes to take place towards their development.

In the development there was an emphasis placed on local identities and on the sense and spirit of place, within the geographical territory of the island, along with the sea and seabed (with a number of significant shipwrecks) surrounding it and certain associated places and sites on the mainland. The Nelson Mandela Gateway Museum on the Victoria and Alfred Waterfront and the maximum security prison building with its exhibitions on the island now act as 'hubs' from which visitors can obtain information about the island's different landscapes and natural and cultural heritage sites and resources.

The 'conservation' work that has been done so far continues to focus on the ongoing documentation of both the tangible immovable and movable cultural heritage *in situ*, along with the intangible cultural heritage. A really important part of this documentation work has centred on the recording of the oral testimonies and memories of the ex-political prisoners and ex-wardens, with the 'cell stories' exhibition being an early outcome of this. In this exhibition, a single object important to a particular individual prisoner has been placed in a single cell and the ex-prisoner's oral story related to the object is played over the intercom system in that cell.

The research that has been done on the island is both interdisciplinary and multidisciplinary and has brought together the natural and cultural landscapes and the heritage resources. In addition, the research has not solely been done by perceived academic 'experts'. Local people have been involved in the research and dissemination processes. For example ex-political prisoners have researched and developed the storylines and have acted as tour hosts for visits to the island.

Indeed, the Robben Island Museum can be seen as an example of where ecomuseological-like approaches have been used in the redevelopment and rebranding of sets of over-layered landscapes, including changing cultural landscapes, for the benefit of all stakeholders. What once was a landscape of banishment has now become a landscape with the symbol of hope and freedom, which is promoted as a tourism destination. In this particular case, it is interesting to note how the redevelopment of Robben Island has in many ways challenged the old 'official' lists of what was deemed to be significant heritage in Apartheid South Africa, whilst at the same time becoming a showcase in the 'official' new lists of the democratic South Africa. In this respect, it may differ from the other examples in this chapter.

Conclusion

The six examples described above indicate that the use of ecomuseological-like approaches and the '21 Principles' foster dynamic processes through which communities are able to identify, conserve, interpret and manage their natural and cultural heritage resources for sustainable development. Community involvement does not mean that state and local government administrations, heritage management practitioners, academics, businesses and other stakeholders are irrelevant or excluded, but simply that local people and these other stakeholders need to cooperate in whatever ways are appropriate within the decision-making processes and actions. In ecomuseology, caring for and communicating the scope of local natural and cultural heritage resources should provide new, more meaningful interpretations and raise territorial self-awareness and profile. Ecomuseological approaches and principles demand that heritage reflects aspects of the cultural landscape, including the 'natural' environment, where it has been invested with cultural values, significance and meanings by local people. It includes the histories of inhabitants and all the sources of evidence, tangible and intangible, that have been socially identified and are considered of lasting value.

It cannot be denied that ecomuseological-like approaches and processes transform places, nature, people, traditions and artefacts, as they identify heritage resources to be protected, celebrated and interpreted. However, ecomuseums and integrated and participatory heritage management initiatives are different in the way that they engage with cultural landscapes in that they often provide an alternative vision to 'official' or 'traditional' methods simply because the selection of what is deemed to be heritage – a significant part of the cultural landscape – is decided by local people working together. Ecomuseums are an antidote to the globalisation of culture by acting at the local or regional level, drawing on their own cultural and natural assets, devising a distinctive and self-defined heritage-scape.

The one characteristic that appears to be common to all ecomuseums and heritage initiatives that follow similar approaches and principles is their 'pride in place' – that is in the cultural landscapes that they represent and in the new cultural landscapes that they sometimes create. This is true whatever the nature of the ecomuseum or heritage project, whether it be linked to a scattered group of heritage sites in Alberta; abandoned terraces in northern Italy; a rural farming community in Turkey; areas of rainforest, wetlands and savannahs in Guyana; or, in a contentious space like Robben Island, which celebrates the triumph of the human spirit over trials, tribulation and social and political injustices. This pride is expressed in a variety of ways. It can be seen in the local citizen's contribution to an exhibition, in the sheer pleasure people take in performing local music and dance, or the satisfaction in demonstrating craft skills such as carpentry. It can be found in indigenous people affirming their belief systems and cultural identities and how these link to physical, natural and economic environments. It can be associated with people sharing about their painful experiences and memories, but also sharing about how they overcame adversity. Ecomuseums and similar integrated and democratic heritage projects encourage dialogue between local people as well as inviting visitors to explore their territory; these factors can only serve to promote a better understanding of the changing values and meanings associated with cultural landscapes as they are constantly adapting to meet the shifting needs of people.

Note

1 This meeting was the result of an invitation for PD to give advice and support for the development of the Hüsamettindere Ecomuseum, and was led by the Ecomuseum's Director and academics from Canakkale Onsekiz Mart University (Tourism and Travel Management Programme) Bozcada. The meeting involved site visits and detailed discussions with local residents and key political leaders in the city of Mudurnu and the region.

References

Balan, J. (1994) 'The Kalyna Country Ecomuseum: An Exercise in Community Building in Alberta', *Together* 6, 3: 10–12.

Borrelli, N. and Davis, P. (2012) 'How Culture Shapes Nature: Reflections on Ecomuseum Practices', *Nature and Culture* 7, 1: 31–47.

Bowers, D.J. and Corsane, G. (2012) 'Revitalising Amerindian Intangible Cultural Heritage in Guyana and its Value for Sustainable Tourism', in M.L. Stefano, P. Davis and G. Corsane (eds) *Safeguarding Intangible Cultural Heritage*, Woodbridge: The Boydell Press, pp. 201–212.

Clifford, S. and King, A. (2006) *England in Particular*, London: Hodder & Stoughton.

Corsane, G. (2006) 'Using Ecomuseum Indicators to Evaluate the Robben Island Museum and World Heritage Site', *Landscape Research* 31, 4: 399–418.

Corsane, G. and Bowers, D.J. (2012) 'Sense of Place in Sustainable Tourism: A Case Study in the Rainforest and Savannahs in Guyana', in I. Convery, G. Corsane and P. Davis (eds) *Making Sense of Place: Multidisciplinary Perspectives*, Woodbridge: The Boydell Press, pp. 249–260.

Corsane, G., Davis, P., Elliott, S., Maggi, M., Murtas, D. and Rogers, S. (2007) 'Ecomuseums Evaluation: Experiences in Piemonte and Liguria, Italy', *International Journal of Heritage Studies* 13, 2: 101–116.

Davis, P. (2007) 'Ecomuseums and Sustainability in Italy, Japan and China: Concept Adaptation Through Implementation', in S. Knell, S. MacLeod and S. Watson (eds) *Museum Revolutions: How Museums Change and are Changed*, London and New York: Routledge, pp. 198–214.

Mandela, N. (1997) 'Robben Island, 24 September 1997: Address by President Mandela – Heritage Day', *Ilifa Labantu: Robben Island – Heritage of the People* 1, 9: 3.

Murtas, D. and Davis, P. (2009) 'The Role of The Ecomuseo Dei Terrazzamenti E. Della Vite (Cortemilia, Italy) in Community Development', *Museums and Society* 7, 3: 150–186.

Rivard, R. (1985) 'Ecomuseums in Quebec', *Museum* 37, 4: 202–205.

Rivière, G.H. (1985) 'The Ecomuseum: An Evolutive Definition', *Museum* 37, 4: 182–183.

Robben Island Museum (2001) *Robben Island Museum; Strategic Plan for the 2001/2002 Financial Year*, Cape Town: Robben Island Museum.

Smith, L. (2006) *Uses of Heritage*, London: Routledge.

8

DESPERATION, DELIGHT OR DEVIANCE

Conflicting cultural landscapes of the urban poor in developing countries

Suzanne Speak

Introduction

This chapter provides a picture of the rich relationship between rural migrants of the Global South and the urban land and landscape they occupy to produce their organically evolving settlements. It explores the cultural values embedded within the informally planned landscapes of the urban poor, highlighting how these are undervalued by authorities.

There is much ambiguity about the definition of 'urban', with a lack of understanding of the complexity and interplay of 'urban' and 'rural' activities (Tacoli 1998). This ambiguity and the different interpretations of 'urban living' causes conflict between migrants and city authorities. This chapter highlights the way in which authorities manage and control the use of space and impose a new orthodoxy of the urban(e) over what they perceive as the deviant behaviour of rural to urban migrants.

In cities of the Global South two new and conflicting cultural landscapes are emerging. First, there are the new, globally recognisable landscapes of modernity, formally planned by governments of developing countries to present their cities as stages for global economic investment and activity. In contrast, there are the informally planned landscapes of urban poor migrants, which evolve to service their everyday needs for shelter and livelihood. The former are developed largely to support neo-liberal, macroeconomic policies and the needs and desires of the aspiring middle classes who are most likely to benefit from such policies. They follow a 'new orthodoxy' of the urban landscape which is spreading across the developing world. The latter are borne out of a combination of desperation and delight by those who such policies are failing. These conflicting rationales are leading to tensions between migrants and policymakers about the use and form of urban land and what is appropriate behaviour in the urban area.

The once colonial cities of the developing world have long experienced conflict over the use of their space. Designed to represent power, order and social control they were bifurcated landscapes, laid out to protect Europeans from the perceived disease, dangers and 'deviant' behaviour of indigenous people (Mitchell 2002). They were not only sites of government and trade, but also islands of sanitation and sanctuary from the local environmental and social conditions, protected from overcrowding by population control, urban planning and land laws which kept indigenous people at bay (Christopher 2001; Dick and

Rimmer 1998; Christopher 1988). Those few indigenous people allowed in, to support the governing activities of the colonial authorities, were heavily controlled. Landscape was a key element in that control. As Stock (1988) notes, the model for British cities in tropical colonies was developed in India, where the health of British officials and troops was protected by a 'cordon sanitaire', a building free zone, separating British and native areas. Unable to own or inhabit land within the boundary of colonial cities, local people settled on the periphery. As long as settlements were sufficiently far away from colonial cities as to pose no health threat, there was little concern about planning for the physical or social conditions of the workers or the resources upon which they were living.

With the collapse of European colonial control, particularly in Africa and Asia, during the middle of the twentieth century, newly independent governments were unable, and unwilling, to restrict the influx of rural people to the city. Urban populations grew rapidly through migration, and informal settlements, such as the much-documented Kibera in Nairobi (Umande Trust Kibera 2007) or Dharavi, Mumbai (Dyson 2012), expanded as their conditions deteriorated. The migrants in such settlements left behind not only their physical land but also the activities and practices which had formed the basis of their survival mechanisms and value systems and which imbued that land with a specific culture. These settlements, and the many others which have sprung up both as a result of, and in support of, economic growth in the developing world in recent years, are now the sites of conflicting landscape cultures. This chapter suggests that the sociocultural control, managed through planning and land laws of colonial governments, can be seen again in the manipulation and control of the landscapes of the urban poor by city authorities adopting neo-colonial ideals.

Conflicting landscape rationales

In recent years, globalisation and international trade have brought economic growth to many cities of the Global South, with resultant rapid physical development. This has dramatically affected the form and use of landscape, not least by increasing urban land prices in many developing cities. For example, India's economic liberalisation, and the arrival of multinational corporations, raised land prices in Mumbai to be amongst the highest in the world by the middle of the 1990s (Nijman 2006). However, the city was also, and remains, home to some of the poorest people in the world, many of whom are rural to urban migrants who live in locations which are becoming increasingly economically significant for commercial development (Mukhija 2001; Payne 2001). It is, therefore, a city of contrasts not only in terms of economy but in terms of cultures and people's relationships with the urban landscape.

Despite economic growth in many countries, governments have been unable to ensure adequate housing or livelihood opportunities for many, if not most, of their rapidly growing urban populations. Poverty, once associated with rural agricultural life, has urbanised, as it did as a result of the Industrial Revolution in Europe in previous centuries (Dercon 2008; Ravallion et al. 2007). In the absence of adequate formal housing or employment, the urban poor do what they can to ensure their shelter, livelihoods and food security. However, their activities are at odds with the image of affluent modernity many city authorities seek to project. This has given rise to conflicts over access to, and use of, urban space born of what Watson (2003) refers to as the 'conflicting rationales' between different groups in the urban arena. These conflicting rationales are seen starkly in the clash of cultures which are thrown up in the context of the informal urban settlements and livelihood activities of rural to urban migrants.

Duncan (1989) argued that urban landscapes are culturally produced models of how the environment should look and behave. It could be argued also that they are culturally produced models of the way in which *people* should behave within them. They are not static, inert entities, but formed both to accommodate human behaviour and activity and as a result of these. This is now clearly recognised in the European Landscape Convention (CoE 2000) which understands change as an integral part of all landscapes. It is right, therefore, that urban landscapes should be constantly changing and evolving. However, difficulties arise in the prioritising, management and control of that change, particularly because of the speed at which it is occurring in cities of the Global South.

The urban cultural landscapes of the poor in the Global South are products of their collective memory, social networks and the logic of their survival behaviour within the city. They can be read as mental maps, drawn from personal experience and shared knowledge of locations good for trading and sites of potential daily employment (Figure 8.1). They are navigated through settlements where those with similar ethnic and cultural backgrounds might be found and through known places of safety for shelter (Tipple and Speak 2009). These landscapes include public spaces for growing crops or tethering animals for grazing (Mlozi 1997) and are crossed by a network of social relations and reciprocity which supports poorer people's daily lives (Speak 2011). The features, functions and processes of these landscapes are imbued with intangible, often religious, meanings, personal and communal

FIGURE 8.1   Men waiting on the roadside in Delhi, India, in a location where they know, through word of mouth, that they will receive handouts of food and news of potential labouring work for the day (Suzanne Speak).

memories and spiritual continuity, sometimes made tangible through rudimentary shrines. In short, the poor have a very visceral connection with their new urban landscapes, which relate directly to their physical and spiritual survival in the same way as the rural landscapes of their places of origin.

In contrast, in the major cities of the developing world, very different new cultural landscapes are being shaped and constructed, both conceptually and physically, by municipal authorities seeking to promote their cities as 'World Class' (Roy 2008). They are character-ised by the 'flagship' buildings of internationally renowned architects, stadia for international events, such as the Olympics or Commonwealth Games and sites of investment opportunity and development potential. Providing a canvas for the cultural landscapes of the new 'middle class' elites, they are constructed on commercial locations for the consumption of global products and services, and contemporary social and recreational activity such as nightclubs, restaurants and gyms (Atkinson 2003). They can be mapped by new, often gated, residential locations which are as much about residents' identity as part of a 'new elite' as they are about shelter, sustenance or home (see also Chapter 11). Thus, the new cultural landscape of the urban affluent is about public representation to the outside world rather than the ability of the landscape to support livelihood.

In some cases these new elite landscapes form the template for entirely new places. This is evident in both India and China, where economic growth has spawned a wave of new cities. For example, Gurgaon, near Delhi, is a new commercial and residential sub-city built in what was previously a rural location. It entirely reflects a globalised economic and aesthetic age. Although in a once rural location, it is entirely urban in nature and this 'manufactured' city shows no vestige of traditional Indian urban culture.

Planning and conflicting cultural landscapes

New and conflicting cultural landscapes are being negotiated in the built fabric of cities through spatial policies which prioritise the needs and desires of the more affluent (Fernandes 2004). These policies have become the guiding norms of planning, spread by an international flow of ideas and key discourse on, for example, sustainability or economic development (Healey and Upton 2010). However, Adger *et al.* (2001: 683) note that the use of dominant values within discourse to justify official actions may be inappropriate:

> since global discourses are often based on shared myths and blueprints of the world, the political prescriptions flowing from them are often inappropriate for local realities.

The use of international discourse to inform planning processes, policies and tools, without regard for their value or impact, allows little room for accommodating what Watson (2003) identifies as the 'deep difference' evident amongst urban populations. She identifies two types of difference. The first is inter-group difference, growing from social, religious, economic, gender and ethnic roots. The second 'deep difference' is that between the state and its citizens. This stems from the different value systems under which citizens and governments operate in many countries.

Despite the new affluence described above, many less affluent citizens in the Global South are operating within traditional value systems based on kin, religion, ethnicity and their relationship with nature (Groenfeldt 2003; Escobar 1995). However, Escobar argues that planning policy in previously colonised territories is increasingly driven by the imposition of values based on neo-liberal, market-driven rationality. Similarly, Fernandes (2004) notes that such rationality is manifested in the built fabric of cities through spatial policies which favour the needs and desires of the affluent. This ideology is encouraged by the policies of international agencies including the IMF and World Bank (Slater *et al.* 2006).

As a result, around the world, such urban policies have led to millions of urban poor people being evicted and/or relocated to newer, more peripheral locations, to release now commercially valuable land for development. However, beyond the demands of the market, evictions are also driven by political ambitions to promote cities as attractive, modernising global locations, internationally recognisable and culturally acceptable. Recognising this, Fernandes (2004) raises concerns that the poor, and other marginalised groups, are not simply excluded to free up valuable land but that their marginalisation is embedded within a political-discursive process which seeks to make them invisible. Sibley (1995) refers to this as 'spatial purification'. The urban landscape must be purified not only of the visual presence of the urban poor but of their daily actions, activities and cultures. These activities serve as constant reminders of the fact that the new cultural orthodoxy of the urban landscape – commerce, consumption and globalised aesthetic – has failed to eradicate poverty or to bring about a sociocultural shift in a significant proportion of the population.

Case studies of cultural landscapes of the urban poor

The following two case studies highlight the way in which poor rural to urban migrants establish themselves in the city, creating new cultural landscapes relevant to their needs, skills, knowledge and values. The case studies focus first on the landscapes of housing in India and then on landscapes of livelihood in Peru. However, the issues they highlight are relevant across the developing world. The case studies, and voices within them, are drawn from over a decade of fieldwork in informal settlements.

Case study 1: Kusumpur Pahari, India, and the cultural landscapes of housing

India's recent economic boom offers limited formal employment for rural migrants and housing policy has failed to produce adequate, affordable housing. As a result, out of a degree of desperation, the migrants must construct their own dwellings and grasp at any livelihood opportunity they can find. It was against this backdrop that, in the city of Delhi by 2000, nearly 50 per cent of the housing stock comprised of illegal, informal development, much of it in slum settlements erected by migrants. One such settlement is Kusumpur Pahari, a well-established, 30-year-old slum and home to around 15,000 people.

The landscape of Kusumpur Pahari has grown organically in a location offering easy access to work. It assumes a form quite different from the compartmentalised spaces of affluent areas. In the formally planned landscape of the city, the different activities of production, consumption or social interaction are increasingly given their own locations (office centre, shopping mall, gym, club) which are detached from the dwelling and often from the neighbourhood (Ellin 1997). In Kusumpur Pahari no such compartmentalisation is evident. Domestic, caring and productive activities are conducted in shared public space, which forms a significant arena for the development of reciprocity so vital to a broad range of daily life functions. The layout comfortably accommodates the overspill of daily household activities into a multifunctional, supportive urban landscape, where domestic activities merge with productive, social with political, public with private. New knowledge learned in the city blends with old to provide livelihoods. Activities such as drying produce before taking it to market, preparing, cooking and selling food, tailoring, small-scale manufacturing, and the very urban activities of rag picking and recycling, all take place in the public areas outside the private dwelling. Tipple (2005) notes similar situations in a range of developing countries.

In Kusumpur Pahari, as in most slum settlements, the dwellings are small and private space extremely limited. The public space of the street becomes part of a household's semi-private arena such that it is perceived as a safe and secure place much as it would be in the rural villages from which migrants came. Thus, public space becomes valuable storage and domestic space where people feel at liberty to leave their belongings, trusting that they will not be taken. Although the streets are public, they constitute the private 'territory' of extended households so that they become almost part of the houses. In the evenings, they are used for socialising and, at festival times, for celebration. Kellett and Bishop (2006) note this also in Kampung settlements in Bali.

The small, organically developed landscape in Kusumpur Pahari fosters the cultures of reciprocity and intergenerational, inter-household support. For example, Figure 8.2 shows an

FIGURE 8.2   An older lady who is cared for in the public space of the settlement (Suzanne Speak).

older lady who spends her days resting on a *charpoi* (traditional bed frame) outside her family's house while the family are out at work. She is cared for by neighbours who pass the time of day, bring food and ensure she is comfortable. She commented:

> it is good, I am happy here ... I can call to my neighbour if I need anything. People always come to talk with me, bring me my food ... I keep an eye on the children. I like to see the sky, people, not be inside all the day.

In this lady we see a culture of engagement with, and support through, the landscape of the settlement very far removed from the new gated estates of single-family dwellings and high-rise apartments which are constructed for the new, aspiring, urban middle classes.

Although born of desperation, the new landscapes of the urban poor are not merely a representation of their struggles for shelter and survival. They also embody and express joy and delight, as we seen in the response of the older lady above. As the cultural landscapes of social and spiritual communities, they are imbued with the resonance of merged histories and sometimes lost locations. In an era of commercialised leisure and cultural activity, they offer free sites for the observance of religious and spiritual traditions, festivals and celebrations. For example, Figure 8.3 shows how some female migrants from Southern India decorate the area outside their houses in Kusumpur Pahari with salt at festival time.

Case study 2: Villa el Salvadore, Peru, and the cultural landscapes of agriculture

In 1995, the President of Peru, Alberto Fujimori, introduced a land law designed to stimulate and reward development through private sector investment. It resulted in a significant change

FIGURE 8.3 Salt decoration on the ground in Kusumpur Pahari (Suzanne Speak).

to the rural landscape (Zimmerer 2002; Escobar 1995). Smaller farms in fertile lowlands were bought out and converted for large-scale, intensive food production. Coupled with this, the country experienced over three decades of civil unrest brought about by the 'Shining Path', a Maoist guerrilla insurgent organisation. The result was large-scale rural to urban migration as people moved to cities, especially Lima, in search of safety and work. Against this backdrop, the failure of successive governments to provide adequate housing has resulted in the development of major informal settlements in the desert around Lima. One such settlement on Lima's fringe is that of Villa el Salvador (Figure 8.4), which is the result of mass land invasions which began in 1970 as many migrant families left the Peruvian highlands. The district is 35 km² situated in the vast, empty sand flats around 32 km south of the city. The land is poor quality, arid, barely fertile sand, sloping from the hills inland to the Pacific coast. It is now home to over 380,000 people.

Although it has established itself as a permanent residential area, many people still have no legal tenure to the land. Services, including electricity and sanitation, are available in the more well-established areas, thanks to the efforts of the settlers. However, the settlement is continually evolving and life in the desert is harsh for new households. Yet their very existence there alters the nature of the landscape from a peripheral, deserted place to a place of intense human activity; urban, if not urbane. Nevertheless, it offers little in the way of employment. Thus, the settlers have multiple and complex livelihood activities, including paid labour in the city, self-employment, reciprocity, hawking and urban agriculture, which form a significant part of livelihood strategies.

Although the occupation of Peru's desert coastline can be traced back many millennia, in modern times it has been a barren land (Moseley 1992). Nevertheless, within this harsh environment, the urban poor are now creating a new cultural landscape through settlements and, in particular, from agriculture and horticulture, through collective activity, indigenous knowledge and a shared desire to 'green' the desert, not only for food but for a sense of community and delight.

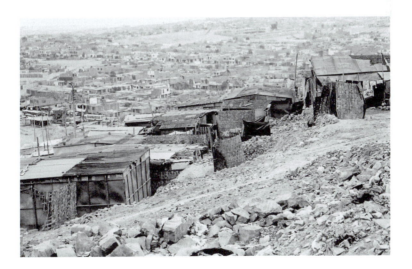

FIGURE 8.4   Villa el Salvador, Peru (Suzanne Speak).

The term 'urban agriculture' covers a range of farming and animal rearing activities at different scales within the urban and peri-urban area (see for example Mougeot 2000; Quon 1999). It can include everything from a household's subsistence farming on their own plot or a scrap of public land, to production in excess of household need being sold to supplement other income, to larger-scale commercial farming for profit (Mwalukasa 2000). It has been common in countries of the developing world for centuries, where climate and transport conditions meant that food had to be produced locally.

Scholars have noted the value of urban agriculture in coping with the negative economic impacts of structural adjustment programmes (Rogerson 2003; de Zeeuw 2002; Binns and Lynch 1998); temporary emergencies such as civil war, economic crisis and natural disasters (Nugent 2002: 86–87; Mlozi 1997); and food crises (Abdulsalam-Saghir and Oshijo 2009: 38); as well as the longer-term pressures resulting from climate change (Stringer *et al.* 2010). All these factors are present in Villa el Salvador, making agriculture a logical livelihood activity.

As new groups of households move in to the settlement, despite their rudimentary dwellings, lack of services, insecurity and poor livelihoods, one of the first activities to take place is planting at both household and community levels. The strong presence of NGOs in the settlement encourages this. Over time, individual and collective agricultural and horticultural activities in the desert produce a hybrid cultural landscape where new urban living and facilities mesh with traditional cultures and beliefs about the land and landscape as provider – Pachamama – Mother Earth.

Working with one NGO, the environmental network 'Red Ambiental', community members have collaborated to design public gardens and growing spaces. The plan they provided was what, in contemporary cities of the developed world, would be labelled as a community garden (see Figure 8.5).

FIGURE 8.5 Community model for 'common field' growing areas in Villa el Salvador (Suzanne Speak).

However, in conversation about the rationale for the plan, it became clear that it more accurately reflected the traditional 'common field' agriculture of the rural Andes. The common field tradition originated, in part, as a means of support during colonial times, when peasant farmers were required to pay labour tribute to the ruling elites. Having shared, common fields allowed herders to be located closer to the village, reducing the need to travel and freeing time for them to undertake agricultural tasks and share the labour tribute required. It was also a means of 'periodically reallocating land among the have-nots so all could bear an equal share of the tribute burden' (Godoy 1991: 409). This history is echoed in the words of one woman interviewed about the plan for the community garden who noted that, by having a community area for growing food:

> people can support each other, some have to go to the city for work, some have no time, we all have a hard life here . . . This way we can look after each other's crops . . . we can all share the land, working together, it's better.

The logic which underpinned the development of common field agriculture centuries ago is the same which maintains the culture in Villa el Salvador today. People still need to split their time between labour in the city and working the land, and not all households have the same access to land or the same ability to work and maintain it. Thus, a collective approach is as relevant now, on the city's fringe, as it was 200 years ago in the rural Andes.

Agriculture is established for food security, certainly; but equally, if not more, importantly, it is established for delight. The growing of flowers, particularly at an individual household level, seems as important to some settlers as building a better dwelling. Figures 8.6 and 8.7

FIGURE 8.6 Flowers planted 'for Pachamama' in the garden of a rudimentary dwelling of straw mats in Villa el Salvador (Suzanne Speak).

FIGURE 8.7 Flowers planted to differentiate the road from the 'claimed' land of the dwelling plot and to identify the dwelling (Suzanne Speak).

show how people have planted flowers in and around their most basic dwellings. This requires the investment of time and some, albeit little, money.

When the author asked why flowers had been grown and not food, the resident of the house in Figure 8.6 commented: 'Food you take; flowers are for giving, for the land, for Pachamama.'

The resident of the dwelling in Figure 8.7 commented: 'people should know, this is my home, my land now. I am proud of my land, the flowers are to say that this is mine'.

Landscape, control and the perception of deviance

Despite the logic of their construction the housing and livelihood landscapes of rural migrants are perceived, and often treated by the authorities, as deviant. This is demonstrated by the way in which official policies deal with informal housing and livelihood activities, especially urban agriculture.

Informal housing, such as that in Kusumpur Pahari, is under constant threat of demolition, especially when the eyes of the world are focused on the city, because the settlement is seen as an eyesore. In an example where demolition has actually taken place, Newton (2009) argues that the major housing and relocation project of the 'Breaking New Ground' strategy in Cape Town, which purported to be an effort to adequately house the urban poor, could more accurately be seen as a beautification project ahead of the 2010 FIFA World Cup.

Similarly, in Delhi in the run-up to the 2010 Commonwealth Games at least 140,000 people were evicted from slums around the city to support efforts to improve the city's image (Hazards Centre 2005). Some were relocated to what was presented as a 'better' location. In November 2002, the Municipal Corporation of Delhi (MCD) began moving the residents of several slum settlements on the edge of the Yamuna River to a relocation colony at Bhalaswa Jahangir Puri, some 25 km from their original location in the city. The relocation settlement is on 193 acres of low-lying, poor-quality land. No services, facilities or housing were provided and the area offers no form of employment. People were moved there with no consideration for the grouping of households by cultural, ethnic or religious background.

Eventually a more structured plot allocation was put in place and households were allocated dwelling plots of between 12 and 18 square metres for an average household size of six people. This is less space than most had in their city slums. People have struggled in the decade since then to construct their own dwellings and a new community. Some have managed to construct reasonable, brick-built houses. Equally, many remain in makeshift dwellings of tarpaulin and board. Figure 8.8 shows the extremes of these dwellings. Where possible, residents have recreated some of the more organic public spaces of the slum settlements and re-established a sense of community.

However, worse may yet be to come. The MCD has developed plans to overlay the area with a grid pattern of three- or four-storey blocks of flats, with stair access but no lift. These will provide around 16,987 flats of the same small size as the original plots (with no possible addition of a second floor). The plans for the settlement also include major and minor roads of standard dimensions (for an area where virtually no one has a car) and a number of large, formal parks and public areas. This demonstrates a complete lack of understanding of the housing and livelihood cultures of the urban poor and their relationship with the land

FIGURE 8.8   Rudimentary and better dwellings in Bhalaswa relocation colony, Delhi (Suzanne Speak).

and landscape of their neighbourhoods. It compartmentalises the domestic, caring, social and productive activities into the same rigid spatial layout that suits more affluent communities. It does little to support or encourage the vital reciprocity and community spirit which develops through the shared use of public space and which enables the older lady in Kusumpur Pahari (discussed earlier) to be cared for by neighbours. Indeed, one might ask how, without the benefits of a lift, such a lady would be able to leave her home in the type of new housing proposed.

The Peruvian migrants in Villa el Salvador fare better in that they may escape eviction, but this is largely because their settlements are already in peripheral locations on land of little commercial value and which is difficult to build upon. Nevertheless, even here, the official intervention is not to provide water and sanitation but to overlay the settlement with a formal layout and impose regulated plot sizes. Figure 8.9 shows one part of Villa el Salvador

FIGURE 8.9 Lines in the sand drawn by municipal authorities setting out plots in Villa el Salvador (Suzanne Speak).

where the plot demarcation lines can be seen drawn in the sand. While this may improve conditions in the longer term, in the short term such intervention in informal settlements can often be damaging to livelihoods and cultural heritage by overlaying a series of unhelpful conditions. Kamete (2007) suggests that such conditions may be based on residual ideas of a utopian urban form embedded in planning systems inherited from colonial governments.

Relocation settlements are inevitably sited on the periphery of the city. Their very location exacerbates the residents' poverty, limiting their ability to access the low-paid, low-skilled work as labourers and domestic workers, which they have come to the city to access. Different livelihood strategies therefore must emerge in these peripheral places. People establish small enterprises, but distance from the city means that small manufacturing or tailoring are not viable as goods cannot be taken to market. In Bhalaswa, residents established a small, informal market at the edge of the road near the settlement in an attempt to earn money and provide a service to their own community. However, the authority had the small makeshift stalls demolished and removed, saying that the settlers should use the formal market which was too far away and therefore too expensive to be viable.

As we have seen in the case of the Peruvian settlers, urban agriculture has an important role to play. However, the regularisation of their settlements brings not only formal plot sizes but also some regulations about appropriate, acceptable behaviour. While not all urban agriculture is prohibited, keeping of livestock is restricted, ostensibly for public health reasons.

As in the Peruvian case, people in Bhalaswa expressed a desire to undertake small-scale urban agriculture for food security. When this was discussed with officials, one noted:

Interviewee: [Bhalaswa] is an urban extension, not a rural place, it's not appropriate, they can go to the market to buy their food, they don't need to grow it, beside, the land is not good.
Interviewer: surely, with a little help and investment it could be improved a little, so that they could grow some crops, or even just if you provided some fencing to help control the livestock that might help?
Interviewee: This is not a farming area, we don't want to encourage them to be farming and keeping livestock, this area is for housing . . . they are not in the slums now, *they must learn to live properly*.

Conclusion

As cities of the Global South develop and expand, there exists a cultural struggle for territory between the urban poor migrants, who are essential to this development but excluded from it, and city authorities and more affluent groups for whom it is designed. The struggle involves an overlapping of physical structures, memories and narratives as each group seeks to express both their real, and their desired, cultural identity within the landscape.

The contraction and control of the realm of the urban poor is frequently presented as an economic decision. The justification is that the land is needed for the physical development associated with economic growth. However, the expulsion of migrants from the city space in Delhi to free up valuable development land does not require them to be relocated so far from their livelihoods in the city. Other approaches are available and well documented as good practice. For example, *in situ* upgrading, as undertaken in some other cities can maximise the value of the land for a range of income groups, while retaining the valuable services of rural migrants for the city and its more affluent occupants.

In situ upgrading also helps to retain the social networks and sociocultural relations which have developed in informal settlements. Some informal settlements can be relatively long lived. For example, Dharavi in Mumbai, India, began in the early years of the twentieth century and Kibera, in Nairobi, Kenya, dates back to the late 1800s when the Imperial British East Africa Company forced native Kenyans out of the city. Just as any long-term formal settlement, they can develop both tangible and intangible heritage. Indeed, some have called for Dharavi to be given World Heritage Site status (Brugman 2009).

If relocation of settlers is essential, there are a range of alternative methods of ensuring adequate housing, rather than overlaying upon them a rigid land use and housing design. Jain (2003) considers the planning system in Delhi to be too inflexible to support the urban poor. Certainly this singular approach, compartmentalising productive and domestic arenas, does not work for rural migrants, whose relationship with the landscape outside the dwelling is more fluid and critical to their survival strategies.

Peruvian migrants might escape eviction, but even here the official intervention is not to provide water and sanitation but to overlay the settlement with a formal layout. The priority, it appears, is not to provide rural migrants with the benefits of an urban lifestyle but to 'tidy up' the settlement in line with what is perceived as the development of an urban landscape appropriate to their vision of the new, modern city, stipulating plot sizes, building regulations and acceptable activities. In doing so, they condemn migrants to a hybrid landscape of liminality (Speak 2011). They are not able to aspire to the promise of the contemporary urban and are forbidden from recreating the rural past. They are, effectively, once more excluded from the landscape of the (neo-)colonial city.

However, what is truly revealed by examining authorities' reactions to the new cultural landscapes of the urban poor, is a lack of recognition of the cultural value of the continual, dynamic moulding and remoulding of urban landscapes of survival. The European Landscape Convention upholds a broad understanding of 'cultural landscapes' which validates not only the outstanding but also the ordinary as being central to the formation of shared heritage and identity. This validation is lacking in the approach of many governments in the Global South. Indeed, it might be argued that their approach sees landscape not as a valid representation of cultural identity, incorporating a story of both desperation and delight, but as a political tool with which to eradicate shared cultural identity and re-craft a prescribed new one in line with a globally recognised aesthetics. All those landscapes which do not subscribe to this, and the behaviours which lead to them, are perceived as deviant.

References

Abdulsalam-Saghir, P.B. and Oshijo, A.O. (2009) 'Integrated Urban Micro Farming Strategy Mitigation against Food Crises in Odeda Local Government Area, Ogun State, Nigeria', *Journal of Agricultural Extension* 13, 1: 35–44.

Adger, W.N., Benjaminsen, T.A., Brown, K. and Svarstad, H. (2001) 'Advancing a Political Ecology of Global Environmental Discourses', *Development and Change* 32, 4: 681–715.

Atkinson, R. (2003) 'Domestication by Cappuccino or a Revenge on Urban Space? Control and Empowerment in the Management of Public Spaces', *Urban Studies* 40, 9: 1211–1245.

Binns, T. and Lynch, K. (1998) 'Feeding Africa's Growing Cities into the 21st Century: The Potential of Urban Agriculture', *Journal of International Development* 10, 6: 777–793.

Brugman, J. (2009) 'Bestow Heritage Status on Dharavi', *Economic Times of India*, 19 March.

Christopher, A.J. (2001) 'Urban Segregation in Post-Apartheid South Africa', *Urban Studies* 38, 3: 449–466.

Christopher, J. (1988) 'Roots of Urban Segregation: South Africa at Union 1910', *Journal of Historical Geography* 1, 4: 151–169.

CoE (Council of Europe) (2000) *The European Landscape Convention* text, online. Available at: www.coe.int/europeanlandcapeconvention.

De Zeeuw, H. (2002) *The Role of Urban Agriculture in Social and Community Development*, online. Available at: http://www.ruaf.org (accessed 02 February 2012).

Dercon, S. (2008) *'Rural Poverty: Old Challenges in New Contexts', GPRG-WPS 072*, Global Poverty Research Group, Oxford: Economic and Social Research Council.

Dick, H.W. and Rimmer, P. J. (1998) 'Beyond the Third World City: The New Urban Geography of South-east Asia', *Urban Studies* 3, 12: 2303–2320.

Duncan, J.S. (1989) 'The Power of Place in Kandy: 1780–1980', in J.A. Agnew and J.S. Duncan (eds) *The Power of Place: Bringing together Geographical and Sociological Imaginations*, Winchester, MA: Unwin, pp. 185–201.

Dyson, P. (2012) 'Slum Tourism: Representing and Interpreting "Reality" in Dharavi, Mumbai', *Tourism Geographies* 14, 2: 254–274.

Ellin, N. (ed.) (1997) *The Architecture of Fear*, New York: Princeton Architectural Press.

Escobar, A. (1995) *Encountering Development*, Princeton: Princeton University Press.

Fernandes, L. (2004) 'The Politics of Forgetting: Class Politics, State Power and the Restructuring of Urban Space in India', *Urban Studies* 41, 12: 2415–2430.

Godoy, R. (1991) *The Evolution of Common-Field Agriculture in the Andes*, Cambridge: Cambridge University Press.

Groenfeldt, D. (2003) 'The Future of Indigenous Values: Cultural Relativism in the Face of Economic Development', *Futures* 35, 9: 917–929.

Hazards Centre (2005) *Blueprint for an Apartheid City*, New Delhi: Hazard Centre.

Healey, P. and Upton, R. (2010) *Crossing Borders: International Exchange and Planning Practices*, London: Routledge.

Jain, A.K. (2003) 'Making Planning Responsive to, and Compatible with, Reforms', *Cities* 20, 2: 143–145.

Kamete, A.Y. (2007) 'Cold-hearted, Negligent and Spineless? Planning, Planners and the (R)Ejection of "Filth" in Urban Zimbabwe', *International Planning Studies* 12, 2: 153–171.

Kellett, P. and Bishop, W. (2006) 'Reinforcing Traditional Values: Social, Spatial and Economic Interactions in an Indonesian Kampung', *Open House International* 31, 4: 58.

Mitchell, W.J.T. (2002) *Landscapes and Power*, Chicago: University of Chicago Press.

Mlozi, M.R.S. (1997) 'Urban Agriculture: Ethnicity, Cattle Raising and Some Environmental Implications in the City of Dar es Salaam, Tanzania', *African Studies Review* 40, 3: 1–28.

Moseley, M.E. (1992) *The Incas and their Ancestors, the Archaeology of Peru*, London: Thames and Hudson.

Mougeot, L. (2000) 'Urban Agriculture: Definition, Presence, Potentials and Risks', in N. Bakker, M. Dubelling, S. Gundel, V. Sabel-Koschella, and A. Zeeuw (eds) *Growing Cities, Growing Food: Urban Agriculture on the Policy Agenda*, Feldafing: Food and Agriculture Development Centre (ZEL), pp. 1–42.

Mukhija, V. (2001) 'Enabling Slum Redevelopment in Mumbai: Policy Paradox in Practice', *Housing Studies* 16, 6: 791–806.

Mwalukasa, M. (2000) 'Institutional Aspects of Urban Agriculture in the City of Dar es Salaam', in N. Bakker, M. Dubelling, S. Gundel, V. Sabel-Koschella, and A. Zeeuw (eds) *Growing Cities, Growing Food: Urban Agriculture on the Policy Agenda*, Feldafing: Food and Agriculture Development Centre (ZEL), pp. 147–159.

Newton, C. (2009) 'The Reverse Side of the Medal: About the 2010 Fifa World Cup and the Beautification of the N2 in Cape Town', *Urban Forum* 20: 93–108.

Nijman, J. (2006) 'Mumbai's Mysterious Middle Class', *International Journal of Urban and Regional Research* 30, 4: 758–775.

Nugent, R. (2002) 'The Impact of Urban Agriculture on the Household and Local Economies', in N. Bakker, M. Dubbeling, S. Guendel, U. Sabel-Koschella and H. de Zeeuw (eds) *Growing Cities,*

Growing Food: Urban Agriculture on the Policy Agenda – A Reader on Urban Agriculture, online. Available at: http://www.ruaf.org (accessed 13 January 2012).

Payne, G. (2001) 'Urban Land Tenure Policy Options: Titles or Rights?', *Habitat International* 25, 3: 415–429.

Quon, S. (1999) *Planning for Urban Agriculture: A Review of Tools and Strategies for Urban Planners, Cities Feeding People Report 28*, Ottawa: International Development Research Centre.

Ravallion, M., Chen, S. and Sangraula, P. (2007) 'New Evidence on the Urbanization of Global Poverty', *Population and Development Review* 33, 4: 667–701.

Rogerson, C. (2003) 'Towards Pro-Poor Local Economic Development: The Case for Sectoral Targeting in South Africa', *Urban Forum* 14, 1: 53–79.

Roy, A. (2008) 'The 21st-Century Metropolis: New Geographies of Theory', *Regional Studies* 42, 4: 69–86.

Sibley, D. (1995) *Geographies of Exclusion*, London: Routledge.

Slater, R., Ashley, S., Tefera, M., Buta, M. and Esubalew, D. (2006) *PSNP Policy, Programme and Institutional Linkages*, London: ODI.

Speak, S. (2011) 'Point of No Return: Exploring the Issues which Trap Migrants in a State of Homelessness in the City', *International Development Planning Review* 32, 3–4: 225–243.

Stock, R. (1988) 'Environmental Sanitation in Nigeria: Colonial and Contemporary', *Review of African Political Economy* 15, 42: 19–31.

Stringer, L., Mkwambisi, D., Dougill, A.J. and Dyer, J.C. (2010) 'Adaptation to Climate Change and Desertification: Perspectives from National Policy and Autonomous Practice in Malawi', *Climate and Development* 2, 2: 145–160.

Tacoli, C. (1998) 'Rural-Urban Interactions: A Guide to the Literature', *Environment and Urbanization* 10, 1: 147–166.

Tipple, A.G. (2005) 'The Place of Home-based Enterprises in the Informal Sector: Evidence from Cochabamba, New Delhi, Surabaya and Pretoria', *Urban Studies* 42, 4: 611–632.

Tipple, G. and Speak, S. (2009) *The Hidden Millions: Homeless in Developing Countries*, London: Routledge.

Umande Trust Kibera (2007) *The Right to Water and Sanitation in Kibera in Nairobi, Kenya*, Nairobi: Umande Trust.

Watson, V. (2003) 'Conflicting Rationalities: Implications for Planning Theory and Ethics', *Planning Theory and Practice* 4, 4: 395–407.

Zimmerer, K.S. (2002) 'Common Field Agriculture as a Cultural Landscape of Latin America: Development and History in the Geographical Customs of Land Use', *Journal of Cultural Geographies* 19, 2: 37–63.

9

LANDFILL AND DISASTERSCAPES IN THE WASTELANDS OF INDONESIA

Joe Duffy

Introduction: ideas of place, land and identity

As an artist my own practice is concerned with ideas of place. I consider how assumptions of landscape and identity can be addressed and questioned in film and photography and how they can be represented and investigated through visual exploration and documentation. This has led to a body of filmic, installation and photographic work focusing on natural and man-made disasters in the Indonesian archipelago. In this chapter I examine issues that arise when the landscape and environment are considered through creative media fields and academic research. I pose questions about how space is constructed and changed, how cultural relationships can be informed by such work and how the invisible can be made visible. The area of focus is the garbagescape;[1] how it is used as a resource and its relationship to urban poverty in Jakarta. My main case study is the landfill site of Bantar Gebang on the outskirts of Jakarta, the attendant trash-picking communities and the illegal settlement of Senen where many of these workers live. The chapter then moves from this man-made disasterscape to consider the landscapes created by natural disasters such as the Merapi and Krakatau volcanic eruptions in Indonesia and to examine how economic considerations and tourism coexist with concepts of the contemporary sublime and apocalypse.

My consideration is of place as 'not just a thing in the world but a way of understanding the world' (Creswell 2004: 11) while exploring concepts of location and context. In my practice I use artist approaches that map human experiences and process emotional encounters through moving images, photography and installation-based art forms. I examine issues of disaster, urban poverty, community and recycling in Indonesia and then use my own work to discuss how the contemporary sublime can be found in the wastelands explored, how sense of place can be understood and the plight of the urban poor revealed.

The context of place

Indonesia, with its estimated population of 239 million people, 17,500 islands and 600 languages, has its political economic and administrative centre in Jakarta. The 25 million population of this sprawling megacity expands over a huge area of 6,418 km²

(Cybriwsky and Ford 2001: 199). As it has grown, this city has fused together many areas in the region including Depok, Bogor, Jakarta, Bekasi, Tangerrang Puncak and Cinanjur, giving rise to the acronym *Jabodetabekpunjur* (Sassen 2001). Resulting in an urban environment, 'most of the time without blueprint' (Kusumawijaya 2005: 23), Jakarta then appears as a massive conurbation, extending and expanding over a number of municipal zones with new forms of landscape emerging. The growing population of this expansive urban space produces thousands of tonnes of garbage daily and aids the development of new material topographies. The waste ends up dumped in the landfill site of Bantar Gebang in Bekasi at the city's periphery with its attendant manual recycling industries forming communities, activities and engagements that link and aid the growth of the city.

To understand the formations of Jakarta's topographies Stephen Cairn's work on 'Desa Kota Urbanism'[2] provides an innovative way to look at Jakarta's city structure. This term refers to the combination of rural and urban uses found through examining a cross section of the city. In Jakarta it includes such places as the landfill site at Bantar Gebang, the farming areas nearby, the kampongs (settlements), shopping malls, gated communities, ministry buildings and highways. The rural urbanity found in Jakarta reflects the way different cultures have come together within this large urbanised area, and the way this city acts as a mirror of the Indonesian republic and a 'city-world' (Augé 2008: xii). The structure and functioning of the city is influenced by the influx annually of 250,000 migrants to Jakarta from other parts of the Indonesian archipelago, bringing with them different dialects and cultural expressions. Many of these migrants have arrived from rural areas and now live in makeshift shelters, tents and illegal settlements, joining the existing high numbers of urban poor and forming new squatter kampongs (Cybriwsky and Ford 2001).

An estimated 5 per cent of the Indonesian population are slum dwellers. They live under highway overpasses, between railway tracks and riverbanks, they face insanitary conditions, lack of access to education, contend with health and safety hazards, and eviction from the settlements by the police. In many cases they occupy sites outside those that anthropologist Marc Augé has described as non-places (Augé 2008). These spaces can be described as the non-relational sites of transaction, the locations of movement, of transit, of shopping and consumption such as hotels, motorways and airports. The non-place of the railway system is the train station, with the slum area by the side of its tracks in Senen, Jakarta, partially characterised as being outside this non-place, and inhabited by outsiders; people that do not belong anywhere. These spaces are contested, occupied by migrant workers from Sumatra and the Sunda area, speaking a mixture of Sundanese and Javanese, rural migrants from the Merapi volcano area, the margins of Yogyakarta, and other industrialised cities of Indonesia, from Surabaya to Manado. The train track community exists on the margins of established urban villages, precariously placed as temporary dwellings in danger of eviction and the hazards of the passing trains.

The moulding of the scattered archipelago into a unified modern nation has brought together characteristics of the global and local within the kampongs. These are traditionally understood to refer to villages, but are now found as settlements within the city. This local/global duality or 'glocality' (Meyrowitz 2005: 21) can be seen in the informality, poverty and rural traditions of the kampong within the urban domain. The layout of these spaces comprises low houses, shacks with tin roofs, narrow gangs (alleyways) and open sewers: a visually eclectic layout, as revealed within my photographic work and discussed in detail later. More affluent and middle-class housing is found within gated communities, apartment blocks and suburban housing strips interspersed between the illegal settlements and slums.

The reflection of this glocality is found within the temporary shelters of the informal settlements represented in my photograph 'Dwelling' (Figure 9.1). It is an image of home in the illegal squatter settlement next to the train tracks in Senen, Jakarta, the occupants of which work informally as *pemulungs*, trash-pickers collecting and recycling waste. The Jakarta area is estimated to have between 350,000 and 450,000 trash-pickers working informally, with two million of the nation's population surviving on a living made from the waste-recycling activity.

'Dwelling' (Figure 9.1) shows the site of two homes against the wall that separates one urban village from the train tracks. The detritus of recycled trash is evident in the shack structures, homes made of cardboard, wood, polystyrene sheets and plastic; these are objects of waste salvaged from the streets and landfill sites. Domestic environments with clothes hanging out to dry and potted plants reveal the living conditions of the urban poor in an area where older couples, solo old women, and young families survive in abject poverty.

'Dwelling' (Figure 9.1) reveals the eclectic formation of urban living where the inhabitants show resourcefulness in the hybrid use of materials and bricolage tactics to reuse and recycle the outputs from the 'product-system' (de Certeau 1984: xxiv). This bricolage is expressed in a collage-like appearance of the material structures that makes place and form identities from the reused debris and waste. Thus the urban sprawl here is loaded with textures, details and traces of the past that can be seen in the architecture, in layered forms of detritus and the hybridity of the makeshift kampongs. Capturing the layout of the

FIGURE 9.1 Dwelling (Joe Duffy 2011).

FIGURE 9.2   Irene: still from *Landfill* (Joe Duffy 2011).

settlement is a particular concern within my photographic works, which reveal the materials of waste used as a resource and in the development of community and home.

This understanding of home is further informed through interviews with the local population and evidenced in the still from my film *Landfill* (Figure 9.2). This image shows Irene sitting outside her home, a structure made of salvaged materials, placed just a few feet from the trains that frequently pass by. Like many people in this settlement, she listens out for the warnings of a bell ringing to indicate the coming trains; a repetitive sound that can be heard every few minutes that forms part of an acoustic ecology (Schafer 1977). This sound punctuates the other sounds of working activities such as the noise of plastic cups being cleaned for recycling, the chatter of play and motorbikes on the streets nearby.

Irene was in her late teens when she followed her friends to Jakarta from the rural area outside Cankrindgan. She worked as a maid to a wealthy family for a number of years, helping them to raise their children until she was no longer needed within the household. With no skills, no family and no financial means to return home she found herself destitute and she drifted into work as a *pemulung*, collecting trash such as plastic cartons and cardboard. Now, Irene can no longer return home since her village was destroyed by the volcanic eruption of Merapi. As part of the older generation which is devoid of internet and social media skills and therefore marginalised from the chain of communication, she no longer knows if she has other relatives in the Kaliaurang area; she relies on writing letters to addresses that may no longer exist.

The 120-hectare landfill site of Bantar Gebang in Bekasi, West Java, is the dumping ground of most of Jakarta's waste, at least 6,500 tonnes daily. The landscape of rotting rubbish here extends as far as the eye can see with more than 8,000 trash-pickers working the site to collect aluminium tins and cans, glass items, plastics and paper while bulldozers on the top of the mounds move rubbish forever forwards. The still image in Figure 9.3 shows the working

FIGURE 9.3 *Landfill* still (Joe Duffy 2011).

zone of the site which is the newly forming landscape of trash created by the waste trucks arriving from Jakarta. The quadrant is the name given to the busiest section of this garbages-cape where masses of individuals work through the waste to collect materials for recycling and for collection and transportation to the villages at the edge of the landfill site.

Non-organic waste such as plastics and metals is collected and sold to *Lapaks* (middlemen) in Bantar Gebang (*Jakarta Post* 2010). One of them, Ngadenin, aged 42 of Ciketing Udik, a village next to the site, buys recyclable objects such as toys, cardboard boxes and plastic bottles, depending on the material, for between Rupiah (Rp) 700 and 1,800 per kilogram, from the garbage pickers. He remarks, 'I manage 15 trash-pickers who are skilled at sorting recyclables ... the final products are sold to recycling factories across Java'. The informal economy of *pemulung* and structures built around the recycling of waste help to establish a network of contacts through the city stretching to areas such as Senen. This also forms a hierarchy of trash culture; of middlemen and bosses, of exploited labour, of rural to urban migration with the trash-picking acting as an incentive for the urban poor to earn income.

This use of the landscape of trash as a resource also creates a visually layered landscape, ordered and structured according to the colours of different materials. The image 'Sorting Zone' (Figure 9.4) depicts this hierarchical layout of place, and indicates the process of recy-cling and use of space by illustrating the tactic of appropriation and bricolage mentioned earlier. This trash-picking is a continuous operation in a landscape once characterised by paddy fields and agricultural land but now *desa kota*, a hybrid space of kampongs and recycling sites that includes cemeteries and mosques, homes made of rummaged items from the tip and now comprising a housing area of small one-room huts and 2,000 family units.

Garbage becomes a metaphor for the difference between the rich and poor, where, as revealed in an interview with the *Guardian* (Hodal 2011), riches can be found in trash. 'For a long time, it was hard to go back home', says Sar Jok, 59, a gangmaster who sells items found

FIGURE 9.4   Sorting Zone (Joe Duffy 2011).

in the landfill to recycling companies. 'People would say, why do you live on the dump? It smells bad, you smell bad.' The stench of rotting garbage in 35-degree heat is extreme, as are the swarms of flies and the cesspit pools that collect during the rainy season. The reminder of abjection is thus palpable and it acts as a social stigma for the trash-pickers. 'When we smell we are taken over by otherness. Hence the sense of smell is considered a disgrace in civilization the sign of lower social strata' (Adorno and Horkheimer 1979: 184). Sar Jok's comments indicate the attitude to those who work with the trash, but his response sheds light on the financial opportunities that trash provides that helps him overcome the social stigma: 'when they saw I made good money, their opinions changed'. The mountain of rotting waste thus offers a living to those enterprising enough to take it on and is enough to prevail over the adverse perceptions of working in the tip.

Visual representations of waste and poverty

The representation of the relationship between the urban poor and waste within visual culture can communicate information about alternative ways of living because 'art exhibitions and anthologies are primary vehicles for the production and dissemination of knowledge today' (Greenberg *et al.* 1999: 1). The relevance of art in this context offers the possibility of new perspectives and ways of looking at the world, 'without coming to terms with our art, we can scarcely understand ourselves' (Danto in Freeland 2001: 13). One of the roles of art is its ability to question and define culture and our understanding of the world. This viewpoint of artists and film-makers is of key importance in my discussion.

The CP Biennale[3] of 2005, with its subject of Urban/Culture curated by Jim Supangkat,[4] provided a contextual and artistic interpretation of the urban domain from Indonesian artists responding to issues of the environment, politics and realities of the city space. The contextualisation of the urban/culture subject resulted in a number of viewpoints and perspectives that have enabled artists' work to be considered as creating dialogue regarding the issues and representations of Indonesia. As an observer, *flâneur* and witness, I am an outsider and present such a viewing position on the trash-pickers' situation. My work provides images of the experience of being immersed in the senses, sights, smells and sounds of the wastelands and sites of disaster visited. The extension of the experience to an audience is discussed later through Jonas Bendiksen's (2012) installation that takes slum environs as its subject. Other forms of documentary and narratives of waste can also be found in work such as Lucy Walker's *Waste Land* (2010). This is based around the experiences of Brazilian trash-pickers. The only projects that deal specifically with Indonesia or the Global South in detail include *Bantar Gebang* (2005) by Jeroen de Rijke/Willem de Rooij. As a detached, objective, one-shot, ten-minute film it observes life slowly taking shape over the garbages-cape. It uses a fixed camera position that borrows its aesthetic from landscape painting. The slow unfolding movement of activity in the landfill gives a 'sense of discontinuity and on the viewer's part probably a slight sense of shame at deriving aesthetic pleasure from such a picture' (Lütticken 2000 unpag.). The film is contemplative and peaceful and the opposite to the harsh reality depicted. It is this contradiction of beauty, horror and otherness found by the voyeur that invokes the sublime and creates such an uneasy aesthetic and uneasy viewing experience. *Position Among the Stars* (2010), directed by Leonard Retel Helmrich, is the final in a trilogy of films that depict urban poverty in the slums of Indonesia through the eyes of a Jakarta family. These films chart daily life from the historical events of Soeharto's downfall through the rise of Islamic power with this latest film showing aspects of corruption and the widening inequalities and gaps in the social fabric of Indonesia. Visually they provide a view on consumerism within the family, with single, fluid camera movements travelling over the landscape and characters. The realities of urban living and slum environs connect with the dialogue, the voices and snippets of conversation with residents and their views.

Jonas Bendiksen's documentation of slums takes place as an artistic installation entitled *The Places We Live* (2005). This recreates the experience of a personal encounter with slum dwellers where the Jakarta slum is represented in one room with all four walls built of rear projection screens. The space that is created in this installation is occupied by five households while a sound recording containing statements from the inhabitants is showered down from the overhead speakers. Between each display of a household, images and soundscapes of the outside environment surround the visitor in an immersive environment. The cramped space is tidy and domesticated, organised like most homes, with pictures, wallpaper and other decoration indicating that 'no matter what economic condition people are living in, not only do we need to create shelter over our head, but to create a home' (Bendiksen 2012). Even under the most extreme living conditions, the familiarity of home and of images which indicate a need to belong can be found.

In the Peripheries exhibition that took place in Manchester in 2011,[5] my own work was a 12-minute film *Landfill* (2011), created by following the tactic of walking and mapping the urban character from the landfill site to the squatter settlements using film, photography and Global Positioning System (GPS) tracking. A multi-screen installation with a projector/monitor was set up using visual information composed of moving images and animated

GPS tracking data. The GPS data was recorded so as to reveal the spaces from a mapping and satellite perspective and then intercut with films of the landscapes. The work was then structured using narratives recorded from the inhabitants and layered sounds from the environments encountered. The photographic body of work is also formed using images taken while walking along the pathways and rubbish mounds tracing homes and the remnants of home; the *unheimlich*[6] of the garbagescape.

This work provides images that relate to architectural historian Anthony Vidler's use of the term 'uncanny' to represent imagining the loss of home in a post-industrial society. The feelings of powerlessness in certain spaces are pivotal to understanding the relation between the identity and psyche through a subjective sense of place within the city (Vidler 1992). The wastescape can be seen as combining these paradoxical ideas of the urban/rural, incorporating ideas of absence/presence and thus formulating an uncanny geography (Rogoff 2000). The relationship of the uncanny to landscape can be better understood by referring to Rogoff's use of Freud's original notion of *unheimlich* or the uncanny as 'that class of the frightening which leads back to what is known of old and long familiar' (Freud 1955 [1919]: 220). When this concept of the uncanny is applied to geographical under-standings it enables us to reflect on the visual dislocation of ruined landscapes, abandoned, contaminated and waste sites. Images based on such thinking can reveal another view of the landscape; its abjection and its ability to be read as socially significant text. It can also help us reflect on the effect that such visual images have on us and on our lifestyles in a consumer-based society.

Wastescapes display the unwanted material of society, but also the socially constructed cultural residue along with the broken child's bag on the landfill site and the rotting rubbish. In images of wastescapes, the 'dark and the unsanitary is transmogrified into the sublime and the beautiful' (Shohat and Stam 2002: 52) and objects evoke an uncanny sense where the everyday and familiar are made strange. Viewing partial objects can induce apocalyptic anxiety by apparently returning, as if from some great catastrophic event, altered and removed from their natural state. The objects are resurrected by the trash-pickers from discarded and subverted items and the excess of waste. In my images and installations the objective is to reveal the relationship of the viewer to the images, not only as one of a perceiving subject and to display landscape as constructed, but to remind us that we are both a result of environment and that we make the environment. The landfill and its waste are here social text revealing the redemption of the low and the marginal which are resurrected and reinvented in the hybrid bricolage of the place-making activities of home and settlement.

This landscape of residue is therefore also one of much ambiguity as it signifies consumer demand, economic and technological progress but also the excess of this through waste and the issues of its removal. The constantly changing landscapes that are the garbagescapes represent the materiality of economic and cultural conditions and inequalities. Artistic explorations of these landscapes highlight notions of population increase, consumerism, recycling and sustainability as well as the lives of those who rely on such landscapes for their livelihood.

Natural, man-made disasters and the sublime

One of the first writings on the sublime effect of the landscape is found in Edmund Burke's *A Philosophical Enquiry into the Sublime and the Beautiful* (1988 [1759]). The discourse is of awe, terror and horror, strong emotions, a strange unsettling aesthetic, developed by the tourist gaze of the eighteenth century in which stormy seas, craggy mountains, war, horror and violence were part of an aesthetic spectacle. Traditionally these feelings were linked to the body being overwhelmed by nature, overpowering the senses, resulting in 'a sort of delightful horror, a sort of tranquility tinged with terror' (Burke 1988 [1759]: 101). Natural disasters and man-made catastrophes create specific forms of landscapes that are marked physically but can also render a subjective effect on the viewer. The nineteenth-century ideas of the sublime highlighted anxieties about the destruction of nature through industrial forces and the industrialising economy of Western Europe. In a similar way, in the wastescape of Bantar Gebang there is a sense of nature becoming denaturalised, of artificial hills made up of the detritus of consumption and the waste as a surrogate of nature.

When considering the idea of the apocalyptic landscape in Indonesia it is possible to consider both natural and man-made disasterscapes. The 2010 Maplecroft Natural Disaster Risk Index (NDRI) ranked countries in order of economic exposure to natural hazards and listed Indonesia as second below Bangladesh. Its location on the 'ring of fire' (the name given to the chain of islands situated on a geological fault line) makes it prone to tectonic shifts and movement in the earth's plates. The earthquake and resulting tsunami of 2004 and the volcanic eruption of Merapi in 2010 are examples of particularly severe recent natural catastrophes. The infamous Krakatau volcanic eruption of 1883 killed an estimated 30,000 people and has become etched on cultural memory, replayed through fiction and detailed through historical and geological fact. There have also been numerous man-made disasters created as the result of industrial activity such as the Porong mud volcano of 28 May 2006. This was caused during the search for oil by a company, Lapindo Brantas, which drilled into the geological crust triggering an eruption of boiling mud. This catastrophe displaced over 75,000 people and destroyed a number of villages.

Some of these man-made catastrophes have created brownfield sites, or contaminated spaces now unfit for occupation due to human activity, industrial use and pollution. These large areas of land are often seen to be outside the spatial order of the urban but they have also been recognised as being linked, thus 'the brownfield site is continuous with the fabric of the city, as the city is likewise continuous with the slum' (Himanshu quoted in Gans and Weisz 2004: 4). Such thinking connects to the notion of the wastescape and slum settlements of the *pemulung* which does not regard such areas as apart, but integral to the city and its functioning. Portrayal of such landscapes of waste and disaster can help provoke increased Western awareness of the environmental crisis, of waste management, capitalist excess, poverty in the Global South and of nature being replaced by our packaged detritus. Apocalyptic narratives are also created from current concerns of melting ice caps, climate change, global warming, landscapes of industrialised pollution, nuclear waste dumps, brownfield sites, oil spills and expanding megacities. When visually confronted with such sights they have the ability to induce feelings of awe and fear and provide an encounter with the sublime (Thompson 2007). Here political, physical and social disruptions are reflected in the impacts on the landscape, and link back to Burke's original conception of the sublime and issues of industrialising society. The cataclysmic here is found in the apocalyptic images of the landfill and the wastescapes of Indonesia as metaphors for the end of the world, the result of economic policies and structures. The effects of capitalism are highlighted by Zizek as the end of value, the collapse of communities, the death of the spiritual and veneration of nature. He says: 'We talk all the time about the end of the world but it is much easier for us to imagine the end of the world than small change in the political system, life on earth maybe will end, but somehow capitalism will go on' (Mead 2012). The irony of this is that when faced with the harrowing effects of capitalism, of supply and demand, exploited labour and environmental degradation, we seem to be able to create narratives of the end of existence more easily than the end of capitalism.

The impacts of capitalism on the landscape are found in the brownfield sites, in the extremities of urban poverty and even in the detritus washed up on the shores of Krakatau island. The scarred landscape evokes the sublime in 'Krakatau' (Figure 9.5) with its spewed volcanic debris from the Krakatau volcano and its visual delineation of organic and inorganic matter. This is reflected in the debris in 'Rakata' (Figure 9.6) seen as shipwrecked remnants of the end of the world. Washed up on the shoreline are sandals, bags, clothes, televisions, all manner of waste thrown overboard, waste from shipwrecks, or rubbish spills from the Sumatran or Javan mainlands. Along with the landfill sites of Bantar Gebang and Senen and the destroyed villages around Merapi where the economic reality, the sublime and uncanny landscapes meet, I find the material for my work. It is here that I also find the apocalyptic reminders of volcanic disaster which act as visual prompts for the end-of-the-world narratives.

Wastescapes and tourism

While traversing the slums of Jakarta, the landfill of Bantar Gebang and the sites of natural disasters in Indonesia I do so as a *flâneur*. Placing myself at these sites I, like other tourists,

FIGURE 9.5 Krakatau (Joe Duffy 2012).

FIGURE 9.6 Rakata (Joe Duffy 2012).

encounter an apocalyptic sense of dread in the sublime awe of such sites. There is also the pleasure of being witness to this otherness, presented in works such as the short film *Merapi* (Figure 9.7).

The scene in Figure 9.7 is of a journey with the viewer being led through the forest which is burnt and eroded by the volcanic eruption of Mount Merapi which occurred in November 2010. The portrayal is aided by narrative excerpts provided by Christian Awuy, the Merapi Volcano rescue team. The image in Figure 9.8 ('Trees') signifies this charred landscape, and the violent force of nature, but also evokes the uneasy aesthetic which renders a strange beauty to the landscape.

An estimated 400,000 people were displaced from their villages which were destroyed or made unsafe by the 2010 volcanic eruption lava flows, pyrotechnic blasts and ash clouds. Many of the displaced villagers spent weeks in temporary shelters and football stadiums, while others migrated to the cities in search of work. In the narrative excerpts in the film *Merapi*, the local mountain rescue guide expresses views on landscape relationships, the eruption as signifier of dissatisfied nature and the excesses of greed and consumer frenzy; they blame capitalism for the disaster. Spaces and temporalities collide as a second screen reveals the tragic effect of the natural disaster on the nearby villages, the burnt motorbikes, melted radios, broken cutlery, ash-filled birdcages, roofs and walls blown away. The displaced familiar objects found in photographs such as Figure 9.9 ('Teapot') are reminiscent of the

FIGURE 9.7 Stills from *Merapi* (Joe Duffy 2011).

FIGURE 9.8 Trees (Joe Duffy 2011).

waste images of the landfill site found in Figure 9.10 ('Footwear') which refers to the displaced icons of home and domesticity now rendered obsolete, decayed, dead and haunted by absence of normality.

The wasted, ruined, destroyed landscapes also provide opportunities for a more voyeur-istic strand of tourism often described as dark tourism, grief tourism or poverty tourism. Research on dark tourism has been informed and encouraged by the impact of a global-ised media to compress, digitise and forward news and images instantly. Representations of disaster are quickly circulated around the world. Other new forms of leisure activity are emerging such as the tours of brownfield sites and disaster zones. These so-called dark tourist experiences provide a sense of identity and realisations of the fragility of survival 'in the

FIGURE 9.9 Teapot (Joe Duffy 2011).

FIGURE 9.10   Footwear (Joe Duffy 2011).

face of violent disruptions of collective life routines' (Rojek and Urry 1997: 110). Such access to places where death, destruction, tragedy or historical events took place, or are still taking place, can have a significant effect on our lives (Tarlow 2005).

The destroyed village of Kaliurang is preserved as a memorial and site for tourist visits with many of the remaining villagers inviting visitors to photograph their homes for a fee or to buy DVDs of a short documentary on the subject of Merapi. The organisation of these tourist visits to the Merapi volcano site is carried out by local travel agencies in the nearby city of Yogyakarta in Java. As far away as Jakarta and Surabaya trips are offered to the 'Merapi eruption Special'. Edwin Himna of the Association of the Indonesia Tour and Travel Agencies is reported as suggesting that demand is high for such experiences: 'In the new volcano tour package, we'll take customers to explore the closest village to the peak and see how bad the devastation is, then we'll take them to a river to watch cold lava flood past' (Rondonuwu 2010). A tourist who travelled to see the site of destruction remarked 'I drive everywhere to witness such things because by seeing them I am always reminded to be thankful that God still spares me' (Rondonuwu 2010). The pleasure of the visit illustrates awe of the sublime and thankfulness for survival.

The 'poorism' tours in Jakarta run by Ronny Poluan of Jakarta Hidden Tours visit slum areas. Participants in the tours are guided around a number of communities to visit health centres, offices, homes, factories and schools to discuss social issues and poverty concerns with workers and inhabitants. In doing so they can observe how communities work together. Money charged for the tours goes towards the school, local community, officials and tour guides with some portion of the fees going to slum guides, the non-governmental organisations (NGOs), the families in the slums and the community groups visited. As a visitor to the Hidden Jakarta Tour stated, 'It was refreshing to escape from all the shopping malls!'. The tour offers an insight into the conditions of the urban poor in Jakarta far away from the shopping centres, bars and hotels that tourists commonly frequent and the opportunity to learn about the hidden aspects of Jakarta. While providing some financial assistance to slum communities, it also aims to educate tourists to experience the city in a new way and also to see beyond the sense of otherness in the slums; community, home and place is valued the same here as elsewhere.

Gotong Royong and community action

Amidst the wastescapes of environmental disaster, landfill sites, urban slum settlements and volcanic disaster sites there is a sense of hope. The clichéd view of the countries of the Global South from a Eurocentric perspective is that aid, agency and knowledge are needed to deal with a perpetual state of social and economic crisis caused by corruption and disorder. Aid from Western countries is seen as a saving force. The reality is that successful self-help and invention takes place locally. This is often supported by the work of NGOs and team building within communities. *Gotong Royong* is the term given in Indonesian for this reciprocal exchange of assistance which was promoted under Soekarno's regime from 1945 to 1967. This was traditionally applied to rural tasks such as agricultural planting and house building, but it is now witnessed in the community action projects of the Urban Poor Linkage (Uplink), the Mercy Corp, Urban Poor Consortium and projects rebuilding live-lihoods and homes in the disaster zones of Aceh and Merapi. One programme in Merapi is the Go Green Campaign which involves tourists buying seeds and plants from locals to plant in the villages to encourage regrowth of vegetation.

Uplink is one of the groups working to develop pro-poor social and cultural systems. It has economic networks throughout 14 Indonesian cities which aim to establish a national network of urban poor communities. Uplink works to help survivors of disasters rebuild their communities, to set up emergency shelters and to work through *gogur gunung*, mutual cooperation or teamwork strategies to clear rubble. The proactive approach of these organisations such as Uplink and Urban Poor Consortium enables a community approach for the reconstruction of lives and communities rather than providing charity or food handouts. The concern is with development at the local level; an approach especially useful when government involvement is minimal.

The result of such projects is to invest emotionally into the well-being of communities and to alter perceptions of the environment. It also helps people shape their own landscapes. It means that communities keep ownership of the economic means of production of goods made from recycled materials. An example of this is the small factory structure of the Sekolah Kami School. This site in Bekasi, West Java, is built on brownfield land, reclaimed from waste ground comprised of the residue of trash collected and sorted from the landfill site. The school includes gardens, a fish pond, classrooms, music rooms and a small factory where the children of trash-pickers and informal economy workers learn transferable skills and crafts. The school gains funds from the sale of the products made by the children.

In another project based in Jakarta, the Healthy Places, Prosperous People/Lingkungan Sehat Masyarakat Mandiri project (HP3), set up by Mercy Corps, aims to improve sanitation issues and extend local knowledge and problem solving. The outcomes of the project included photographic exhibitions of work carried out by the children in the Penjaringan slum who have drawn their environment and photographed the garbage. The aim is to encourage others in the community to improve their landscape.

Conclusion

As national garbage management coalition head Bagong Suyoto claims: 'The 2008 Waste Management Law requires the city to encourage the grass roots to manage waste independently, but in reality, they have failed' (*Jakarta Post* 2010). This means more projects like HP3 are needed to create liveable landscapes and manage the growing problem of waste, estimated to be around 53.5 million tonnes a year by 2020, and the expansion of the site at Bantar Gebang, which has already grown to 200 hectares.

In Western countries we hide waste in large holes; in Indonesia the waste produced is seen as a resource. The waste and the people whose livelihoods depend on the waste build a new landscape, not of consumption but of recycling. These landscapes provide a living, have meaning, can be seen to have beauty, particular sounds, smells and a sense of place. All this can be revealed and is being revealed by artists in innovative ways which can reach both insiders in these landscapes and those outside, to whom such landscapes are often seen as representations of the apocalypse. Such activities can show how a new living is provided for communities out of material that is rejected by others. The garbage creates a new landscape where beauty and many meanings can be found. But this is very different to the rural landscapes which new colonists of the garbagescapes have been forced to leave.

In my work I hope to indicate that something positive can be found even in such places of apparent ugliness and disaster. Through my examination of these garbagescapes and the natural and man-made disasterscapes of Indonesia the characteristics of these new landscapes can be understood and the cultures which create and are created by such landscapes examined. The environmental crisis and expanding growth of cities such as Jakarta, the landscape of natural and man-made disasters and the effect these have on place-making, on mobility, and concerns for the future leave the potential for artistic narratives to be continually unfolding.

Notes

1 Garbagescape refers to the physical landscapes comprised of detritus, trash and garbage, with disasterscape as a topography marked by cataclysmic events that affect the environs or human communities. Disasterscape is used here to indicate the landscape affected by natural disaster as well as the effects of economic and ecological disruption.
2 For more information on the *desa kota* and other projects examining the planning and mapping of Jakarta see Urban Archipelagos (2011).
3 The CP Biennale is organised by the CP Foundation. It aims to focus on hidden, marginalised or dismissed realities, particularly in Asia (see www.biennale.cp-foundation.org/index.html).
4 http://biennale.cp-foundation.org/2005/cpb_2005_essays.html.
5 The Peripheries exhibition, co-curated by Joe Duffy and Tongyu Zhou, included work from artists exploring concepts of place in Asia. www.peripheries.co.uk.
6 *Das Unheimliche* – the opposite of what is familiar; a Freudian concept which indicates that something can be familiar and foreign at the same time thus providing perception of something being uncanny, or uncomfortably familiar (see Freud 1955 [1919]).

References

Adorno, T. and Horkheimer, M. (1979) *The Dialectic of Enlightenment*, London: Verso Editions.

Augé, M. (2008) *Non-Places: Introduction to an Anthropology of Supermodernity*, London: Verso.

Bendiksen, J. (2012) *The Places We Live*, online. Available at: http://www.theplaceswelive.com/ (accessed 10 February 2012).

Burke, E. (1988 [1759]) *A Philosophical Enquiry into the Origins of the Sublime and Beautiful*, Oxford: Oxford University Press.

Cresswell, T. (2004) *Place: A Short Introduction*, Oxford: Blackwell.

Cybriwsky, R. and Ford, L. (2001) 'City Profile: Jakarta', *Cities* 18: 199–210.

de Certeau, M. (1984) *The Practice of Everyday Life*, Berkeley: University of California Press.

Freeland, C. (2001) *But Is It Art? An Introduction to Art Theory*, New York: Oxford University Press.

Freud, S. (1955 [1919]) 'The Uncanny', in J. Strachey (ed.) *The Standard Edition of the Complete Psychological Works of Sigmund Freud*, Volume XVII, London: The Hogarth Press.

Gans, D. and Weisz, C. (2004) *Extreme Sites: The Greening of Brownfield Sites*, London: John Wiley & Sons.

Greenberg, R., Ferguson, B.W. and Nairne, S. (1999) *Thinking about Exhibitions*, New York: Routledge.

Hodal, K. (2011) *Living off the Landfill: Indonesia's Resident Scavengers*, online. Available at: http://www.guardian.co.uk/world/2011/sep/27/indonesia-waste-tip-scavengers (accessed 23 October 2011).

Jakarta Post (2010) *Bantar Gebang Trash Mountain gets 4,500 Tons Bigger Daily*, 23 July, online. Available at: http://www.thejakartapost.com/news/2010/07/23/bantar-gebang-trash-mountain-gets-4500-tons-bigger-daily.html (accessed 18 March 2013).

Kusumawijaya, M. (2005) 'Indonesian Urbanity: A Project in Progress, without Blueprint', in J. Supangkat (ed.) *Urban/Culture*, CP Biennale 2005, CP Foundation, Museum Bank Indonesia: Kepustakaan Populer Gramedia.

Lütticken, S. (2000) *The Fictions of De Rijke/De Rooij*, online. Available at http://www.smba.nl/en/newsletters/n-56-bantar-gebang/ (accessed 9 February 2011).

Mead, R. (2012) 'The Marx Brother: How a Philosopher from Slovenia Became an International Star', *The New Yorker*, online. Available at: http://www.lacan.com/ziny.htm (accessed 5 February 2012).

Meyrowitz, J. (2005) 'The Rise of Glocality: New Senses of Place and Identity in the Global Village', in K. Nyiri (ed.) *A Sense of Place: The Global and the Local in Mobile Communication*, Vienna: Passagen, pp. 21–30.

Rogoff, I. (2000) *Terra Infirma: Geography's Visual Culture*, London: Routledge.

Rojek, C. and Urry, J. (eds) (1997) *Touring Cultures*, London: Routledge.

Rondonuwu, O. (2010) *After Eruption Indonesia Turns to Disaster Tourism*, online. Available at : http://www.thejakartaglobe.com/home/after-eruption-indonesia-turns-to-disaster-tourism/412073 (accessed 15 January 2011).

Sassen, S. (2001) *The Global City*, 2nd edn, Princeton: Princeton University Press.

Schafer, M. (1977) *The Tuning of the World*, Toronto: Knopf.

Shohat, E. and Stam, R. (2002) 'Narrativizing Visual Culture: Towards a Polycentric Aesthetics', in N. Mirozoeff (ed.) *The Visual Cultural Reader*, London: Routledge, 2nd Edn. pp. 36–59.

Tarlow, P. E. (2005) 'Dark Tourism: The Appealing "Dark Side" of Tourism and More', in M. Novelli (ed.) *Niche Tourism – Contemporary Issues, Trends and Cases*, Oxford: Butterworth-Heinemann.

Thompson, K. (2007) *Apocalyptic Dread: American Film at the Turn of the Millennium*, Albany: Millennium State University of New York Press.

Urban Archipelagos (2011) *Cultures of Legibility Project*, online. Available at: http://archipelagos.eu/description.html (accessed 10 May 2011).

Vidler, A. (1992) *The Architectural Uncanny*, Cambridge, MA: MIT Press.

10

ALTNEULAND

The *old new land* and the new-old twenty-first-century cultural landscape of Palestine and Israel

Shelley Egoz

Introduction

Israel has seven cultural properties meeting the requirement of Outstanding Universal Value on the UNESCO World Heritage List.[1]

Despite the existence of several outstanding and culturally significant properties within the occupied Palestinian territories (oPt), a list of recommended Palestinian sites faced challenges that were not related to criteria eligibility or any UNESCO procedures for inscription of properties. The Palestinians had not been full members of the cultural body of the United Nations, UNESCO, until 1 November 2011 when, in spite of political objections of the United States and Israel, the General Conference voted to admit Palestine as a member. The move now allows the Palestinian government to apply for historic monuments and locations to be classified as World Heritage. And indeed, the city of Bethlehem's Church of Nativity and Pilgrimage Route have since been inscribed (29 June 2012).[2] Yet, the ramifications of the results of the November 2011 vote embody more than a bureaucratic change. The meanings embedded in old and new landscapes of Israel and Palestine are fraught with ideologies, emotions and nationalistic contestation.

The dialectics ingrained in the New versus Old motif are a predominant component in the narrative of Zionism, the foundation ideology of the State of Israel and the landscape narratives of the region. The Middle Eastern coastal area known as Palestine until 1948 when the State of Israel came into being, is a historic geopolitical asset.[3] The geographic location of the region, at the crossroads of Africa, Asia and Europe, is a passage between East and West, offering a considerable strategic advantage for empires and colonisers. Contestation and transformations of dominations for thousands of years have left a rich and diverse array of cultural landscapes, many of them 'recycled' on the same sites. The place is also a geotheologic centre, known as the 'Holy Land' for Christians around the world and the focus of spiritual and emotional significance in particular for Jews and Muslims, culminating in the potent symbolism of Jerusalem, the main sacred city. The place labelled by Israelis *Eretz Israel* or *Eretz Zion*[4] is perceived as the Jewish ancestral promised biblical land; it is both a pervasive abstract ideal in Jewish tradition and has been tangible contested political territory between immigrating Jews and indigenous inhabitants over the last 100 years. The unusual status of the State of Israel, a state established for a particular ethnicity/religion, revolves around the New/Old binary. The old cultural landscapes are set in mythological Jewish antiquity (Zerubavel 1995), existing along with modern twentieth-century resettlement by Jews. Through potent ideological education a complementary relationship between the new and old landscapes is naturalised into Israeli consciousness to represent historic ownership side by side with a pioneering ethos, a modern national revival and progressive future-oriented development. Past and present are combined through what is promulgated as 'Jewish Heritage' or 'Biblical Archaeology' and the Zionist vision: investment in the landscape that includes modern town planning, architecture and infrastructure to support a growing Jewish population. In between these two discourses lies another, unacknowledged, landscape layer: that of the Palestinian villages destroyed in 1948 that are at the core of the Israeli–Palestinian conflict today (see Egoz 2008, 2011a; Kadman 2008; Benvenisti 2000; Khalidi 1992).

Palestine, in the twenty-first century, is known as the West Bank (of the Jordan river) and the Gaza Strip, territories that have been occupied by Israel since 1967.[5] In this chapter I will use the term occupied Palestinian territories (oPt) when discussing contemporary Palestine, so to avoid confusion between the area historically named 'Palestine' which includes the land of the State of Israel. The 'old' cultural landscape of oPt is similar to that of Israel as these two competing national entities are part of one historic region inducing contestation over heritage claims to that landscape (Ibrahim 2011).

The twentieth and twenty-first centuries' new landscape of the occupied Palestinian territories (oPt) is significantly different in character to the new cultural landscape of Israel underpinned by the Zionist vision of progress. The dynamics of the Zionist enterprise drove the establishment of two new landscape types in oPt: refugee camps and Israeli settlements. Refugee camps, a landscape of overcrowding and poor infrastructure, are the result of the 1948 war in which hundreds of thousands of Palestinians were displaced from their towns and villages in the land that became Israel. The new cultural landscape of oPt is also typified by a growing number of Jewish settlements since the 1970s. The illegal building and ongoing expansion of Jewish settlements in oPt, controversial as its moral justification might be within centre-left Zionist political discourse in Israel and the eyes of the international community, is in line with the Zionist ethos of creating a modern developed landscape to accommodate Jews.

The new and old landscapes of Israel and oPt are thus intertwined, attesting to the impossibility of landscape to be confined within political boundaries (Egoz *et al.* 2011; Egoz 2010) (Figure 10.1).

Zionism and the landscape of Palestine

Zionism, the ideology validating the existence of the State of Israel as an ethnically Jewish state, was a national-cultural revolutionary movement that began in the nineteenth century among the European Spring of Nations and movement for nations' self-determination.[6] At the time several Jewish thinkers in Eastern Europe shared the political approach to the Jewish Problem (defined by Jews as anti-Semitism erupting in their persecution). Austro-Hungarian Jewish journalist Theodor Hertzl (1860–1904) is considered the visionary philosopher of the idea to materialise attachment of territory to a Jewish entity. In 1897 he convened the first Jewish congress in Basel, Switzerland, in which the revolutionary idea was launched. In 1902 Hertzl published his utopian novel *Altneuland* (*Old New Land*) in Germany. The idea of a new Jewish home in the traditional land of Palestine[7] gained momentum in the twentieth century

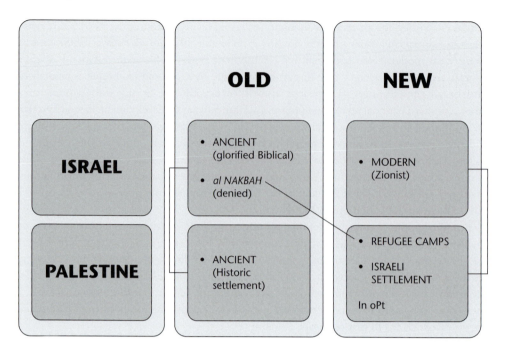

FIGURE 10.1   Relationships between the old and new landscapes of Israel and Palestine (Shelley Egoz).

with the ideological foundation of what is termed 'modern Zionism'.[8] It materialised in the 1948 establishment of the State of Israel in Palestine in the aftermath of the Nazi Jewish holocaust. Small-scale ideological colonisation of Palestine by Jews began as early as the 1880s after the assassination of the Russian Tsar Alexander the Third triggered violence and massacres of Jewish communities. In the course of the twentieth century, Zionist ideology gained momentum among secular Jews and drove further settlement. Despite the relatively small actual numbers of colonisers during the first half of the twentieth century, Jewish-European colonisation had a significant influence in terms of modernisation and its effect on the indigenous population and the landscape (Pappe 2004).

Zionism was also a revolutionary movement; it endorsed utopian ideals and visions and was in search of a new identity to substitute for Jewish religious values. During the twentieth century the indigenous landscape that was being dramatically transformed by Europeans became an identity-builder for the newly arrived Jewish immigrants. The new-old landscape theme became a means to try to root those who left the familiarity of their home landscapes and settle in a mostly desolate Middle Eastern landscape. Landscape and homeland are prevalent motifs in *Volk* nationalism. Yet Zionism differed from other nineteenth-century national movements, which strived to liberate people settled in their own land. In contrast the ideal of creating a new homeland in a faraway land had to be associated with an old ancestral land. At the beginning of the modern era, following Enlightenment, many Jews became secular and the traditional religious way of life that had bound Jews throughout the ages was losing its power. In order to mobilise as many Jews as possible, Zionism had to create new values and imagery that would maintain a Jewish identity (Liebman and Don-Yehia 1983). Equally, new values would have to support attachment to territory. One of these was the invention of a new Jewish stereotype, an antithesis to the exilic *wandering Jew* that has no roots. By giving primacy to working the land, the *New Jew* would become rooted. Land and farming land-scapes in particular thus gained symbolic dimensions (Egoz 1997). Transformation of landscape took on the notion of *Binyan* (building) both as a national ideal and a tangible activity and object (Chowers 2002). A pioneering ethos and its challenging engagement with an adverse landscape later became one of the modes that constructed a narrative of modern Israeli sense of place (Schnell 1998). The revolutionary liberation idea of the new Jew in the new landscape also diffused into the building of urban settlement.

Zionism saw in the international Garden City movement a utopian model to follow (Elhyani 2004). Tel Aviv, the first Hebrew town, was founded in that spirit in 1909 on the outskirts of the ancient town of Jaffa. In the mid 1920s, while Palestine was under British Mandate, Scottish town planner Patrick Geddes drew the master plan for Tel Aviv. During the 1930s and 1940s several Zionist immigrant European-trained architects contributed modernist designs, notably Bauhaus-inspired architecture (Figure 10.2). In 2003 Tel Aviv, coined 'The White City', was inscribed on the UNESCO World Heritage List due to its 'synthesis of outstanding significance of the various trends of the Modern Movement in architecture and town planning in the early part of the twentieth century' (Criterion ii) and epitomising an 'outstanding example of new town planning and architecture in the early

FIGURE 10.2 Mid-twentieth-century Bauhaus design in Tel Aviv, 2011 (Shelley Egoz).

FIGURE 10.3   Palestinian run-down neighbourhood in Jaffa, 2011 (Shelley Egoz).

twentieth century, adapted to the requirements of a particular cultural and geographic context' (Criterion iv).[9] The new White City, however, stands in contrast to the old Black City (termed so by Rotbard 2005), Palestinian Jaffa, that is included in the same municipality jurisdiction known as Tel Aviv Jaffa. While the White City of Tel Aviv earned its World Heritage status, the Black City is a denied *al Nakbah* landscape (Egoz 2008). The neighbourhoods of Jaffa, which still house parts of the indigenous Palestinian marginalised population who were not displaced in 1948, are relatively run down (Figure 10.3), whilst in contrast the core of the Palestinian Ancient City area has been appropriated and gentrified to accommodate an Israeli artistic tourist precinct. Gentrification of former Palestinian neighbourhoods is ongoing due to the aesthetic value and attractiveness of an Arab architectural style and the proximity to the Mediterranean Sea as a landscape asset (Figure 10.4).

All in all, under Zionism rural and urban settlement patterns were primarily based on European modernising paradigms which drove an effort to transform what was seen as a desert wilderness into a utilitarian landscape. The early twentieth-century settlers ascribed heroic value to the draining of wetlands, for example. Awareness of wetlands' biodiversity function and ecological value was lacking and the understanding of unsustainable consequences of greening the desert and increased development was limited at that time. In that respect, Zionists shared the conquest of the wilderness pioneering ethos of other settler societies such as New Zealand for example, that perceived an existing ecology as wilderness and valued dramatic landscape modification as progress (Egoz and Bowring 2004). At the same time, in Palestine, a similar attitude to landscape was coupled with a romantic reading of the local indigenous primitive landscape ascribing it to be the *biblical landscape*, thereby forming another symbolic vehicle to create an identity of Jewish belonging to an ancient land.

FIGURE 10.4 Gentrified Jewish neighbourhood in Jaffa, 2011 (Shelley Egoz).

The old 'biblical' landscape motif

The perception of the local landscape as *biblical* is rooted in an historic Christian European view of the land of Palestine. The landscape of Middle Eastern Palestine has lured Europeans for many centuries. Verbal and pictorial descriptions dating back as far as the end of the fourth century form evidence of its religious significance. Christian pilgrims' accounts of Palestine contained scenery descriptions that composed religious biblical narratives (Leyerle 1996). In cartography, the first printed maps of Jerusalem that were published between the fifteenth and eighteenth centuries reflected an ideological concept of the Holy City (Rubin 1992). At the beginning of the eighteenth century, the four-volume historical geography of the Old and New Testaments by Dr Edward Wells, a Church of England clergyman, published in Oxford, reinforced the construction of the biblical image of the landscape of Palestine (Butlin 1992). During the nineteenth-century age of reconnaissance, developments in travel facilitated visits to Palestine by many Western explorers such as geographers and archaeologists, several of whom produced graphic expressions depicting biblical place imagery. Some particularly worth mentioning here are British Royal Engineers Charles Wilson and Charles Warren, American biblical geography scholar Edward Robinson and British archaeologist Flinders Petrie. Artists William Barlett and David Roberts and architects Charles Barry and Thomas Allom visited Palestine and produced many biblical landscape illustrations (Figure 10.5). Other artists such as William and Edward Finden and J.M.W. Turner never set foot in Palestine but produced a biblical imagery based on Roberts' illustrations and the drawings of British architect Charles Barry. With the invention of the medium of photography in 1839, the first landscape photographs to appear in books were of Palestine, notably of biblical sites. Nineteenth-century

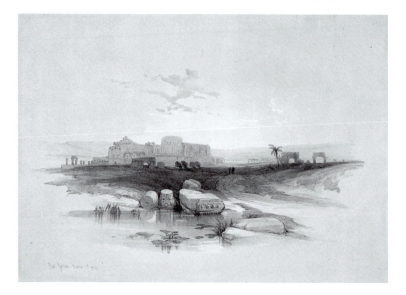

FIGURE 10.5 Painting of Beit Jibrin, Palestine, by David Roberts (1796–1864), Louis Haghe, lithographer (Public domain from Library of Congress).

British photographers, however, also utilised their cameras to depict the local Palestinian agricultural landscapes, villages and towns, which they believed represented the biblical landscape (Nir 1985). This Christian view provided fertile ground for a naturalisation of the old Biblical landscape theme into the new Zionist narrative (Egoz 2008).

Antiquity, ruins and the biblical landscape

The building of national identity was aided by an effort to ground Jews in the old landscape through the presentation of tangible archaeological findings. This provided evidence of the 'concrete documentation of the continuity of a historical thread' (Yeivin cited in Benvenisti 2000: 11) and legitimised the ideology of a *return to a fatherland*. Such a phenomenon is prevalent within nationalism; it was typical of nineteenth-century *Volk* ideologies in their search for a historical account of a connection to territory. In Zionism, 'Antiquity' was depicted as a glorious period in Jewish national history as opposed to the period of exile (Zerubavel 2002). Ideals strived to erase a recent past of exile and create a sense of belonging in a new setting through ascribing ancient biblical dimensions to the landscape. Bible mythology was promulgated as Jewish history, instilling a sense of belonging for Jews where land and land-scape are of particular significance. Today, the majority of Zionist Israelis, whether religious or secular, share the belief that the land they call *Eretz Israel* is first and foremost the historic land of the Jewish people.[10]

The ancient landscape came into public focus through archaeology, a discipline that gained extraordinary cultural prominence within Zionist values, later developing into a cult in Israeli society (Elon 2000). In 1928 settlers of a Kibbutz,[11] Beit-Alfa, in the Jesrael Valley in northern Palestine discovered a mosaic floor of a Jewish Synagogue dated back to the sixth century while digging an irrigation channel. This serendipitous finding became an opportunity to enlist religious Jewish themes, formerly rejected by modern Zionism that began as a secular movement, and to dig up 'remnants and relics of the glorious Jewish past' (Elon 2000: 300). The nation-state's political use of archaeology to claim territory based on historical continuity is not unusual but the extent of popular interest and cult-like enthusiasm for archaeology in Israel especially between the 1950s and the 1970s is unprecedented. 'Jewish' and 'Biblical' archaeology gained a secular-religion dimension. Similar to values embodied in landscape such as working the land (farming), archaeology became another symbolic glue to ingrain an attachment to land and claim historical ownership. Findings did not necessarily have to portray Jewish themes for Israelis to claim them; antiquities were described as biblical if they could be associated with Bible stories. Public interest in participation in archaeological diggings, collection of artefacts, museums and books published on Jewish archaeology helped to instil the sense of ownership of the land. Throughout the years the significance of archaeological finds became taken for granted and unquestionable. This has set in place a powerful ideological dimension, providing a sense of place which has bolstered communal Jewish nationalist identity grounded in the landscape.

Archaeological remnants of Ancient Jewish presence were also decisive elements in the creation of some of Israel's national parks (see Egoz and Merhav 2009). The cultural landscapes of these parks hold a didactic role in moulding identity through 'figuratively illustrating Jewish history while cultivating a new Israeli culture of recreation' (Efrat 2004: 81). Numerous of the sites have been occupied by various cultures throughout the centuries of settlement in Palestine. One such recent past landscape layer is that of what is known as the Palestinian *al-Nakbah* (the catastrophe)[12] (see Egoz 2008, 2011a). Over 100 sites of tourism and recreation in Israel include vestiges of depopulated Palestinian villages (Kadman 2008), but in contrast to the emphasis on Jewish heritage these landscapes are not considered worthy of preservation in Israel, despite the outstanding architectural value of some of the sites (Figure 10.6). This

FIGURE 10.6   The depopulated Palestinian village of Lifta on the outskirts of Jerusalem in 2006 (Shelley Egoz).[13]

approach to ruins of Palestinian villages is backed by protocols of the Israel Department of Antiquities and Museums that was established in July 1948. The department adopted the 1922 British Mandate definition of antiquities which referred only to man-made objects created before 1700 CE (Benvenisti 2000). Dwelling on antiquities reinforced a nationalist claim for the land and facilitated the denial of the last three centuries of an indigenous Palestinian landscape (ibid.). In the mid twentieth century those who were displaced from that landscape layer were resettled in refugee camps in Palestine.

The new landscape of oPt

Among the everyday lived-in contemporary landscape of oPt are two distinct landscape types: refugee camps and Israeli settlements (Figures 10.7 and 10.9). The original residents of the camp shown in Figure 10.7 came from the destroyed village of Beit-Jibrin on the western hills of Hebron. The village site is depicted on David Roberts' eighteenth-century painting of the biblical landscape (see Figure 10.5) and due to the site containing an array of ancient ruins and landscape assets from a diversity of cultures, most notably the Hellenistic period (third–second centuries BCE) and bell-shaped chalk caves from the Arab Period (seventh–eleventh centuries CE), it is today the declared Israeli National Park of Bet-Govrin.

Refugee camps

The refugee camps now house some of the 1948 uprooted persons from the lands that became the State of Israel. There are close to 800,000 refugees in the West Bank, a quarter of them live in 19 camps while the rest reside in towns and villages. In Gaza there are more

FIGURE 10.7 The refugee camp of Beit-Jibrin in Bethlehem, oPt, 2011 (Tim Williams).[14]

than one million refugees comprising three-quarters of the entire population; about 500,000 inhabit eight camps. The agency responsible for their well-being is UNRWA (United Nations Relief and Works Agency for Palestine Refugees in the Near East). UNRWA provides education, health services and some food distribution to the needy. Yet, refugee camps are landscapes of poverty. They are typified by high unemployment, unfit infrastructure of sewage and roads, shortages of water, overcrowding of housing and schools, and lack of open spaces[15] (Figures 10.7 and 10.8).

More than 60 years on from the 1948 displacement, the collective identity of Palestinian refugees and their descendants is comprised of the yearnings for and memories of their past homes' landscape (Peteet 2005). The ghost *Nakbah* landscape within Israel and the refugee camps in oPt share inherent paradoxes, the former as an unacknowledged Palestinian landscape where ruins have been appropriated to represent an Israeli biblical landscape (Egoz 2008), and the latter in their eternalised 'temporary' status. This duality is fundamental to understanding the complexity of the contemporary Palestinian landscape:

> Both the demolished villages and the refugee camps are extraterritorial spaces, not fully integrated into the territories that surround them. The former is [*sic*] legally defined as absentee property and the latter as a United Nations administered area, a sphere of action carved out of state sovereignty.
>
> Refugee life is suspended between these two ungrounded sites. Always double.
>
> *(DAAR 2011: 6)*

At the same time the overall landscape in oPt is fragmented. The 1993 Oslo agreement between Israel and the Palestinians guaranteed the occupied entity a right for self-governing

FIGURE 10.8 *Dheisa* refugee camp south of Bethlehem, oPt, 2011 (Tim Williams).

by a Palestinian Authority (PA). That area, however, is controlled by Israel through a division into three categories:

- Area A is in total control of the PA for civil affairs and security/law and order.
- Area B is under PA control for civil affairs and Israeli control for security.
- Area C, which includes 60 per cent of the land area, is under total Israeli control.

For Israel, breaking up any Palestinian territorial contiguity is seen as assuring its own security. Thus landscape structure is used as a form of social and cultural control and access is restricted through administrative and physical barrier landscape elements: checkpoints, roadblocks, fences and walls.[16] The most prominent invasive landscape feature is that of the Jewish settlements.

Jewish settlements in oPt

The Jewish settlements are strategically planned and located, and their expansion is managed according to long-term political and military agendas.

Settlement in oPt began after the 1967 war and Israeli conquests of neighbouring countries' territories. It started with right-wing ideologists, *Gush Emunim* (which translates as 'a Community of Believers'), a messianic group that was inspired by Rabbi Zvi Yehuda Kook's ruling that what they termed as the 'Liberated Territories' were holy parts of the land of Israel not to be handed over to non-Jewish sovereignty in any circumstances. As time went on Israeli governments encouraged non-ideological civilian settlement through the provision of economic benefits and mostly by supplying affordable housing. In 2011 there were about 120 settlements that varied in scale and character, from city neighbourhoods (e.g. around Jerusalem) to small ideological outposts, community settlements, small towns and three cities. Around 500,000 Israelis live in these settlements.

The landscape of the Israeli settlements of oPt is distinctly different from its indigenous surroundings. It stands out in its modern architectural character and the developed infrastructure that services its Jewish inhabitants. In terms of sustainability, these building developments have had significant negative impacts on the local ecology and human physical health. Deforestation and large-scale excavations (see Figure 10.9) and construction of roads carved into the hilly terrain resulted in destruction of local flora and fauna habitats (Isaac 2000). Sewage from settlements has been dumped onto neighbouring Palestinian land and in several cases wastewaters seeped into groundwater, polluting springs used by Palestinians (ARIJ 2008; UNEP 2003).

The Israeli developed landscape in oPt is coherent with the Zionist settlement ideology of the early part of the twentieth century that utilised the technique of *Homa Umigdal* (Tower and Stockade). *Homa Umigdal* is a Zionist settlement strategy that creates facts *in situ* in the context of a national struggle over land. The concept was conceived in the mid 1930s during the British Mandate in Palestine. Tensions evolving from the Arab Revolt of 1936, the first organised violent expression of Palestinian nationalist aspirations, drove the British to restrict Jewish settlement. In response, the Jews developed a 'defensive' settlement type to facilitate seizing land that was previously purchased by Jewish National Funds. Its goal was to create a physical geographic continuity of Jewish settlement in the landscape along the

FIGURE 10.9 The Israeli settlement of Modi'in Elite, built on Palestinian lands in oPt, 2010 (Courtesy of activestills.org).

valley axes. All operations were planned to materialise swiftly, in one day or overnight, to avoid British authorities preventing the establishment of settlements. The idea is ascribed to communal settlement member Shlomo Gur and was developed by architect Yohanan Ratner. Between 1936 and 1939, 57 such settlements were erected. The method was based on expeditious erection of a wall, 1.80 m in height, made of prepared wooden moulds to be filled with gravel and surrounded on the outside with barbed wire thus creating a 35 by 35 metre courtyard. A wooden tower that was also prepared in advance was erected and used as a guarding lookout. Inside the walled courtyard there were four sheds that could host 40 troops. Tactically, *Homa Umigdal* operations had three main objectives: enable defence to hold up until reinforcement would arrive; be in eye contact with other settlements; and make sure roads maintained free access.

Sharon Rotbard (2008, 2005, 2003) argues that *Homa Umigdal* has become an overarching paradigm of Israeli architecture, manifested in the design of neighbourhoods and settlements, planning of cities and also the underpinning metaphor of what he terms the industry of facts on site: the translation of political agendas into deeds. These include seizing of territories through a spatial positioning of settlements and infrastructure as well as the prioritisation of military and security considerations above any others and a skilled use of tools of modernity such as organisation, administration, prefabrication logistics, and media (Rotbard 2008: 36).

Homa Umigdal gained a mythological heroic dimension in Israeli society. Taught in schools as part of a glorified Zionist ethos, it has become ingrained into a national psyche as a positive symbol and a heritage legacy. The Zionist yearning has thus been transformed into a concrete landscape which is further reinforced by that action of the Society of Preservation of Israeli Heritage Sites (SPIHS), which includes a *Homa Umigdal* museum at *Gan Hashlosha* national park catering for domestic and international tourists and educational programmes.

At the same time, the new and old are intertwined in the landscape of oPt and the Palestinian rural landscape surrounding the Israeli landscape is also seen as a biblical landscape. Eyal Weizman (2007) comments on the paradoxical and ironic dimension of the way Jewish settlers in oPt view the landscape:

> The landscape, imbued with religious signification, establishes the link that helps people relive and re-enact religious-national myths in a way that juxtaposes, on the very same land, ancient with modern time . . . Within this panorama lies a cruel paradox: the very thing that renders the landscape 'biblical' or 'pastoral' – its traditional habitation and cultivation in terraces, olive orchards, stone buildings and the presence of livestock – is produced by the Palestinians, the very people whom the settlers would like to displace.
>
> *(Ibid.: 135–137)*

However this compound political nature of new and old landscapes is also present in the current heritage discourse of the PA.

The old heritage landscapes in oPt

The United Nations had in 1974 granted the Palestinian Liberation Organization (PLO) a United Nations observer, rather than member, status (Gelfond-Feldinger 2011). UNESCO and local Palestinian heritage experts had been working in the past few years on a list of potential heritage landscape sites in accordance with a 2002 Budapest World Heritage Committee's acknowledgement of the exceptional universal value present in Palestinian cultural and natural heritage landscapes (Daibes 2011). Yet, until 1 November 2011 the Palestinian proposal of the fourth-century Church of the Nativity in Bethlehem was unable to proceed because Palestine is not a State Party to the World Heritage Convention. While this prominent cultural property has since, as earlier mentioned, been inscribed, the account of Palestine's challenges in trying to nominate places to the World Heritage List is but one example of the political nature of the discourse on heritage between Palestine and Israel. The old cultural landscapes in oPt, similar to those of Israel, are universal treasures that represent the diversity of cultures that had through the ages inhabited the land of Palestine (Figure 10.10). Yet, according to UNESCO (2010) the promulgation of the Jewish antiquity motif and denial of Palestinian rights to heritage in oPt are a part of the strategies adopted by the Israeli occupiers in order to assert their holdings in this disputed territory. In March 2010 an item on the provisional agenda for UNESCO Executive Board's session presented an overt accusation regarding the old landscape of oPt:

> Since Israel's occupation of the West Bank and Gaza Strip in 1967, hundreds of Palestinian archaeological sites and cultural property have been systematically confiscated, looted and excavated by Israeli authorities, endangering Palestinian cultural heritage and denying Palestinians their cultural patrimony, as well as denying development and access to heritage sites and historic places of worship . . . [T]he Israeli Government has attempted to highlight the Jewish character of archaeological and heritage sites in the

FIGURE 10.10 A significant landscape mark in Palestine is the fifth-century Greek monastery of Mar Saba east of Bethlehem, 2011 (Tim Williams).

occupied Palestinian territory, while erasing or neglecting the universal character of these heritage sites and denying access to all people of faith.

(UNESCO 2010: 1)

These poignant words epitomise the strong emotions embedded within the concept of World Heritage properties. While UNESCO World Heritage sites endeavour to encapsulate Outstanding Universal Value, the complexity and tensions embedded in significance and value, whether outstanding, ancient, new or ordinary, are paramount in the case of the intertwined new and old cultural landscapes of Palestine and Israel and the politics that underpin them.

Conclusion

UNESCO states that 'Cultural landscapes . . . testify to the creative genius, social development and the imaginative and spiritual vitality of humanity. They are part of our collective identity' (UNESCO 2012).

Collective identity, however, is a slippery and controversial notion (see for example Anderson 1991) and so is 'Heritage', as Laurajane Smith (2006) articulated in her coining of Authorized Heritage Discourse (AHD). Heritage is a social construct rather than a found object; the value of cultural landscapes is often embedded in the meanings ascribed to them rather than the tangible artefacts themselves (Taylor and Lennon 2012). Meanings are also influenced by power, political ideologies and territorial contestation over resources. Similarly, the shifting of political boundaries across the landscape are artificial human constructs and ownership of iconic cultural landscapes is fluid.

Notwithstanding the integrity of ICOMOS expert evaluation of cultural heritage sites for World Heritage nominations and the process of addressing selection criteria, there remain political hurdles when looking at the ancient, old and new landscapes of Israel and Palestine. In a place of ongoing bloody conflict, the landscape is recruited for a struggle over resources and identity. While Israel practises its 'selective amnesia' policy in the case of the ruined Palestinian landscape on which it had created a new modern landscape, Palestinians in refugee camps have recreated an identity based on memory and yearnings for their lost landscapes (Peteet 2005).[17] The role of landscape as an active political determinant and a tool to maintain power might not be unique to the case of Israel and Palestine but in this context it is intensified. In a place where a dominant culture holds hegemony and creates a new landscape reinforced by ancient cultural landscapes' myths while denying another people's connections to the same landscape, the 'universal value' of cultural landscapes is problematic. Expressions of power, exclusion and lack of justice come through clearly in the Old/New Zionist motif of *Altneuland* and are mirrored in the cultural landscape of Israel and Palestine.

Cultural landscapes are repositories of societies. Like those who create or destroy them, they are complex and often far from the ideals we might wish them to incorporate. World Heritage cultural landscapes are indeed a testament to 'the great diversity of the interactions between humans and their environment' (UNESCO 2012) but hardly a mirror of tolerance to cultural diversity.

The World Heritage Committee of UNESCO selects cultural landscapes according to their Outstanding Universal Value and cultural significance. The European Landscape Convention (ELC) supports the protection of the everyday ordinary lived-in landscape. The preamble of the ELC states the goal 'to achieve sustainable development based on a balanced and harmonious relationship between social needs [and], economic activity' (CoE 2000). This suggests that the new cultural landscapes of the twenty-first century should play an active role in supporting not only Outstanding Universal Value but also ethics of democracy, social justice and human well-being.

Notes

1 http://whc.unesco.org/en/culturallandscape/.
   Whilst a number of these include landscape settings, only one property, *Incense Route: Desert Cities of the Negev*, is specifically listed as a cultural landscape.
2 http://whc.unesco.org/en/list/1433.
3 The name Palestine is derived from 'Provincia Syria Palaestina', the Eastern Mediterranean administrative unit under the Roman Empire (named in 135 CE).
4 *Zion* is the traditional Jewish name for Jerusalem.
5 In terms of Gaza the situation is different. In August 2005 Israel disengaged from the Gaza Strip and evicted all Israelis from the Gaza Strip and from four settlements in the northern West Bank, demolishing the Israeli residential buildings. Gaza, governed by the Hamas organisation, is hostile to Israel and in return, to date (July 2012), is under siege.
6 The term 'Spring of Nations' refers to a period of revolutions and conflicts in mid-nineteenth-century Europe; these are regarded as the events that eventually shaped the modern nation-state model and its ideologies.
7 First under Ottoman rule and after the First World War under a British Mandate.
8 Modern Zionism is the term ascribed to the political movement which aims to mobilise Jews from all parts of the world to settle in Palestine as opposed to 'Zionism' as an abstract idea of yearnings of the exiled Jews to their lost land as expressed in prayers and poetry.
9 http://whc.unesco.org/en/list/1096/.
   For more detail on the UNESCO selection criteria see: http://whc.unesco.org/en/criteria/.
10 The grounding of the notion of the Bible as the history of the Jewish people is ascribed to Jewish German-born historian Heinrich Graetz's (1817–1891) seminal work *History of the Jews*, who was influenced by European Volk traditions of his time. Graetz's work has been widely criticised for its

lack of academic rigour but that did not impede its popularity or the ideological hegemony that it still today holds in Israeli secular society.

11 *Kibbutz* is a collective settlement influenced by socialist utopian ideals that were part of the ethos underpinning twentieth-century Zionist settlement.

12 al-Nakbah is the term for the 1948 Palestinian catastrophe in which 700,000 Palestinians were displaced. About 400 villages were destroyed during and after the course of Israel's War of Independence. Many of the displaced that are still alive 60 years on, and their descendants, reside in refugee camps in the West Bank, Gaza, South Lebanon, Syria and Jordan.

13. The story of Lifta has attracted much media attention and controversy due to its unique architectural and Palestinian Heritage values and an Israel Land Administration (ILA) plan for a gentrified high-end residential neighbourhood on this site (see more on Lifta in Egoz, 2008).

14. This camp's original residents came from the destroyed village of Beit-Jibrin, on the western hills of Hebron.The village site is depicted in David Roberts' 18th century painting of the Biblical landscape (see figure 10.5) and due to the site containing an array of ancient ruins and landscape assets from a diversity of cultures, most notably the Hellenistic period (third-second centuries BCE) and bell-shaped chalk caves from the Arab Period (seventh-eleventh centuries CE), it is today the declared Israeli National Park of Bet-Govrin.

15 http://www.unrwa.org/etemplate.php?id=86.

16 For a detailed analysis of the effects of the occupied landscape on Palestinian well-being see Egoz and Williams (2010) and Egoz (2011b).

17 Several of the refugee camps, as well as their neighbourhoods and streets, are named after the villages from which inhabitants had been displaced.

References

Anderson, B. (1991) *Imagined Communities: Reflections on the Origin and Spread of Nationalism*, London: Verso.

ARIJ (2008) *Monitoring Israeli Colonization Activities in the Palestinian Territories*, Jerusalem: Applied Research Institute. Available at: http://www.poica.org/editor/case_studies/view.php?recordID=1295 (accessed 13 March 2012).

Benvenisti, M. (2000) *Sacred Landscape: The Buried History of the Holy Land since 1948*, Berkeley: University of California Press.

Butlin, R.A (1992) 'Ideological Contexts and the Reconstruction of Biblical Landscapes in the Seventeenth and Early Eighteenth Centuries: Dr Edward Wells and the Historical Geography of the Holy Land', in A. Baker and G. Biger (eds) *Ideology and Landscape in Historical Perspective*, Cambridge: Cambridge University Press, pp. 31–62.

Chowers, E. (2002) 'The End of Building: Zionism and the Politics of the Concrete', *The Review of Politics* 64, 4: 599–626.

CoE (Council of Europe) (2000) *The European Landscape Convention* text, online. Available at: http://conventions.coe.int/Treaty/en/Treaties/Html/176.htm.

DAAR (2011) 'Decolonizing Architecture Art Residency', *Sedek* 6: 4–7.

Daibes, K. (2011) 'Our Gift to Eternity: Securing Protection for Palestine's Heritage Sites', *This Week in Palestine* 155.

Efrat, Z. (2004) 'Mold', in H.Yacobi (ed.) *Constructing a Sense of Place: Architecture and the Zionist Discourse*, Aldershot: Ashgate, pp. 76–88.

Egoz, S. (1997) 'The Pardess: An Israeli Symbolic Landscape', *Landscape Research* 22, 2: 175–189.

Egoz, S. (2008) 'Deconstructing the Hegemony of Nationalist Narratives through Landscape Architecture', *Landscape Research* 33, 10: 29–50.

Egoz, S. (2010) 'The European Landscape Convention: A Close View from a Distance', Key Address, in Proceedings of The Council of Europe (CoE) 8th International Workshop for the Implementation of the European Landscape Convention, *European Spatial Planning and Landscape* 93: 25–31, Strasbourg: Council of Europe Publishing.

Egoz, S. (2011a) 'Claiming a Right to Landscape: Rooting, the Uprooted and Re-Rooting', in S. Egoz, J. Makhzoumi and G. Pungetti (eds) *The Right to Landscape: Contesting Landscape and Human Rights*, Aldershot: Ashgate, pp. 165–181.

Egoz, S. (2011b) 'Landscape as a Driver for Well-being: The ELC in the Globalist Arena', *Landscape Research* 36, 4: 509–534.

Egoz, S. and Bowring, J. (2004) 'Beyond the Romantic and Naïve: The Search for a Complex Ecological Aesthetic Design Language for Landscape Architecture in New Zealand', *Landscape Research* 29, 1: 57–73.

Egoz, S. and Merhav, R. (2009) 'Ruins, Ideology and the Other in the Landscape, the Case of Zippori National Park, Israel', *JoLA* 8: 56–69.

Egoz, S. and Williams, T. (2010) 'Co-existent Landscapes: Military Integration and Civilian Fragmentation', in C. Pearson, P. Coates and T. Cole (eds) *Militarized Landscapes, from Gettysburg to Salisbury Plain*, London: Continuum, pp. 59–79.

Egoz, S., Makhzoumi, J. and Pungetti, G. (eds) (2011) *The Right to Landscape: Contesting Landscape and Human Rights*, Aldershot: Ashgate.

Elhyani, Z. (2004) 'Horizontal Ideology, Vertical Vision: Oscar Neimeyer and Israel's Height Dilemma', in H. Yacobi (ed.) *Constructing a Sense of Place: Architecture and the Zionist Discourse*, Aldershot: Ashgate, pp. 89–115.

Elon, A. (2000) *A Blood–dimmed Tide: Dispatches from the Middle East*, London: Allen Lane.

Gelfond-Feldinger, L. (2011) 'UNESCO Rejects Palestinian Heritage Proposal', *The Art Newspaper* 225.

Ibrahim, N. (2011) 'The Politics of Heritage in Palestine: A Conflict between Two Narratives', *This Week in Palestine* 155.

Isaac, J. (2000) *The Environmental Impact of Israeli Occupation Media Monitors Network*. Available at: http://www.mediamonitors.net/isacc2.html (accessed 13 March 2012).

Kadman, N. (2008) *Erased from Space and Consciousness: Depopulated Palestinian Villages in the Israeli-Zionist Discourse*, Jerusalem: November Books (in Hebrew).

Khalidi, W. (1992) *All that Remains: The Palestinian Villages Occupied and Depopulated by Israel in 194*, Washington, DC: Institute for Palestine Studies.

Leyerle, B. (1996) 'Landscape as Cartography in Early Christian Pilgrimage Narratives', *Journal of the American Academy of Religion* LXIV, 1: 119–143.

Liebman, C.S. and Don-Yehia, E. (1983) *Civil Religion in Israel*, Berkeley: University of California Press.

Nir, Y. (1985) 'Cultural Predispositions in Early Photography: The Case of the Holy Land', *Journal of Communication* 35, 3: 32–50.

Pappe, I. (2004) *A History of Modern Palestine*, Cambridge: Cambridge University Press.

Peteet, J. (2005) *Landscapes of Hope and Despair*, Philadelphia: University of Pennsylvania Press.

Rotbard, S. (2003) 'Wall and Tower', in R. Segal and E. Weizman (eds) *A Civilian Occupation: The Politics of Israel's Architecture*, London: Verso, pp. 39–56.

Rotbard, S. (2005) *White City, Black City*, Tel-Aviv: Babel (in Hebrew).

Rotbard, S. (2008) 'Homa Umigdal: The Mold of Israeli Architecture', *Sedek* 2.

Rubin, R. (1992) 'Ideology and Landscape in Early Printed Maps of Jerusalem', in A. Baker and G. Biger (eds) *Ideology and Landscape in Historical Perspective*, Cambridge: Cambridge University Press, pp. 15–30.

Schnell, I. (1998) 'Transformations in the Myth of the Inner Valleys as a Zionist Place', in A. Light and J. Smith (eds) *Philosophy and Geography III: Philosophies of Place*, Lanham: Rowman & Littlefield, pp. 97–116.

Smith, L. (2006) *Uses of Heritage*, London: Routledge.

Taylor, K. and Lennon, J. (eds) (2012) *Managing Cultural Landscapes*, London and New York: Routledge.

UNEP (2003) *United Nations Environmental Programme Desk Study on the Environment in the Occupied Palestinian Territories*, New York: UNEP. Available at: http://postconflict.unep.ch/publications (accessed 13 March 2012).

UNESCO (2010) *Fact Sheet on Israeli Consolidation of Palestinian Heritage Sites in the Occupied Palestinian Territory: The Case of Hebron and Bethlehem*, Paris: Executive Board Doc. 184 EX37.

UNESCO (2012) *Cultural Landscapes*. Available at: http://whc.unesco.org/en/culturallandscape/ (accessed 8 March 2012).

Weizman, E. (2007) *Hollow Land: Israel's Architecture of Occupation*, London: Verso.

Zerubavel, Y. (1995) *Recovered Roots: Collective Memory and the Making of Israeli National Tradition*, Chicago: University of Chicago Press.

Zerubavel, Y. (2002) 'The "Mythological Sabra" and Jewish Past: Trauma, Memory and Contested Identities', *Israel Studies* 7, 2: 115–144.

11

NEW SPATIAL CULTURES

A landscape story from Egypt

Tamer M. Abd El-Fattah Ahmed

Introduction

There are many definitions of landscape which encompass both landscape as territory and landscape as something much more than just the physical environment. Common and customary understandings indicate that landscapes are understood to be physically real as well as something that can be viewed, perceived and imagined (Wylie 2007). Landscape can be conceived in terms of a mixture of the past, present and future; as something which is spatially distributed over the earth's surface as well as above and below that surface (Kaplan 2009). Landscapes are definable through social, visual and ecological understandings that encompass community, justice, nature and environmental equity (Mels 2003) and exchanges between the natural, cultural, social and economic systems (Wood and Handley 2001). Within the context of these various understandings of landscape, this chapter uses the term landscape to refer primarily to the designed landscape and it aims to examine the emerging upmarket designed housing landscapes of Cairo and to discuss how these new landscapes reflect changing cultures and people's relationships with ideas and ideals of landscape in Egypt.

The struggle against aridity in the Middle East has influenced social and political organisation and shaped religious and cultural values. This is largely as a result of the duality of the Middle Eastern landscape character; on one hand, the ordered, inhabited space of settlements and cultivated land and, on the other, what is seen as the more hostile dry desert (Makhzoumi 2002). Dutton (1992) noted that aridity has also influenced the management of landscapes under Islamic Law which recognises two categories of land, *Ard-Amar* (developed) and *Ard-Mawat* (dead or undeveloped) (Makhzoumi 2002). Thus, *Ihya-al-mawat* (making life flourish in dead lands) has always been a central value in Middle Eastern culture (Llwellyn 1992). *Ihya-al-mawat* indicates that there is a fundamental understanding that the desert can be changed and transformed by development.

Of relevance in considering these understandings is Warnock and Brown's (1998) landscape strategy model, echoed by Wood and Handley (2001) and elaborated by Selman (2006) (Figure 11.1). This draws attention to the importance of considering character and condition in developing appropriate tools for landscape development. Character and condition are seen to be undermined by 'dysfunctions', where land uses are introduced

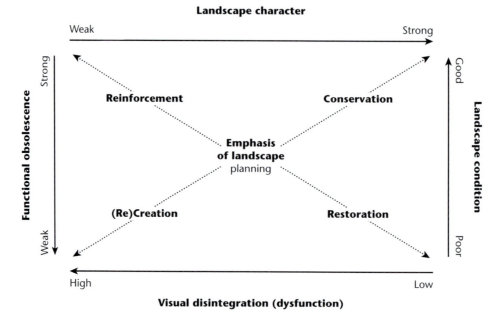

FIGURE 11.1 Developing landscape strategies to the landscape status and trends (Selman 2006: 38).

that do not relate to that landscape's ability to function, and 'obsolescence', where the economic forces that have given the landscape a coherent character are losing their viability. The landscape strategy model indicates various remedies for such changes based on four key approaches: landscape restoration, landscape conservation, landscape reinforcement and landscape (re-)creation. Such approaches are useful in the consideration of the landscapes of the Middle East where in many places the landscape character is a constructed one in which nature has been tamed, ordered and controlled.

Motloch (2001: 8) stated that '[t]o design more responsively in any culture, we can begin by reading that culture's autobiography – its landscape'. Thus a landscape reflects the desires and concerns of the cultures that lie within it. Makhzoumi (2002) suggests that in environments that are often hostile to human habitation, such as those found in the Middle East, human-modified or created landscapes are designed to provide environments that reflect a need for comfort and security as well as to express cultural understandings of beauty. These needs are now commonly described as relating to the liveability of a landscape. Under this kind of analysis it would be possible to see the creation of new landscapes in Cairo as needing to relate primarily to a cultural reaction to the difficulties that the natural environment presents and a need to tame, order and control the desert.

But why does the landscape look the way it does and what clues does the landscape itself present? It has been suggested that it is in fact not always possible to read the landscape directly, but understanding the development of landscape requires research and analysis to explore its function, understand its history and therefore to find out what it says regarding the status of a just world in the here and now. These questions were addressed by Lewis (1979) when he suggested seven axioms for understanding and reading landscapes. Almost 30 years later,

Mitchell (2008) argued the need for renewed attention to the nature of the struggle in and over the landscape in a capitalist era. Mitchell presented a new set of axioms for understanding and reading landscapes. To begin to see 'how' and 'why' landscapes exist, Mitchell turns away from a focus on meaning towards one on production. He suggests that his new axioms for landscape 'are designed to form an analytical and normative basis, by providing a historical materialist methodological foundation for what landscape is and does' (2008: 33). While Lewis emphasises landscape as process, Mitchell seems to emphasise landscape as production.

While landscape can be understood in numerous ways, so people's experience of landscape can also be interpreted in various ways (Antonson *et al.* 2009). Meinig (1979) argued that landscapes comprise both what we actually see and our perception of what we see at the same time. Landscape is interpreted by the mind, therefore, the reader of the landscape is integral to its meaning; the same landscape may mean different things to different people. He listed ten possible aspects of a landscape as: nature, habitat, artefact, system, problem, wealth, ideology, history, place and aesthetic. The importance of Meinig's ten versions of the same scene, as Motloch (2001) points out, is that it presents a comprehensive overview of the range of landscape interpretations that people are prone to perceive. This chapter takes up these ideas of interpretation and uses case studies from Cairo to examine how the new designed landscapes are perceived in different ways. This chapter suggests that the fundamental point in reading landscapes is that it allows us to understand cultural concerns such as the need to respond to the aridity of the environment.

Context (place and people)

Egypt occupies the north-eastern corner of the African continent. With a surface area of just over one million square kilometres (1,019,600 km^2) or about 3 per cent of the total area of Africa (Zahran and Willis 2009) most of the country falls within the temperate zone, and is situated in the centre of the largest, driest desert regions on the globe. Average temperatures are high (mean: summer 20–30^{0}C, winter 10–20^{0}C) and the mean annual rainfall is less than 10 mm. The most significant feature of Egypt's landscape is the River Nile, which is the largest and most important source of fresh water in the country (Figure 11.2). The Nile divides Egypt into two parts; Egypt east of the Nile shows significant relief, including the country's highest mountain peaks; west of the Nile the landscape is generally featureless, largely made up of vast expanses of deserts dotted with scattered oases. The Nile valley has been described as a lotus flower with Cairo occupying and strangling the throat of the flower (Golia 2004). The evolution of Cairo and its urban structure perceived from socio-economic and socio-political standpoints has been a subject widely researched and analysed (Abu-Lughod 1971; Beattie 2005; Golia 2004; Khadr *et al.* 2010; Raymond 2007; Stewart 1999).

The city can be seen to be divided into adjacent and often overlapping social spaces. It is not easy to distinguish between the strata in society or the different social spaces in Cairo, but people living in these areas can be grouped by their education level, their business activities and the density of their living accommodation, property cost and quality of amenities (Bayat and Denis 2000; Denis 1996; Fahmi and Sutton 2008; Stewart 1999). Raymond (2007) estimated that the lower stratum of society forms about 56 per cent of Cairo's population and shares only 12 per cent of the aggregate income, while the middle forms 39 per cent with 34 per cent of the income, and only 5 per cent form the upper stratum with about 54 per cent of the income. Singerman (1995: 30) recorded that rich and poor in Cairo live 'cheek by

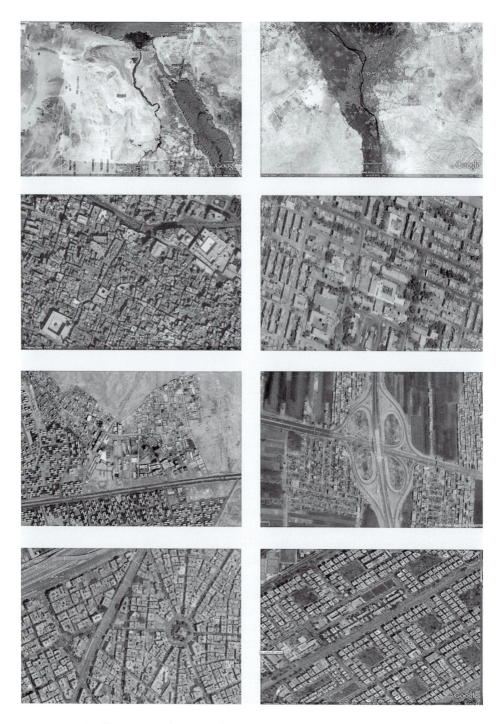

FIGURE 11.2   Satellite images of Egypt and Cairo captured July 2010. Top left: Egypt; top right: Cairo; upper–middle left: Inner Cairo; upper–middle right: Inner Cairo cooperative housing; lower–middle left: desert informal settlement; lower–middle right: green land informal settlement; bottom left: Wayli district satellite image; bottom right: Heliopolis satellite image (Google Earth accessed 5 August 2012).

jowl' in some areas and are not totally segregated. However, Harris and Malak (2002: 71) noted that this is not the norm and '[i]n class terms, and by western standards, Cairo is a highly segregated city'.

The landscape characteristics found in Egypt based on lush green valleys and harsh desert clearly show human imprints and the impacts of the interaction between cultural and natural forces. Culture has been considered as an important agent of change in this landscape with nature as the medium; the result can be described as the cultural landscape (Sauer 1963). It is the continuous effort by people to manage the Egyptian desert landscape that has made the most important impact on its character. For example, there are many grand projects which have had a significant effect on landscape change and which reflect the culture and aspirations of the time. One of these was the Suez Canal built in the late nineteenth century and the High Dam in the mid twentieth century which affected not only the River Nile landscape physically, but also Egypt's political structures, social activities, economic organisation and almost every other aspect of Egyptian life. Landscapes are recognised as continually changing because of the dynamic interactions inherent in natural and cultural systems and changing societal demands (Antrop 2005). In Egypt the attempts to manage the landscape at both national and regional scale have had a direct influence on urbanisation by turning the generally uninhabitable desert plains into areas now habitable by millions of people.

The growing concern over the quality of urban life in Cairo resulting from population growth and the deterioration of the urban environment due to the industrialisation in the 1950s led to a series of attempts to master-plan the city in 1956, 1970, 1983, 1990, 1995 and 1998. The first serious attempt was the 1970 Greater Cairo Master Plan which proposed the accommodation of population growth through a super agglomeration consisting of satellite towns. The plan had two major objectives: (1) to contain the city within its built-up area by means of a surrounding circular road and a green belt; and (2) to divert any further population to new satellite towns to the east and west on desert land away from the green north and south (Yousry and Aboul Atta 1997). This plan was not fully implemented in the 1970s, yet it formed the basis for the 1983 Greater Cairo Master Plan, which remains to date the basemap for urban development in the region. In 1981, the 1970s plan was updated and launched in response to deteriorating urban conditions, which were evident in its overcrowded population, its proliferation of small enterprises, housing shortage, poor infrastructure and environment.

Together the 1970 and 1983 Greater Cairo Master Plans and subsequent modifications in the 1990s pushed the urban growth out of the city towards the east and west rather than the historic north–south expansions. Urban sprawl continued to move towards the north but more slowly than before (Sutton and Fahmi 2001). Such infrastructure improvements led to negative as well as positive outcomes and divided Cairo into six different spatial patterns as highlighted by Sutton and Fahmi (2001: 148):

> **First:** the ruralisation of urban fringes and the emergence of spontaneous informal settlements around the city peripheries. **Second:** the urbanization of rural villages on the outskirts . . . **Third:** the densification of the west bank of the Nile . . . of the south . . . and of the northeast . . . triggered a mass residential mobility to the suburbs. **Fourth:** saturation of the CBD [Cairo Business District] and the decline of the inner old city as people seek to move out from core areas to the fringes. **Fifth:** inefficiency of new desert settlements in providing housing for low-income population. **Sixth:** population growth in the suburban master planned estates within the desert new settlements.

It can be noted that what Sutton and Fahmi (2001) called the 'mastering' of Cairo's population growth is clearly shown in the decline in the size of the inner-city population. The outward movement of population included people from all different socio-economic classes. An example of this was the rapid unforced relocation of people to 'New Cairo City' in the east and to '6th of October City' in the west. The development of these new desert settlements was based on the concept of Master Planned Estates (MPEs). These are a recent manifestation of urbanisation based on utopian place-making ideals deriving from the Garden City movement found in the UK in the late nineteenth century. The expectation is that this form of development can produce a better place to live than that found in the high-density urban core within Cairo. In particular, the new developments are based on the idea that ideal communities can be achieved by the extensive provision of infrastructures and a suburban-style landscape which is completely different to that found within most other residential areas in Cairo.

The city of New Cairo is in fact a gigantic suburban development built up of a mosaic of MPEs. The city lies to the east of the Greater Cairo Ring Road between the Cairo–Suez Road to the north and the Cairo–El-Sokhna Road to the south. New Cairo has developed incrementally since the mid 1980s as a result of new urban polices which represent a radical change to the previous planning objectives, urban population and city structure (Figure 11.3).

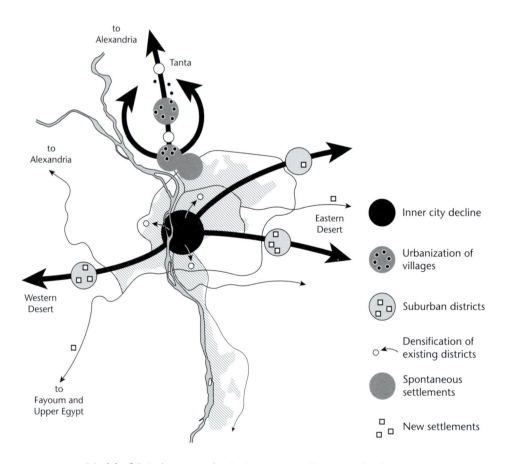

FIGURE 11.3 Model of Cairo's recent urbanisation patterns (Sutton and Fahmi 2001: 148).

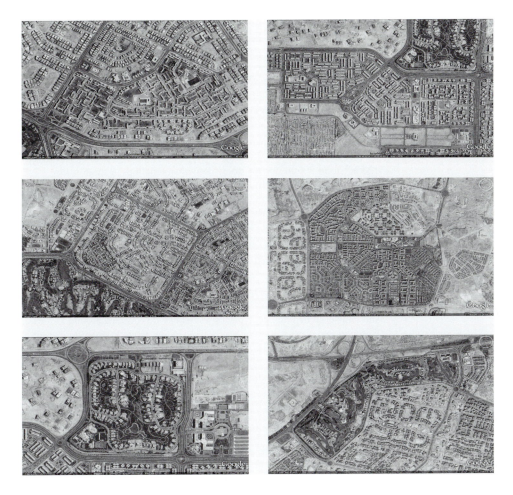

FIGURE 11.4   Satellite images of the six MPEs in New Cairo. Top left: Cooperative MPE;
top right: Improved Cooperative MPE; middle left: Self-build MPE;
middle right: Controlled MPE; bottom left: Gated MPE; bottom right:
Golf MPE (Google Earth accessed 5 August 2012).

Six forms of MPEs can be identified in New Cairo, including: Cooperative; Improved
Cooperative; Self-build; Controlled; Gated; and Golf (Figure 11.4). These forms of MPE not
only have different characteristics but they are intended to cater for different social groups. In
addition, they are developed and promoted by both the public and private sectors through
different strategies (Table 11.1).

The key question here is how can we read the new spatial culture that is created by
the new developments? And how can we understand the reasons behind its rise? The
following discussion is based on data and analysis from fieldwork undertaken between 2006
and 2008 and structured around information obtained from interviews with planners and
developers of these six MPEs.

TABLE 11.1 Characteristics and physical structure of Master Planned Estates in New Cairo

Master Planned Estate	Characteristics and physical structure
Cooperative and Improved Cooperative	The developers provide ready-made affordable housing to the low-income social stratum. Housing units are in the form of flats, ranging from 65 m² up to 90 m² in five-storey blocks. These blocks are usually clustered around a common green space. Population density is set to 64,000 residents/sq. mile.
Self-build	The developers provide plots for self-build homes to middle- and high-income social strata. The dwellings are in the form of flats ranging from 120 m² up to 300 m² in five-storey residential buildings or three-storey detached and semi-detached houses ranging from 400 m² to 840 m². The residential buildings and the houses are usually lined along streets, and are located in the middle of 600 m² fenced plots. Population density is set to 44,800 residents/sq. mile.
Controlled	The developers provide ready-made dwellings to middle- and high-income social strata. The controlled MPEs are developments with marked entry ways, but no methods for preventing access. Dwellings are in the form of flats or houses. Flats range from 35 m² to 320 m² in five-storey blocks and houses range from 256 m² to 660 m² in the form of two-storey detached and semi-detached houses. Typically the blocks are clustered around a common green space and the houses lined along streets. Population density is set to 44,800 residents/sq. mile.
Gated and Golf	The developers provide ready-made and sometimes customised dwellings to the high-income social stratum. These are fully gated to limit access but without restricting it. Dwellings are in the form of two-storey detached and semi-detached houses ranging from 400 m² to 1,100 m². The houses are clustered around a picturesque park or a 27-hole golf course. Population density in both cases is set to 19,200 residents/sq. mile.

The new cultural landscape

Earlier in this chapter the idea of reading a culture's landscape was introduced. Lewis (1979) suggests that landscape is an unwitting record of our tastes, values and aspirations and thus the key point in the creation of cultural landscapes is that landscape is a process by which identities are formed. The landscape practices and spatial arrangements in the MPEs have been offered to people as 'ready-made' products thus the key question is what can be interpreted from the landscape practices in these arid-zone MPEs if we consider them as both process and product of contemporary culture.

In New Cairo, the MPE landscape is actively planned and produced; it can be conceived as a pure physical intervention into the desert plains surrounding Cairo and thus it is an act of determination. This determination is usually operated solely by developers and without any involvement from residents. To interpret 'what a landscape is, what it does and why it looks the way it does we need to pay attention to both the broad and the narrow relations of production ... that are always struggled over' (Mitchell 2008: 34). Landscape practices in the MPEs can be seen through the lens of relations of production, as both a consequence of struggle over the aridity of the region and a way to end this struggle by transforming its harsh nature. These new designed landscapes can be seen as products which are produced as a service that is essential for the existence and convenience of humanity (De Groot et al. 2002).

Like any aspect of the built environment, the designed landscape structure in the MPEs is planned to accommodate particular functions. Any landscape is functional by nature; functions can be translated into services when they are valued by people, although, functions might exist in the absence of people (Termorshuizen and Opdam 2009). In New Cairo, the primary, if not the most obvious, function of the landscape for the developers' point of view is either to directly realise value (i.e. profits) or to establish the conditions (i.e. liveability) under which value can be realised. Accordingly it is not surprising to see that the private sector developers are taking the quality and provision of newly designed landscapes more seriously than the public sector. This is articulated well by the improved-cooperative housing officer at NCDA (New Cairo Development Agency):

> Those private companies have the means to spend on their developments ... it is what they do ... they spend and in return they gain high profits ... we can't do this ... although we are trying but our resources at the end of the day are limited ... of course there is no way to compare developments that are purely dedicated to profit with ones like ours which are dedicated mainly to helping people with housing.
>
> *(Interview)*

The new residential landscape in New Cairo has been produced through a process of speculative investment that is coordinated through multifaceted fiscal market actions. It can therefore be seen to reflect the values, aspirations and tastes of a sector of Cairo's contemporary affluent community. Like any investment it is speculative. In general developers invest in the creation of the new designed landscape in the belief that it will create conditions for the realisation of greater profits than could be otherwise anticipated.

For example the cooperative housing officer at NUCA (New Urban Communities Authority) pointed out that the provision of more attractive buildings and vast green areas in the Improved Cooperative MPEs is more expensive in the short term but in the long term can secure increased profit since the landscape structure helps sell the houses: 'yes it cost slightly more than the old schemes but it would cost more to have empty cheaper ghost communities' (interview). Similarly in the Controlled MPE, the developer's marketing officer explained:

> We are more generous than our competitors in terms of spending on the details of the outdoor features in our developments ... the type of people who want to live in a community like Al-Rehab want more than a flat or a villa ... such people want a package of services that comes with the flat or the villa.
>
> *(Interview)*

These kinds of replies confirm that the designed landscapes in the MPEs are seen as valuable for the functions they can perform. Nonetheless, for developers the realisation of monetary value is the main incentive for considering the landscape structure and, as Harvey (2007: 234) argued, 'all aspects of the production and use of the built environment are brought within the orbit of the circulation of capital'. Some developers sink capital into landscape projects in order to increase the revenues they gain through house sales. There are clear examples of this in the practices followed in the establishment of both the Gated and Golf MPEs. In one Gated MPE studied, capital was used to develop a park and, in another, a golf course; in

FIGURE 11.5 Identifying landscape practices in New Cairo as artefact and as wealth.

both cases the developers responsible used the new designed landscape as a promotional tool for selling each MPE.

Landscape development practice in New Cairo can be interpreted in the terms that Meinig (1979) identified; that is as both 'artefact' and 'wealth' (Figure 11.5). The developers have reshaped nature for their own purposes and consider their new MPE landscapes superior to the desert landscape which they have replaced. It is of course not new to find that landscape designers consider it possible to improve on nature in various ways. This new landscape is completely different to that which pre-existed the development and the development is based on increasing the primary value of the landscape and thus the investment of the landowners. Landscape practice here is about the translation of landscape into economic units, with the greatest consideration given to market forces in accommodating the infrastructure necessary to service and promote the MPEs.

These new landscape creations face critiques from those who see the developers as aggressive despoilers of nature. But there is also an important cultural dimension to this change which is also of some public concern. The influence of the context on a particular cultural behaviour might explain many landscape practices because cultures dictate that certain activities should occur in certain places (Lewis 1979). The desert symbolises the realm of the dead in Egyptian culture and remains associated to this day with cemeteries (Singerman and Amar 2006). Thus deserts are not only places that are hostile in terms of environmental comfort, but they still hold associations for Egyptians which hinder the incursion of the living into what is a space that is seen to belong to the dead. Therefore MPE developers in New Cairo have had to work hard to turn the desert's ochre soil to green, both metaphorically and literally, in order to render the desert attractive to people, and to dispel the idea that the desert is for the dead rather than for living. The cooperative housing officer at NUCA (New Urban Communities Authority) explained:

> For many years people called the desert new-cities the *torab* cemeteries … to be honest they were pretty much alike … we had to change this centuries' old idea in people's minds … for thousands of years Egyptians lived in the green valley and buried their dead in the desert, [for this reason we are now providing] attractive buildings in attractive settings with vast green spaces in between.
>
> *(Interview)*

Lewis' argument, that landscapes make little cultural sense if studied outside their context, can thus be seen to be helpful here; both the local and regional context is important. Landscape practices in the MPEs in New Cairo will appear in one light if studied only in relation to the context of providing new housing, but can be seen in a number of other ways culturally if related to the wider context of the region and traditions relating to the desert.

In creating new housing landscapes, many MPE developers in New Cairo are also keen to hark back to the positive image of Khedive Isma'il's Cairo with its (Haussmannian-Paris-like) tree-lined boulevards, public squares, parks, villas and apartment blocks which characterised a vanished late nineteenth-, early twentieth-century 'liberal era' of Egypt. In many cases this nostalgia has become an important argument in the promotion of the desert developments. The developer's marketing officer of the Gated MPE explained:

> We provided our customers with what they needed ... we returned them once again to the golden age of Ismailian Cairo ... when Cairo was called 'Paris on the Nile' ... with many parks ... clean ... and chic buildings ... actually many of our customers were brought up in Zamalek or the Garden City ... of course the Zamalek and Garden City of the past not the current ruined ones.
>
> *(Interview)*

This representation of history in landscape practices is not immanent in the physical landscape, which reflects a very different style than that fondly recalled by developers. However it is an association which again indicates the importance of the construction of meanings that are attached to landscape and the way these are used and manipulated for particular objectives. Developers have tried to alter existing associations, as in the desert associations with the dead, where they feel that a reframing of landscape is required, but also align the new designed landscape with past ideals of an elegant and desirable green city. Thus following Meinig's (1979) proposed different ways of seeing the same scene, landscape practitioners in New Cairo regard the new landscape as both 'habitat' and 'ideology' (Figure 11.6). The landscape practices of the MPE developers can be seen as the physical expression of contemporary culture. The developers are, by their actions, changing not only the landscape, but also changing the cultural association of the landscape.

Many MPE developers in New Cairo adopt an intense interventionist approach to their estates in order to maintain their position in the real estate market. The aim is usually to ensure that the quality of their developments is not compromised during and after the

FIGURE 11.6 Landscape practices in New Cairo as habitat and as ideology.

construction phase. This mainly involves ensuring the implementation and the upkeep of the estates' landscape to the highest standards so that it will continue to attract potential residents both to it and to the developer's future projects. While the communal spaces are relatively easy to manage in terms of the developer's objectives, the private spaces are harder to control. To overcome this, some developers control the estates by setting legally endorsed restrictions on any alteration to the new landscape by the residents; these include modifications to buildings and street front appearances. Residents who deviate from these guidelines receive notice of their legal obligations to maintain the landscape to the status designed by the developers. Failure to do so might subject residents to legal action by the developer. As the developer's marketing officer of the Controlled MPE explained:

> We are doing here [in the Controlled MPE] what the local authority is failing to do in the rest of New Cairo . . . in the sale contracts we clearly state that any modification to the buildings, facades or private gardens should be approved by and through us or at least under our supervision . . . this is to ensure the quality of the development's appearance, not just for us but also for its residents.
>
> *(Interview)*

Landscape practices in the MPEs in New Cairo can also be seen therefore as an expression of power. A desire for power over the definition of meanings to be read into and out of landscape practices, and to determine just what will exist both in and as the landscape (Mitchell 2008).

Despite the neoliberal-authoritarian political system in the past 30 years in Egypt, the exercise of rule is no longer exclusive to the state, especially in urban development, but is increasingly enacted by different actors as is illustrated in these new settlements. Therefore, the expression of power by some landscape practices in New Cairo can be understood as a governance tool which the MPE developers use to deal with the development and its residents. These practices could be seen as undermining individual freedom of expression, yet research suggests that these restrictions are welcomed by residents as a desirable aspect of living in a MPE. This is expressed by a respondent (male, 30–40 years old) who has lived in the Controlled MPE since 2002:

> Here in this community [Controlled MPE] you can't install even a satellite dish or an air conditioning unit without getting permission from the developer . . . and you might get fined if your front garden is not tidy and clean . . . they are very strict most of the time about whatever might hinder the overall appearance of the community . . . this makes it a different place to live . . . we would be worried if they started to be more relaxed about the upkeep of the community.
>
> *(Interview)*

Hence, the lack of enforcement and control in some cases was a prime issue of concern as articulated by a respondent (male, 50–60 years old) who has lived in the Self-build MPE since 2002:

> They [the developers] need to enforce the standards they set when they advertised this estate [Self-build MPE] . . . people should not be left to do whatever they want in their

houses, facades and street frontage … this affects the look of the whole estate as well as our property value and our quality of life … they [the developers] do not follow through on any standards they promoted when we built here … they are not doing what they need to do [for the upkeep of the estate] … they are not enforcing any standards on people.

(Interview)

These excerpts show that there is a strong interest by both residents and MPE developers in the enforcement of local landscape regulations. It seems that the interventionist approach of some MPE developers to their estates no longer needs to be justified as it is welcomed by the residents themselves. It is the lack of intervention that is likely to require justification. The landscape practice here can be seen as an expression of underlying processes. In Meinig's (1979) terms, landscape practices in New Cairo can be seen as both 'system' and 'tool' (Figure 11.7). The interpretation of landscape practices in MPEs in New Cairo as an expression of underlying processes is based on the holistic view of landscape as a system. In this interpretation, MPE developers consider the quality of landscape as an essential consideration. The development is sold to potential residents as an expression of a high quality of life. But this is on the understanding that natural and human-made elements of the built environment require constant intervention and correction to maintain a required ideal. The landscape practice of the MPE developers can be described as functional, infrastructural, behavioural and aesthetic problem-solving tools.

FIGURE 11.7   Landscape practices in New Cairo as system and as tool.

Concluding remarks

The discussion in this chapter aims to reveal that the agendas behind the MPEs developers' landscape practices are mainly determined by a desire to maximise profits and by establishing the conditions for doing so. Nevertheless, these practices can also be understood in terms of the cultural context which is about a struggle against the aridity of the region. Hence, the new designed landscapes are also being used as a tool to change the harshness of the desert into a liveable place. Landscape practice in the MPEs can therefore be viewed as a tool and as a generator of a new spatial culture.

By understanding how landscape character in Egypt is now being created and changed we can begin to understand how the perceived meanings of landscapes can be manipulated by different actors. It also shows the importance of understanding not only the context, but the complex social, ecological and economic drivers that can alter the interactions that people have with the landscape and the new spatial cultures that can result. Cairo's landscapes are changing because of these dynamic interactions and alterations, and are the result of consecutive reorganisations of land in order to adapt land use and spatial structure to changing societal demands.

References

Abu-Lughod, J.L. (1971) *Cairo: 1001 Years of the City Victorious*, Princeton: Princeton University Press.

Antonson, H., Mårdh, S., Wiklund, M. and Blomqvist, G. (2009) 'Effect of surrounding landscape on driving behaviour: a driving simulator study', *Journal of Environmental Psychology* 29, 4: 493–502.

Antrop, M. (2005) 'Why landscapes of the past are important for the future', *Landscape and Urban Planning* 70, 1–2: 21–34.

Bayat, A. and Denis, E. (2000) 'Who is afraid of ashwaiyyat? Urban change and politics in Egypt', *Environment and Urbanization* 12, 2: 185–199.

Beattie, A. (2005) *Cairo: A Cultural History*, Oxford: Oxford University Press.

De Groot, R.S., Wilson, M.A. and Boumans, R.M.J. (2002) 'A typology for the classification, description and valuation of ecosystem functions, goods and services', *Ecological Economics* 41, 3: 393–408.

Denis, E. (1996) 'Urban planning and growth in Cairo', *Middle East Report* 20, 2: 7–12.

Dutton, Y. (1992) 'Natural resources in Islam', in F. Khalid and J. O'Brien (eds) *Islam and Ecology*, London: Cassell, pp. 51–57.

Fahmi, W. and Sutton, K. (2008) 'Greater Cairo's housing crisis: contested spaces from inner city areas to new communities', *Cities* 25, 5: 277–297.

Golia, M. (2004) *Cairo: City of Sand*, Cairo: The American University in Cairo Press.

Harris, R. and Malak, W. (2002) 'The urban geography of low-income housing: Cairo (1947–1996) exemplifies a model', *International Journal of Urban and Regional Research* 26, 1: 58–79.

Harvey, D. (2007) *The Limits to Capital*, Oxford: Blackwell.

Kaplan, A. (2009) 'Landscape architecture's commitment to landscape concept: a missing link?', *Journal of Landscape Architecture* 4, 1: 56–65.

Khadr, Z., Nour el Dein, M. and Hamed, R. (2010) 'Using GIS in constructing area-based physical deprivation index in Cairo Governorate, Egypt', *Habitat International* 34, 2: 264–272.

Lewis, P.F. (1979) 'Axioms for reading the landscape', in D.W. Meinig (ed.) *The Interpretation of Ordinary Landscapes*, New York: Oxford University Press, pp. 11–32.

Llwellyn, O. (1992) 'Desert reclamation and conservation in Islamic Law', in F. Khalid and J. O'Brien (eds) *Islam and Ecology*, London: Cassell, pp. 87–97.

Makhzoumi, J.M. (2002) 'Landscape in the Middle East: an inquiry', *Landscape Research* 27, 3: 213–228.

Meinig, D.W. (1979) 'The beholding eye: ten versions of the same scene', in D.W. Meinig (ed.) *The Interpretation of Ordinary Landscapes: Geographical Essays*, New York: Oxford University Press, pp. 33–48.

Mels, T. (2003) 'Landscape unmasked: Kenneth Olwig and the ghostly relations between concepts', *Cultural Geographies* 10, 3: 379–387.

Mitchell, D. (2008) 'New axioms for reading the landscape: paying attention to political economy and social justice', in J.L. Wescoat and D.M. Johnson (eds) *Political Economies of Landscape Change*, Dordrecht: Springer, pp. 29–50.

Motloch, J.L. (2001) *Introduction to Landscape Design* (2nd edn), New York: Wiley.

Raymond, A. (2007) *Cairo: City of History*, Cairo: The American University in Cairo Press.

Sauer, C.O. (1963) *Land and Life: A Selection from the Writings of Carl Ortwin Sauer*, Berkeley: University of California Press.

Selman, P.H. (2006) *Planning at the Landscape Scale*, London: Routledge.

Singerman, D. (1995) *Avenues of Participation: Family, Politics, and Networks in Urban Quarters of Cairo*, Chichester: Princeton University Press.

Singerman, D. and Amar, P. (2006) *Cairo Cosmopolitan: Politics, Culture, and Urban Space in the Globalized Middle East*, Cairo: The American University in Cairo Press.

Stewart, D.J. (1999) 'Changing Cairo: the political economy of urban form', *International Journal of Urban and Regional Research* 23, 1: 103–127.

Sutton, K. and Fahmi, W. (2001) 'Cairo's urban growth and strategic master plans in the light of Egypt's 1996 population census results', *Cities* 18, 3: 135–149.

Termorshuizen, J. and Opdam, P. (2009) 'Landscape services as a bridge between landscape ecology and sustainable development', *Landscape Ecology* 24, 8: 1037–1052.

Warnock, S. and Brown, N. (1998) 'A vision for the countryside', *Landscape Design* 269: 22–26.

Wood, R. and Handley, J. (2001) 'Landscape dynamics and the management of change', *Landscape Research* 26, 1: 45–54.

Wylie, J. (2007) *Landscape*, London: Routledge.

Yousry, M. and Aboul Atta, T.A. (1997) 'The challenge of urban growth in Cairo', in C. Rakodi (ed.) *The Urban Challenge in Africa: Growth and Management of its Large Cities*, Tokyo: United Nations University Press, pp. 111–149.

Zahran, M.A. and Willis, A.J. (2009) *The Vegetation of Egypt*, London: Springer.

12

CHINA

New cultures and changing urban cultures

Mary G. Padua

So far, we are still somewhere between chaos and celebration, and no further.

(Liu 2008: 81)

Landscapes are made and remade.

(Reed 2005: 14)

Introduction

China's vast physical landscape is defined by its steep mountain ranges, fertile valleys and alluvial plains drained by a network of rivers that emerge into its long coastline. The first cities in China were located in the fertile basins and river valleys and then, following the influence of foreign trade, further urbanisation was concentrated along the coastline. The spatial pattern of human settlement was a result of thousands of years of political territorialism, urbanisation and periods of disunity, war and peace (Elvin 2004; Yu 1992; Skinner 1977) (Figure 12.1). Thus, although the process of hyper-rapid urbanisation in the People's Republic of China has resulted in the emergence of new cities in just three to five years, the creation of the present-day urban landscape is the continuation of a process that has ancient roots (Figure 12.2).

The recent remarkable urban growth can be represented numerically: 1978 = 190+ cities; 1984 = 290+ cities; 2010 = 650+ cities. The threefold expansion during this period has been attributed to Deng Xiaoping's late 1970s policy launch of the *Four Modernisations* relating to agriculture, industry, science and technology, and national defence, and the *gaige kaifang* (reform and opening up). The nation's recent urban transformation is remarkable given the extent of the societal fragmentation and destruction China experienced during Mao's Cultural Revolution (1966–1976). During this period there was a government-led expulsion of the nation's urban population to the countryside for 'moral reform', economic isolationism, a ten-year closure of schools and the removal of many expressions of China's ancient cultures from both society and the landscape. The 1970s reforms accelerated the modernisation of Mao's peasant-based society and created a crucible for

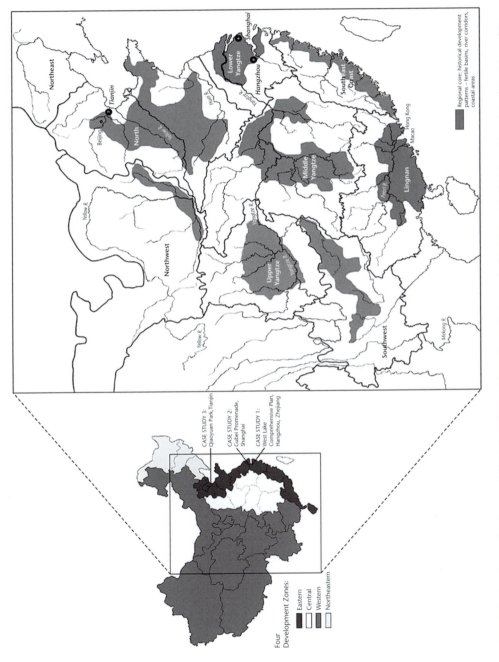

FIGURE 12.1 Generalised map of China's settlement patterns and case study locations (graphic by author based on Ma and Wu 2005 and Skinner 1977).

	Neolithic		1200–2000 BCE
Ancient China	Xia		2100–1800
	Shang		1700–1027
	Western Zhou		1027–771
	Eastern Zhou 770–221 BCE	Spring & Autumn period 770–476 BCE	
		Warring States period 475–221 BCE	
Early Imperial China	Qin		221–207 BCE
	Han		206 BCE –220 CE
	Three Kingdoms		220–280
	Jin		265–420
	Sixteen Kingdoms		304–439
	Southern and Northern		420–589
Classical Imperial China	Sui		581–618
	Tang		618–907
	5 Dynasties and 10 Kingdoms		907–960
	Song 960–1279	Northern Song 960–1127	
		Southern Song 1127–1279	
Later Imperial China	Yuan		1271–1368
	Ming		1368–1644
	Qing		1644–1911
Modern China	Republic of China		1912–1949
	People's Republic of China [New Era 1982]		1949–

FIGURE 12.2   A general chronology of Chinese history (based on Clunas 1997 and Fairbank 1957).

urban experimentation and the emergence of new cultural landscapes in contemporary Chinese cities.

The focus of this chapter is the new designed landscapes that have emerged during the twenty-first century in selected cities in China's eastern region. The chapter's trajectory extends Yu and Padua's (2007) discussion of China's production of cosmetic cities. It also builds on Padua's (2010, 2007) theory of hybrid modernity that is reflected in late twentieth-century public parks in secondary Chinese cities. Hybrid modernity, reflective of the hybrid modernisation process, provides a framework for understanding the interaction of global and local forces in shaping culture and society along with a third element in China: notions of Chinese nationality and identity. It expands on Appadurai's (1990) commentary on alternative modernity and positions China in the world view as a long-standing civilisation and nation that is socioculturally distinctive. In this context, China is interpreted on its own and not within the 'advanced/advancing' or 'developed/developing' dichotomous narrative for nations.

The notion of Chinese nationality builds from Anderson's (1991) premise that national identity is essentially a mythological construction that largely serves political purposes. Nationalism or nation-building – Chineseness as local identity – is interrelated with

Anderson's notion of a reimagined post-Mao national identity. While discussion of cosmetic cities (Yu and Padua 2007) addresses the superficiality of China's post-Mao urban fever, hybrid modernity theorises that by the end of the twentieth century China's new public parks represented a tripartite fusion of global and local design influences along with nation-building and evolving Chinese identity. In building the theory for hybrid modernity, several transformations were involved. These included the shifts from Mao's isolationism to the opening to the world from central government and then local government autonomy; from socialism to the capitalist market economy; from the collective to the individual; from poverty and ruralism to wealth and urbanism with the rise of China's middle class. This provides the context for China's new designed landscapes built in the first decade of the twenty-first century.

This chapter considers what the most valued landscapes are likely to be in China in the future. It also reflects on the influences of future urban landscapes, particularly given the central government's target to build 400 additional cities by 2020 (Liauw 2008). The investigation is guided by two key questions:

- How does the contemporary designed landscape represent China's new urban culture?
- Will these designed landscapes continue to have meaning in China's urban future into the twenty-first century?

The examination is predicated on the fact that designed landscapes are cultural by-products of a particular society. It follows in the intellectual tradition fostered by Hayden (1997), Jackson (1994), Treib (1993), Meyer (1991) and other scholars where the method of research into the cultural landscape (designed or vernacular) is design inquiry and the interpretation of its physical form within its social, cultural, economic and political contexts.

The first part of the chapter is organised to help orientate the reader to contemporary conditions in China given the complexity of its ongoing hyper-rapid urbanisation. The key issues that affect the consideration of new urban landscapes are then established through the discussion of three case studies. Finally, the chapter examines how the recent designed urban landscapes reflect today's urban cultures and speculates on the implications of this for the development of future cultural landscapes.

Landscape development and new urban culture

A focus on selected designed landscapes in twenty-first-century urban China reveals that 'urban' is the operative word and is fundamental to understanding China's changing culture. In China's top-down central government, 'urban' and 'rural' are formal legislative land use planning terms used in the governance of populated areas. Under each of these terms, there can be found a particular set of bureaucratic regulations, but the situation is made more complex by the overlap between the various government agencies that have administrative responsibility. Generally, during the Mao Zedong era, circa 1949–1976, the government focus was on the development of rural society with industrialisation occurring primarily in the countryside. During the post-Mao reform period the focus was on modernising and re-building the nation through urbanisation (see Kram *et al.* 2012; Xu and Yeh 2009; Ma and Wu 2005; Yeh 1999). As this change continues to evolve there is also now a growing environmental agenda and a need to deal with the dire environmental destruction created by hyper-rapid urbanisation, climate change, and the fundamental need for agricultural expansion to feed the growing population through rural development and cropland cultivation.

The development of China's cultural landscapes

Cultural differences between northern and southern China arose as the result of regional settlement patterns. A north–south boundary was created by the Yangtze River's east–west alignment where wheat and coarse grains were generally grown in the north and rice in the south (Skinner 1977; Hsieh 1973). Historically, southern China was considered the more urban and sophisticated and this was where the important cultural and trading centres of Hangzhou, Suzhou and Shanghai were located. The Grand Canal was an important trading route. It drew water from China's main east–west rivers and linked the south to Beijing, it also contributed to the area's livelihood and urban identity. By the late 1800s China's eastern coast in particular had become urbanised as a result of the influence of foreign trade. The following selected designed landscape case studies are located in this important eastern region.

West Lake Comprehensive Master Plan, Hangzhou, Zhejiang province

The first case study is the West Lake Comprehensive Master Plan (WLP), Hangzhou, Zhejiang province. WLP was developed between 1999 and 2001 by the local Hangzhou Design Institute (HDI). Primarily this was a landscape protection strategy for nearly 13 square kilometres covering the lake and adjacent environs. It included lakefront renovation plans for the Southern Scenic Area and Hubin Street Lakefront, the Western Scenic Area and North Scenic Area built by 2004. Deputy Mayor Zhang Jianting spearheaded this revitalisation project with the expectation to improve the city, remake its cultural identity, promote the development of tourism and provide high-quality urban open spaces for the local community. In line with Zhang's goals, HDI focused on ways to restore the West Lake environment, rejuvenate and preserve its cultural identity, and regenerate Hangzhou for the new century (W. Chou, pers. comm., 7 May 2007). To accomplish this, HDI sought to re-envision the previous image of imperial West Lake defined by 'one lake, two pagodas, three islands, two causeways' set within a three-sided mountainous perimeter and viewed from its urban fourth edge, with the contemporary concept: 'hot east, prosperous south, secluded west, elegant north, and beautiful centre' (W. Chou, pers. comm., 7 May 2007) (Figure 12.3).

The surface area of the freshwater lake extends over 5.5 square kilometres and is surrounded on three sides by mountains with the fourth side bounded by Hangzhou. The waterscape composition is a result of centuries of dredging practices necessary to maintain the lake's water quality. This idyllic landscape, a lake with three islands and dramatic mountainous backdrop along with imperial palace gardens and Suzhou's hundreds of traditional scholar-official gardens – the so-called Gardens of the Literati designed and created by imperial court scholar-officials in Suzhou during their retirement (Keswick 1978) – provides an archetypal example of the Chinese Picturesque genre in landscape design.

Originally West Lake was the site of a small bay near the mouth of the Qiantang River. With later alluvial sedimentation blocking the river's mouth, it became a lagoon, and eventually over 1,400 years ago during the Sui dynasty it evolved into an inland lake (Chen 2003).

FIGURE 12.3 West Lake Comprehensive Plan, location of ten classical scenes and major visual elements of West Lake's iconic imagery, based on HDI 2002 Plan (courtesy HDI).

It is part of one of the original 44 national-level scenic parks, known as the West Lake National Scenic Area, designated by China's State Council in 1982 that recognised the mountainous area surrounding West Lake, provided limited funding for the restoration of religious temples located in the mountains and covered the former Song dynasty capital city known as Lin'an.

Hangzhou's West Lake National Scenic Area lies in Zhejiang province within the historic Jiangnan region. This region was considered the most urbane, highly cultured and intellectual centre during China's imperial period. Today it spans Zhejiang and Jiangsu provinces along the eastern coast. Hangzhou, capital city of Zhejiang province, Suzhou, major city in Jiangsu province and its capital city Nanjing, nearby Shanghai, and various other cities in the historic Jiangnan region are reclaiming their heritage and cultural identities through the regeneration of historic landscapes and the establishment of new designed landscapes.

The merchant class of Hangzhou financially supported the building boom of both Buddhist and Taoist temples in the mountains surrounding the West Lake (Little 2000). These religious sites became destinations for pilgrimages by scholar-officials and the families of the elite who travelled for days and nights during religious holidays. Nyiri (2006) maps the cultural development of scenic areas and leisure travel as the inspiration for poets, storytellers, musicians, artists and leaders throughout China's classical history. The traditions for long travels and pilgrimages through the mountains to cultural heritage sites can be considered as early forms of tourism. It has been suggested that this ritual travel became embedded in the Chinese psyche and can explain the character of current domestic tourism (Sofield and Li 1996).

West Lake's iconic imagery was the inspiration for China's classical artists and poets, and various political leaders who visited the area. Artists from the Hangzhou-based Song Imperial Painting Academy produced many landscape paintings from which ten were selected, given poetic titles and deemed the 'Ten Scenes of West Lake' circa 1127–1129 CE (Chen 2003). These ten classical scenes spurred more inspiration for artists, garden designers and poets for many years; and West Lake became a pilgrimage site for China's leaders throughout history. During a visit to West Lake in 1699, the Qing emperor Kangxi formalised the names of the ten scenes with four character inscriptions. Later, the local governor had ten stone tablets engraved with Kangxi's imperial inscriptions, and housed them in outdoor pavilions at ten physical sites around West Lake. Later Emperor Qianlong, Kangxi's grandson, wrote poems during his various visits to West Lake and his poems were engraved on his grandfather's stone tablets (Chen 2003).

Generally, the designed landscape in the Mao era (1949–1976) dealt primarily with utilitarianism, the factory commune (Lu 2006) and the agricultural collective (Zhao and Woudstra 2007) and later mass-scale destruction of traditional gardens during the Cultural Revolution (1966–1976). However, like previous leaders in China, Mao visited West Lake on numerous occasions; he wrote poetry, hiked in the mountains and like Emperor Qianglong wanted to leave his legacy there. In the early 1950s, Mao commissioned Beijing Forestry Professor Sun Xiaoxiang, a Zhejiang province native, to design a so-called modern park at one of the classical ten scenes of West Lake called 'Viewing Fish at Flower Pond'. According to Sun (X. Sun, pers. comm., 18 June 2008), a modern park should have Western design elements; he pointed out that his design was the first park in China to incorporate the open lawn and grassy meadows from the English Picturesque garden tradition. His design incorporated scenes that represented different traditional garden styles: Japanese, Chinese and English.

As Hangzhou revitalised itself after the Cultural Revolution, the water in West Lake had become badly polluted with sewage by the mid-1980s. Concerns in the 1990s grew steadily about the condition of the West Lake area as Hangzhou became more affluent in the wave of post-reform economic development (X. Wang, pers. comm., 30 June 2008). Hangzhou's local officials wanted to improve tourism to the West Lake area and were concerned about the city of Hangzhou's image in relation to the encouragement of urban development. The local administration took a radical first step and demolished the garden walls around the 1920s–1930s lakefront villas. The goal was to create a continuous lakefront promenade with free public access. Until then most urban parks in China required an entry fee; providing free access for the proposed new lakefront promenade was a radical move. Local officials wanted to modernise the West Lake area's post-Mao identity and encourage local and national tourism, especially China's nouveau riche in nearby Shanghai.

In keeping with China's modernisation, Hangzhou's officials established high-technology zones with one located in the urban area near the West Lake in the late 1990s.

Urban revitalisation was seen as a useful tool to attract foreign investment. Local leaders commissioned the Hangzhou Design Institute (HDI) to assess the environmental situation at the West Lake. They were aware that their city's image was tied to its urban cultural heritage. However, the older leaders now felt politically free from the tyranny of central government and the oppression of the Cultural Revolution; their younger cadres were ready to reclaim the city's classical urban heritage.

WLP planning 1999–2001 and construction 2001–2004

HDI formulated the WLP as an action-based preservation strategy that sought to remediate the pollution affecting West Lake, improve its water quality and rejuvenate Hangzhou's urban heritage. By 2004 completed projects in the WLP included: the Southern Scenic Area and Lakefront at Hubin Street, Western Scenic Area and Northern Scenic Area (Figure 12.3). In HDI's research of the lake's dredging maintenance records (over hundreds of years) and assessment of conventional water quality analysis, the lake was found to have poor water quality. This was due to the accumulation of pollutants from sewage from the farmers and rural collectives that emerged in the Mao period, industries built in the 1980s and 1990s, and deforestation. Overcrowding throughout West Lake's various scenic areas within and around the lakefront by local, regional and national tourists also contributed to the water's poor quality. HDI concluded that West Lake's Qing dynasty perimeter along its western edge provided the key to dealing with the pollution, as well as improving the lake's water quality. HDI's renovation plans were complex and called for dredging West Lake and a complete re-articulation of the western and southern perimeters of the lake to mimic the Qing dynasty lakefront edge; minor renovations were proposed for the lake's northern perimeter area and the lakefront promenade along Hubin Street.

In the re-articulation of the lake's perimeter at the Western Scenic Area, HDI's design called for the relocation of over a thousand families in village areas and rural collectives, and the closure of industrial factories. The lake was dredged and new water bodies created along with a new lakefront alignment. HDI implemented a modern public infrastructure and mechanical system that filtered the lake water as part of the city's storm water management. The design of the Western Scenic Area was based on an interpretation of imperial paintings including a naturalised lakefront edge with wetland plantings and a contiguous system of open spaces along the West Lake's waterfront (Figure 12.4). A new village in the style of Qing and Ming architecture housed small-scale commercial retail shops, and teahouses with vacation residential hotels.

The Southern Scenic Area covers over 35 hectares and the aims focus on refreshing the West Lake urban edge and Hangzhou's city heritage (Figure 12.4). Using primarily contemporary design language, the lakefront's edge was reconstructed to reflect the city's ancient, imperial and modern heritage. Imperial paintings and city archives helped identify the locations of small bays, lagoons and canals at the lake's edge. HDI created a contiguous lakefront promenade with a system of parks and plazas that contain references to local history, folklore and mythology. The inspiration was drawn from a Qing dynasty painting depicting a Ming dynasty scene of West Lake's urban edge adjacent to the ancient city walls that contained one of the Song dynasty's ten classical scenes. HDI's lakefront design also celebrated the locations of the historic gates for the ancient walled city (Figure 12.5). Historic lakefront buildings were renovated for commercial uses along with construction of a new restaurant retail complex

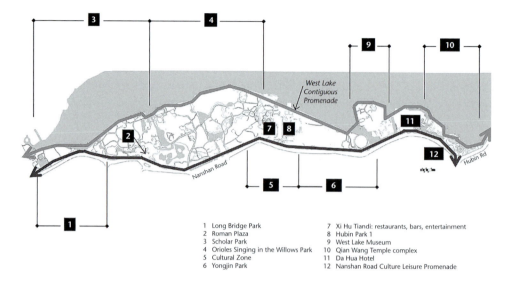

1 Long Bridge Park
2 Roman Plaza
3 Scholar Park
4 Orioles Singing in the Willows Park
5 Cultural Zone
6 Yongjin Park

7 Xi Hu Tiandi: restaurants, bars, entertainment
8 Hubin Park 1
9 West Lake Museum
10 Qian Wang Temple complex
11 Da Hua Hotel
12 Nanshan Road Culture Leisure Promenade

FIGURE 12.4   Southern Scenic Area plan illustrates the re-articulated lakefront edge alignment, series of new and renovated parks and plazas, programme elements and their locations (based on HDI 2002 plan, courtesy HDI).

FIGURE 12.5   Reconstructed lakefront alignment at Yongjin Park marks the historic location of Yongjin gate of the ancient walled city and the mouth of a natural stream that traversed into the imperial city (Mary Padua 2007).

known as Xi Hu (West Lake) Tiandi; it was modelled on commercial development first built in Shanghai that merges new and historic buildings. Extending northward from the lakefront at the Southern Scenic Area, HDI continued its contemporary design with the renovation of the lakefront promenade at Hubin Street, also adjacent to the city.

HDI's chief engineer indicated that one of the sources of this newly synthesised landscape design along West Lake's urban edge was based on web research of projects by foreign contemporary landscape architects in Japan, the United States, France and Germany. Thus, although this team of designers was educated in China, this design was strongly influenced by internet access to international designs. Using an international contemporary design vocabulary, HDI's design of the West Lake's urban edge pulled together, celebrated and brought back references to the area's cultural heritage.

HDI's design for the Northern Scenic Area include minor renovations that preserved the hilly backdrop, part of the three-sided mountainous backdrop in West Lake's iconic landscape. Its Chinese Picturesque design vocabulary is taken from the adjacent contemporary design of the Hubin Street Lakefront Promenade along the Hangzhou's urban edge. Upgrades were made to the existing lakefront pedestrian path system including new timber boardwalks and expanded paths. The design also reorganised the area's visual access and overall visual quality; it created new sight lines to the mountain scenery through the use of new tree planting and vegetation, as well as the removal, relocation and transplanting of trees and vegetation.

HDI's design approach combined considerations of the area's local culture and ecology when they employed contemporary international design language, environmental technology and the Chinese Picturesque genre in their implementation of the WLP. The Western and Northern Scenic Areas preserved the mountain scenery of West Lake's iconic cultural landscape. The Southern Scenic Area and Hubin Street Lakefront Promenade were primarily conceptualised as major renovation projects for the city to improve tourism and attract foreign investment. This helped to remake Hangzhou's cultural identity and preserve West Lake's heritage, and improved its facilities as a national-level tourist destination. It also contributed significantly to mitigating the environmental problems affecting West Lake's water quality. It is likely to have contributed to the achievement in 2011 of the UN World Heritage inscription of the West Lake Cultural Landscape of Hangzhou; the newly designated area overlaps the West Lake National Scenic Area and the lake's urban perimeter.

Gubei Pedestrian Promenade, Shanghai

The four municipalities of Shanghai, Tianjin, Beijing and Chongqing are controlled directly by the central government in China. The second case study is the Gubei Pedestrian Promenade (Promenade) which is located in Shanghai. Shanghai's ascent as a major city has been linked to Hangzhou's decline beginning with the Taiping Rebellion (Wang 1999). The two cities experienced colonial modernisation during the late 1800s when foreign businessmen financed a private railway that linked Hangzhou to Shanghai's port open for foreign trade. While Hangzhou was the city known as 'paradise on earth', Shanghai emerged as the city known as 'Paris of the East'.

The new Promenade, by the SWA Group (2005) a US-based international consultancy, was designed as an urban oasis for Gubei, a densely populated luxury community originally planned for foreign professionals and their families. The Promenade is flanked by luxury high-rise residential buildings spanning three city blocks and is part of the Gubei second development phase located at the western edge of Shanghai's urban centre. The residential towers contain ground-floor commercial uses.

SWA's design concept for the approximately one-kilometre-long outdoor pedestrian spine built on Shanghai's heritage as a cosmopolitan city where foreigners lived, its local small-scale urban street typology of lanes and alleyways for the local community, and the classical garden tradition from nearby Suzhou. The scheme was also designed to meet sustainability goals including wellness and urban healthy living standards for the Gubei community. The client was frustrated by the experience with three previous design firms whose work they found unsatisfactory. SWA was given a set of programme parameters for each block including high-end retail stores and art galleries, a large community assembly area for recreation and seasonal entertainment, and restaurants and cafes with alfresco dining. The client also demanded that SWA adhere to the European garden design language established in Gubei's first development phase.

The city of Shanghai is spatially organised around the Huangpu River, a major tributary of the Yangtze and officially comprises 16 administrative districts and one county. Gubei lies within the boundaries of Changning, one of eight sub-districts that define Puxi, which is one of Shanghai's 16 administrative districts. Puxi contains the city's historic urban centre with an Art Deco style riverfront skyline known as the Bund. Opposite the Bund is the Pudong area, another one of Shanghai's 16 administrative districts on the east bank of the river with a skyline purported to rival Hong Kong. Gubei, covering over 130 hectares, was originally planned for the international community of professionals and their families who worked in the Hongqiao Economic Development Technology Zone (EDTZ), established in 1984 near the Hongqiao airport. Gubei is to the west and physically adjacent to the historic area in Shanghai known as the International Settlements, a district that was designated for foreign businessmen and their families to reside when the city became one of the first five port cities in China to open for foreign trade under the 1842 Treaty of Nanking. The built environment of Gubei's first phase reflected the 1980s design trend towards a neo-classical Western European tradition. By 2005 the first phase of the Gubei community housed over 15,000 residents from China, Japan, Korea, Hong Kong, Taiwan, Singapore, as well as from the West. These residents lived in a dense urban environment made up of pseudo-European buildings with landscapes designed in the French classical tradition. However the trend for neo-classical Western style was changing in other areas of Shanghai and cities throughout China. A number of hybrid modern designed landscapes had already been completed that drew from China's local history and ecological design principles. Therefore, aware that innovation in landscape design had occurred in Shanghai, other places in China and the world in general, SWA felt compelled to educate their client about possible design alternatives to the French classical garden language depicted in the first phase of Gubei.

After a one-week design workshop in Shanghai, SWA was able to satisfy the client to accept their new design concept that was based on the synthesis of two design languages expressed in French Renaissance gardens and contemporary parks in Paris. Their design also incorporated the intimate scale found in Shanghai's urban heritage of streets, courtyards and alleyways, as well as the private traditional scholar gardens found in Suzhou. The 'Cultivar Gardens' concept (Y. Hung, pers. comm., 2 July 2012) drew from the formal botanical notion of the 'cultivar', a new plant species created by genetically blending different plant species, and was described as combining 'the French traditional garden design with French modern

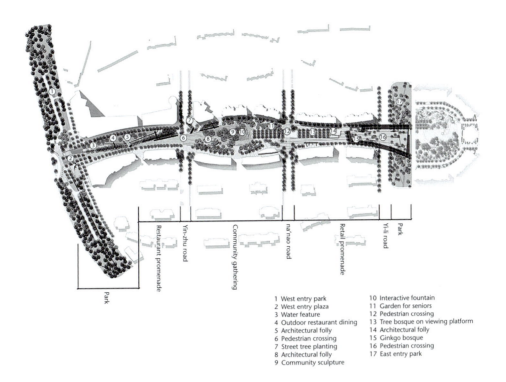

Restaurant promenade

Yin-zhu road

Community gathering

na'nao road

Retail promenade

Yi-li road

Park

Park

1 West entry park	10 Interactive fountain
2 West entry plaza	11 Garden for seniors
3 Water feature	12 Pedestrian crossing
4 Outdoor restaurant dining	13 Tree bosque on viewing platform
5 Architectural folly	14 Architectural folly
6 Pedestrian crossing	15 Ginkgo bosque
7 Street tree planting	16 Pedestrian crossing
8 Architectural folly	17 East entry park
9 Community sculpture	

FIGURE 12.6   Gubei Pedestrian Promenade Master Plan by SWA (courtesy SWA).

design to essentially create a new species of landscape' (Hung *et al.* 2005: 11). It also called for the inclusion of three separate buildings in the guise of architectural follies at each block which were intended to animate the pedestrian environment and enhance the human scale largely dominated by high-rise towers. SWA saw this concept as a way to create a new identity for Gubei (Figure 12.6).

With the client's authorisation to proceed with design development, SWA returned to their US west coast office to develop their concept into a detailed master plan (Figure 12.6). With distance and more time, SWA focused their strategy on addressing the needs of the Gubei community living in a dense urban environment. While retaining the notion of the Cultivar Gardens concept, the landscape master plan strategy called for the provision of 'a contiguous pedestrian open space that is safe, multifunctional, sustainable, fun and exciting for all ages involved the layering and integration of five distinct considerations: cultural infrastructure, environmental sustainability, healthy living, interpretive nature and inventive design' (Y. Hung, pers. comm., 2 July 2012).

SWA's final design strategy created a multipurpose path and series of public spaces that served the residents, visitors, Shanghai community and emergency vehicles. Using trees and vegetation along with architectural follies, water features and different paving materials in various patterns, the design established an open space system and hierarchy of spaces for activities including: an urban gateway plaza with monumental water features at Gubei Street as the main north–south commercial corridor along the Promenade's western boundary;

FIGURE 12.7 Bosque of trees photograph (courtesy Tom Fox 2010).

a large elliptically shaped multipurpose paved area for the Gubei community; raised platforms shaded with *bosques* of trees; intimate-sized areas set in lushly planted areas for passive uses; outdoor seating plazas for alfresco dining; and a series of natural vegetated bioswales to introduce nature and educate the children. The ground plane of the small intimate areas was defined using permeable paving made up of custom-made unit pavers whose forms were based on the curvilinear Chinese roof tile. This paving design allows surface water to drain directly into the soil; it meets environmental sustainability principles and best management practices for stormwater management. An urban forest with over 1,000 trees was planted naturalistically as well as formally in *bosques* and *allées,* typical of French classical gardens. The intention for the urban forest was environmental sustainability, healthy living and community well-being through the creation of a shady pedestrian environment, and reduction of the urban heat island effect (Figure 12.7).

Gubei Pedestrian Promenade represents an elegantly crafted series of outdoor public open spaces for the luxury high-rise residential community in Shanghai. It reflects Shanghai's urban and colonial heritage as a place for foreigners to live but it is also a new multipurpose pedestrian street and form of cultural infrastructure that expands from Shanghai's unique public space and street typology. This includes the *Tianzifang* historic complex of *shikumen* residential buildings, small-scale lanes and alleyways located off Taikang Road in Shanghai's French Concession area, the outdoor pedestrian mall along Nanjing Road, Xintiandi's mixed use entertainment district completed in 2003, and the riverfront promenade and its various renovations along the historic Bund.

Qiaoyuan Park, Tianjin

Within a few hours' drive east of Beijing is Tianjin, another of China's four municipalities controlled directly by central government. Tianjin is located within a delta area in China's eastern region and was one of the host cities for the Beijing 2008 Olympics. In the period leading to the Olympics the authorities in Tianjin replaced a 1990s elevated expressway interchange with a larger expanded version. The remnant lands beneath the elevated regional expressway interchange were developed quickly, except for one quadrant which contained a large drainage basin, military shooting range and ad hoc rubbish dump with a stench recognisable within a half-kilometre radius. The nearby residents regarded this area as a 20-hectare eyesore and complained to the local Tianjin authorities. A high-ranking central government official who commuted daily into Tianjin's urban centre also complained. Very soon after the complaints were heard the landscape architect Professor Kongjian Yu and his firm Turenscape were commissioned to design a new park to mitigate the problems: it was later called Qiaoyuan Park, named after Tianjin's local reputation as a city with many bridges that crossed the Hai River (Padua 2013).

Yu was familiar with the area's local ecology and he often travelled along the road. His strategy was to use the area's delta ecology for his design inspiration. He transformed the area though a design based on using the ecosystem services of the site and by creating a place for ecological experimentation. This project represents a mastery that Yu built up over ten years in ecological design. The site had several environmental challenges: shallow alkaline soils, stormwater drainage problems and the landfill site. The new park design was filled with vegetation but it certainly did not feel or look naturalistic. The dominant design element was the field of 21 organic-shaped basins. However these ponds had a uniformity that was too perfect to be mistaken for a naturally evolved setting. Yu's design goal was to improve the soils through this system of vegetated wet and dry demonstration ponds (Figure 12.8). The raised topography along the perimeter of the basins created a visual effect similar to the large moguls found on a ski run and this hilly quality was exaggerated by the verticality of some of the wetland plants.

Yu is not the only designer in China now using ecological principles as a key basis for design combined with inspiration founded on the importance of sense of place and local identity. The funding of the case study projects in West Lake, Hangzhou and Gubei, Shanghai illustrates an example of a new ecological awareness and a new understanding by those funding new public spaces that sense of place and cultural heritage as reflected in the landscape is important.

Overview

The discussion of the three projects demonstrates the growing importance of place-based design, local cultural heritage and environmental sustainability concerns in China's recent landscape designs. Each reflects challenges faced by China's city leaders to preserve their city's competitive economic edge within the ongoing hyper-urbanisation, as well as keep in step with central government's nation-building efforts. China's market economy, globalisation and capitalism have created societal shifts that have given rise to consumerism, a rising middle class, more leisure time and new lifestyles. The conceptualisation of these projects has progressed from the superficiality of the cosmetic city urban landscapes discussed by Yu and Padua (2007). Through radical change to West Lake's urban edge, HDI has deepened its hybrid modern

FIGURE 12.8   Aerial view of Qiaoyuan Park showing system of wet and dry ponds (courtesy Kongjian Yu/Turenscape 2008).

approach through its temporal-spatial exploration of Hangzhou's ancient, imperial and twentieth-century modern past with an underlying desire to improve the lake's water quality. In Shanghai, SWA's fine-grain design of the Gubei Pedestrian Promenade creates a new type of cultural infrastructure and serves the community needs by creating a comfortable outdoor urban oasis that builds on the city's unique hybrid identity as Paris of the East, its historic urban morphology and its urban heritage. Yu's work in Tianjin and elsewhere continues on an environmental trajectory that also creates new spatial forms and effectively addresses China's new urban milieu.

The case study projects discussed here emphasise the rapid transformation of the designed landscapes in China's twenty-first-century urban areas since the so-called urban fever of the 1980s. Exposed to the outside world, whether via the internet, mass media, foreign travel or overseas education, and conscious of the environmental destruction created by hyper-rapid urbanisation, China's vanguard of designers, whether home-grown or foreign, recognise the need to make meaningful designed landscapes for China's rapidly changing society and contemporary urban culture.

Reflections on future directions of urban landscapes in China

As has been shown briefly, the direction of China's urban landscape design is presently taking a number of different routes. There is evidence to show that some of these attempt to reflect contemporary Chinese culture, however the direction of future landscape design in China is less clear. Will the protected status of the West Lake area be sustained? Will the contemporary design along the urban lakefront be able to withstand the throngs of people that will be attracted to it, and survive the test of time? Will new buildings, whether high-rise hotels, residential or office towers, within the designated urban buffer zone laid out in the World Heritage site inscription create negative environmental impacts on the lake's water quality? HDI claims that the present reconstruction of the lakefront's edge to its Qing dynasty alignment is an ecologically sound decision, but will future designers agree? HDI's design essentially demolished all of the Mao-era park spaces along the lakefront in the Southern Scenic Area. Will future designers question this loss? If so, will the reimagining of Mao's park go against the spirit of UNESCO's standards for the historic urban landscape? In relation to the theme of new cultural landscapes, does this new landscape represent contemporary culture's desires and needs? Does this interpretation of historic features and cultural meanings within a framework inspired by a contemporary international design language really reflect contemporary Chinese urban cultures and retain what is really valued from past cultural landscapes?

As an already recognised cultural landscape, HDI's projects around the West Lake, Hangzhou are perhaps the least likely to be lost to redevelopment during the fever for urban landscape change which is very present and most likely to increase in all China's burgeoning cities. The West Lake's designation as a National-level Scenic Park and Historic site provides some safeguard against immediate change and perhaps its recent inscription as a cultural landscape on UNESCO's World Heritage list will provide further protection. However, while HDI's designs for the lake's perimeter areas, Western Scenic Area, North Scenic Area, the Lakefront at Hubin Street and the Southern Scenic Area, appear to have been well executed and are within the designated cultural landscape boundary, there seems to be little to prevent a future modification of the work. Such change might result from the encroaching urban development, which although outside the boundary of the West Lake cultural landscape, could be detrimental to the lake's water quality and require a radically altered edge condition.

SWA's Shanghai project builds on the city's cosmopolitan identity urban heritage. It also reinterprets the scale of the Chinese Picturesque gardens from nearby Suzhou. At first glance, the Promenade may seem highly commercial, but it represents innovative design that allows flexibility of use by providing a range of outdoor open spaces for everyday leisure and recreational needs, as well as for seasonal events for Gubei residents and the Shanghai community. New nature has been inserted within the Promenade's very dense urban environment. It is a new type of multidimensional, flexible pedestrian-based corridor that expands Shanghai's heritage of community public space and urban street typology. Given the shade of the urban forest, the various spaces within the Promenade are heavily used. In the future, will designers recognise the project as a new type of cultural infrastructure that acknowledges a certain type of lifestyle and outdoor living? Will future designers give value to the Promenade's contemporary design language; will they consider it worthy of SWA's claim that it contributes to Shanghai's urban street typology? The hope is that the urban forest will mature enough to be valued as a functional and valued open space achieving SWA's concept to create flexible multipurpose spaces.

It could be that Yu's work, SWA's work, and perhaps the work of other designers such as Damon now working in China, could be considered as a reflection of a new Chinese

FIGURE 12.9 Organic-shaped sculptures used in the water cleansing process at Living Water Park, Chengdu, Sichuan province (Mary Padua 2003).

cultural phenomenon, or *eco-urban poetry* within landscape design. This eco-urban poetry is particularly obvious in Damon's Living Water Park at Chengdu, with its sinuous alignments of the organic sculpted stone flow forms that oxygenate the water as part of the cleansing process (Figure 12.9). The rest of the park represents the Chinese Picturesque design genre with a few attempts at contemporary plaza design. SWA's contemporary international design introduces swathes of vegetated bioswales with a system of pedestrian bridges designed to overlook the vegetation; naturalistic but highly constructed, it represents a new nature for the residents living in the dense urban environment (Figure 12.10) and new opportunities for introducing children to natural ecology. SWA's urban forest, as a major eco-urban gesture, also demonstrates the importance of environmental sustainability and urban ecology.

Yu's Qiaoyuan Park, with its ecologically inspired design, takes Damon's ideas and elevates them into another dimension that dispels the Chinese Picturesque (Figure 12.11). The relationship between poetry and garden-making were intertwined in China's classical literati *shan-shui* tradition (Feng 1992; Keswick 1978). Perhaps Yu's work represents a truly novel Chinese design genre that deals with the present ecological design trend that draws from the natural sciences to regenerate China's urban leftover spaces, while fully embracing the importance of visual quality and design aesthetics that respect *genius loci* and local history. The visual narrative he has been pursuing could be described as an evolved form of what Keswick (1978) calls magical realism, used to describe Chinese classical gardens. Such Chinese gardens, designed by retired officials, were artificial constructions of nature, dominated by scenes of various forms of rockery, a main water body and individual plantings; these

FIGURE 12.10   Pedestrian bridge overlook of vegetated bioswale along SWA's Gubei Pedestrian Promenade, Shanghai (courtesy Ying-Yu Hung 2010).

designs were driven by metaphysical concerns and Daoist notions of harmony with nature. Keswick interpreted the Westerner's appreciation of these gardens as magical realism or other-worldly in that the aesthetics were new, difficult to grasp, yet visually provocative. Yu's Qiaoyuan Park set within an urban context is an artificial construction of a second or new nature; adaptive regenerative processes in a new type of public park composed of wet and dry circular forms set among earthen mounds never seen or experienced before in China (Figure 12.11). Yu's park could be interpreted as an example of China's twenty-first-century magical realism. While it is a science-based naturalistic park, it is largely a geometric composition rather than authentic as a natural wetland and is very popular for the local residents.

Yu is quite sincere about exploiting people's leisure time in his parks in order to teach them about ecological design, as well as raising environmental consciousness. His work, as does SWA's and HDI's, contributes to China's emerging twenty-first-century urban form and the community needs of the rapidly changing society. It is important to note that a high proportion of China's current urban population now consists of young professionals who were born in the city and are now raising their families there. They have little or no experience of rural life except through oral histories or stories of their parents or grandparents. The parks and public open spaces discussed here have the potential to provide important experiences of the landscape that become positive memories of their early twenty-first-century urban life.

FIGURE 12.11 Pond with viewing platform and interpretative signage at Qiaoyuan Park (courtesy Kongjian Yu/Turenscape 2008).

Conclusion

Navigating the landscapes in China that are presently considered to be of high cultural value and considering the future of such landscapes is a complicated task in the ever-changing milieu of government control. Further difficulties arise when this is overlain with the speed of spatial change and the appetite for hyper-rapid urbanisation now occurring in China. The new cultural landscapes such as those discussed in this chapter have been agents for transformation in China's urban revolution and have potential for influencing the lives of many young urban dwellers. The selected designed landscapes are revolutionary in China in that they find ways to combine the site's cultural heritage with its local ecology. These projects build on innovations that began in the hybrid modern parks in China's late twentieth century but they are much more attuned to China's rapidly changing urban culture. Some are highly constructed and referential to China's zeitgeist; for example, Yu's Qiaoyuan Park in Tianjin dominantly depicts an eco-urban narrative. Other designers, like HDI as shown at West Lake, Hangzhou, have created elegant new cultural landscapes where the threads of the urban present and the ecological past are woven together with contemporary expressions of an urban cultural heritage. The new design manages to sit lightly within West Lake's iconic scenery.

SWA's sophisticated design expands Shanghai's typology of public space and urban heritage as a place for international residents and local communities with their elegantly crafted project. Notions of identity in these case study urban landscapes are linked to emblems of a mythologised past and contemporary symbols of China's material achievements. In these various ways, perhaps the innovations of those creating today's new cultural landscapes will help carry forward a revolution that will create an urban future that is able to synthesise China's historic landscapes awakened by outside influences and developed within a Chinese context that deals with China's complex identity. This complex and sometimes contradictory nature of Chinese identity could be understood when reflecting back on the opening ceremonies of the 2008 Beijing Olympics. It ranged from ersatz imperial splendour to an appearance by the Chinese astronaut; it was staged to have maximum impact in mobilising and uniting the Chinese public; its effectiveness was demonstrated in an outpouring of nationalist fervour across China. It was also meant as a demonstration to the world that China had fully integrated into global society. While the Mao era attempted to erase all things to do with imperial China and Confucianism, the 2008 Beijing Olympic opening ceremonies and the urban landscapes illustrated in this chapter celebrate China's contemporary urban society and have reimagined and mythologised China's past – imperial, colonial and early twentieth-century modern China. Outside influences will no doubt continue to have an impact upon Chinese identity and it may prove challenging for some to define authentic Chineseness in the future. This is already affected by the many international design consultancies working in China, the overseas education and professional experience of prominent Chinese designers and the increasing influences of technology, mass media and the internet. Foreign design influences are likely to continue, given the economic uncertainty in the European Union and the United States, and the growth of China's globally influenced design industries, particularly given central government's forecast for a population growth of 0.5 billion by 2020 and expectations for the building of an additional 400 cities (Liauw 2008). While the engagement with ecological concerns within the design community in urban areas can be seen as very positive, the disposition of the projects discussed here and the acceptance of the ongoing interplay of local and global influences in China's urban future points to the need for China's professional communities to ensure that they are aware of the challenges in trying to achieve the responsible production of new urban cultural landscapes that are sensitive to China's evolving identity, the desire to be more ecologically sensitive and the consideration of the community values embedded within historic and traditional landscapes.

References

Anderson B. (1991) *Imagined Communities: Reflections on the Origin and Spread of Nationalism*, London: Verso.

Appadurai, A. (1990) 'Disjuncture and Difference in the Global Cultural Economy', *Theory, Culture, and Society* 7, 2: 295–310.

Chen, G. (2003) *Hangzhou*, Beijing: Foreign Language Press.

Clunas, C. (1997) *Art in China*, Oxford: Oxford University Press.

Elvin, M. (2004) *The Retreat of the Elephants: An Environmental History of China*, New Haven and London: Yale University Press.

Fairbank, J.K. (1957) (ed.) *Chinese Thought and Institutions*, Chicago: University of Chicago Press.

Feng, J.Z. (1992) 'Mutual Nutrition of Man and Nature: An Outline of the Comparative History of Landscape Architecture', *Spazio e societe* 57: 62–77.

Hayden, D. (1997) *The Power of Place: Urban Landscapes as Public History*, Cambridge, MA: MIT Press.

Hsieh, C.M. (1973) *Atlas of China*, New York: McGraw-Hill.

Hung, Y., Aquino, G. and Ma, K.C. (2005) *Shanghai Gubei Gold Street*, Shanghai, PRC, Client Presentation Technical Report 12 July 2005, SWA Group, Sausalito, California USA.

Jackson, J.B. (1994) *A Sense of Place, a Sense of Time*, New Haven: Yale University Press.

Keswick, M. (1978) *The Chinese Garden: History, Art and Architecture*, London: Academy.

Kram, M., Bedford, C., Durnin, M., Luo, Y., Rokpelnis K., Roth B., Smith, N., Wang, Y., Yu, G., Yu, Q. and Zhao, X. [ed. N. Smith] (2012) *Protecting China's Biodiversity: A Guide to Land Use, Land Tenure, and Land Protection Tools*, Beijing: The Nature Conservancy.

Liauw, L. (2008) 'Introduction to New Urban China', *Architectural Design* 78, 9: 6–15.

Little, S. (2000) *Taoism and the Arts of China*, Berkeley: University of California Press.

Liu, D.H. (2008) 'After the Pearl River Delta: Exporting the PRD – a View from the Ground'. *Architectural Design* 78, 9: 78–81.

Lu, D. (2006) *Remaking Chinese Urban Form: Modernity, Scarcity and Space, 1949–2005*, London and New York: Routledge.

Ma, L.J.C. and Wu, F. (2005) *Restructuring the Chinese City*, London and New York: Routledge.

Meyer, E. (1991) 'The Public Park as Avante-Garde', *Landscape Journal* 10, 1: 16–26.

Nyiri, P. (2006) *Scenic Spots: Chinese Tourism, the State, and Cultural Authority*, Seattle: University of Washington.

Padua, M. (2007) 'Hybrid Modernity: Framing the Park in Post-Mao China', *Council of Educators in Landscape Architecture (CELA) Negotiating the Landscapes Proceedings*, Penn State, pp. 65–80.

Padua, M. (2010) *Hybrid Modernity: Late 20th Century Landmark Parks in China*, unpublished PhD thesis, Edinburgh College of Art, University of Edinburgh, Edinburgh, Scotland, UK.

Padua, M. (2012) 'This Way, Shanghai', *Landscape Architecture* 102, 12: 52–65.

Padua, M. (2013) 'Bridge to Somewhere Else', *Landscape Architecture* 103, 2: 80–87.

Reed, P. (2005) *Beyond Before and After: Designing Contemporary Landscape, Groundswell: Constructing the Contemporary Landscape*, New York: The Modern Museum of Art.

Skinner, G.W. (1977) 'Regional Urbanization in Nineteenth Century China', in G.W. Skinner (ed.) *The City in Late Imperial China*, Stanford: Stanford University Press, pp. 214–215.

Sofield, T.H.B. and Li, F.M.S. (1996) 'Rural Tourism in China', in S.G. Page (ed.) *The Business of Rural Tourism*, London: Routledge, pp. 57–84.

Treib, M. (1993) 'Axioms for a Modern Landscape Architecture', in M. Treib (ed.) *Modern Landscape Architecture: A Critical Review*, Cambridge, MA and London: MIT Press, pp. 36–67.

Wang, L. (1999) 'Tourism and Spatial Change 1911–1927', in J.W. Esherick (ed.) *Remaking the Chinese City: Modernity and National Identity, 1900–1950*, Honolulu: University of Hawaii, pp. 107–120.

Xu, J. and Yeh, A.G.O. (2009) 'Decoding Urban Land Governance: State Reconstruction in Contemporary Chinese Cities', *Journal of Urban Studies* 46, 3: 559–581.

Yeh, A.G.O. (1999) 'The Transformation of the Urban Planning System in China from a Centrally-Planned to Transitional Economy', *Progress in Planning* 51, 3: 167–252.

Yu, K. (1992) 'Experience of Basin Landscapes in Chinese Agriculture has led to Ecologically Prudent Engineering', in L.O. Hansson, and B. Jungen (eds) *Human Responsibility and Global Change: Proceedings of the International Conference on Human Ecology*, University of Gothenburg, Sweden, pp. 289–299.

Yu, K. and Padua, M. (2007) 'China's Cosmetic Cities: Urban Fever and Superficiality', *Landscape Research* 32, 2: 225–249.

Zhao, J. and Woudstra, J. (2007) 'In Agriculture, Learn from Dazhai, Mao Zedong's Revolutionary Model Village and the Battle against Nature', *Landscape Research* 32, 2: 171–205.

13

CULTURAL LANDSCAPES AND CLIMATE CHANGE

Protecting resources that matter in a future of uncertainty

Robert Z. Melnick

Introduction

The healthy and robust future of cultural patrimony, especially as affected by changing global climate conditions, should be of great concern to our society, our diverse communities, and each of us as individuals. It is impossible to consider seriously the future protection of cultural resources, and especially the future of cultural landscapes, without recognising, accepting and responding to the clear trajectory of climate change. While climate change is a global phenomenon with local implications, there is no longer any doubt that there is an evolving set of ecological modifications as a direct result of human activity and climate change (Intergovernmental Panel on Climate Change 2007; Epstein and McCarthy 2004).

While it is not the goal of this chapter to present an argument supporting the scientific concept of climate change, it is evident that it remains a point of controversy in a number of countries, including the United States of America. This controversy is often grounded in a political and philosophical/religious foundation, and has resulted in climate change becoming a cultural issue instead of primarily an arena for scientific investigation and societal response (Hulme 2009; Steyn 2006; Flannery 2005). As has occurred throughout human history, insights in scientific endeavours, especially revolutionary insights that challenge the normative thinking, are often met with derision, scorn and doubt. This is no less so for the science of climate change, even in light of growing evidence and rigorous scientific inquiry.

Heritage conservation, as a field, has also often been challenged by unforeseen developments, too often with traditional, defensive and predictable responses that have not always advanced the goal of resource protection. The field is now faced with some difficult choices, opportunities, challenges and decisions in the coming years (Carroon 2010). Attention needs to be turned to a range and scale of issues beyond the traditional tasks of resource identification, documentation and conservation intervention, either at a planning or site scale. Heritage conservation and protection, and especially cultural landscape protection, need to go far beyond what has been achieved in the past, facing a future filled with certain uncertainty. New cultural landscapes will be shaped as much by climate change as they will be by traditions, practices and human intervention.

Some perspectives on the value of heritage conservation

Heritage conservation,[1] especially as it has been practised in the USA, is often too narrow in scope, too bound in tight silos, and too unwilling to change in response to shifting contexts, whether environmental, cultural or political. This has been especially limiting in work with cultural landscapes and often results in traditional approaches to nontraditional circumstances. While long-held and well-developed values should not necessarily be relinquished, there is an essential human need to understand context in both time and place, both temporally and geographically. This need is, in the very best sense, what propels the efforts by individuals, community and by society towards heritage conservation. At the most fundamental level, people throughout the world are driven by a desire to know, understand and protect multiple cultural and historic contexts. Like the landscape, the capacity to evolve and change will provide greater opportunity for true sustainability and a greater opportunity for the new cultural landscape. Scholarly and professional foundations are important, but rigid adherence to so-called established truths is limiting and can be dangerous. The nature of scientific revolutions and paradigm shifts demands that methods, techniques and theories are regularly tested.

For example, it is necessary in the context of climate change to reconsider dramatically what is meant by significance and historic fabric, and how the conservation community strives to protect valued cultural landscapes. How realistic is it to try to conserve landscapes that will recede or even disappear under the weight of climate change? If these landscapes are protected, is it appropriate to stress a rigid adherence to the historic fabric of these places, or do we need to think more broadly about what is meant by historic integrity, at least in the USA?

Disasters, heritage resources and climate change

In this context, there are many ways to think about climate change, especially with respect to cultural landscapes. One way is that it is and will be a disaster, and result in a set of changes that cannot be easily predicted. It is, fundamentally, a matter of circumstance, relationship and a matter of judgment of degree. What may seem like a disaster to some may appear routine to others.

For those in a developed country, a disaster may present itself when the local grocery is out of your favorite cheese, or you cannot find the keys to your automobile. For those who live on the edge of starvation, the lack of any food at all is truly a disaster. These extreme, and admittedly simplistic, examples are reminders that this is a world of relative metrics and not absolutes. Hot in one location is mild in another, and wet in one landscape may just be the normal winter somewhere else. While context is not everything, it is the societal framework within which these landscapes thrive. When the framework evolves, the landscape will as well.

Heritage resources never exist out of context, except, perhaps, when they are stolen or removed. Arguments around the Elgin Marbles are familiar (King 2005). In the USA the removal of Native American artefacts to big city, out-of-situ museums presents similar issues of rightful ownership and protective stewardship (Brown 2004). Taking resources out of context, even thinking about them out of context, turns them into objects rather than dynamic resources. These resources are then considered and appreciated in what is, quite literally, a foreign culture. The same can be said for climate change and cultural landscapes. Climate change response, or anticipation, is best activated when contextual, as well as the particular, issues are engaged.

Disasters that will define cultural landscapes come in many forms and shapes, and from many causes and origins. There are disasters that cannot be foreseen, and which are most often the result of the normal and cyclical processes of natural systems. They are disasters to humans, but not if the natural, as opposed to the human, systems are the primary consideration. The 2011 earthquake and tsunami that hit northern Japan was, by any measure, a disaster impacting upon the human systems of settlement, energy and food production, and, of course, life itself. It was also a normal and expected, if not anticipated, event in geologic time. In the Cascade mountain region of the western USA,[2] the next volcanic eruption is fully expected, if not anticipated; only the date is unknown (Figure 13.1). The 2011 Japanese tsunami was only a surprise because of its timing, not because of its occurrence.

In 2005, Hurricane Katrina was also a disaster, one that dramatically affected heritage resources across the Gulf Coast of the USA (McCarthy 2011). As with many disasters, this was also catastrophic, in that it was quick, overwhelming and devastating in its impact. The best that could be done, at the time, was to watch it unfold as it overtook that landscape (Figure 13.2).

Even in 2012, the US Gulf of Mexico coastal area is still recovering from those events of 2005. Although Katrina looked like a natural disaster, there is ample scientific thought that it was caused by a combination of events, by both human actions and the usual and expected cycles of natural systems. These are disasters that result from a combination of natural forces and human actions that aggravate those systems and inflict lasting damage.

FIGURE 13.1   The Cascade mountains, in the western USA, comprise a young range in geologic time, with the potential for expected eruption as part of the normal patterns of natural systems. This image is of Mount Hood in Oregon, looking south (Robert Melnick).

FIGURE 13.2   New Orleans, Louisiana, after the Katrina disaster of 2005, reflected both human
and natural impacts on this urban cultural landscape. Recent years have seen
a rash of unusual weather events throughout the USA and elsewhere
(Robert Melnick).

Many scientists believe that Katrina was an aggravated storm, intensified by changes in ocean
temperature.

Another very good example of a natural disaster aggravated by human intervention is
the dust bowl of the 1930s, a period of severe dust storms causing major ecological and agricultural damage to American and Canadian prairie lands (Egan 2006). Although droughts had
occurred in this region on and off for centuries, the story of the dust bowl is an instructive
lesson to understand the relationship between human actions and natural forces that often
result in calamity. Why, in the 1930s, did so much soil literally fly away, sometimes as far as
Washington, DC, over 1,500 miles (2,400 km) to the east?

The direct explanation is that, in the 1920s, wheat, as well as the long-established cotton,
became the most popular and economically rewarding crop in the region, so much so that
there were millions of acres of grazing land ploughed for wheat production. For previous
centuries, this landscape was held in place by the deep roots of native grasses. But when the
drought hit in the late 1920s, the temperatures rose and the winds blew, and the grass was
gone, ploughed under (Figure 13.3). The problem was compounded because wheat is a
seasonal crop, with shallow roots, that is harvested every season. The topsoil took flight, no
longer secured by natural vegetation, and the decade turned into a disaster by any measure,

FIGURE 13.3   The dust bowl in the USA had a severe impact on people's lives and the landscapes they had nurtured and tended for years, as illustrated in this 1936 Dorothea Lange photo of a farmstead near Dalhart, Texas (Library of Congress, Prints & Photographs Division, FSA/OWI Collection, LC-DIG-fsa-8b32396 DLC).

a disaster that could have been averted. There still would have been a drought, but not a dust bowl, with its ensuing damage and harm to so many people, families, communities and cultural landscapes. The 1930s dust bowl had a dramatic impact upon the cultural landscape of the middle one-third of the continental USA and portions of Canada. Out of this disaster rose the US Soil Conservation Service, as well as other programmes, to engage in long-term efforts to avoid another dust bowl.

These two examples suggest that there is a need to think of the varieties of disaster that severely impact upon heritage resources, and especially the uncertainty about occurrence, intensity and human response. In order to anticipate the shape of the new cultural landscape in the future, it is valuable to think about these types of events before they happen, even if the specifics are unknown, as there will inevitably be the need to respond rapidly.

Climate change and its impact on cultural landscapes

Another type of disaster exists, one that is often unseen because it is not immediate and it is not generally considered catastrophic. This is the slow erosion of heritage resources as they are affected by forces outside the purview or control of heritage conservation. Management of the impacts of these forces and dynamics is needed if the goal of providing future generations the opportunity to locate themselves within the time and space context of the landscape is to be achieved.

Climate change is complex and too often simplified, rather than clarified. It is not yet fully understood, yet is already the target for political fights and dire predictions from multiple directions. The sky is not falling,[3] but it may be changing shape and colour. In many ways, most, if not all, disasters are unforeseen and unanticipated; they are both natural and man-made (see Chapter 9). While these are usually sudden and dramatic, disasters can also occur in a more subtle way, revealing their impact as time unfolds and there is the opportunity to reflect on what has occurred. Perhaps the most important of these globally is climate change for those directly concerned with heritage resources and, perhaps more importantly, how it will affect the endeavour of defining and protecting these significant places (Cullen 2010).

In a topic dominated by science – climate change studies – it is instructive to consider this arena from a humanities and conservation perspective. While science is of course concerned with people, understanding the potential impact of climate change on both the planet and our societies is a valuable endeavour. Confronting the human impact of these forces, in addition to the biological, ecological and environmental scenarios, allows for a more measured and considered response. To begin with, climate change is an idea, not just a physical phenomenon. As Hulme states: 'our cultural, social, political and ethical practices are reinterpreting what climate change means' (Hulme 2009: xxv). Given the controversies surrounding climate change in the public press, it is important to recognise some essential beliefs about this topic.

Based on the scientific evidence (both anecdotal and longitudinal) human action is changing the climate of this planet. While the pace or even extent of change is not always clear, scientific evidence demonstrates that climate change is happening. Climate, however, is not the same as weather. Weather is today and tomorrow; climate is long term and cyclical, with greater impact on societal and cultural systems. Climate is also more difficult to see, beyond the generalisations, which are often too broad and lack sufficient detail to be useful. For example, it is prevalent to believe that the Pacific Northwest of the USA is wet and rainy, as are the British Isles. Hawai'i, like Bali, is always sunny and warm. The Antarctic is bitter, windy and unbearably cold.

Furthermore, it is a mistake always to consider climate change in a catastrophic context, as this does not advance the understanding of climate change and societal impacts. There are broad human and societal impacts of climate change, just as there are for any other disaster, and these are often overlooked in the popular literature. Among these are the impacts on heritage resources, which are most valuably evaluated critically, and not dogmatically.

Scholarship in the recognition and protection of cultural and historic resources, especially significant cultural landscapes, has expanded considerably in recent years. These landscapes have evolved and changed over time in response to essential human needs of settlement, habitation, food production, economic viability, and security, in the very broadest meaning of that term. These dynamic systems evolve as their living features (e.g. trees, shrubs, grasses, vines) grow and die as part of the normal and expected life cycle (Laird 1998), and other components (e.g. river systems, topographic features and coastlines) are restructured through natural ecological processes. In this sense, landscape is always a noun *and* a verb.[4] Landscape is something that *exists*, but is also something that is *evolving*. There is perhaps no greater natural force than climate, which has an impact upon the direction of change in cultural landscapes. One cannot think about a landscape without considering what it is now, but also how it is always changing, always evolving. This is especially so when climate change is considered, but the idea of evolution is a fundamental understanding of cultural landscapes as well.[5]

Ongoing scientific research explains that climate change is both a global and local phenomenon, geographically and temporally. Climate change cannot be affirmed or denied due to warmer or wetter weather from one year to the next, or because one valley shows signs of decaying native plants and another valley does not. A broader and more expansive understanding is needed, as well as the scientific evidence to support those observations. The work of landscape architects, and even many landscape historians, is essentially, but not exclusively, prescriptive. In the very broadest meaning of the terms, these professionals seek out environmental opportunities and propose responses, most often rational solutions. Sometimes there is success, while at other times the challenges are more difficult to resolve. Embodied in this work is the understanding that the landscape is dynamic and never static. This is not a new or unique idea, of course, but it is essential to grasp, in order to engage both the long and short view on issues of heritage resource protection and disasters.

Like much science, research in climate change is as much an art as it is an exact discipline, and it focuses on the quality of life, especially as it is integrated with the quality of the planet. Through lifelong training and endless propaganda, society has come to expect that scientists inevitably have the right answers to the world's pressing problems. At best, this is an unreasonable expectation with which to burden those who experiment, take intellectual and professional risks, and seek answers that are often unimaginable or outside accepted worldviews. While it has become commonplace to refer to 'paradigm shifts' (Kuhn 1962), these are really revolutions in thinking, not merely shifts. It may be argued, as discussed below, that what is needed is a revolution, and not merely a shift, in the thinking about, and approach to, historically significant cultural resources, and especially landscapes, as their conservation or protection is confronted, and the response to human-inflicted changes to ecological systems is embraced.

The best science, it would seem, expects and accepts many errors, mistakes and miscalculations on the way to establishing new understandings, new paradigms and new truths. Of course, there is no way to know what is truth and what is misunderstanding in relation to the natural world, while standing too close to the problem or event. Kuhn's (1962) description and analysis of both Copernicus' and Galileo's endeavours, for example, supports this notion. It takes distance and perspective to evaluate the veracity of an idea, the importance of a theorem or the significance of a breakthrough.

The same can be said for work in heritage conservation. Temporal distance and contextual perspective are necessary even to begin to assess the importance or significance of historic buildings, sites, structures, objects and landscapes, regardless of the location. The so-called '50-year rule' of the National Register of Historic Places in the USA, for example, emerged from this argument. Under this rule, which is not really a rule but more of a guideline, a property, such as a building or landscape, must be at least 50 years old before it is eligible to be nominated to the National Register. There are exceptions to this, but this guideline expects the temporal distance of two generations before the meaning and value of a place can truly be determined. This is not really a new idea but it confirms that significance, whether in history or in science, requires critical perspective and analytical judgment. It also reasserts that strategies and protocols, for both science and history, are best re-examined on a regular and consistent, basis. This is particularly so as contextual conditions change and perceptions and understandings are modified.

This discussion is meant to establish the backdrop for exploring the consequences of climate change on the ways history is approached, and even more so, the societal necessity and even urgency to protect those places that visibly reflect and reveal the poetics of the human condition. In the heritage conservation community, cultural landscapes have only relatively recently been recognised, and attention to them often still challenges conservation dogma (UNESCO 2003). Although the study and protection of significant cultural landscapes is now generally accepted within intellectual and governmental frameworks internationally, this has not always been the case. Most importantly, in many ways these significant places are strangers in a strange land (Heinlein 1961).

Although this chapter primarily discusses climate change issues in the United States, it is important to recognise that other nations have been more proactive in confronting these problems. The International Council on Monuments and Sites (ICOMOS), for example, has held a number of invaluable workshops and General Assemblies that convene international experts to tackle these basic questions (ICOMOS 2009, 2007, 2005, 2003). The ICOMOS resolutions from New Delhi (ICOMOS 2007) and Xi'an (ICOMOS 2005) are especially important recognitions that we can no longer consider heritage conservation outside of the changing global climate. Likewise, English Heritage has been a leader in the recognition that cultural resources, including landscapes, are seriously threatened by the impacts of climate change (English Heritage 2008).

In many ways, cultural landscapes are outside of conservation orthodoxy, which is built on the traditions of history, historic architecture and prehistoric and historic archeology. In those fields, especially as they intersect with heritage conservation, primary emphasis is most often placed on both cultural origins and resource stability. While these principles have developed an elasticity in recent years, the origins of heritage conservation, especially in the USA, are grounded in the need to know a place's earliest moments, and the need to resist change to its structure, attributes and details.

These principles are expressed in many ways, primarily through the criteria for the National Register of Historic Places and the Secretary of Interior's Standards for Historic Preservation Projects (Birnbaum 1994). In both of these documents, for example, a property's integrity is of primary value. As is known, in this context integrity is a measure of a property's present condition as compared with what it was during the period from which it gains significance. The closer a property is today to its original condition, the greater its integrity. What does this have to do with climate change, protecting cultural landscapes and understanding what new cultural landscapes might be? More importantly, how might climate change lead to a re-examination of what is meant by integrity? Can the argument be made that cultural landscape integrity does not carry the same criteria as that for other heritage resources, particularly architecture or archeological sites?

In order even to attempt to answer these questions, it is instructive to look carefully at the burgeoning interest in cultural landscapes, and the relationship of these landscapes to the larger heritage community. Taking the USA as an example, it can be seen that since the late 1970s there has been increased interest in understanding and protecting places that reflect the dynamics of American life, and the ways in which the land has been settled and used over time. This has resulted in much greater attention to cultural landscapes, and the development of strategies for understanding their significance and planning for their protection and continued presence in society. These methods were adapted to fit into heritage conservation practice, and in many cases adhered to the stricture that oldest is best, and change is explicitly undesirable.

While a landscape is protected in order to understand its cultural value and meaning, the processes of landscape dynamics are often overlooked in this conversation. In light of sobering climate change predictions and realities, rethinking and re-envisioning strategies for protecting, and perhaps even understanding, significant cultural landscapes is required. Unlike the established conservation orthodoxy, historic *landscape conservation* is often based on embracing change, rather than resisting it (Shoard 1981). This is fundamental to landscape studies, and, in many cases, still anathema to traditional conservation practice, especially in the USA. The US Secretary of Interior's Standards for Preservation, for example, specifies that '*preservation* is defined as the act or process of applying measures necessary to sustain the existing form, integrity, and materials of an historic property' (US Department of the Interior 1992). It is a system and ideal based on the desire to stabilise a resource (i.e. building, structure or object) so that its historic form and details are never lost.

Landscapes present a different challenge, insofar as the landscape is composed of elements and character-defining features that are inherently dynamic, such trees, shrubs, vines, soil, tectonic plates, gravel paths, and even the colour and mood of the sky. As established by the US National Park Service, the lead federal agency for heritage conservation, landscapes are identified, analysed, recorded and evaluated using standardised methods. There is a perceived need to codify the approach to historic resources, in order to ensure, at a national scale, that such resources are considered and treated comparatively. This ensures that within the USA recognition and heritage designation carry equal weight across the country. In light of US federal funding of these activities, as well as some levels of intervention, this is a necessary component of the system. No two resources are ever exactly the same, but the approach to them, as evidenced through the codified standards of the National Register, for example, assists scholars to avoid the tendency to wander from standardised criteria in response to specific circumstances. These methods, many of which are founded on architectural and archaeological principles, are also applied to landscapes. Whether it is through National Register Bulletin 30 on rural landscapes (McClelland *et al.* 1990), Guidelines for the Treatment of Cultural Landscapes as set forth in the Secretary of Interior's Standards for the Treatment of Historic Properties (US Department of the Interior 1992), or NPS Technical Preservation Brief 36 on cultural landscapes (Birnbaum 1994), the goal is to provide uniform standards by which to achieve the goal of historic landscape conservation or protection.

All of these documents, however, consider the landscape within a constant or predictable context and fail fully to appreciate or duly recognise the dynamic nature of the larger environmental milieu. The codified criteria assume that the larger ecological context is static, within an acceptable dynamic range, such as seasons, warm or cold years, or wet or dry summers. Thus, each of the directions for recognising, evaluating and treating cultural landscapes, in heritage conservation parlance, assumes a greater level of constancy than it is now experienced or reasonable to anticipate. This results in an approach to landscapes that is not fully adaptable to systemic variations and idiosyncrasies, and which, by its broad distribution as official imprimatur, affects a wide range of efforts and activities. More importantly, perhaps, it sets unrealistic expectations and aspirations. This is a complex system, but one which generally does not account for impacts of climate change, or especially regional variations of those impacts. This system is in the process of changing, and there is now attention to climate change within the US National Park Service (US National Park Service 2012; Hoffman and Mielbrecht 2007). Nonetheless, the established approaches to cultural landscape conservation have not yet reached the levels needed to address these issues.

Changing context and rethinking historic integrity

Two big issues emerge in this discussion, beginning with that of context. When considering the future of cultural landscapes, context, in the very broadest meaning of that term, is a defining factor. Traditionally it has been valuable to recognise multiple contexts: political, geographical, geomorphological, cultural, historical and ecological. Environmental context, loosely interpreted, refers to the larger ecological systems within which a cultural landscape exists. While the consideration of cultural landscapes in the USA has always included contextual understanding and analysis, the ecological context is perhaps the most important frame from which to engage the cultural landscape. Unlike a historic structure, for example, a cultural landscape cannot be 'weather-proofed' from the prevailing climate.

However, what happens if that context is no longer as predictable as it once was? What might be the appropriate proactive response, and what can be done? This applies to all cultural resources (as it does to the health of natural systems), and not just cultural landscapes. Context is an idea, however, that is too easily forgotten, pushed aside, or left for the next scholar or practitioner. There is no way to avoid the changing contexts, as the furore around climate change, and potential disasters that could result from climate change (e.g. increased storms, coastal erosion, lengthening droughts, etc.), plays out in the scientific communities, social interactions, everyday activities and political debates. This does not affect only landscapes, but landscapes change at a rate and pace that is noticeably different from that of structures and most archeological sites. In many ways cultural landscapes are the 'canary in the mine' when it comes to the impact of climate change on other cultural resources.

In addition to context, the other big issue is the idea and implementation of historic integrity criteria. As defined by the US National Register of Historic Places, integrity is analysed using seven factors: location, design, setting, materials, workmanship, feeling and association. There has been argument about this concept and these criteria since they were first introduced following the 1966 historic preservation legislation and the later amendments. While scholars and practitioners are familiar with these criteria, they have also engaged in a debate about the difficulty of their application and the seemingly endless discussion about what they really mean and how to apply them. In terms of cultural landscapes, this may be the weakest part of the American system of analysing heritage resources and especially cultural landscapes. In contrast internationally, similar criteria under the heading of authenticity introduced in *The Nara Document on Authenticity* (ICOMOS 1994) and also incorporated into the *Operational Guidelines for the Implementation of the World Heritage Convention* (UNESCO 2011: para 88, p. 22) are increasingly taken into account in determining heritage values.

Linked to the changing global context, the determination of authenticity, as those in the heritage conservation community understand it, must be re-examined. It is beneficial to accept the idea that authenticity, like cultural landscapes, is a dynamic concept; it is valuable to go beyond the landscape frame to engage its meaning. Additionally, the field of cultural landscape analysis and protection needs to move beyond the historic and outdated notion of strict resource stability and fully engage with the reality that landscapes, and most other cultural resources, tangible and intangible, are dynamic and evolving. While this is often addressed more successfully internationally, in the USA it is still an issue that has yet to be fully confronted.

While integrity or authenticity as an idea may be viable, it is necessary to adopt a flexible and creative approach to its application, especially for cultural landscapes. For example, it is often more revealing to identify the character-defining features of a cultural landscape, rather than the detailed and specific material culture. In many ways, this raises more questions than answers, yet the work of understanding cultural landscapes is, to a great extent, filled with queries.

If an agricultural field has been in seasonal crop rotation for 100 years, does it really matter if it is not the same crop as it has always been? If a significant designed garden is losing its trees as the climate warms, ever so slightly, should those same trees be replaced with the same genus and species, thereby ensuring their future demise? Alternatively is it more creative to search for a new variety that provides a parallel degree of shade, canopy cover, branching pattern, leaf size and deciduous detritus? The question that should be asked is, what really matters? Does it matter more, in conservation terms, that a landscape retains the exact tree genus and species or that the spatial and visual consequences of those trees are maintained? How can the ecological consequences of the use of different species be considered alongside the cultural implications? Would it be better to plant replacement trees that are more resistant to warming, or to re-plant trees that will not survive their twenty-first-century environment?

Threats to cultural landscapes and adaptations to climate change

In order to advance beyond the generalities of climate change concerns, it is instructive to consider specific threats that present challenges to how we think about these places, but also how we formulate rational responses and constructive actions (English Heritage 2008: 6–7). These threats include:

- Rising sea levels and a possible increase in storm intensity.
- Increased extremes of wetting and drying that heighten the risk of ground subsidence.
- More frequent intense rainfall that causes increased erosion and damaging flooding.
- Changes in hydrology that put well-preserved agricultural and other wetlands at risk.
- Changes in vegetation patterns that threaten the visibility and integrity of cultural landscapes.
- A warming climate that makes some historically authentic tree plantings difficult to conserve.
- Changes in the distribution of pests that threatens the integrity of designed landscapes.
- Possible increases in the frequency or geographical range of extreme weather that could pose an increased risk of damage to some historic landscapes.

In addition, some adaptive responses to climate change may themselves have an impact on the historic environment, for example:

- 'Hard' coastal defence (such as the construction of sea walls) is seen as untenable on much of the undeveloped coast and has led to a new emphasis on selective managed realignment

FIGURE 13.4   The parade ground at Civil War-era Fort Monroe National Monument, in Virginia, may be heavily impacted by increased salinisation due to the change in groundwater levels, with risk to historic vegetation (Robert Melnick).

and 'soft' defences (such as managed retreat to allow flooding of low-lying land), posing a possible risk to cultural landscapes.

- The design integrity of some historic landscapes could be damaged by the need to provide new and more effective rainwater disposal or storage systems or flood protection features (Figure 13.4).
- Alteration of agricultural and forestry practices, resulting from changes in crop, stock-keeping or species viability, could pose a risk to traditional farm sites and historic landscapes.

There are a number of adaptations that can be considered as the vision of landscape conservation is altered in response to these new realities and challenges (Melnick 2009). These potential adaptations should not be taken as answers, and are perhaps best considered as an agenda for future research, scholarship and intervention.

It is fundamental to accept the premise of an uncertain but certainly variable future for all heritage resources, especially cultural landscapes (Millar *et al*. 2007). Flexibility in approaches to cultural landscapes is essential, as well as frequent reassessment of cultural resource conditions, especially landscapes, and allowing for the need to alter direction as conditions change. These are not easy strategies, as they demand a dynamic approach, including a tolerance for change. It may mean, for example, a reconsideration of what is meant by 'character-defining features' or even what is most valued in these resources (Gates 2002).

When addressing these challenges, it will be important to adapt to change and ways to mitigate it. It is important to consider both short- and long-term efforts. While in some cases changes may mean a great deal and in other cases not as much, it will be as instructive to think about 'protection' rather than simply 'conservation'.

Promoting resilience to change is a substantial challenge but one that should be addressed.[6] This strategy may mean greater proactive intervention, rather than waiting until undesired change has occurred, in certain highly valued landscapes. This, in turn, implies the setting of priorities. For example, there are positive steps that can be taken, such as engaging in greater seed-banking or intensive management during revegetation, a labour-intensive and costly process that nonetheless may enable the protection of critical landscape features (English Heritage 2008).

Additionally, the selection of vegetation for replanting should consider resilience issues such as drought and heat tolerance, life span, regular monitoring of vegetation change, habitat modification, scale of landscape area impact, biodiversity conservation, and others (US National Park Service 2012). For example, in the traditional kalo lo'i (or taro patches) of Hawai'i, cyclical plant selection may be most heavily influenced by those species of kalo that thrive in brackish water rather than freshwater (Figure 13.5). While this may be a variation from traditional Hawaiian agricultural practices, it would also provide greater opportunity for the protection of defining cultural landscape characteristics.

Perhaps the most difficult actions will be decisions about which resources to try to save, which landscapes are salvageable, and which landscapes are not (Laird 2005). In extreme terms, this may mean a form of cultural-landscape triage, choosing to save certain places while letting others remain only in the historical record. This is not a long-term response but may be necessary as a short-term step while the science for more lasting solutions is refined. This may also be the most contentious suggestion. What is the basis for triage decisions? Who makes them, and are they based primarily on available *fiscal* resources as opposed to the significance of historic *landscape* resources? As often happens, political issues and blatant nostalgia can probably not be avoided.

FIGURE 13.5   Taro, or kalo, patches in Hawai'i have been traditionally planted with primarily freshwater-resilient species, as in this recently re-established patch at He'eia, on the island of Oahu. As sea levels rise, it may be necessary to plant species that are resilient to brackish water, a mixture of fresh and seawater (Robert Melnick).

In the USA, especially, it will be instructive to learn from how others are approaching this issue, such as ICOMOS and the Noah's Ark project in Europe, which

> aims to improve [the protection of cultural resources] through a deeper understanding of the behavior and response of immovable cultural heritage and historic materials to the [impacts of climate change], discovering possible endangering synergistic processes and providing cultural heritage managers, decision makers and legislators with scientifically sound data and models.[7]

This cannot be an emotional or humanistic argument alone, as engaging the scientific community and scientific literature in this essentially humanist quest should be an inherent part of the process.

Finally, the long, or broad, view is valuable, as the historical ranges of variation are recognised (Millar and Woolfenden 1999). Taking both the long and short views relating to the past, present and future is vital in this effort. While it is often tempting or convenient to look at the most recent past, landscape time, and heritage resource time, demands the consideration of variations over a long period. Taking only the immediate snapshot in the rearview mirror can result in a failure to recognise the nature and impacts of climate change, relying too much, perhaps, on last year's rainfall gauges, this year's storm data or next year's temperature graph. Weather, of course, has not been constant, but there have been understandable and identifiable normal ranges of variation that can be used as a baseline (Del Tredici 2007).

FIGURE 13.6   Historic tree plantings and traditional Hawaiian religious sites at Pu'uhonua o Honaunau National Historical Park on the Island of Hawai'i, are threatened by rising seawater and changes in the occurrence and intensity of storms (Robert Melnick).

FIGURE 13.7   Traditional fishing areas, both fishponds and fish traps, at Kaloko-Hanokohau
National Historic Park, Hawai'i, are pressured by rising seawater, and a potential
change in other water characteristics, such as temperature and wave action
(Robert Melnick).

FIGURE 13.8   Fort Jefferson, is on Garden Key in Dry Tortugas National Park, Florida, where the
Atlantic Ocean and the Gulf of Mexico meet. It is in threat of deterioration from
rising seawater levels, changing storm occurrences and intensity, and potentially
altered wave patterns (Robert Melnick).

How do all heritage resources, not only landscapes, respond to the subtle changes that are presently threatening and are likely to continue to threaten them with potential disaster in the future? It is not sufficient to merely sit on the sidelines and observe as these cultural landscapes and other heritage resources, like Pu'uhonua o Honaunau (Figure 13.6) and Kaloko-Honokohau National Historical Parks in Hawai'i (Figure 13.7), or Fort Jefferson in Dry Tortugas National Park in Florida (Figure 13.8), are slowly overwhelmed by rising sea waters. The changing nature of the climate will, without a doubt, impact upon the way that landscapes of great cultural value evolve, and also affect the ways in which they are seen, understood and protected.

The field of cultural landscape studies needs to be challenged as it confronts these issues. Heritage conservation, even historic landscape conservation, can be very staid and even predictable. This is no longer a viable option in a world in which drastic change seems inevitable, if not always predictable.

Notes

1   Although the practice in the USA is to refer to 'historic preservation', in this chapter that term has been replaced, primarily, with 'heritage conservation'.
2   The Cascade Range is a major mountain range of western North America, extending from southern British Columbia, Canada, through Washington and Oregon to Northern California in the USA. All of the known historic eruptions in the contiguous USA have been from Cascade volcanoes. The two most recent were Lassen Peak (California) in 1914 to 1921 and a major eruption of Mount St. Helens (Washington) in 1980. Minor eruptions of Mount St. Helens have also occurred since, most recently in 2006.
3   Chicken Little is a folk tale with a moral in the form of a cumulative tale about a chicken who believes the world is coming to an end. The phrase 'The sky is falling!' features prominently in the story, and has passed into the English language as a common idiom indicating a hysterical or mistaken belief that disaster is imminent.
4   It is a verb in the way Mitchell suggests since there is a need 'to change "landscape" from a noun to a verb [to see it] as a process' (Mitchell 1994: 1). See also Taylor's (2012) critique of landscape as a cultural product and process.
5   See also Safina (2010: 9) who takes us on a journey through his landscapes and reminds us, as he wanders through the marshes of eastern Long Island, NY, that 'every walk is a product of the present and a relic of the past'.
6   In their discussion of climate change and forests, Millar *et al.* define resilience: 'Resilient forests are those that not only accommodate gradual changes related to climate but tend to return toward a prior condition after disturbance either naturally or with management assistance' (Millar *et al.* 2007: 2147). That is the general definition used in this chapter.
7   Noah's Ark distributes information and materials through a website. For more information see: http://noahsark.isac.cnr.it/overview.php.

References

Birnbaum, C.A. (1994) *Protecting Cultural Landscapes: Planning, Treatment and Management of Historic Landscapes.* Available at: http://www.nps.gov/tps/how-to-preserve/briefs/36-cultural-landscapes.htm (accessed October 28, 2013).
Brown, M.F. (2004) *Who Owns Native Culture?*, Cambridge, MA: Harvard University Press.
Carroon, J. (2010) *Sustainable Preservation: Greening Existing Buildings*, Hoboken: John Wiley & Sons.
Cullen, H. (2010) *The Weather of the Future: Heat Waves, Extreme Storms, and Other Scenes from a Climate-Changed Planet*, New York: Harper.
Del Tredici, P. (2007) 'The Role of Horticulture in a Changing World', in M. Conan and W.J. Kress (eds) *Botanical Progress, Horticultural Innovations and Cultural Changes*, Washington, DC: Dumbarton Oaks, pp. 259–265.

Egan, T. (2006) *The Worst Hard Time*, Boston: Houghton Mifflin.

English Heritage (2008) *Climate Change and the Historic Environment*. Available at: http://www.english-heritage.org.uk/publications/climate-change-and-the-historic-environment/climate-change.pdf/ (accessed October 28, 2013).

Epstein, P. R. and McCarthy, J.J. (2004) 'Assessing Climate Stability', *Bulletin of the American Meteorological Society*, 85, 12 (December) pp. 1863–1870.

Flannery, T. (2005) *The Weather Makers: How Man is Changing the Climate and What It Means for Life on Earth*, New York: Atlantic Monthly Press.

Gates, P. (2002) *Gardening in the Global Greenhouse: The Impact of Climate Change on Gardens in the UK*, Oxford: UK Climate Impacts Programme.

Heinlein, R. (1961) *Stranger in A Strange Land*, New York: Putnam Books.

Hoffman, J. and Mielbrecht, E. (2007) *Unnatural Disaster: Global Warming and Our National Parks*, Washington, DC: National Parks Conservation Association.

Hulme, M. (2009) *Why We Disagree About Climate Change*, New York: Cambridge University Press.

ICOMOS (1994) *The Nara Document on Authenticity*. Available at: www.international.icomos.org/nara_eng.htm.

ICOMOS (2003) *The Hoi An Declaration on Conservation of Historic Districts of Asia*, Paris: ICOMOS.

ICOMOS (2005) *Xi'an Declaration on the Conservation of the Setting of Heritage Structures, Sites and Areas*, Paris: ICOMOS.

ICOMOS (2007) *International Workshop on Impact of Climate Change on Cultural Heritage*, New Delhi, Paris: ICOMOS.

ICOMOS (2009) *Thematic Workshop on Cultural Heritage and Climate Change*, 16th General Assembly and Scientific Symposium, Quebec, Paris: ICOMOS.

Intergovernmental Panel on Climate Change (2007) 'Summary for Policymakers', in S. Solomon, D. Qin, M. Manning, Z. Chen, M. Marquis, K.B. Averyt, M.Tignor and H.L. Miller (eds) *Climate Change 2007: The Physical Science Basis. Contribution of Working Group I to the Fourth Assessment Report of the Intergovernmental Panel on Climate Change*, Cambridge and New York: Cambridge University Press, pp. 1–18.

King, D. (2005) *The Elgin Marbles: The Story of Archaeology's Greatest Controversy*, London: Hutchinson.

Kuhn, T.S. (1962) *The Structure of Scientific Revolutions*, Chicago: University of Chicago Press.

Laird, M. (1998) 'Climate, Weather and Planting Design in English Formal Design of the Early 18th Century', *Die Gartenkunst des Barock*, ICOMOS Journals of the German National Committee 28: 14–19.

Laird, M. (2005) 'The Impacts of Climate Change on Historic Landscapes', in *The Significance of Setting: Conserving Monuments and Sites in Changing Canadian Cultural Landscapes*, Toronto: ICOMOS Canada, pp. 33–36.

McCarthy, D. (2011) 'Assessing Cultural Resources in the Wake of a Disaster', paper presented at the George Wright Society Annual Conference, 15 March 2011. Cultural Resource GIS Facility, National Park Service, Washington, DC.

McClelland, L., Keller, J.T., Keller, G.P. and Melnick, R.Z. (1990) *Guidelines for Evaluating and Documenting Rural Historic Landscapes*, Bulletin No. 30, National Register of Historic Places, National Park Service, US Department of the Interior, Washington, DC.

Melnick, R.Z. (2009) 'Climate Change and Landscape Preservation: A Twenty-First-Century Conundrum', *APT Bulletin: Journal of Preservation Technology* 40, 3–4: 35–42.

Millar, C. and Woolfenden, W. (1999) 'The Role of Climate Change in Interpreting Historical Variability', *Ecological Applications* 9, 4: 1207–1216.

Millar, C., Stephenson, N. and Stephens, S. (2007) 'Climate Change and Forests of the Future: Managing in the Face of Uncertainty', *Ecological Applications* 17, 8: 2145–2151.

Mitchell, W.J.T. (1994) *Landscape and Power*, Chicago: University of Chicago Press.

Safina, C. (2010) *The View From Lazy Point*, New York: Henry Hold and Company.

Shoard, M. (1981) 'Why Landscapes Are Harder to Protect Than Buildings', in D. Lowenthal and M. Binney (eds) *Our Past Before Us: Why Do We Save It?* London: Maurice Temple Smith, pp. 83–108.

Steyn, M. (2006) 'Climate Change Myth', *The Australian*, 11 September 2006.

Taylor, K. (2012) 'Landscape and Meaning: Context for a Global Discourse on Cultural Landscapes Values', in K. Taylor and J. Lennon (eds) *Managing Cultural Landscapes*, London and New York: Routledge, pp. 21–44.

UNESCO (2003) *World Heritage Papers 7 Cultural Landscapes: The Challenges of Conservation*, Paris: UNESCO World Heritage Centre. Available at: www.unesdoc.unesco.org/images/0013/001329/132988e.pdf.

UNESCO (2011) *Operational Guidelines for the Implementation of the World Heritage Convention*, Paris: UNESCO World Heritage Centre.

US Department of the Interior (1992) *Secretary of Interior's Standards for Preservation and Guidelines for Preserving Historic Buildings*. Available at: http://www.nps.gov/hps/tps/standguide/preserve/preserve_index.htm (accessed 23 January 2011).

US National Park Service (2012) *Climate Change Response Program*. Available at: http://www.nature.nps.gov/climatechange/index.cfm (accessed 15 May 2012).

14

EXPLORING FUTURE CULTURAL LANDSCAPES

Maggie Roe

> *Landscape means an area, as perceived by people, whose character is the result of the action and interaction of natural and/or human factors.*
>
> *(European Landscape Convention, Article 1, COE 2000)*

> *For all landscapes ask the same question in the same whisper. 'I am watching you – are you watching yourself in me?'*
>
> *(Durrell 1960: 158)*

> *Food you take; flowers are for giving, for the land, for Pachamama.*
>
> *(in Speak, Chapter 8, p. 146)*

Introduction

The idea of cultural landscape continues to inspire researchers, philosophers, poets, policymakers and others, increasingly in cross-disciplinary and interdisciplinary areas. This focus does not ignore the difficulties that the terminology raises (see e.g. Jones and Daugstad 1997; Roe *et al.* 2008) but, as suggested in Chapter 2 (Taylor and Francis), there is now a substantial body of academic literature discussing how cultural landscapes might be defined, identified and managed, and many other means to express what cultural landscapes mean to ordinary people.[1] In conceptual terms, the influence of human cultural systems on 'natural' systems in the landscape can be illustrated as a continuum (Figure 14.1) with the types of landscape most often labelled as cultural usually seen as those more dominated by human activities. In the past, landscape categories often include 'wilderness' or areas which supposedly exhibit no human impact or interaction (Figure 14.2). The enduring use of wild and wilderness as concepts linked to ideas of a 'pristine' nature (with no human interaction) do not seem to be helpful in a world where there is little evidence to suggest such a state presently exists. Within a holistic concept of cultural landscape, landscape is no longer seen simply as a view or scene, a static background within which activities and actions occur or a tableau upon which change is imposed. Although change has become a useful focus in many

Natural Culture dominates
Landscapes where the impact of humans may apparently be small or hidden or non-human processes may dominate, e.g. Antarctica.

Symbiotic Relationship
Landscapes created by the intertwining of human and natural processes in some kind of harmony or symbiotic relationship.

Human Culture dominates
Landscapes that are dominated by human artefacts, buildings and where natural processes have been severely modified by human control, e.g. large cities.

FIGURE 14.1   Cultural landscapes: the relationship between humans and natural processes in the landscape can be seen as a continuum where at one end of the scale human impact or relationships may be difficult to discern or understand, at the other it may be more difficult to see the relationships between humans and natural processes and the human impact may be dominant. In between these extremes are many different kinds of relationship between humans and natural processes that may be seen or unseen (tangible and intangible).

First Nature
Landscapes that are regarded as unaffected by human activities within which humanised landscapes can sit. These may be referred to as 'wilderness'.

Second Nature
Landscapes created as a result of human needs or purposes, generally without aesthetic intent, or where aesthetic concerns were subsidiary to economic or functional concerns e.g. agricultural landscapes, towns and cities and all other infrastructures that support human habitation.

Third Nature
Landscapes that are designed with specific aesthetic and functional intent e.g. parks, gardens, town squares.

FIGURE 14.2   The three 'natures' as indicated by Cicero according to John Dixon Hunt and discussed in Thompson (2012). The second 'nature' is a humanised landscape that sits within the first nature, and the third nature is intentionally designed so that 'nature and culture are deliberately mixed' (p. 159) and features are borrowed from both first and second natures.

different disciplines to conceptualise and understand landscape (Muir 2003), the vibrancy that change in the landscape brings is still not always reflected in the way management and policy is devised in Western countries in particular. Chapter 2 (Taylor and Francis) provides the basis for asking if a more dynamic and holistic understanding of landscape could be gained, how would this affect our relationship with it and our perception of it?

In this book the authors have explored a number of ideas around the concept of cultural landscape, but have focused clearly on the 'new' aspect. The aim is to examine the nature of a variety of physical and psychological bonds developing between people and landscapes, and in particular, to try to identify how value is created from such living connections and processes. Authors were asked to: discuss what constitutes a new cultural landscape; identify how landscapes develop into cultural landscapes; suggest what possibilities there are for new types of cultural landscape and new relationships with the landscape; and consider the ordinary and everyday relationships with landscape in particular.

A number of important questions were raised during this process based on the key concept that ideas, features, elements, processes and uses create cultural landscapes. In the introduction a number of issues are identified related to the importance of understanding both the relationship between individuals and the landscape and communities and landscapes. In particular, how far does the concept of future cultural landscapes relate to the perception of management and manipulation, and how far is it about the experience of landscape? If the latter is particularly important in creating new cultural landscapes, what kind of experiences or relationships provide the basis for the perception of a cultural landscape, and does it matter if the use changes?

There seems to be a split in outlook between those in academia and practice focusing on cultural landscapes and much of the literature relating to a key area of landscape studies; that is landscape architecture. In the former there is a good understanding of many of the key issues discussed in this book, particularly the links between past, present and future values, issues such as intangible heritage values, human rights and the tensions inherent in considering management of cultural landscapes (e.g. Taylor and Lennon 2012). However in landscape architecture literature the term cultural landscape still seems to be used primarily to relate to visual quality to discuss the preservation of heritage and the material manifestation of past human values. In the UK there has been an increasing influence and emphasis on historic and archaeological landscape conservation through funding bodies and agencies providing work for landscape architects and in much general landscape architectural practice. Planning policy also continues to have a strongly protectionist and restrictive stance in the UK (Roe *et al.* 2009). This suggests that in some important areas landscapes are primarily regarded as material, created by past uses which embed more desirable values than those of the present. More innovative thinking may be found in other parts of the world (e.g. see Taylor and Lennon 2012) where values and attitudes to landscape are very different. This unevenness in attitudes, policy and practice, particularly in terms of awareness of the opportunities in the future planning and management of cultural landscapes, would indicate that greater connection needs still to be made between disciplines and between academia, policy-makers and practitioners on these issues, and much can be learned from the alternative relationships with landscape as shown by the contributors to this book. The key point here is, how can the changing views and values of society and culture be reflected in healthy and meaningful landscapes of the present and future without losing what is valued from the past?

The World Heritage Convention (1992) was the first international instrument to recognise and to offer protection for cultural landscapes of Outstanding Universal Value. Rössler (undated: 7) reports that the aim of World Heritage designation for cultural landscapes is to recognise landscapes which embody 'past ways of life' but which also have 'continuing relevance today'. Future relevance and management are also addressed in Mitchell *et al.* (2009) where successful management planning is seen to be about 'concerns and future alternative courses of action, and [an examination of] the evolving chains of causes and effects likely to result from current decisions' (p. 38). In particular, developing shared visions for determining the future direction of management is important and transmission of knowledge, developing governance regimes and protecting existing capital are highlighted. Consideration of the World Heritage Convention categories may be useful as a starting point for thinking about new cultural landscapes (as illustrated in Figure 1.1) but are there other potential categories which, for example, reflect the 'commodification' of landscapes and the contexts (physical and other) within which new cultural landscapes develop?

If we understand that human actions do not only mould but are moulded by the environment, it thus follows that 'mutual moulding' or interaction in some form or another is likely to be a key component of the development of new cultural landscapes. The question is what kind of interaction could be relevant (such as those that might occur from a distance, i.e. not physical at all) to develop significant meaning, or is a close material relationship necessary? Interaction indicates activity, whereas relationship is a connection, a correlation, a link, bond or association. The contributions in this book suggest that many different types of interaction are possible as the basis for new cultural landscape development and that in management and policy we need to consider and find new ways to consider a more complex set of relationships or connections than is presently the case.

Categories: what are new cultural landscapes?

The chapters have revealed a number of possible conceptions of new cultural landscapes:

1. *The cultural landscape as layer*, where landscapes may be highly valued because of the way they reflect relationships with past and present culture(s), values and ways of seeing. The time depth of human influence is often suggested as a series of identifiable layers upon the landscape like geological layers in rock formations, which show the influence of environmental effects. The problem with this is that such layers rarely indicate the real complexity of influence and the unevenness of connections and relationships that have impact upon the material landscape; the 'cycles of change that ripple and rebound' (Muir 2003: 401), the reverberations that alter relationships within the landscape. In particular, it does not show the mutual moulding of landscape and humans or the relationships which leave no material impact. However there are some examples where this concept may be useful.
2. *The everyday cultural landscape*, where landscapes hold potential value in relation to commonly recognised indicators of cultural landscape quality, but are not presently protected or recognised under a legislative system because they are considered as 'ordinary' or partially degraded. The ELC provides us with the basis for considering all landscapes as potentially valuable, particularly ordinary landscapes, but there still seems to be much resistance against this understanding. Through the categories it uses, the ELC itself seems to uphold the existing hierarchy of landscape value, even though this may bear little resemblance to people's connection with the landscape. Everyday, people may have a close relationship with particular landscapes (e.g. through farming systems, or dog walking) (see Chapter 3, Davies), but such everyday relationships may not be seen as important until there is a risk that they may disappear.
3. *The invisible cultural landscape*, which is not recognised as 'landscape' because our present ways of seeing may be limited for various reasons. Although those inhabiting the landscape may value the landscape, outsiders may not. This may be related to the way the landscape itself is perceived to be materially ugly, derelict, polluted or degraded and, in some cases, these invisible places are not even recognised as *potential landscapes* because the landscape values that are based on ocular-centric quality indicate that such places have no, or negative, value and are often offensive. There are many examples where landscape is transformed, 'cleaned up' or sanitised through material redevelopment, through the expulsion of cultures and/or the overlaying of new material and non-material culture (see Chapter 5, Bell). But perhaps the answer is not to change the physical landscape, but change our awareness – our way of seeing the landscape. Chapter 9 (Duffy)

provides an example where new initiatives reveal the qualities of a refuse *garbagescape*; a landscape type that is commonly treated as 'invisible'.

In addition there is a category which lies somewhere between the real and the imaginary; this is:

4.   *The imaginary or representative cultural landscape*, which is cultural because of the real or perceived events that have occurred there (e.g. films or real battles, etc.), and where the relationship is that the landscape has become a setting for particular events. These events may be real or imaginary, but the landscapes have become symbolic. As symbols they may also then generate a new kind of relationship, such as tourism. Some of these places have similar properties to those described under the UNESCO World Heritage 'associative landscapes' category, which are landscapes that have cultural/artistic associations with natural elements and the symbolic landscapes created as a result of actual events, or myths and stories of particular cultures in the past. However, in the new kinds of association described in Chapter 6 (Jewell and McKinnon) the cultural value is constructed by virtual communities whose relationship with the physical place is often minimal; the conception of such landscapes may in fact bear little relationship with the actuality of the place (Figure 14.3).

FIGURE 14.3   'Sycamore Gap', Hadrian's Wall, Northumberland. Hadrian's Wall was listed as a World Heritage Site in 1987, and in 2005 it was inscribed as part of the transnational Frontiers of the Roman Empire. Sycamore Gap became more widely famous as 'Robin Hood's Tree' as a result of the film *Robin Hood: Prince of Thieves* (1991) which relocated the landscape somewhere in the south of England.

How are new cultural landscapes created?

In the introduction five major themes are identified and it is useful to return to these themes in trying to think about the conceptions of landscape identified above.

1. Landscape as process: quality and relationships

The physical form of cultural landscapes emerges primarily as intentional products of human activity and ideologies as 'cultural landscapes represent changing relationships between humankind and the environment, as well as major historical or cultural events or processes' (Mather and Jensen 2010: 342). Intended actions also result in unintended or unforeseen products of human activity or 'downstream' impacts. Human actions may not achieve desired intentions for a myriad of reasons. The chapter contributions echo these various ideas. In the provision of catalysts for new cultural landscapes or in providing conditions for landscapes to emerge it is possible to recognise a very broad range of processes and connections, for example when devising management regimes which will affect the future development of the landscape. There are considerable difficulties where heritage values from different cultures create relationships with the landscape that differ so dramatically that it makes collaborative working impossible, even where there is a strong desire to come to some kind of compromise. In Chapter 2, Taylor and Francis provide an example from Australia where 'Western' sensibilities find the intangible values of indigenous peoples hard to understand and/or the commercial considerations/values blind those involved to the importance of such values. The question here is if in spite of common interest the different understanding of landscape based on particular cultural paradigms means that no consensus can be reached, whose values should drive future management? If a solution emerges that reflects particular cultural values and not others, is this a sustainable management solution?

Chapter 10 (Egoz) suggests that revolution and migration can be a means of instigating the development of new cultural landscapes. Displaced and/or fragmented cultures may create 'cultural landscapes of exile' as well as past landscapes of memory where displacement has occurred. This has resonance with the analysis in Chapter 8 (Speak) concerning squatter settlements and urban agricultural landscapes in India and other countries of the Global South. Cultures that are forced to give up a landscape, then move and create a home somewhere else are likely to reinterpret old landscape values in a different location and remould the new landscape to reflect those values. Chapter 8 indicates how landscape knowledge (agricultural production) is transported and reapplied, or reinterpreted and thus new cultural landscapes are created from a synthesis of old values and new experience in a new location. In Chapter 10 (Egoz) Jewish settlers were able to return to ancient knowledge based on myths of the 'biblical landscape' because the new location afforded them this possibility of regaining something that was long valued and perceived in a particular way. The new cultural landscape was based upon existing cultural tradition or perhaps reinvented cultural traditions, rather than reinterpretation, or something much more novel. Here it seems that utopian or idealised concepts have provided the basis for remoulding the landscape. In the examples in Chapter 8 (Speak) from the Global South, memory of the physical and the relational have played a part in constructing a new cultural landscape with productivity the main consideration.

Present landscapes are sometimes considered to be highly representative of a particular past point in time rather than a continuing process of change. An example is the gardens of Versailles, France, which in many ways reflect the desire for control of King Louis XIV and the cultural context of seventeenth-century France. These gardens, the most extensive in the Western world, were established as a monument to and by a powerful individual, but they can also be regarded as 'the embodiment of France' (Thompson 2006: 330) and require particular management practices to maintain their form. Present landscapes may be protected by legislation of some kind and may already have a management regime worked out based on maintaining the landscape in a way so that it remains valued (by a community, or communities of stakeholders). Such landscapes may be facing considerable change because of conditions (such as climate change) which may result in a new kind of landscape structure with different requirements as regards management. Geographers sometimes label our present age as the 'anthropocene' because of the dominance of humans and the extent of the impact we are having on the environment, particularly on climate. We may evolve alternative relationships with landscape through responses to climate change as discussed in Chapter 13 (Melnick) depending on whether humans or natural forces are really the primary agents of change. Chapter 13 shows a very clear example of how humans are actively involved in the creation of landscape at a very large scale, indeed globally, but where local knowledge and interaction will be of critical importance for human survival. Another example of this new heritage-in-the-making is seen in Chapter 6 (Jewell and McKinnon) which illustrates how new practices and relationships with landscape are created *by* and *for* film tourism. A key question here is: how much can present landscapes change before the qualities that make the landscape relevant to present cultures are lost? The loss of landscape features, meanings and ecological richness clearly is an issue that has provoked various policies and actions around the world, however the consideration of how present cultures might add meanings to the landscape has had much less consideration. Can a more positive approach provide us with a way of helping to understand past, present and future potential relationships with landscape? Some of these themes are revealed in Chapters 4 (Mitchell and Barrett), 7 (Davis and Corsane), 10 (Egoz) and 13 (Melnick). In Chapter 6 (Jewell and McKinnon) it is suggested that new views may help to redefine people's (or group) identities. However such identity may be an illusory construct over time rather than something based on a physical relationship with landscape. Film enthusiasts develop an identity apart from their everyday culture through attending film-related events, visiting places, connecting to others with a particular 'community of interest' which may or may not have an enduring effect on the landscape. As with past cultures that had no discernible material impact on the landscape, but may have passed on intangible meanings, the enduring qualities of such things are difficult, if not impossible, to predict.

There is presently much emphasis and argument concerning the need to establish landscape quality objectives, particularly in relation to maintaining and enhancing landscape character (see Selman 2012) and as set out in the ELC. High landscape quality is seen to be directly linked to high value, with value generally considered to be a 'social construction arising from the cultural contexts of a time and place' (Stephenson 2008: 129). However the chapter contributions suggest that for managers and policy construction it may be more useful to think in terms of qualities (rather than quality) of landscape as this may provide the opportunities that are needed for interactions with landscape to develop. Opportunities are sometimes articulated as affordances[2] in landscape studies (see Gibson 1979; Kyttä 2002). The chapters suggest that constructing affordances rather than quality in landscape might also provide a useful basis for planning and design of landscapes since it is not always the high quality of landscapes that determine whether landscapes are highly valued, but the relevance to and mirror of a particular culture that seems to be important.

People hold 'values' and also express 'value' for things – thus it is important to understand how values are developed and how things are valued. Stephenson's (2008) cultural values model is helpful here. The model indicates the dynamic nature of interactions – i.e. the overlapping nature of values that people commonly express, and the way they express the values in terms of relationships and practices as well as forms. Immediate values are expressed as 'surface values' while other values can be identified as those that are 'embedded', i.e. are experienced over time. In Chapter 13, Melnick suggests that distance (in time) is needed before judgements of value can be made, so we cannot judge whether the landscapes that are valued today will be valued in 50 years' time. However if we think about past values in relation to landscape, there are many things that we did not value in the past that we value now – perhaps mostly in relation to scarcity value – and thus this may provide us with some insights as to future value judgements.

The processes by which new cultural landscapes are created suggest that both personal and collective understandings are important, but, although cultural knowledge and understandings are passed on through individuals, we generally consider culture to be a collective attribute. The intangible value identified in World Heritage designations are often expressed by 'insiders' as developed through personal experience and knowledge of place over time. The accessibility to outsiders would appear limited, and as related in the account in Chapter 2 (Taylor and Francis) the transferability of such understandings between cultures can be impossible. This would indicate that the collective understanding of what constitutes a cultural landscape is important rather than an individual response even though it is suggested that a collective understanding of landscape requires personal experience and interpretation (Treib 2009). Thus change in an individual's way of life may not be relevant for the emergence of new cultural landscapes while significant change in the collective ways of life in contemporary (and likely future) lifestyles may be of considerable significance.

Meaning and association

In thinking about the potential of new cultural landscapes, we may begin to comprehend the more complex hybrid ideas of landscape that Wylie (2007) labels as 'topographical, visual, phenomenal and synthetic associations' (p. 205). It is often suggested that cultural landscapes are particularly important because of the associations or meanings they hold for people. The terms often used rather suggest that cultural meaning is applied to the landscape from the outside (see discussion in Wylie 2007: 99) but for many cultures the landscape is not figurative or symbolic it is actual: the rock does not just look like a turtle, it *is* a turtle (Figure 14.4).[3] What emerges is comprehended by an understanding based on Ingold's view that landscape is part of us and we are part of the landscape (see Ingold 2000). If this is correct then whatever landscapes we are creating today, pleasing or not, are cultural; they reflect us and we are made by them. The salinity-ravaged landscapes of the shrimp industry in Asia, and Disneyland Paris are as much our cultural landscapes as the World Heritage Sites of Durham Cathedral, UK, or the Forbidden City, Beijing, because all reflect our present culture and values; our relationships. The question is really not whether these are cultural landscapes, but whether they will be valued by future generations?

Changing values determine what is kept and what is destroyed in the material landscape and there has been much removal of what present culture would like to try to forget of the

FIGURE 14.4. The Melkhi Khad (Turtle Rock), Gorkhi-Terelj National Park, Mongolia (Maggie Roe).

past. Certainly Chapter 9 (Duffy) indicates that there is a growing fascination with landscapes that past generations would not even have recognised as landscape. Evidence for this change is the growth of the grief tourism market and the work of artists who are revealing the potential of *garbagescapes* and *disasterscapes*. However the recognition of the potential of such places in landscape policy and management is rare. Chapter 3 (Davies) also indicates how management regimes of sites are reflecting these kinds of changing values and meanings. Existing characteristics are retained rather than removed in order to create a more sanitised version of landscape which might provide a surface view of economic and cultural values. The difficulty is in determining what in landscape reflects enduring and what reflects surface cultural values (Figures 14.5a and 14.5b).

Chapter 11 (Ahmed) describes how landscape value has become monetarised in the new landscapes of Cairo where a new cultural landscape has been made out of the desert. Culture here equates to making the desert liveable. These new landscapes represent changing social and economic conditions and in particular changing ideas of social exclusion. Here there is willingness on the part of the rich to appropriate areas that had an association with those that were culturally forbidden (desert/burial areas) and reinvent them as green areas for living. The developers are replacing cultural exclusion for social exclusion since the new areas are not places that poorer communities can access, nor do they have a say in the transformation of these landscapes.

FIGURES 14.5a and 14.5b Eurodisney, Paris: a new cultural landscape? (Maggie Roe)

Connections

There is now in many spheres of life a feeling that we need to find a new way to connect with each other, to build connections between communities at a local and global scale, and also to connect with other species and what is commonly labelled as the 'natural world'. Our awareness of the potential of networks and connections has grown with the development of technological networks and understanding of the importance and complexity of physical networks such as those seen in ecological systems and the networks that humans build, such as communication infrastructures. The focus is now also on those networks that are much more difficult to define, the intangible social and cultural connections that have an impact on the way we feel and behave, which in turn changes the way we alter the material world. Connectedness is now also often expressed as something that is desirable for sustainable human development, and something that has been lost through development processes; thus a political 'reconnection agenda' has grown, particularly in Westernised countries, but also in many countries around the world. Exploration of themes of connection, complexity and networks is very much the zeitgeist of our time.

In particular, the desire to connect with and experience landscape is providing increasing numbers of people with a way, not only to connect physically and psychologically with the materiality of the environment, but also to engage with landscape as the basis for self-insight and the possibility of imagining a different way of life. In engaging with landscape, communities and individuals can gain an understanding of the significance of the intangible associations that provide a sense of place, identity, some kind of stability and meaning. Through the study of these ideas, landscape can be seen as a cultural process; something more than a topographical material entity, and more than something external to the individual to be perceived as 'a view'.

In reconnecting with landscapes, people may gain new links with other individuals, with their own or other communities and with heritage and natural cycles and changes; aspects of living that are commonly labelled as 'culture'. The feelings that connections bring may affect behaviour and thus in a time where there is much talk of society fragmentation, destruction of and disconnection from the environment we need to use all our imagination, resourcefulness, experience and skill to find cultural connections that provide ways to address contemporary material and psychological challenges.

Culture as a term signifies both physical and psychological consciousness and connection, comprehensible as dynamic and evolving through both individual and shared practice (Ingold 2000). Landscape is often described as 'perceived by people' and is thus inherently a cultural construct of the mind or emotions (CoE 2000; Fairclough 2012), but also the materiality of many landscapes has predominantly resulted from human interactions carried out over many years. Thus cultural landscapes are material and intangible, they are a process and an opportunity; the characteristics and understandings of what they constitute are myriad and complex. Bringing together the terms (cultural and landscape) provides opportunities to consider these interrelationships between people and the land in the past and present and, most relevant for this book, into the future.

2. Change

In this book there are many interpretations of what a new cultural landscape might be. As suggested at the beginning of this chapter, it may be the physical creation of a new landscape, but it may also be a reinterpretation of what 'cultural landscape' is, thus it is a change in a way of seeing landscape. Chapter 2 (Taylor and Francis) suggests that in creating a new outlook on landscape we allow for the possibility of finding better ways to strengthen the materiality and understanding of cultural landscapes. This can alter the often-present contested relationships that damage landscape processes and the identities of local or indigenous peoples. The use of landscapes in films can influence and construct both new communities – or cultures – of interest and new communities – or cultures – of place. These cultures become real for participants and become of real influence. Those who inhabit the landscapes are affected by the tourist visitors and their requirements and changes in the identity of the landscape, which is subsumed under the new film culture through association (e.g. Gallipoli in Turkey, the Lord of the Rings locations in New Zealand, and Alnwick Castle – the setting for part of the Harry Potter series – in England).

There are many examples of past cultural landscapes that have been destroyed (e.g. see Diamond 2005). Immediate examples that spring to mind are the Marsh Arab reedlands which were drained by Saddam Hussein, destroying a way of life in Iraq that Gavin Maxwell so vividly portrayed.[4] Another example is the communist landscapes in Eastern Europe, many of which are being replaced as described in Chapter 5 (Bell). The issue here is how can new landscapes emerge from such destruction? Can lessons be drawn from the landscapes of destruction such as those affected by war, the building of dams, spread of disease, invasive species, climatic events, etc.? Bell (Chapter 5) suggests that in the Eastern bloc a completely different landscape is developing with little or no vestige of the traditional cultural landscape from the pre-communist era because of the destruction of culture and landscape by the communists. The loss of surroundings and (meaningful) landscapes is recognised as important by Albrecht (2005) who coined the term *Solastalgia* to describe the pain or sickness caused by the loss of, or inability to derive solace from, the present state of one's home environment. Such feelings may exist when places that are important to you are under some kind of threat and he suggests these can be contrasted to the spatial and temporal dislocation and dispossession experienced as nostalgia. Albrecht suggests that environmental damage and other threats have made it possible for people to feel dislocated, undermined, have feelings of loss of value and be homesick without leaving home. Cultural landscapes can be seen as constantly changing mosaics with humans as part of the mosaic and as a driver of change. Thus, how much change is acceptable before the landscape stops providing identity and meaning? In Chapter 5, Bell suggests that there is considerable risk of losing all sense of identity in a landscape with a population where there has been, and still is, massive change occurring.

The themes that emerge in Chapter 13 (Melnick) relate to loss prevention, risk assessment and aversion. If cultural landscapes are created by the intersection of culture and nature, then climate change will affect the development of cultural landscapes as much as traditions, practices and other human interventions. In Chapter 13 Melnick emphasises the importance of understanding and working with the context (time and place) and developing traditional approaches to nontraditional circumstances. We need to identify what is significant in cultural landscapes and devise strategies to cope with unpredictability, disaster and risk; in particular to identify the degree of acceptable change, the subtle and cumulative impacts at a range of long and short timescales, and identify whether anything can be done to ensure that these levels of change are not exceeded. Melnick stresses the importance of integrity in cultural landscapes and that good landscape conservation is about embracing change to retain integrity.

He suggests that, in the USA, assessment methods for recognising cultural landscapes do not embrace understandings of change, context, peculiarity or difference, or the complexity of systems that create cultural landscapes. Davies (Chapter 3) also emphasises the importance of considering the cumulative impacts of change. In the UK the community forests movement has provided large areas of new landscapes based on an incremental planting-up and by gaining public access to small parcels of former derelict and other land. These now provide large areas of publicly accessible woodland on many urban fringes in the midlands and north of England in particular.

3. Interaction, consumption and practice

Interaction has emerged as a particularly important feature of cultural landscapes and this is both tangible and non-tangible, primarily based on physical relationships. The exploration of new cultural landscapes suggests that the interactions may include meanings and associations gained at a distance and as a landscape imaginary. Wylie (2007) suggests landscape is experienced, seen, is a projection of cultural meaning and is something 'with which we act and sense' (Wylie 2007: 245). Thus perhaps we do not need any kind of physical interaction to create the idea or way of seeing landscape; to act and sense it. Incorporating the basic premise set out in the introduction that humans are, as other species, not separate from the natural world, but part of it, then it is conceivable that we may find other examples of interaction with landscape in the natural world which act at a distance or without a specific physical relationship.

   In the chapter contributions, there are many links made to food and productivity in the landscape. This indicates that there is a special message to be read about how landscapes that can be considered productive provide special meaning. Productivity is perhaps the most fundamental expression of interaction with landscape for humans and other species (Figure 14.6). Many landscapes that are specially noted as cultural landscapes, that are protected as World Heritage Sites and those that are rapidly being lost almost unnoticed around the world (e.g. Estonian, Spanish and Portuguese farm landscapes being reclaimed by natural processes) are those that have been agriculturally productive or were primarily cultivated pastoral landscapes. Agriculture is regarded to be as potentially important for cultural identity as it is for economic development. Food is seen as a key bearer of tangible and intangible cultural and aesthetic values linked to both people and their natural and built, rural and urban landscape environment. Although food is not separately recognised as a contribution under the Outstanding Universal Value (OUV) criteria, UNESCO World Heritage assessment now includes landscapes that reflect a particular identity based on food heritage. An example is the Lavaux vineyard terraces which stretch from Montreux to Lausanne in Vaux, Switzerland. These were inscribed in 2007 as a landscape which is 'an outstanding example of a centuries-long interaction between people and their environment, developed to optimise local resources so as to produce a highly valued wine'.[5]

   Settled agricultural landscapes are not the only important productive landscapes. For example, landscapes that remain primarily used for purposes of hunting and gathering are also now recognised as valuable cultural landscapes. Many productive landscapes hold important intangible values and undoubtedly the fundamental provision of food and the places where food could be grown and where good, clean water could be gained became significant because of the need for survival. What then of today's productive landscapes?

FIGURE 14.6   The importance of productivity in landscape interactions: a farming family in Southern China carrying out daily tasks of food production and clothes washing (Maggie Roe).

Do these have real potential as new cultural landscapes? The agricultural landscapes of today in many countries such as the UK are a good indicator of our culture; think of the hedgeless wide open arable lands we have created that reflect our culture of reliance on technological and mechanical ability, on dense urban living and large populations, and on the landscape as primarily a productivist tool. While we may now be looking at a 'post-productivist' landscape (Macfarlane 2007), as set out in Chapter 7 (Davies and Corsane) the increasing pressures for food indicate that there is likely to be considerable scope in relation to new cultural landscapes related to food production (see also Chapter 4, Mitchell and Barrett, and Chapter 8, Speak).

Food advertising and labelling commonly use images of landscape, and by so doing encourage a particular way of seeing the landscape. These images represent the stories (and often myths and imaginaries) of the productive landscapes or the associative landscapes of production. Olwig (2008) considers how representations of landscape have encouraged the subject–object, society–nature binaries often embedded within it. Food advertising today can be seen to be helping to create new stories of commercialism and consumerism (see Estulin 2004) that indicate a belief in attainable ideals. Advertising and other promotional materials help to frame the nature of places by shaping them as commodities to be desired. Conversely, by producing these kinds of images (many of which may be unattainable) are we storing up trouble for the future? Are we producing a culture where we in fact create disillusionment

FIGURE 14.7 Ice cream landscape at Northumberland County Show, UK: does the production of ice cream really result in the kind of landscape illustrated on the van? (Maggie Roe)

because we cannot produce or replicate in reality the image of sustainability (Figure 14.7) that we have produced on the label?

Indeed, does the success of modern advertising indicate that we have created a culture that has chosen illusion over reality? These ideas echo the discussion in Chapter 6 (Jewell and McKinnon) concerning film landscapes. Such advertisements appear to be trying to combat what Lister (2008: 150) suggests is the disappearance of the 'elemental knowledge of what we eat' and the growing problem of placeless food. Food awareness and marketing has undergone considerable cultural alteration in recent years in the UK, but representations do not appear to reflect the dynamic and often non-rural, cultural and aesthetic public values, but more of an idealised landscape imaginary.

The culture(s) and communities that grow up around the growing of food have been explored by a number of people (e.g. Crouch 1991). Food has an important cultural impact on landscape in other ways, e.g. the creation of food outlets (shops, cafes, etc.) and the creation of urban cultural landscapes (e.g. South Street Seaport, Boston) and, increasingly, the growing of food in and around urban areas, as suggested in Chapter 3 (Davies). In urban contexts cultivation of food and timber growing has been used to involve communities as a transformative experience in degraded areas. Such interaction with landscape is recognised as the basis for building lifelong attitudes to community working and environmental awareness.

A key message concerning the agricultural landscapes of North America as discussed in Chapter 4 (Mitchell and Barrett) is the importance of recognising flux as part of the cultural landscape character and structure, as well as the agricultural communities that depend upon and live in the landscapes. Landscape character is often described as a product of farming systems in rural landscapes and thus is helpful in thinking about future cultural landscapes. In the UK the movement towards partnerships and cooperatives of small-scale growers and local farmers' markets may reduce the likelihood of change to homogenised and large-scale farming practices. Chapter 4 (Mitchell and Barrett) illustrates how city–country working is producing new agricultural landscapes that are increasingly crossing cultures in North America. Economic viability is clearly important, but so are traditional values. Telling the story of productivity and how the interaction of communities with the landscape supports cultural identity can act as a considerable pull to tourists. Cultural identity as a result of food is perhaps nowhere more obvious than in relation to the culture of wine growing in France where the 'appellations mix the natural environment of the region with the "raw materials" (grapes) used and the skill involved in production and processing, thus ensuring a tie to a place' (Bell and Valentine 1997: 17). English cheeses have a similar association with particular landscapes and community identities; there is a considerable movement in the UK and other countries to market foods based on the culture of the landscape from which they come and develop linked tourism opportunities. Chapter 4 (Mitchell and Barrett) discusses how tourism is seen as a way of affirming the importance of developing more sustainable practice as well as understanding how culture is reflected in the landscape. However, increasing pressures in relation to food security are likely to ensure that agricultural landscapes continue to change and food production will become increasingly a feature of non-rural landscapes as shown in Chapter 8 (Speak) in the picture of a critical need for food in poor settlements of the Global South.

In the new urban poor settlements of countries such as India, the speed of change is astonishing. Here migration has meant that rural poverty has moved with populations to urban areas as it did in England in the Industrial Revolution of the 1800s. In the Global South populations have a 'very visceral connection' with their landscape which relates directly to the need for both physical and spiritual survival, as it did in the rural landscapes that they abandoned. Thus although these new cultural landscapes appear very different, the basis upon which they have evolved relate directly to the same drivers or needs by the communities that live within them and they operate on traditional value systems. The new landscapes that are created exhibit multifunctionality in the way that planned settlements such as those described in Chapter 11 (Ahmed) in the rich suburbs of Cairo do not. The inhabitants of these new settlements of the urban poor value their land in a very different way to those for whom landscape acquisition is simply an economic investment.

In the consideration of how new cultural landscapes might emerge, it would seem that it is important for there to be a place where people have the opportunity to interact as well as to interact with the landscape. As Thompson (2012) suggests, a new generation of public park landscapes may not afford the opportunities for direct encounters between people, nature, weather and the changing seasons that older, highly valued parks and gardens provided and which make them places that people care about and contribute to their distinctiveness. The understanding that a landscape provides opportunity or affordance may be important in the way it is valued, as well as the taking up of those opportunities. Highly valued cultural landscapes often show evidence or remains of interaction: this may be material as in buildings, land reshaping, etc. or associative as in stories, books, language, etc. As shown in the chapter contributions, there are often various kinds of interactions in valued landscapes. While landscapes that are designed may provide extensive and planned change, many of the landscapes presently recognised as 'cultural' have developed through more chaotic relationships between communities and natural forces, one where the primary objective was not landscape change per se, but simply survival.

Present studies of past cultural landscapes involve the study of patterns in human behaviour that are reflected in the landscape. In Chapter 8, Speak's analysis of urban landscapes of the Global South suggests that these are not static or inert places, but are evolving and formed to 'accommodate human behaviour and activity and as a result of them' (p. 138). Such landscapes are constructed anew driven by collective memory, social networks and the logic of survival behaviour within the city. Antrop (2005) suggests that local knowledge and traditions combined with landscape ecology understandings could produce new cultural landscapes and agro-systems. Traditional patterns of behaviour and knowledge are often conserved through management practice and can be used to develop new cultural land-scapes such as described in Chapter 7 (Davis and Corsane). The ecomuseum approach suggests the importance of understanding local needs and drivers, the peculiarity of landscapes and the local experience and interactions with landscape that makes landscape particular. It also often reflects the importance of food cultures and folk traditions and these are reflected in literature, musical and artistic 'products' and customs. Such an approach provides the opportunities to critique the relevance of knowledge of the past rather than taking for granted that all landscape management techniques increased landscape sustainability (see Emmelin 2000). The ecomuseum approach encourages active engagement between local communities and visitors and the environment; often a change in behaviour. It is a dynamic way to respond to the challenges of the ongoing creation of new landscapes using rebranding to reveal historical significance and the potential of the present and future.

4. Power and control: justice, politics, involvement and democracy

IUCN and ICOMOS are the global bodies responsible for reviewing nominations by States Parties for World Cultural Landscapes. Information is then used by ICOMOS and IUCN to advise the World Heritage committee. All participants in these processes hold considerable influence on how a 'cultural landscape' is presently conceived. The examination of power relations and justice issues in the development and meanings that attach com-munities to landscape provide rich pickings for researchers and help build up the picture of the complexity of the relationships behind our perception of what cultural landscapes are and can be. Issues of power and control are frequently referred to in the chapter contributions. In Chapter 10 (Egoz) the issue of ownership of land and power over the cultural landscape is of considerable importance. In Palestine the landscape is imbued with ancient significance much of which has to do with ownership. Lands in this region have been taken over and 'owned' by the creation of new uses over many years by various different cultures. In Palestine new cultural landscapes are created that reinforce the removal or construction of national/political boundaries, and which produce new boundaries. In Palestine Israeli communities have colonised landscapes with material features and new cultivation techniques which transform the desert landscape (see also Chapter 11, Ahmed). Colonisation is also through the revival of biblical myths and the creation of new ones which suggest that the pastoral landscape moulded by Palestinian settlers has been produced by Israelis. Palestine is seen as a landscape of denial; the present Israeli denial of a Palestinian indigenous landscape and in some cases the removal of the vestiges of Palestinian inhabitation. New boundaries are created in the landscape that transcend the generally accepted boundaries of justice power and equality and there is selective amnesia by one culture and yearning for a different reality by another. Can new cultural landscapes be constructed where a known part of the cultural heritage of a landscape is misappropriated or deliberately denied? Alternatively, are such attempts doomed to long-term failure? The Jewish story is one of returning to a significant cultural landscape and making something new from it, which is perhaps unusual. However the long-term sustainability of a system that does not provide justice to other cultures who may have rights over the land is questionable. Not only would a new cultural landscape that emerged as a combination of the sensibilities and desires of all relevant cultures be extraordinarily rich, but as is suggested in Chapter 2 (Taylor and Francis) and by other authors (e.g. Wild *et al.* 2010) landscape change can play a significant role in instigating demand for community rights relating to control over resources. Reaction to change can help build community cohesion and heighten the awareness of differences between cultures of attitudes to landscape.

Many cultural landscape ownerships are contested, as are the memories and associations of landscapes and there are many examples of constantly shifting cultural/political boundaries that involve issues of power in the landscape. Another example is given in Chapter 2 (Taylor and Francis) in relation to Australian landscapes. Can Outstanding Universal Value of landscape be understood in such cases? Landscape justice issues seem to emerge strongly and the need for new governance structures are required to ensure integrated management practice. In Chapter 8 Speak suggests that many governments in the Global South recognise the power of landscape as a representation of cultural identity and use it as a political tool with which control can be exerted. Cultural identity that is regarded as 'deviant' can be removed or new identities constructed through forced change in the landscape.

Empowerment is commonly regarded as a characteristic felt by communities who gain increased control over their landscape, or participation in landscape decisions (Roe 2007). In Chapter 9 (Duffy) rubbish landscapes have been given new meanings and new uses through which poor communities gain feelings of ownership and control. Chapter 3 (Davies) describes how degraded landscapes reflect damaged communities that are dislocated from the landscape. But there is now a green 'gold' emerging from the black of former coal-mining sites in the form of species–rich landscapes and culturally significant sites. These emerging cultural landscapes indicate a local enthusiasm and desire for a new social and economic culture and an understanding of how improving health and regeneration of landscape is seen to reflect that of empowered communities.

Speak (Chapter 8) and Ahmed (Chapter 11) suggest that the new urban landscapes of the more affluent individuals of society are about public representation to the outside world; the need to see and be seen in particular settings, places and doing certain activities that indicate a place in society. These cultural landscapes are far removed from those of the urban poor and reflect global tastes of commerce and consumption rather than local identities and cultures. Furthermore there is a constant threat to those living in poor settlements and towards land that is regarded as 'empty', such as the Cairo desert, from the urban rich as the demand for building development space increases. Thus new cultural landscapes, as old cultural landscapes, reflect social exclusion, political and power relations and the ever-increasing need for the consumption of what is seen as underused or 'derelict' land.

5. Linkage – past, present and future values

Speak (Chapter 8) notes the importance of understanding the speed of change in many landscapes, particularly those of the urban poor in the Global South. Schneeberger *et al.* (2007) suggest that understanding the drivers of change is important and relatively few drivers decelerate the rate of change. One of the characteristics of many new cultural landscapes discussed in the chapter contributions is fast change. Certain landscape types appear to be particularly associated with 'fast' change. Selman (2007) and Selman and Knight (2006) identified that where landscapes exhibit a 'virtuous circle', or relationships that reinforce social, economic and ecological capital, they are largely self-sustaining, with the pursuit of social and economic livelihoods contributing to landscape distinctiveness and character. In changing landscapes the contribution of serendipity is acknowledged in the synergies between people and nature that result in the cultural landscapes that are highly valued. These landscapes have evolved because of intimate and fortuitous associations between communities, livelihoods and environments over time fulfilling what seems to be a deep-seated spiritual need to connect to the environment in ways that are meaningful (Selman 2012; Roe *et al.* 2010; Verschuuren *et al.* 2010). In 2001 Green and Vos identified a number of landscapes that were transformed rapidly that are now valued cultural landscapes (Table 14.1). The indication is that it takes considerable time, at least a generation in the examples given, before such landscapes are valued. A number of contributions in this book would seem to challenge the assumption that recent fast change landscapes are little or less valued than older, slow change landscapes, but further assessment is required into the veracity of this assumption. Planning the kind of landscape transformation that will produce new cultural landscapes – highly valued landscapes – seems to be a somewhat hit or miss affair, but planning for the opportunities that bring communities and individuals into some kind of engagement with landscape, in under-valued existing landscapes and in the planning of new landscapes, may be an important way of providing opportunities for chance interactions to occur that lead to the perceptions of value recognised in cultural landscapes.

Examining the nature of the past landscape reveals much about the functioning of society, but it cannot hold the full story of conflict, meaning, experience and the transitional and intangible values of communities and societies. Chapter 10 (Egoz) indicates that the Jewish new cultural landscape of Palestine projects both biblical myth (story) and material culture without apparently learning any particular lessons from either tradition and being selective about the traditions reflected in both the material and intangible landscape. Traditio-nal values of landscape are always reinterpreted by present communities to suit their own requirements, even where it is suggested that the present landscape reflects a smooth continuum of past and present values. There is a creation of individual or shared patterns of meanings that are influenced by the relationship with landscape; these meanings change over time to provide a framework for perspective and perception; a person's sense of identity may be inherent or constructed; for example through childhood connections and/or emotional response. In many Western cultures until recently our day-to-day life was lived at a relatively small scale in the landscape. This changed with increased communications, the exchange of goods and services and globalisation. More nomadic cultures often travelled significant distances according to seasons; some still do (Jordan 2001). These landscapes can be analysed in terms of significant 'nodes' and 'links' with sense of place developing from interactions with seasonal change and the affordances of the landscape, the resulting activities and the customs that grew up. The environment was moulded by the use and the modification of natural processes which

TABLE 14.1 Examples of 'fast change' landscapes

Location	Driver of change	Landscape transformation	Useful sources of information
Establishment of the Shenandoah National Park, West Virginia, USA. Authorised in 1926 and fully established in 1935.	• Initially, the desire to establish a National Park area by Federal government to create a 'wilderness' only 75 miles from Washington DC. • Later, a public works programme to boost confidence during the Great Depression.	Overall 196,466 acres with 79,579 acres of designated wilderness area. The Blue Ridge area has been inhabited by humans for over 9,000 years. European settlers had been there since the eighteenth century but over 450 families were moved in order to establish Shenandoah National Park. The interpretation of the culture and lifestyle of these families has changed enormously over time. Shenandoah National Park was pieced together from over 3,000 individual tracts of land, confiscated, purchased from or abandoned by settlers. The new landscape was created by fire suppression, road construction, wildlife protection, removal of human inhabitants, new engineering and landscape works. Former pastures and orchards were abandoned and buildings removed. Recreation facilities were built by Roosevelt's Civilian Conservation Corps. The natural process of vegetative colonisation occurred so quickly that in 1976 Congress designated two-fifths of the park as a wilderness.	Shenandoah National Park information, National Park Service, US Department of the Interior. Available at: http://www.nps.gov/shen/index.htm Frazier, B. (2007) The Eminent-Domain Origin of Shenandoah National Park, Future of Freedom Foundation. Available at: http://fff.org/explore-freedom/article/eminentdomain-origin-shenandoah-national-park/

Lignite Mining in the Rhineland, Germany, since the 1940s.	• Brown coal (lignite) extraction.	Lignite is mined in various areas of Germany. In the Rhineland, to the west of Cologne it covers an area of approximately 2,5000km². The mining works have removed forests, fields, roads, towns and watercourses and produces a new landscape visible from space. Whole communities have been moved; since 1948 30,000 people or 70 per cent of the population have been affected by the mining operations. Landscape change consists of preparation for mining, mining operations and restoration. In this area some of the land has been restored to farm land and forest, and lakeland landscapes have been created in other areas for recreational use.	European Association for Coal and Lignite Information. Available at: http://www.euracoal. be/pages/layout1sp. php?idpage=72 Reich, J. (2001) 'Re-creating the wilderness: shaping narratives and landscapes in Shenandoah National Park', *Environmental History* 6, 1: 95–117. Powell, K.M. (2007) *The Anguish of Displacement: The Politics of Literacy in the Letters of Mountain Families in Shenandoah National Park*, Charlottesville: University of Virginia Press. Rhenish Lignite Mining – Landscape Change, Diercke International Atlas. Available at: http://www. diercke.com/kartenansicht.xtp?artId=978-3-14-100790-9&stichwort=well&fs=1
Oostvaardersplassen Nature Researve, Netherlands 1974.	• Land reclamation, sea defences and drainage; • The 'rewilding' of the Flevoland polder.	The Oostvaardersplassen reserve was created when the Southern Flevoland polder was reclaimed from Lake Ijssel. The area of the reserve was originally to be developed for industry, but because of the economic situation of the time, this did not happen. Now human intervention is kept to a minimum. Often described as 'rewilding' project, this area is grazed by feral herds of Heck cattle, Red deer and Konik horses. The new landscape consists of 6,000 ha of open water, marshland, wet and dry open grasslands and flowering communities with trees and shrubs. It exhibits a high degree of biodiversity near to a heavily populated area of the Netherlands.	Vera, F.M.W. (2009) 'Large scale nature development the Oostvaardersplassen', *British Wildlife*, pp. 28–36. Available at: http://diaplan.ku.dk/pdf/large-scale_ nature_development_the_Oostvaardersplassen.pdf/ BirdLife International (2011) *Rewilding May Offer a Sustainable Alternative to Traditional Management*, presented as part of the BirdLife State of the world's birds website. Available at: http://www. birdlife.org/datazone/sowb/casestudy/415 Herrmann, M., Royffe, C. and Millard, A. (2000) 'Sustainable landscape design in practice', in J.F. Benson and M.H. Roe (eds) *Landscape and Sustainability*, London: Spon.

TABLE 14.1 (*Continued*)

Location	Driver of change	Landscape transformation	Useful sources of information
Shenzhen Special Economic Zone, Guangdong Province, China, 1980.	• Creation of a Special Economic Zone which allowed foreign investment and economic development.	Shenzhen was a small market centre surrounded by rice fields founded in the seventeenth century. In the 1970s it consisted of less than 3 km² of small businesses and one-story houses. It was a hilly area, with fertile agrarian land. Shenzhen was 20–30,000 people in 21 communes. In 2013 it covers an area of 2,050 square kilometres including urban and rural areas, with a population of 15 million. After becoming a special economic zone in 1979, Shenzhen underwent tremendous change in landscape. The once hilly area is now replaced by mostly flat ground. Landforms have been removed and the coastline and low-lying marshlands have been altered by fill material to provide building areas. The area is highly urbanised with infrastructure, parklands, industrial parks, businesses and residential areas.	Seto, K.C. and Fragkias, M. (2005) 'Quantifying spatiotemporal patterns or urban land-use change in four cities of China with time series landscape metrics', *Landscape Ecology* 20: 871–888. Yeung, Y.-M. and Kee, G. (2009) 'China's Special Economic Zones at 30', *Eurasian Geography and Economics* 50, 2: 222–240. Available at: http://www.espre.cn/111/manage/ziliao/China%26_039.pdf O'Donnell, M.A. (2013) *Laying Siege to the Villages: Lessons from Shenzhen*, Shenzhen noted blog. Available at: http://shenzhennoted.com/2013/03/29/laying-siege-to-the-villages-lessons-from-shenzhen/ Clark, C. (1998) 'The politics of place making in Shenzhen, China', *Berkeley Planning Journal* 12, 1: 103–125. Available at: http://www.escholarship.org/uc/item/99w9p6w2#page-1
Alqueva Reservoir project in the Guadiana Valley, Alentejo region. Completed in 2002 and filled in 2012.	• Creation of a strategic water reserve in a dry region. • Irrigation for intensive agriculture • Hydro-electric power generation • Job creation (tourist market including golf industry).	A new 160 square mile reservoir landscape (96 square miles of water) created from one of the largest deforestation projects in Portugal (one million trees, including many cork oaks), 10 dams, 3,000 miles of irrigation canals, new roads, bridges and pumping stations. The reservoir is the largest man-made reservoir in Europe. It submerged 160 stone age rock cave paintings, archaeological sites, valuable wildlife habitats related to the Iberian Lynx, wild boar and bird species. Aldeia da Luz village was demolished in 2002 and submerged and a new village (350 buildings) built on the edge of the reservoir.	BBC report (2002) 'Portugal opens Europe's largest dam'. Friday 8 February. Available at: http://news.bbc.co.uk/1/hi/world/europe/1808734.stm Rose, C.D. (2012) *Aldeia da Luz*, Untitled Books, Issue 50. Available at: http://www.untitledbooks.com/fiction/short-stories/aldeia-da-luz-by-c-d-rose/ Entre Duas Terras (Entre Deux Villages/Between Two Villages) 2003, a film by Muriel Jaquerod and Eduardo Saraiva Pereira. Available at: http://www.cultureunplugged.com/play/5502/Entre-Duas-Terras--Entre-Deux-Villages--Between-Two-Villages- Museum of Luz, Aldeia da Luz, Portugal.

(Based on Green and Vos 2001).

in turn affected the cultures and activities: as Nassauer (1995: 229) observed, 'culture changes landscapes and culture is embodied by landscapes'.

Concepts of sense of place and place identity are useful in considering how past, present and future values link and are transferred. Place identity is the way an individual or group constructs or inherits feelings, memories, concepts and ideas about particular landscapes as well as a particular landscape type (Jewell and McKinnon 2008). Such feelings may induce a feeling of belonging or being an outsider in certain landscapes. Attempts to create certain place identity also indicate a need to control and even conform to others' perceptions of identity (e.g. mowing lawns in suburbia). Contemporary and future life-styles may be changing the way we construct identity (of ourselves and the landscape) and the influence of commodification through advertising and marketing may have a more significant role than in the past. Change will not necessarily destroy the special character of place but the qualities may be built upon, changed or others created. Fluctuation is an inherent part of the perception of landscape character – whether it is in relation to physical changes such as seasonal or small incremental changes, or changes such as can be seen by the way a landscape is regarded (the *garbagescapes* of Chapter 9 and the film locations of Chapter 6). How much change of character can there be before there is loss of *genius loci*? The chapter contributions suggest that some new cultural landscapes may arise from fast change with little or no connection to the past landscape character or *genius loci*. While these new landscapes may be distinctive and valued, their lack of connection to past manage-ment practice and speed of change may mean their future sustainability is questionable. However cultural liminality (such as the squatter settlements in Chapter 8, Speak) may not necessarily mean new cultural landscapes are *not* created and many transient cultures may have created significant landscapes that are now lost in the mists of time. Antrop (2005: 21) suggests that 'cultural landscapes are the result of consecutive reorganization of the land in order to adapt its use and spatial structure better to the changing societal demands'. Although this appears to provide a rather one-way picture of cause and effect, an idea of fluidity in cultures and landscapes can be seen as similar to the dynamic picture provided under concepts of resilience. Such landscapes could be seen to be in a constant state of destruction and renewal. In a useful analysis of the potential of the resilience concept[6] in managing cultural landscapes Plieninger and Bieling (2012) suggest that many presently valued cultural landscapes are characterised by periods of considerable change, including remodelling by human management practices which can be seen as unsustainable and degrading. The focus on change management recognises there may be periods of 'rapid change, uncertainty, novelty and experimentation leading to either destructing or creative change in the system' (ibid.: 18). The resilience concept provides a dynamic picture of change and unpredictability relating to past, present and future; it suggests the need for action, collaboration and inter-action in order to achieve some degree of control within changes in the landscape through adaptive co-management approaches.

Throughout the chapters, there are expressions of interaction where people are passionate about places. In particular, displaced peoples often look back on a landscape with fondness or passion, even if the way of life is not. Chapter 8 (Speak) indicates that the memory of interactions and skills learned in relation to rural landscapes are carried with communities and reinterpreted in very different and new locations. Chapter 10 (Egoz) suggests the power of long-term memory, passion for land and imagined interaction (for descendants) with landscapes in the potential creation of new cultural landscapes.

ICOMOS (2009: 7) suggests that 'cultural landscapes often reflect specific techniques of sustainable land use, considering the characteristics and limits of the natural environment they are established in, and a specific spiritual relation to nature'. Chapter 13 (Melnick) suggests that external influences or drivers for change may be more powerful than and subsume many of our existing cultural landscapes. This may include those that we do not presently recognise as particularly valuable or those that have been sustained with little change over a long period. Also lost will be links to the past and the skills and memories contained in many landscapes. The question of what should be conserved as well as how we develop new ways of life that will produce meaningful landscapes becomes more critical. It is also important for policymakers and managers to question how perceptions of cultural landscapes may be changing as a result of new imperatives and the role of changing values in the creation and maintenance of cultural landscapes.

Conclusions: new cultural landscapes?

It states the facts, provides examples, and only at the end presumes to draw conclusions.
(Jackson 1980: 113)

The aim of this book is not to provide the last word on the idea of new cultural landscapes, but to provoke discussion. It reveals some alternative views of what cultural landscapes might be through the research, experience in practice, theory and viewpoint of authors from a variety of disciplinary allegiances and outlooks. In doing so, the objective is to help create a 'new culture of landscape' in the consciousness of policymakers, politicians, landscape managers, academics and others interested in the subject.

The interactive nature of the relationship between humans and landscape has been described in the book as 'mutual moulding', meaning a feedback system whereby humans respond to change in the landscape, how we manage and mould the landscape and how the conditions that arise in the landscape then help determine how we act. This assumes both humans and landscape are agents of change. The chapter contributions indicate that perhaps it is most useful to talk about 'relationships' with landscape rather than 'interactions'. Interaction indicates some kind of activity, while relationship indicates a connection. This might be a link, bond or association, but might not necessarily indicate the kind of physicality that is commonly associated with the construction of closeness between humans and the landscape as reflected in the title 'cultural'. Even where there are intangible associations, the general feeling is that these grow out of physical connections with landscape. Conceptions of new cultural landscapes explored in this book suggest that connections may be generated as much by emotions and distance, including feelings of nostalgia, idealism and romantic yearning for 'something better', as by close physical contact built up over many years. The actual physical features of landscape may be removed, ignored or incorporated into new expressions of culture. Selman (2012: 142) suggests that nostalgia for traditional and imagined landscapes 'can pose a barrier to the emergence of new landscapes that are resilient and adaptive'. He emphasises the need for 'social reconnection' with landscape, but part of such reconnection may indeed require imaginings, the desire to create connections between the past and future that requires valuing things such as traditional attitudes to landscape, expressions of cultural connection within literature, music and painting and performance, recognising the importance of visions and discovering the possibility of new kinds of connections. This idea also brings the understanding of the significance of ecological value; as Pretty (2007: 220) suggests we need a vision of an 'animated connected world where people matter and where nature matters, and where we develop a new interconnected ethic', reminiscent of Aldo Leopold's (1949) writing, but reinterpreted to incorporate ideas that emanate from changes in cultures, connections, technologies and ways of living. We acknowledge that biodiversity richness has much to do with positive human management of landscape and there are good examples of indigenous cultures and Western landscape management systems that provide evidence for this.[7] It is also clear that physical contact remains important to the passing on and reinterpretation of skills and understandings of landscape processes that create biological and cultural richness. The chapter contributions reinforce the view that such contact is particularly important in the creation and perception of ordinary cultural landscapes.

It is also useful for planners, designers and managers that tools are identified to help in the endeavour to plan, design and manage landscapes that will be valued. It has been recognised for some time that the experience of landscape, particularly through traditional agricultural practices, sows the seeds for awareness of its value. Chapter 5 (Bell) shows a very clear visual and spatial effect when traditional management is removed. The increasing loss of what are seen as valuable expressions in the landscape of particular cultural periods is of concern in many countries, not least because of the reduction in biodiversity that often results from changes in management systems that have been used for many years. Landscape character assessment tools are generally seen as useful to capture and understand multidimensional and multi-perceptual landscape interactions and social, economic, ecological and cultural values involved in landscape creation (e.g. Chapter 11, Ahmed).

The chapter contributions are generally optimistic in that although many serious problems are highlighted, there is an increasing interest in the value embedded within ordinary landscapes in particular, and a new awareness and understanding of the need for more holistic approaches to landscape management. There is much good research generally on the forces presently leading to large-scale landscape destruction and the need to create (new) cultural landscapes that are relevant to future generations as well as to embody and provide continuity for present generations. A developing policy language would suggest the realisation that all aspects of landscape need to be brought together in management considerations including indigenous, local and traditional values (particularly in relation to ecosystem knowledge[8]), new approaches based on technology and scientific evidence and social and cultural justice.[9] Part of this is allowing new cultural landscapes to develop as seen in Chapter 8 (Speak), to provide new ways of living that can mesh with traditional cultures and beliefs and landscape as provider. This book does not leave us with a toolkit for developing new, highly valued landscapes, but it reiterates that context is of critical importance. For example, landscapes that are important and highly valued by particular indigenous cultures are very different from the urban agricultural spaces in squatter camps of the Global South. Both are already valued by those communities inhabiting them and therefore have the potential to be seen as 'cultural landscapes'.

The chapter contributions help to extend concepts of landscape. The impacts on and challenges to the development of valued landscapes are many.[10] However this book celebrates new cultures, new tools (Figure 14.8) and ideas – imaginaries, scenarios and participation – new connections, adaptations, expressions of culture and opportunities provided by new environmental conditions. In addition to the ideas emerging in this book, there are notions

These virtual-reality goggles are great!
Right now, I'm sun-bathing in Tahiti...

FIGURE 14.8 New tools are emerging to reimagine cultural landscapes in alternative and creative ways.

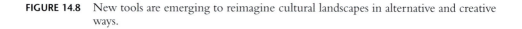

such as those of sky[11] and submerged (sea)[12] landscapes which provide additional opportunities to consider the richness and complexity of human relationships with landscapes in time and space. Reimagining the idea of cultural landscapes as so much more than managing existing relationships with land could provide opportunities for future engagement and expression, building rapport and identity. It could also strengthen existing connections and provide opportunities for building new values upon which the resilience of landscapes and cultures may depend. As Laurence Durrell (1960) put it, landscape expresses itself through the character of the human being 'just as it does through its wildflowers' (p. 156); people themselves are reflections of their landscape and landscapes reflect their management by and relationships with people.

Notes

1 Recent examples of unusual interpretations of this is the King's Singers CD *Landscape & Time*, a collection of works that express 'real and imagined' landscapes (see www.signumrecords.com/catalogue/sigcd090/article.htm), and the *Lakeland Voice* group which carries out 'singing walks' in the South Lakeland District and Yorkshire Dales National Park, UK (see http://www.lakelandvoice.co.uk/). Ancient examples of 'singing the landscape' can be found in Aboriginal traditions of Australia and other indigenous cultures (see Chatwin 1987).
2 Gibson's (1979) theory of 'affordances' interpreted the environment as a series of opportunities implying a complementary process where people and animals are attuned to perceived information and properties of the environment.

3 Brummond (2009) suggests that the ancient pastoralist traditions of Mongolian herders include rituals and knowledge that are specifically linked to local features such as rock formations, and the associated plant and animal life of the area. There is a concept of owning the landscape through interaction, knowledge and experience and there are questions as to whether opening up these landscapes to tourist development will destroy these relationships. See http://www.mongolcc.org/index.php?option=com_content&task=view&id=105&Itemid=1.

4 In *A Reed Shaken by the Wind*, Maxwell (1957) describes his travels with the explorer Wilfred Thesiger through the 2,000 square miles of marshlands of the Euphrates and Tigris north of Basra in Iraq. It was here that Maxwell was given Mijbil, the otter that was made famous by his later book, *Ring of Bright Water* (1960) and a film of the same name based on the story.

5 See http://whc.unesco.org/pg.cfm?cid=31&id_site=1243. On the UNESCO Representative List of the Intangible Cultural Heritage of Humanity (http://www.unesco.org/culture/ich/index.php?lg=en&pg=00011#tabs) are several important references to food landscapes such as the ritual of transplanting rice in Mibu, Hiroshima, Japan, which was inscribed in 2011 (http://www.unesco.org/culture/ich/en/RL/00411).

6 Plieninger and Bieling (2012: 15) define resilience as referring to 'the ability to deal with disturbances or change without altering the essential characteristics of the system in question. Only once certain thresholds are exceeded, profound changes occur, making reorganisation necessary. The resilience approach focuses on the dynamics of change and how to adapt to and shape change'.

7 See for example Taylor's (2013) cases of swidden agriculture in Asia and home gardens in South America (Pulido *et al.* 2008); Jennifer Owen's (2010) 30-year study of a suburban garden in Leicester, England; and the links between genetic diversity in agricultural systems and cultures in many countries as found by Smales' (2006) EU-funded research.

8 Payton *et al.* (2002) for example provide understandings of issues and methods relating to the integration of local and scientific knowledge.

9 See for example the Satoyama Initiative: www.satoyama-initiative.org/en/.

10 Some key impacts on the landscape generally identified in the literature are: internationalisation, high resource dependency, fast change, monetarist values, high consumption, personal gain and individual values, high mobility, aggressive land accumulation, ecological loss, loss of diversity, family change, risk society, religious intolerance, fanaticism, little concern for sustainability in professions or public, communication explosions, inequality, etc.

11 A number of dark skies initiatives and tranquillity assessments that use dark skies as measurements related to landscape are now available, see International Dark Sky Association (www.darksky.org) and Council for the Protection of Rural England (CPRE) Tranquillity mapping initiatives (www.cpre.org.uk). The UNESCO report on starlight reserves and World Heritage scientific, cultural and environmental values is available at: www.darkskiesawareness.org/files/FinalReportFuerteventura SL.pdf.

12 See for example Flatman (2009) and Historic Seascape Character maps developed by English Heritage: www.english-heritage.org.uk.

References

Albrecht, G. (2005) 'Solastalgia, a new concept in human health and identity', *Philosophy Activism Nature* 3: 41–44.

Antrop, M. (2005) 'Why landscape of the past are important for the future', *Landscape and Urban Planning* 70, 1–2: 21–34.

Bell, D. and Valentine, G. (1997) *Consuming Geographies: We are Where We Eat*, London: Routledge.

Brummond, J. (2009) Cultural and Natural Heritage Protection Challenges in Mongolia, Mongolian Cultural Centre [online resource]. Available at: http://www.mongolcc.org/index.php?option=com_content&view=article&id=105:cultural-and-natural-heritage-protection-challenges-in-mongolia&catid=13:latest-research&Itemid=27 (accessed 29 April 2013).

Chatwin, B. (1987) *The Songlines*, London: Picador.

CoE (Council of Europe) (2000) The European Landscape Convention text [online]. Available at: http://www.coe.int/t/dg4/cultureheritage/heritage/landscape/default_en.asp (accessed 30 April 2013).

Crouch, D. (1991) 'Allotment culture', *Resurgence* 145: 38–39.

Diamond, J. (2005) *Collapse: How Societies Choose to Fail or Survive*, London: Penguin.

Durrell, L. (1960) 'Landscape and character', in A.G. Thomas (ed.) *Spirit of Place: Lawrence Durrell Mediterranean Writings*, London: Faber & Faber, pp. 156–163.

Emmelin, L. (2000) 'The confusing multiplicity of futures and the beguiling logic of history', in P. G. Moller, P. Holm and L. Rasmussen (eds) *Aktører i landskabet*, Odense: Odense Universitesforlag, pp. 27–55.

Estulin, D. (2004) *The Age of Reason: Barbie Dolls and G. I. Joes*. Available at http://usa.mediamonitors.net/content/view/full/4004/ (accessed 30 April 2013).

Fairclough, G. (2012) 'Landscape, an archaeology prospect', in S. Bell, R. Stiles and I. Sarlov-Herlin (eds) *Exploring the Boundaries of Landscape Architecture*, Abingdon: Routledge, pp. 83–114.

Flatman, J. (2009) 'Conserving marine cultural heritage: threats, risks and future priorities', *Conservation and Management of Archaeological Sites* 11, 1: 5–8.

Gibson, J.J. (1979) *The Ecological Approach to Visual Perception*, Boston: Houghton-Mifflin.

Green, B. and Vos, W. (2001) *Threatened Landscapes: Conserving Cultural Environments*, London: Spon Press.

ICOMOS (2009) *Description of World Heritage Cultural Landscapes with a Bibliography based on documents available at the UNESCO-ICOMOS Documentation Centre*, Paris: ICOMOS.

Ingold, T. (2000) *The Perception of the Environment: Essays on Livelihood, Dwelling and Skill*, London: Routledge.

Jackson, J.B. (1980) *The Necessity for Ruins and Other Topics*, Amherst: University of Massachusetts Press.

Jewell, B. and McKinnon, S. (2008) 'Movie tourism – a new form of cultural landscape?' *Journal of Travel and Tourism Marketing* 24, 2/3: 153–162.

Jones, M. and Daugstad, K. (1997) 'Usages of the "cultural landscape" concept in Norwegian and Nordic landscape administration', *Landscape Research* 22, 3: 267–291.

Jordan, P. D. (2001) 'Cultural landscapes in colonial Siberia: Khanty settlements of the sacred, the living and the dead', *Landscapes* 2, 2: 83–105.

Kyttä, M. (2002) 'Affordances of children's environments in the context of cities, small towns, suburbs and rural villages in Finland and Belarus', *Journal of Environmental Psychology* 22, 1: 109–123.

Leopold, A. (1949) *A Sand County Almanac and Sketches Here and There*, Oxford: Oxford University Press.

Lister, N.-M. (2008) 'Placing food', in J. Knechtel (ed.) *Food*, Alphabet City Series, Cambridge, MA: MIT Press, pp. 148–185. Available at: http://www.academia.edu/163905/Placing_Food_Torontos_Edible_Landscape (accessed 30 April 2013).

Macfarlane, R. (2007) 'Multifunctional landscapes: conceptual and planning issues for the countryside', in J.F. Benson and M.H. Roe (eds) *Landscape and Sustainability*, 2nd edn, Abingdon: Routledge, pp. 138–166.

Mather, R. and Jensen, J. (2010) *Investigations into Block Island's Submerged Cultural Sites and Landscapes for the Rhode Island Ocean Special Area Management Plan 2010*, University of Rhode Island, June, 20. Available at: http://seagrant.gso.uri.edu/oceansamp/pdf/appendix/05-Mather-Archeology Resources_reduced.pdf (accessed 30 April 2013).

Maxwell, G. (1957) *A Reed Shaken by the Wind*, London: Four Square Books/Landsborough Pubs.

Mitchell, N., Rössler, M. and Tricaud, P. -M. (eds) (2009) *World Heritage Cultural Landscapes: A Handbook for Conservation and Management, World Heritage Papers 26*, Paris: UNESCO.

Muir, R. (2003) 'On change in the landscape', *Landscape Research* 28, 4: 383–403.

Nassauer, J.I. (1995) 'Culture and change landscape structure', *Landscape Ecology* 10, 4: 229–237.

Olwig, K. (2008) 'Has "geography" always been modern?: Choros, (non)representation, performance, and the landscape', *Environment and Planning A* 40, 8: 1843–1861.

Owen, J. (2010) *Wildlife of a Garden, a Thirty Year Study*, London: Royal Horticultural Society.

Payton, R.W., Barr, J.J.F., Martin, A., Sillitoe, P., Deckers, J.F. Gowing, J.W., Hatibu, N., Naseem, S.B., Tenywa, M. and Zuberi, M.I. (2002) 'Contrasting approaches to integrating indigenous knowledge about soils and scientific soil survey in East Africa and Bangladesh', *Geoderma* 111, 3–4: 355–386.

Plieninger, T. and Bieling, C. (eds) (2012) 'Connecting cultural landscapes to resilience', in T. Plieninger and C. Bieling (eds) *Resilience and the Cultural Landscape: Understanding and Managing Change in Human-Shaped Environments*, Cambridge: Cambridge University Press, pp. 3–26.

Pretty, J.N. (2007) *The Earth Only Endures: On Reconnecting with Nature and Our Place in it*, London: Earthscan.

Pulido, M.T., Pagaza-Calderón, E.M., Martínez-Ballesté, A., Maldonado-Almanza, B., Saynes, A. and Pacheco, R.M. (2008) 'Home gardens as an alternative for sustainability: challenges and perspectives', in U.P. de Albuquerque and M.A. Ramos (eds) *Current Topics in Ethnobotany*, Ontario: Research Signpost. Available at: http://www.uaeh.edu.mx/investigacion/icbi/LI_ProdForestales/MaTeresa_Pulido/MTP_7_Pulido.pdf (accessed 30 April 2013).

Roe, M.H. (2007) 'The social dimensions of landscape sustainability', in J.F. Benson and M.H. Roe (eds) *Landscape and Sustainability*, 2nd edn, Abingdon: Routledge, pp. 58–83.

Roe, M.H., Jones, C. and Mell, I.C. (2008) *Research to Support the Implementation of the European Landscape Convention in England*, research report for Natural England (Research Contract No. PYT02/10/1.16).

Roe, M.H., Selman, P. and Swanwick, C. (2010) *The Development of Approaches to Facilitate Judgement on Landscape Change Option*, a research report to Natural England (Research Contract No. 21291).

Roe, M.H., Selman, P., Mell, I.C., Jones, C. and Swanwick, C. (2009) *Establishment of a Baseline for, and Monitoring of the Impact of, the European Landscape Convention in the UK*, research report to Defra (and a Steering Committee) (Research Contract: CR 0401).

Rössler, M. (undated) *UNESCO World Heritage Centre Background Document on UNESCO World Heritage Cultural Landscapes*, prepared for the FAO Workshop and Steering Committee Meeting of the GIAHS project: Globally Important Ingenious Agricultural Heritage Systems, p. 7.

Schneeberger, N., Bürgi, M., Hersperger, A.M. and Ewald, K.C. (2007) 'Driving forces and rates of landscape change as a promising combination for landscape change research – an application on the northern fringe of the Swiss Alps', *Land Use Policy* 24, 2: 349–361.

Selman, P. (2007) 'Landscape and sustainability at the national and regional scales', in J.F. Benson and M.H. Roe (eds) *Landscape and Sustainability*, 2nd edn, Oxford: Routledge, pp. 104–117.

Selman, P. (2012) *Sustainable Landscape Planning: The Reconnection Agenda*, Abingdon: Routledge.

Selman, P. and Knight, M. (2006) 'On the nature of virtuous change in cultural landscapes: exploring sustainability through qualitative models', *Landscape Research* 31, 3: 295–307.

Smales, M. (ed.) (2006) *Valuing Crop Biodiversity: On-farm Genetic Resources and Economic Change*, Wallingford: CABI.

Stephenson, J. (2008) 'The cultural values model: an integrated approach to values in landscapes', *Landscape and Urban Planning* 84, 2: 127–139.

Taylor, K. (2013) 'The challenge of the cultural landscape construct and associated intangible values in an Asian context', in K.D. Silva and N.K. Chapagain (eds) *Asian Heritage Management: Contexts, Concerns and Prospects*, Abingdon: Routledge, pp. 189–211.

Taylor, K. and Lennon, J. (eds) (2012) *Managing Cultural Landscapes*, London and New York: Routledge.

Thompson, I.H. (2006) *The Sun King's Garden: Louis XIV, André Le Nôtre and the Creation of the Gardens of Versailles*, London: Bloomsbury.

Thompson, I.H. (2012) 'Gardens, parks and sense of place', in I. Convery, G. Corsane and P. Davis (eds) *Making Sense of Place: Multidisciplinary Perspectives*, Woodbridge: Boydell & Brewer, pp. 159–168.

Treib, M. (ed.) (2009) *Spatial Recall: Memory in Architecture and Landscape*, Abingdon: Routledge.

Verschuuren, B., Wild, R., McNeely, J.A. and Oviedo, G. (eds) (2010) *Sacred Natural Sites: Conserving Nature and Culture*, London: Earthscan.

Wild, R., Verschuuren, B. and McNeely, J. (2010) 'Conclusions: sustaining sacred natural sites to conserve nature and culture', in B. Verschuuren, R. Wild, J.A. McNeely and G. Oviedo (eds) *Sacred Natural Sites: Conserving Nature and Culture*, London: Earthscan, pp. 280–291.

Wylie, J. (2007) *Landscape*, London: Routledge.

IMAGE CREDITS

1.4 Maggie Roe
1.6 Alistair Jenkins
1.7 Maggie Roe
2.1 National Library of Australia PIC R5689
2.2 Ken Taylor 2010
2.3 Ken Taylor 2012
2.4 Nicholas Hall, 2006
3.1 Hook *et al.* 2010
3.2 After Pahl 1966
3.4 Clive Davies
3.5 Clive Davies
3.6 Clive Davies
4.1 Courtesy of and used with the permission of the US National Park Service
4.2 Courtesy of and used with the permission of Silos and Smokestacks National Heritage Area
4.3 Courtesy of and used with the permission of US National Park Service
5.1 Simon Bell
5.2 Simon Bell
5.3 Simon Bell
5.4 Simon Bell
5.5 Bell *et al.* 2009
5.6 Simon Bell
5.7 Simon Bell
5.8 Simon Bell
5.9 Simon Bell
5.10 Courtesy Mirosław Grochowski
6.1 Sandra Westerbladh
6.2 Susan McKinnon
6.3 © Gail Johnson | Dreamstime.com

6.4   © Maisna | Dreamstime.com

7.1   Jars Balan

7.2   Peter Davis

7.3   Caileen MacLean

7.4   Hüsamettindere Ecomuseum Association

7.5   Gerard Corsane

7.6   Gerard Corsane

8.1   Susanne Speak

8.2   Susanne Speak

8.3   Susanne Speak

8.4   Susanne Speak

8.5   Susanne Speak

8.6   Susanne Speak

8.7   Susanne Speak

8.8   Susanne Speak

8.9   Susanne Speak

9.1   Joe Duffy

9.2   Joe Duffy

9.3   Joe Duffy

9.4   Joe Duffy

9.5   Joe Duffy

9.6   Joe Duffy

9.7   Joe Duffy

9.8   Joe Duffy

9.9   Joe Duffy

9.10   Joe Duffy

10.1   Shelley Egoz

10.2   Shelley Egoz

10.3   Shelley Egoz

10.4   Shelley Egoz

10.5   Beit Jebrin March 7th 1839 by David Roberts (1796–1864) Louis Haghe (lithographer)

10.6   Shelley Egoz

10.7   Tim Williams

10.8   Tim Williams

10.9   Courtesy of activestills.org

10.10   Tim Williams

11.1   Selman 2006: 38

11.3   Sutton and Fahmi 2001:148

12.1   Graphic by author based on Ma and Wu 2005 and Skinner 1977

12.2   Based on Clunas 1997 and Fairbank 1957

12.3   Courtesy HDI

12.4   Graphics by author based on HDI 2002 plan, courtesy HDI

12.5   Mary Padua 2007

12.6   Courtesy SWA

12.7   Courtesy Tom Fox

12.8   Courtesy Kongjian Yu/Turenscape 2008

INDEX

Page numbers in **bold** indicate tables, in *italic* indicate figures and followed by a letter n indicate end of chapter notes.